SIC stands for psychoanalytic interpretation at its most elementary: no discovery of deep, hidden meaning, just the act of drawing attention to the litterality [*sic!*] of what precedes it. A "*sic*" reminds us that what was said, inclusive of its blunders, was effectively said and cannot be undone. The series SIC thus explores different connections to the Freudian field. Each volume provides a bundle of Lacanian interventions into a specific domain of ongoing theoretical, cultural, and ideological-political battles. It is neither "pluralist" nor "socially sensitive": unabashedly avowing its exclusive Lacanian orientation, it disregards any form of correctness but the inherent correctness of theory itself.

SIC

A

series

edited

by

Slavoj

Žižek

Toward a Politics of Truth

Lenin Reloaded

Sebastian Budgen,
Stathis Kouvelakis,
and Slavoj Žižek,
editors

sic **7**

DUKE UNIVERSITY PRESS   Durham and London 2007

2nd printing, 2007

© 2007 Duke University Press

All rights reserved

Printed in the United States

of America on acid-free paper ∞

Typeset in Sabon by Tseng

Information Systems, Inc.

Library of Congress Cataloging-in-

Publication Data appear on the

last printed page of this book.

Contents

Sebastian Budgen, Stathis Kouvelakis, and Slavoj Žižek,
Introduction: Repeating Lenin   1

Sebastian Budgen,	**Introduction:**
Stathis Kouvelakis,	**Repeating**
and Slavoj Žižek	**Lenin**

The project of this book began almost as a provocative gesture, with the conference on Lenin ("Toward a Politics of Truth: The Retrieval of Lenin") held at the Kulturwissenschaftliches Institut, in Essen (Germany) in February 2001. For some commentators in the media, it remained just that. With the essays that comprise this book, some of them papers given at that conference, some others generously offered by their authors to be included in this volume, we want to show that this is something more than an attempt at scandal-mongering in an epoch dominated by the "post-political consensus."

So why focus on Lenin today? Our answer is this: the name "Lenin" is of urgent necessity for us precisely now, at a time when very few people seriously consider possible alternatives to capitalism any longer. At a time when global capitalism appears as the only game in town and the liberal-democratic system as the optimal political organization of society, it has indeed become easier to imagine the end of the world than a far more modest change in the mode of production.

This liberal-democratic hegemony is sustained by a kind of unwritten *Denkverbot* (thought prohibition) similar to the infamous *Berufsverbot* (banning the employment of leftists by any state institution) of the late 1960s in Germany. The moment one shows a minimal sign of engaging in political projects that aim at seriously challenging the existing order, he or she receives the following immediate answer: "Benevolent as it is, this will necessarily end in a new Gulag!" The "return to ethics" in today's political philosophy shamefully exploits the horrors of the Gulag or the Holocaust as the ultimate scare tactic for blackmailing us into renouncing all serious radical commitment. In this way, the conformist liberal scoundrels can find hypocritical satisfaction in their defense of the existing order: they know there is corruption, exploitation, and so forth, but they denounce every attempt to change things as ethically dangerous and unacceptable, resuscitating the ghost of totalitarianism.

Breaking out of this deadlock, the reassertion of a politics of Truth today, should, in the first place, take the form of a *return to Lenin*. But, once again, the question arises: Why Lenin, why not simply Marx? Is the proper return not the return to origins proper?

Returning to Marx is already something of an academic fashion. Which Marx do we get in these returns? On the one hand, in the English-speaking world, we get the cultural-studies Marx, the Marx of the postmodern sophists, of the messianic promise; in continental Europe, where the "traditional" division of intellectual labor remains stronger, we get a sanitized Marx, the "classical" author to whom a (marginal) place can be accorded in the academy. On the other hand, we get the Marx who foretold the dynamic of today's globalization and is as such evoked even on Wall Street. What all these Marxes have in common is the denial of politics proper: postmodern political thought precisely opposes itself to Marxism; it is essentially post-Marxist. The reference to Lenin enables us to avoid these two pitfalls.

There are two features that distinguish his intervention. First, one cannot emphasize enough Lenin's externality with regard to Marx: He was not a member of Marx's inner circle of the initiated. Indeed, he never met either Marx or Engels. Moreover, he came from a land at the eastern borders of "European civilization." This externality is thus part of the standard Western racist argument against Lenin: he introduced into Marxism the Russian-Asiatic despotic principle; at yet a further remove, Russians themselves disown him, pointing toward his Tatar origins. However, it turns out that it is only possible to retrieve the theory's original impulse from this external position. In the same way that St. Paul and Lacan reinscribed original teachings into different contexts (St. Paul reinterpreting Christ's crucifixion as his triumph; Lacan reading Freud through mirror-stage Saussure), Lenin violently displaces Marx, tearing his theory out of its original context, planting it in another historical moment, and thus effectively universalizing it.

Second, it is only through such a violent displacement that the original theory can be put to work, fulfilling its potential of political intervention. It is significant that the work in which Lenin's unique voice was for the first time clearly heard is *What Is to Be Done?* The text exhibits Lenin's decision to intervene into the situation, not in the pragmatic sense of adjusting the theory to the realistic claims through necessary compromises, but, on the contrary, in the sense of dispelling all opportunistic compromises, of adopting the unequivocal radical position from which it is only possible to intervene in such a way that our intervention changes the coordinates of the situation.

Lenin's wager—today, in our era of postmodern relativism, more actual than ever—is that truth and partisanship, the gesture of taking sides, are not only not mutually exclusive but condition each other: the *universal* truth in a concrete situation can only be articulated from a thoroughly *partisan* position. Truth is by definition one-sided. This, of course, goes against the predominant ideology of compromise, of finding a middle path among the multitude of conflicting interests.

For us, "Lenin" is not the nostalgic name for old dogmatic certainty; quite the contrary, the Lenin that we want to retrieve is the Lenin-in-becoming, the Lenin whose fundamental experience was that of being thrown into a catastrophic new constellation in which old reference points proved useless, and who was thus compelled to *reinvent* Marxism. The idea is that it is not enough simply to return to Lenin, like returning to gaze at a painting or visit a tombstone, for we must *repeat* or *reload* him: that is, we must retrieve the same impulse in today's constellation. This dialectical return to Lenin aims neither at nostalgically reenacting the "good old revolutionary times" nor at the opportunistic-pragmatic adjustment of the old program to "new conditions." Rather, it aims at repeating, in the present global conditions, the "Leninian" gesture of reinventing the revolutionary project in the conditions of imperialism, colonialism, and world war—more precisely, after the politico-ideological collapse of the long era of progressivism in the catastrophe of 1914. Eric Hobsbawm defined the concept of the twentieth century as the time between 1914, the end of the long peaceful expansion of capitalism, and 1990, the emergence of the new form of global capitalism after the collapse of the Eastern Bloc. What Lenin did for 1914, we should do for our times.

The texts included in this volume engage precisely with this perspective, not in spite of but because of the multiplicity of positions they occupy and defend. "Lenin" stands here for the compelling *freedom* to suspend the stale existing ideological coordinates, the debilitating *Denkverbot* in which we live. It simply means being allowed to start thinking and acting again.

Chapters 1, 2, 4, 7–9, and 12–17 were delivered as papers at the Essen conference. Chapters 3 and 5 were written specifically for this volume. Chapter 6 originally appeared in Greek and was translated into English by Jeremy Lester of the University of Reading, United Kingdom. Chapter 8 was translated from the original French by Ian Birchall, and chapters 9, 10, and 11 were translated from the original French by David Fernbach. Chapter 16 was translated from the original Italian by Graeme Thomson.

The editors would like to take this opportunity to thank Anne von der Heiden for her inestimable help in organizing the conference, as well as Doug Henwood, Robert Pfaller, and Charity Scribner for their participation.

PART I retrieving Lenin

1

One Divides

Alain Badiou | **Itself into Two**

Today the political *oeuvre* of Lenin is entirely dominated by the canonical opposition between democracy and totalitarian dictatorship. But actually this discussion has already taken place. For it is precisely through the category of democracy that, from 1918 onward, the "western" Social Democrats led by Kautsky have tried to discredit not only the Bolshevik revolution in its historical becoming but also Lenin's political thought.

What particularly deserves our interest is the theoretical response by Lenin to this attack, contained above all in the pamphlet that Kautsky published in Vienna in 1918 under the title "The Dictatorship of the Proletariat" and to which Lenin responded in the famous text "The Proletarian Revolution and the Renegade Kautsky."

Kautsky, in a way that is natural for a declared partisan of a representative and parliamentary political regime, stresses almost exclusively the right to vote. The interesting thing is that Lenin sees in this procedure the very essence of Kautsky's theoretical deviation. This is not at all because Lenin would think that it is a mistake to support the right to vote. No, Lenin thinks that it can be very useful, even necessary, to participate in the elections. He will vehemently repeat this against the absolute opponents of participation in parliamentary elections in his pamphlet on leftism. Lenin's criticism of Kautsky is much more subtle and interesting. If Kautsky had said, "I am opposed to the decision by Russian Bolsheviks to disenfranchise the reactionaries and the exploiters," he would have taken position on what Lenin calls "an essentially Russian question, and not the question of the dictatorship of the proletariat in general." He could have, and should have, called his booklet "Against the Bolsheviks." Things would have been politically clear. But this is not what Kautsky did. Kautsky wants to intervene in the question of the dictatorship of the proletariat in general and of democracy in general. The essence of his deviation is to have done this on the basis of a tactical and local decision in Russia. The essence of the deviation is always to argue on the basis of some tactical circumstances in order to deny the principles, to take the starting point in a secondary contradiction in order to make a revisionist statement on the principal conception of politics.

Let us have a closer look at the way Lenin proceeds. I quote:

> In speaking about the franchise, Kautsky *betrayed himself* as an opponent of the Bolsheviks, *who does not care a brass farthing for theory*. For theory, i.e., the reasoning about the general (and not the nationally specific) class foundations of democracy and dictatorship, ought to deal not with a special question, such as the franchise, but with the general question of whether democracy can be *preserved for the rich, for the exploiters* in the historical period of the overthrow of the exploiters and the replacement of their state by the state of the exploited.[1]

So theory is precisely what integrates in thought the moment of a question. The moment of the question of democracy is in no way defined by a tactical and localized decision, such as the disenfranchisement for the rich and the exploiters, a decision linked to the particularities of the Russian Revolution. That moment is defined by the general principle of victory: we find ourselves, Lenin says, in the moment of victorious revolutions, in the moment of the real collapse of the exploiters. This is no longer the moment of the Paris Commune, the moment of courage and of cruel defeat. A theoretician is someone who addresses the questions, for example, the question of democracy, from the inside of the determined moment. A renegade is someone who doesn't take the moment into account, someone who uses a particular vicissitude as an occasion for what is purely and simply his political resentment.

Here we can see clearly why Lenin is the political thinker who inaugurates the century. He turns victory, the real of the revolutionary politics, into an internal condition of the theory. Lenin thus determines the major political subjectivity of the century, at least until its last quarter.

The century, between 1917 and the end of the 1970s, is not at all a century of ideologies, of the imaginary or of utopias, as the liberals would have it today. Its subjective determination is Leninist. It is the passion of the real, of what is immediately practicable, here and now.

What does the century tell us about the century? In any case, that it is not a century of promises, but of accomplishment. It is a century of the act, of the effective, of the absolute present, and not a century of announcement and of future. The century is lived as the century of victories, after the millennium of attempts and failures. The cult of the sublime and vain attempt, and hence the ideological subjugation, is relegated by the players of the twentieth century to the preceding century, to the unhappy romanticism of the nineteenth century. The twentieth century says: the defeats are over, now it is time for victories! This victorious subjectivity survives all apparent defeats, being not empirical, but constitutive. Victory is the transcendental motive that organizes even the defeat. "Revolution" is one of the names of this motive. The October Revolution in 1917, then the Chinese and the Cuban Revolutions, and the victories by the Algerians or the Vietnamese in the struggles of national liberation, all these serve as the empirical proof of the motive and defeat the defeats; they compensate for the massacres of June 1848 or of the Paris Commune.

For Lenin, the instrument of victory is theoretical and practical lucidity, in view of a decisive confrontation, a final and total war. The fact that this war will be total means that victory is victorious indeed. The century therefore is the century of war. But saying this weaves together several ideas, which revolve around the question of the Two or the antagonistic division. The century said that its law is the Two, the antagonism, and in this sense the end of the Cold War (American imperialism versus the Socialist bloc), which is the last total figure of the Two, is also the end of the century. The Two, however, has to be declined according to three acceptations.

1. There is a central antagonism, two subjectivities, which are organized on planetary level in a mortal struggle. The century is the scene of that antagonism.

2. There is a no less violent antagonism between two different ways of considering and thinking this antagonism. It is the essence of the confrontation between Communism and Fascism. For the Communists the planetary confrontation in the last analysis is the confrontation between the classes. For the radical Fascists, it is the confrontation between nations and races. There is an interlocking here of an antagonistic thesis and of antagonistic theses on antagonism. This second division is essential, perhaps more so than the first one. In fact, there were certainly more anti-Fascists than Communists, and it is characteristic that the Second World War was about this derived opposition, and not about a unified conception of the antagonism, which has only led to a "cold" war, with the exception of the periphery (the Korean and Vietnam wars).

3. The century invokes, as the century of production through war, a definite unity. The antagonism will be overcome by the victory of one of the blocs over the other. One can also say that, in this sense, the century of the Two is animated by the radical desire for the One. What names the articulation of the antagonism and the violence of the One is the victory as the mark of the real.

Let me remark that this is not a dialectical scheme. Nothing lets us foresee a synthesis, an internal overcoming of the contradiction. On the contrary, everything points to the annihilation of one of the two terms. The century is a figure of non-dialectical juxtaposition of the Two and the One. The question here is to know what balance sheet the century draws of dialectical thinking. The driving element for the victorious outcome, is it the antagonism itself or the desire for the One? This is one of the major philosophical questions of Leninism. It revolves around what we understand, in dialectical thought, by the "unity of the opposites." This is the question that Mao and the Chinese Communists have worked the most on.

In China, around 1965, began what the local press, which is always inventive in naming conflicts, calls "a big class struggle in the field of philosophy." This struggle opposes those who think that the essence of dialectics is the genesis of the antagonism and that the just formula is "One divides itself into two"; and those who estimate that the essence of dialectics is the synthesis of the contradictory notions and that consequently the correct formula is "Two unite into one." This seeming

scholasticism conceals an essential truth because it is about the identification of revolutionary subjectivity, its constituent desire. Is it the
desire to divide, to wage war — or is it the desire for fusion, for unity, for
peace? At that time in China all those who supported the maxim "One
divides itself into two" were said to be on the left, and all those who
supported "Two unite into one" were said to be "rightists." Why?

If the maxim of synthesis (two unite into one) taken as a subjective
formula, as desire for the One, is rightist, it is because in the eyes of
the Chinese revolutionaries it is entirely premature. The subject of this
maxim has not gone through the Two until the end; it does not yet
know what the completely victorious class war is. It follows that the
One from which it nourishes the desire is not even thinkable, which is
to say that under the cover of synthesis it makes an appeal to the ancient
One. So this interpretation of dialectics is restorationist. Not to be a
conservative, to be a revolutionary activist nowadays, means obligato-
rily to desire division. The question of the new immediately becomes
the question of the creative division in the singularity of the situation.

In China the Cultural Revolution, especially during the years 1966
and 1967, opposes in an unimaginable fury and confusion the proponents of the One and the other version of the dialectical scheme. In
reality, there are those who, like Mao, who in this period practically
was a minority in the leadership of the party, thought that the socialist
state should not be the polite police-like end of mass politics but, on
the contrary, an incitement of its unleashing under the sign of progress-
ing toward real Communism. And there are those, like Liu Shaoqi and
above all Deng Xiaoping, who thought that economic management is
the most important aspect, that mass mobilization is more harmful than
necessary. School-age youth is the spearhead of the Maoistic line. The
party cadres and a vast number of intellectual cadres oppose it more or
less openly. The peasants remain in a state of expectancy. The workers,
the decisive force, are torn apart in rival organizations so that at last,
from 1967–68 onward, the state, which risks being torn away in the political hurricane, must let the army intervene. Then comes a long period
of extremely complex and violent bureaucratic confrontations, which
does not exclude some popular eruptions; this goes on until the death of
Mao in 1976, which is quickly followed by a Thermidorian coup that
brings Deng back into power.

Such political turmoil is so novel in its stakes and at the same time so obscure that many of the lessons it undoubtedly entails for the future of any politics of emancipation have not been drawn yet, even if it provided a decisive inspiration for French Maoism between 1967 and 1975 — and French Maoism was the only innovative political tendency in France in the aftermath of May 1968. It is clear in any case that the Cultural Revolution marks the closure of a whole political sequence, in which the central object was the party and the major political concept was the concept of the proletariat. It marks the end of formal Leninism, which was in reality Stalin's creation. But maybe it is also what is most faithful to real Leninism.

Incidentally, there is a fashion today, among those willing to indulge in renewed servility toward imperialism and capitalism, to call this unprecedented episode a bestial and bloody power struggle, where Mao, finding himself in a minority in the Politburo, attempted by means fair or foul to regain the upper hand. To such people, we will first answer that to call this type of political episode a power struggle is ridiculously stating the obvious: the militants who took part in the Cultural Revolution constantly quoted Lenin when he said (perhaps not his best effort, but that is another question) that at bottom "the only problem is the problem of power." Mao's threatened position was explicitly at stake and had been declared as such by Mao himself. The "discoveries" of our Sinologists were simply immanent and explicit themes in the quasi–civil war that took place in China between 1965 and 1976, a war in which the truly revolutionary sequence (marked by the emergence of a new form of political thought) was only the initial segment (between 1965 and 1968). Besides, since when have our political philosophers considered as terrible the fact that a threatened political leader tries to regain his influence? Is this not what, day in and day out, they elaborate upon as the exquisite democratic essence of parliamentary politics? Next, we shall add that the meaning and importance of a struggle for power is judged by what is at stake, especially when the means of that struggle are the classic revolutionary means, in the sense that Mao said that the revolution is not "a formal dinner party." It involved an unprecedented mobilization of millions of young people and workers, an entirely unheard-of freedom of expression and of movement, gigantic demonstrations, political meetings in all places of work or study, simplistic and brutal discussions, public denunciations, a recurrent and anarchic use of violence, including armed violence, and so forth. And who could say today that Deng Xiaoping, whom the activists of the Cultural Revolution called "the second of the top leaders who, although members of the party, follow the capitalist path," did not indeed follow a line of development and social construction utterly opposed to Mao's line, which was collectivist and innovative? Did it not become apparent when, after Mao's death, he seized power in a bureaucratic coup that he encouraged in China, during the 1980s and up to his death, a form of neocapitalism of the wildest sort, utterly corrupt and all the more illegitimate as it nevertheless preserved the tyranny of the party? So there was indeed, on every question, and particularly the most important ones (the relationship between town and country, intellectual and manual labor, the party and the masses, and so forth) what the Chinese in their pithy language called "a struggle between the two classes, the two paths and the two lines."

But what about the violence, which was often extreme? What about the hundreds of thousands of people who died? What about the persecutions, particularly against the intellectuals? What we can say about this is what can be said of all the episodes of violence that made a mark on history, including any serious attempts today at constructing a politics of freedom: you cannot expect politics to be soft-hearted, progressive, and peaceful if it aims at the radical subversion of the eternal order that submits society to the domination of wealth and the rich, of power and the powerful, of science and the scientists, of capital and its servants. There is already a great and rigorous violence of thought whenever one no longer tolerates the idea that what people think be held for nothing, that the collective intelligence of the workers be held for nothing, that indeed any thought that fails to conform to the order in which the obscene rule of profit is perpetuated be held for nothing. The theme of total emancipation, when put into practice in the present, in the enthusiasm of the absolute present, is always situated beyond good and evil, because in the middle of the action the only good that is known is the one that bears the precious name whereby the established order names its own persistence. Extreme violence is, therefore, the reciprocal correlative of extreme enthusiasm, since what is at stake is indeed, to talk like Nietzsche, the transvaluation of all values. The Leninist passion for the real, which is also a passion for thought, knows no morality. Morality, as Nietzsche was aware, has only the status of a genealogy. It is a leftover from the old world. Consequently, for a Leninist, the threshold of toleration of what, in our peaceful and old world of today, is to us the worst is extremely high.

This is clearly why certain people speak today of the barbarism of the century. But it is completely unjust to isolate this dimension of passion of the real. Even if it is about the prosecution of intellectuals, disastrous as its spectacle and its effects may be, it is important to remember that what renders it possible is the fact that it is not the privileges of knowledge that dictate the political access to the real. Such was the case in the French Revolution when Fouquier-Tinville condemned Lavoisier, the founder of modern chemistry, to death, saying, "The Republic has no need for scholars." It was a barbaric utterance, completely extremist and irrational, but one has to know how to read it, beyond itself, under its axiomatic, abbreviated form: "The Republic has no need." It is not from need, from interest or from its correlative, or from privileged knowledge that the political capture of a fragment of the real derives, but from the occurrence of a thought that can be collectivized, and only from this. In other words, the political, when it exists, founds its own principle concerning the real, and it does not have any need for anything except for itself.

But perhaps any attempt to submit thought to the test of the real, political or not, would be taken today as barbaric? The passion for the real, strongly cooled down, temporarily gives place to an acceptance of reality, an acceptance that sometimes can have a joyful form and sometimes a sad one.

Certainly the passion for the real is always accompanied by a proliferation of semblance. For a revolutionary, the world is an ancient world full of corruption and treachery. One has constantly to start again with purification, with disclosing the real under its veils.

What has to be underlined is that purifying the real means extracting it from the reality that envelops and obscures it. Hence the violent taste for the surface and for transparency. The century attempts to react against profundity. It puts forward a strong criticism of the fundamental and of what lies beyond; it promotes the immediate and the sensitive surface. It proposes, following Nietzsche, to get rid of the "worlds behind" and to state that the real is identical with the appearance. The thought, precisely because what animates it is not the ideal but the real, has to grasp the appearance as appearance, or the real as pure event of its appearance. In order to arrive at this point, it is necessary to destroy every depth, every presumption of substance, every assertion of reality. It is reality that forms an obstacle against the discovery of the real as a pure surface. There is the struggle against the semblance. But since the semblance of reality adheres to the real, the destruction of the semblance identifies with the pure and simple destruction. At the end of its purification, the real as a total absence of reality is nothingness. This way, taken by numerous attempts of the century—political, artistic, scientific—will be called the way of nihilist terrorism. Since its subjective animation is the passion for the real, this is not consent to nothingness but a creation, and it seems appropriate to recognize in it an active nihilism.

Where are we today? The figure of active nihilism is taken to be completely obsolete. Every reasonable activity is limited, limiting, bordered by the gravities of reality. What one can do best is to avoid the bad and, in order to do this, the shortest way is to avoid any contact with the real. Finally one finds nothingness again, the nothing-of-the-real, and in this sense one is always within nihilism. But since one has suppressed the terrorist element—the desire to purify the real—nihilism is now de-activized. It has become passive nihilism, or reactive nihilism, a nihilism hostile against every action as well as against every thought.

The other way that the century has sketched, the one that tries to keep up the passion for the real without giving way to the paroxysmal charm of terror, I would like to call the subtractive way: it means to exhibit as the real point not the destruction of reality but a minimal difference. The other way set forth by the century is to purify reality, and not to annihilate it in its surface, by subtracting it from its apparent unity in order to detect the tiny difference, the vanishing term that is constitutive for it. What takes place hardly differs from the place where it takes place. It is in this "hardly" where all the affect is, in this immanent exception.

With both routes, the key question is that of the new. What is new? This is the obsession of the century. Since its very beginning, the century has presented itself as a figure of advent or commencement—above all the advent or recommencement of man: the new man.

This phrase, which is perhaps more Stalinist than Leninist, can be understood in two ways. For a whole host of thinkers, particularly in the field of fascist thought (including Heidegger), the new man is in part the restitution of the ancient man, who was obliterated and corrupted. Purification is, in reality, a more or less violent process of return to an origin that has disappeared. The new is a reproduction of the authentic. Ultimately, the task of the century is restitution through destruction, that is, the restitution of origins through the destruction of the inauthentic.

For another group of thinkers, particularly in the field of Marxist Communism, the new man is a real creation, something that has not yet come into existence because it arises out of the destruction of historical antagonisms. It is beyond class, beyond the state.

The new man is either restored or he is produced.

In the first case, the definition of the new man is rooted in mythic totalizations such as race, nation, blood, and soil. The new man is a collection of characteristics (Nordic, Aryan, warrior, and so forth).

In the second case, the new man, in contrast, resists all categorization and characterization. In particular he resists the family, private property, and the nation-state. This is Engels's thesis in *The Origin of the Family, Private Property, and the State*. Marx, too, stressed that the universal singularity of the proletariat is to resist categorization, to have no characteristics, and, in particular, in the strongest sense, to have no particular nationality. This negative and universal conception of the new man, which rejects all categorization, persists throughout the century. It is important to note here the hostility toward the family as a primordial, egoistic kernel of the search for roots, tradition, and origins. Gide's pronouncement—"To all families, I hate you!"—participates in this sort of vindication of the new man.

It is quite striking to see that, at the end of the century, the notion of the family has regained its consensual and almost taboo status. Today the young adore their families and seem not to want to leave the nest. The German Green Party, which considers itself to be oppositional (but this is all relative, as we are talking about the government), envisions a day when it will be able to call itself "the family party." Even homosexuals, who in this century, as we see with Gide, are an oppositional force, are demanding their integration in the family and in the national heritage, and their right to citizenship. This tells us something about where we are today. In the real present of this century the new man was first of all, speaking in progressive terms, the one who would escape from the family and from the tethers of private property, as well as from statist despotism. He was the one who wanted militant subversion and political victory in the Leninist sense. Today, it seems that "modernization," as our masters would put it, consists in being a good little father, a good little mother, a good little son, to become an efficient executive, to profit as much as one can, and to play the role of a responsible citizen. The slogan is now "Make Money, Protect the Family, Win Votes."

The century draws to a close around three themes: impossible subjective innovation, comfort, and repetition. In other words, obsession. The century ends in an obsession for security, it ends under a maxim that is actually rather abject: it is not really so bad to be just where you are . . . there are and there have been worse ways. And this obsession goes completely against the century that, as both Freud and Lenin understood it, had been born under the sign of devastating hysteria, of its activism, and of its intransigent militarism.

We are here—we are taking up Lenin's work—in order to reactivate the very question of theory along political lines. We do this against the morose obsession that is now so prevalent. What is your critique of the existing world? What can you propose that is new? What can you imagine and create? And finally, to speak in the terms of Sylvain Lazarus, what do you think? What is politics as thought?

Note

1   V. I. Lenin, "The Proletarian Revolution and the Renegade Kautsky," in *Collected Works* (Moscow: Progress Publishers, 1974), 28:269.

2

Leninism in the

Twenty-first Century?

Lenin, Weber, and the

Alex Callinicos   **Politics of Responsibility**

"Ceaselessly the thinking man praises Comrade Lenin," wrote Brecht in the 1930s. Nothing could be further from the task the thinking man or woman sets him- or herself today. Demonized and despised, Lenin remains firmly beyond the pale of the politically acceptable, as much in *bien pensant* left-liberal circles as those on the right.

Fashionable historiography faithfully reproduces this attitude. Admittedly the portrait that Orlando Figes paints of Lenin as a macho aristocratic thug in his execrable anti-Bolshevik polemic *A People's Tragedy* is evidently absurd and riddled with inaccuracies.[1] Robert Service's recent biography provides a much more persuasive reconstruction of Lenin's family background, which stresses the Ulyanovs' recent and precarious entry into the gentry but then proceeds down the track of routine denunciation unsupported by any significant revelations from the archives.

Service's treatment of a remark on Lenin by the Menshevik leader Dan during their years in exile is symptomatic of his general method: "there's no such person who is so preoccupied twenty-four hours a day with revolution, who thinks no other thoughts except those about revolution and who even dreams in his sleep about revolution." The obvious reading of this comment is that it ascribes to Lenin unusual single-mindedness—a quality of character that, as numerous platitudes record, involves both strengths and weaknesses. But Service glosses Dan's remark as evidence of Lenin's belief that "only his ideas would genuinely advance the cause of the Revolution"; by the next page this has become straightforward "megalomania."[2] By the time Service reaches the Civil War, all restraint is lost—thus the killing of Nicholas II and his family in July 1918 is attributed to Lenin's "rage," "appetite for revenge," and hatred of the Romanovs without any consideration of the sources or of the kind of instrumental calculations that seem in fact, rightly or wrongly, to have motivated the Bolsheviks' decision to have the imperial family shot.[3]

It is easy enough to dismiss such cases of intellectual shoddiness as examples of the negative impact of post-1989 capitalist triumphalism on historical scholarship. But when we have set this kind of stuff aside, there remains a much more serious question to address: Does Lenin have anything to say to the Left in the twenty-first century? This question is posed at a very important political conjuncture, when resistance to global capitalism is growing, as the succession of demonstrations at Seattle, Washington, Millau, Melbourne, Prague, Seoul, Nice, and Davos shows. Some of the strongest currents in the new Left emerging in these protests are explicitly committed to highly decentralized forms of organizing that seem quite antithetical to the Leninist conception of the vanguard party. Indeed anarchists sometimes seek to exclude from anti-capitalist coalitions anyone who defends this idea, calling them authoritarian.[4]

So does Lenin have anything to say to the new anti-capitalist Left today? We are greatly in Slavoj Žižek's debt for answering this question with an emphatic "Yes!" By using some of the cultural capital his brilliant critical writings have accumulated over the past decade or so to call for a return to Lenin, Žižek has helped to open a space in which serious discussion of Lenin can be renewed on the Left. In seeking critically to interrogate the precise form in which Žižek has issued this call I am (or so I hope) acting in the spirit of solidarity that should inform the work of anti-capitalist intellectuals when they engage in the strategic discussions necessary to confront the common enemy.

As this passage from his announcement of this conference makes clear, Leninism for Žižek marks a division within the anti-capitalist Left:

> Lenin's politics is the true counterpoint not only to the center-left pragmatic opportunism, but also to the marginalist . . . leftist attitude of what Lacan called the "narcissism of the lost cause" [*le narcissme de*

la chose perdue]. What a true Leninist and a political conservative have in common is the fact that they reject what one could call liberal leftist irresponsibility, that is, advocating grand projects of solidarity, freedom, and so on, yet ducking out when the price to be paid for them is in the guise of concrete and often "cruel" political measures. Like an authentic conservative, a true Leninist is not afraid to pass to the act, to take responsibility for all the consequences, unpleasant as they may be, of realizing his political project. Kipling (whom Brecht admired very much) despised British liberals who advocated freedom and justice while silently counting on the Conservatives to do the necessary dirty work for them; the same can be said for the liberal leftist's (or "Democratic Socialist's") relationship toward Leninist Communists: liberal leftists reject Social Democratic compromise; they want a true revolution, yet they shirk the actual price to be paid for it and thus prefer to adopt the attitude of a Beautiful Soul and to keep their hands clean. In contrast to this false liberal-leftist position (of those who want true democracy for the people, but without secret police to fight the counterrevolution, and without their academic privileges being threatened . . .), a Leninist, like a conservative, is authentic in the sense of fully assuming the consequences of his choices, that is, of being fully aware of what it actually means to take power and to exert it. Therein resided the greatness of Lenin after the Bolsheviks took power: in contrast to hysterical revolutionary fervor caught in a vicious cycle, the fervor of those who prefer to stay in opposition and prefer (publicly or secretly) to avoid the burden of taking things over, of accomplishing the shift from subversive activity to responsibility for the smooth running of the social edifice, he heroically embraced the heavy task of actually running the state, of making all the necessary compromises, but also of enacting the necessary harsh measures to assure that Bolshevik power would not collapse. . . .[5]

Žižek here identifies Leninism with what one might call the politics of responsibility. He differentiates this from "liberal leftism," an expression that Žižek uses to refer not to defenders of the Blair-Clinton Third Way and their postmodernist accomplices but rather to those who are genuinely opposed to global capitalism but shrink from the harsh consequences of applying their principles. Tacitly at least, "liberal leftism" thus understood extends to the Trotskyist tradition: are we not meant to recognize Trotsky and those influenced by him among those who fall victim to "hysterical revolutionary fervor caught in a vicious cycle, the fervor of those who prefer to stay in opposition and prefer (publicly or secretly) to avoid the burden of taking things over, of accomplishing the shift from subversive activity to responsibility for the smooth running of the social edifice"?

By contrast, "like an authentic conservative, a true Leninist is not afraid to pass to the act, to take responsibility for all the consequences, unpleasant as they may be, of realizing his political project." This opposition between the "liberal leftist" eager to save his "Beautiful Soul" and the "true Leninist" who sternly accepts responsibility for the consequences of his actions recalls nothing more than the celebrated concluding pages of Weber's lecture "Politics as a Vocation." Here he distinguishes between two basic ways in which ethics and politics may be connected:

> Ethically oriented activity can follow two fundamentally different, irreconcilably opposed maxims. It can follow the "ethic of principled conviction" (Gesinnung) or the "ethic of responsibility." It is not that the ethic of conviction is identical to irresponsibility, nor that the ethic of responsibility means the absence of principled conviction—there is of course no question of that. But there is a profound opposition between acting by the maxim of the ethic of conviction (putting it in religious terms: "The Christian does what is right and places the outcome in God's hands") and acting by the maxim of the ethic of responsibility, which means that one must answer for the (foreseeable) consequences of one's actions.[6]

Delivered in January 1919, in the aftermath of the German Revolution of November 1918 and within days of the unsuccessful leftist rising in Berlin in which Rosa Luxemburg and Karl Liebknecht perished, "Politics as a Vocation" is far from the piece of disinterested scholarship it purported to be. As Perry Anderson has noted, the text brims over with anti-revolutionary and nationalist rhetoric.[7] It is the revolutionary Left that Weber treats as the main instance of the ethic of conviction: valid when authentically experienced—as is not so in "nine cases out of ten," where "I am dealing with windbags, people who are intoxicated with romantic sensations but who do not truly feel what they are taking upon themselves"—it implies a renunciation of this world and of practical success. Any attempt practically to realize absolute principles must

inevitably founder, since it requires the resort to violence that is inherent in all politics, and hence a struggle with "the diabolical powers that
lurk in all violence." Not only are the political acts thereby undertaken
morally compromised, but the revolutionary movement itself becomes
a vehicle for the material interests that will inevitably use its promises
to legitimize themselves, "for the materialist interpretation of history is
not a cab which may be boarded at will, and it makes no exceptions for
the bearers of revolutions!"[8]

The political animus behind Weber's contrast between the ethics of
conviction and of responsibility is best conveyed in this letter to Robert
Michels, written when the latter was still a Marxist syndicalist:

> There are two possibilities. Either: (1) "my kingdom is not of this world"
> (Tolstoy, or a thoroughly thought-out syndicalism . . .) . . . Or: (2) Cul-
> ture—(i.e., objective, a culture expressed in technical, etc., "achieve-
> ments") affirmation as adaptation to the sociological condition of all
> "technology," whether it be economic, political or whatever . . . In the
> case of (2), all talk of "revolution" is farce, every thought of abolish-
> ing the "domination of man by man" by any kind of "socialist" social
> system or the most elaborated form of "democracy" a utopia . . . Who-
> ever wishes to live as a "modern man" even in the sense that he has his
> daily paper and railways and trams—he renounces all those ideals which
> vaguely appeal to you as soon as he leaves the basis of revolutionism for
> its own sake, without any "objective," without an "objective" being
> thinkable.[9]

The ethic of responsibility thus implies the acceptance of the objective realities of the modern world—realities that make democracy as
well as socialism mere utopias. The practitioner of this ethic therefore
renounces revolution and stoically accepts the necessarily compromised
character of all political action that arises from its entanglement in the
unpredictable nexus of cause and effect and its reliance on "morally
suspect or at least morally dangerous ends."[10] The entire construction
and rhetoric of "Politics as a Vocation" makes clear Weber's preference
for this ethical stance, against what he portrays as the destructive dilet-
tantism of his Bolshevik and Spartacist foes.

It is, therefore, highly paradoxical to find Žižek using very similar
terms to Weber: "a true Leninist," let us recall, "is not afraid . . . to
take responsibility for all the consequences, unpleasant as they may be,

of realizing his political project," whereas the ethic of responsibility commands that "one must answer for the (foreseeable) consequences of one's actions." Yet for Žižek this defines the ethical stance of the authentic revolutionary, as opposed to the liberal-leftist "Beautiful Soul" who, in avoiding the messy practical consequences of realizing his ethic of conviction, leaves the world as it is.

Paradoxes are not necessarily to be feared. Indeed, by bringing Weber and Lenin into the same intellectual force-field we may throw light on what is distinctive and valuable in a genuine Leninist politics. Such, at any rate, is what I shall try to do in the rest of this essay.

The Centrality of Theory

The first thing to note is the philosophical presuppositions implied by Weber's contrast. The distinction between the ethics of responsibility and of conviction maps onto a neo-Kantian scission between facts and values. The unconditional character of the normative goals pursued by practitioners of the latter ethic reflects their independence of any actual state of affairs. "My kingdom is not of this world": a life governed by ultimate conviction cannot mix factual appraisals with ethical considerations. Correspondingly, the assessment of consequences involved in the ethic of responsibility irreparably comprises the realistic practice of politics, inherently engaged as this is with the "diabolical powers" of violence.

But Weber's version of neo-Kantianism figures in the contrast in a second form. Common to both ethics is the fact that they cannot be rationally justified: "whether one *ought* to act on the basis of an ethic of conviction or one of responsibility, and when one should do one thing or another, these are not things about which one can give instructions to anyone." [11] The adoption of any set of values is irreducible to a rationally motivated judgment. An inherent gap separates the way the world is from the ends that govern human action: it can only be crossed by a leap, by a decision implied by no set of normative principles, and indeed it is not necessary for a person to recognize the authority of any such principles. Reason can only play at best an instrumental role, identifying the most effective means for achieving ends in whose selection it has played no part. [12]

What Anderson rightly describes as Weber's "decisionism" seems a world away from Lenin's approach to politics.[13] This is best brought out in two stages—first by considering the role played by theoretical analysis in Lenin's politics, and then by confronting the place occupied there by ethical considerations of any kind. The figure of Lenin-the-Machiavellian-opportunist is now well entrenched in mainstream academic discourse. Service is the most recent to express this conventional judgment. Describing the Second Congress of the Communist International in the summer of 1920, he writes of

> the casual fashion in which Lenin treated his Marxism whenever a goal of practical politics was in his sights. Although he thought seriously about social and economic theory and liked to stick by his basic ideas, his adherence was not absolute. In mid-1920 the priority for him was the global release of revolutionary energy. Ideas about the unavoidable stages of social development faded for him. Better to make Revolution, however roughly, than to fashion a sophisticated but unrealized theory. If intellectual sleight of hand was sometimes necessary, then so be it. Even when he stayed close to his previously declared policies, Lenin was mercurially difficult to comprehend. Parties belonging to the Comintern, he declared, should break with "opportunistic" kinds of socialism which rejected the need for the "dictatorship of the proletariat"; but simultaneously he demanded that British communists should affiliate themselves to the Labour Party: Lenin's argument was that communism in the United Kingdom was as yet too frail to set up an independent party.[14]

Yet what a serious intellectual biography of Lenin would reveal is less his casual attitude to theory than the systematic manner in which every significant turn in events drove him to reconsider how best the situation was to be understood from a theoretical perspective.[15] Before the 1905 Revolution a rigorous analysis in particular of Russian agrarian structures in *The Development of Capitalism in Russia* (1899) provided the theoretical basis of Lenin's critique of populist hopes of rural socialism. The capacities for collective action displayed by the peasantry in 1905 forced a reappraisal registered in *The Agrarian Question and the "Critics of Marx"* (1908) and *The Agrarian Programme of Russian Social Democracy in the First Russian Revolution* (1908). The crisis that the outbreak of the First World War precipitated in the international socialist movement prompted Lenin into a more general reconsideration of socialist theory and strategy that was reflected notably in the *Philosophical Notebooks*, which were produced by his reading of Hegel, and in "Imperialism, the Highest Stage of Capitalism." The process culminated in *The State and Revolution*, the incomplete text on the Marxist theory of the state written while he was on the run in the summer of 1917, between the February and October Revolutions.

What this record suggests is neither the cynical opportunist nor the fanatical dogmatist portrayed by conventional historiography. Rather we see a constant tracking backward and forward between theory and practice as new problems force Lenin even in the most pressing of circumstances to step back and to reappraise the situation theoretically. But to say this is not to settle the question of precisely how Lenin himself understood the relationship between theoretical analysis and political practice. Reflecting on the experience of the October Revolution toward the end of his life, he famously quoted Napoleon: "On s'engage et puis . . . on voit." Rendered freely this means: "First engage in a serious battle and then see what happens."[16] This seems to invite a decisionist reading of Lenin's actions in 1917, with the October Revolution a gambler's throw of the dice.

Such a reading would, however, be misleading. Lenin's role in 1917 reflects rather two key themes of his political thought—(1) the complexity and unpredictability of history, and (2) the necessity of political intervention. This first theme is perhaps most evident in the "Letters from Afar" with which Lenin greeted the February Revolution. In the first letter he comments on the apparently miraculous way in which the tsar was suddenly overthrown: "There are no miracles in nature or in history, but every abrupt turn in history, and this applies to every revolution, presents such a wealth of content, unfolds such unexpected and specific combinations of forms of struggle and alignments of forces of the contestants, that to the lay mind there is much that must appear miraculous."[17]

Lenin proceeds to analyze the various elements that came together in February 1917—long-term conflicts in Russian society, the "mighty accelerator" provided by the First World War, Russia's relative weakness among the Great Powers, conspiracies by conservative and liberal politicians who, with Anglo-French encouragement, had concluded that the Romanov dynasty was an obstacle to the effective prosecution of the war, and growing discontent among the workers and garrison of Petrograd. Thus, "as a result of an extremely unique historical situation, *absolutely dissimilar currents, absolutely heterogeneous* class interests, *absolutely contrary* political and social strivings have *merged*, and in a strikingly 'harmonious' manner."[18]

Althusser, of course, used this very text in "Contradiction and Overdetermination" in order to argue for an interpretation of the Marxist dialectic that highlighted the inherent complexity of the historical process, its irreducibility to any simple essence, even the economy.[19] I am, however, more interested here in the implications of this complexity for political action. If "absolutely heterogeneous" elements can form "such unexpected and specific combinations" as those that Lenin analyzes in the "Letters from Afar," then there are strict limits to what even the best social theory can predict. This doesn't mean that historical events are unintelligible, or genuinely miraculous, but the process leading to an "abrupt turn in history" may often be grasped only through retrospective reconstruction—as Lenin did when he sought to understand the February Revolution after it had taken him, along with everyone else, by surprise.

In what passes for contemporary thought, such a recognition of what Merleau-Ponty called the ambiguity of history typically leads to the avoidance of political action and to the passive contemplation of the ironies thrown up by an infinitely complex social world. This was not so in Lenin's case: the very unpredictability of history requires that we intervene to help shape it. In *What Is to Be Done?* (1902), Lenin replies to a claim that, in effect, things are too complicated for his proposed centralized organization of revolutionaries to advance the Russian socialist movement with the famous metaphor of the key link in the chain: "*Every* question 'runs in a vicious circle' because political life as a whole is an endless chain consisting of an infinite number of links. The whole art of politics lies in finding and taking as firm a grip as we can of the link that is least likely to be struck from our hands, the one that is most important at the given moment, the one that most of all guarantees its possessor the possession of the whole chain."[20]

But political intervention is not a blind leap into the dark. Careful analysis is required in order to identify which is the key link, and that in turn involves an understanding of the "whole chain." Thus Lenin writes of "the *actual* political situation" after the February Revolution that "we must first endeavor to define [it] with the greatest possible objective precision, in order that Marxist tactics may be based upon the only possible solid foundation—the foundation of *facts*."[21] "Abrupt turns in history" may be unpredictable, but it does not follow that the circumstances that produce them do not possess certain fundamental contours that it is possible for theoretically oriented analysis to identify correctly in order to guide political intervention.

In the autumn of 1917, when Lenin bombarded the Bolshevik Central Committee with letters demanding that they organize an insurrection, his arguments were based on an analysis of the balance of forces against the background of a rapidly deteriorating military and economic situation. This analysis concluded with the prediction that, if the Bolsheviks did not take power quickly, the ruling class would seek to destroy the revolution either by mounting another military coup like that attempted by General Kornilov in August 1917 or by letting the advancing German armies take Petrograd. "History will not forgive revolutionaries for procrastinating when they could be victorious today . . . , while they risk losing much tomorrow, in fact, they risk losing everything," he wrote on 24 October, on the very eve of the Bolshevik uprising.[22] Thus the political situation has a determinate structure that analysis can reveal; at the same time, contrary to fatalistic interpretations of Marxism, there is more than one possible outcome of the situation; and, finally, which outcome actually prevails depends, in part, on the actions of the revolutionaries themselves.

Of course, any appraisal of the balance of forces may turn out to be at least partially mistaken. It is in this light that we must interpret Lenin's (mis)quotation of Napoleon—"On s'engage et puis . . . on voit." The revolutionaries intervene on the basis of the best available analysis: it is only by thus intervening—seizing what seems to them the key link in the chain—that they discover whether or not this analysis is true. Thus, for example, Lenin was right in predicting a revolution in Germany comparable to the February Revolution, but, in the event, it did not lead to the emergence of a socialist republic in an advanced country that could come to the aid of Soviet Russia. The isolation of the Russian Revolution then dictated the tactical retreats and compromises represented most importantly by the New Economic Policy adopted in 1921 that sought to conciliate the peasantry through a large-scale restoration of market mechanisms in agriculture. Lenin's final reflections on the revolution involve accordingly revised expectations, which anticipate a much more protracted transition to socialism in Russia, in which the Soviet regime will more or less peacefully coexist with rural small producers, gradually seeking to wean them into participating in more collective forms of organization.[23]

The unpredictability of history is thus not equivalent to its indeterminacy. Theoretical analysis may seek to identify the structures and tendencies constitutive of any given situation. But these structures and tendencies, even if accurately conceptualized, do not exhaust the situation. The revolutionary intervenes on the basis of the best take she can get on the situation, attempting to act on what seem to be the decisive factors in it. The inherent limits of even the best theory—its inability even if true to exhaust the situation—compel the constant tracking backward and forward between analysis and action that I argued earlier was an important feature of Lenin's political practice. If things go well (as, of course, they all too often don't), the result is a process of mutual illumination, in which successful interventions allow the refinement of theory, which in turn may contribute to better practice.

The rational kernel of decisionism is that no theory can unambiguously entail or uniquely determine a course of political action. This is so not merely for the reason given above—the fact that, given the complexity of their causes, "abrupt turns in history" are hard to predict. Kant's theory of judgment and Wittgenstein's remarks on rule-following both show that the application of a principle is never an automatic process; it always invites mutually inconsistent interpretations. But such considerations do not reduce political action to an unmotivated leap in the dark. Certainly, in Lenin's case, a developing body of theoretical analysis constituted a critical element of the context in which he acted, even if it was always a matter of judgment how actually to carry on in the light of this analysis.[24]

The Ethics of Revolution

In any case, the picture that I have painted of a continual dialogue between theoretical analysis and political action implies that reason plays more than the instrumental role to which Weber reduces it. But this conclusion may only be properly supported by addressing the second question referred to above, namely that of the place occupied by ethical considerations in Lenin's thought. It has to be said that there is very little of much interest to be gleaned by his explicit remarks on the subject. Like other orthodox Marxists he rejected appeals to abstract normative principles both on philosophical grounds that derive ultimately from Hegel's critique of Kant and for more directly political reasons—for example, that talk of justice and rights concealed class antagonisms and thereby impeded the development of the revolutionary movement required to abolish them.[25]

Had Lenin sought to offer a sustained ethical defense of the October Revolution he would almost certainly have relied on arguments of the kind used by Trotsky in *Their Morals and Ours* (1938). Here Trotsky defends a form of consequentialism, arguing that, "from the Marxist point of view, which expresses the historical interests of the proletariat, the end is justified if it leads to increasing the power of humanity over nature and to the abolition of the power of one person over another."[26] Talk of consequences brings us back to Žižek, for whom "a true Leninist is not afraid to pass to the act, to take responsibility for all the consequences, unpleasant as they may be, of realizing his political project."

The consequences on which Žižek focuses are, however, less the future outcome that might justify our actions in the present than the means necessary to achieve this outcome. He warns us against sliding easily over the ugly things that must be done to rid the world of exploitation and oppression. Such warnings are valuable inasmuch as they provide a corrective to wishful thinking, but they can themselves—unless set carefully in the appropriate context—take on an apologetic role.

This can be illustrated by considering perhaps the most sophisticated apologia of the Moscow Trials, Merleau-Ponty's *Humanism and Terror* (1947). This book defends what Steven Lukes calls "a kind of ultra-consequentialism, in which the very meaning of an action is determined by its results."[27] It does so on the basis of a conception of history in certain respects similar to the one I have attributed to Lenin above. History, as Hegel argues in the dialectic of master and slave, is a struggle to the death: the institutionalized violence of class society can only be removed through revolutionary violence. The future, however, is unknown. Faced with the contingency of history, we must decide on the basis of probabilities. But the consequences of these decisions may turn out to be quite different from those that we intended. Bolshevik leaders such as Bukharin may have sincerely believed that they were saving the revolution in opposing Stalin, but anything that weakened the Soviet Union when faced with Nazi Germany was a counterrevolutionary act: "In a period of revolutionary tension or external threat there is no clear-cut boundary between political divergences and objective treason."[28] The fact that the prosecution's charges of conscious conspiracy with the Gestapo and other foreign secret services were false was beside the point, as is reflected in Bukharin's collaboration with his accusers. In contrast, Trotsky, in going into root-and-branch opposition to Stalin, "acted as though there were no contingencies, and as though the ambiguity of events, cunning, and violence had been eliminated from history," taking refuge in an abstract rationalism.[29]

That this represents an extraordinarily naïve view of the Moscow Trials should go without saying.[30] But it also implies a philosophy of history in which an actor must await future events to condemn or vindicate her morally. What is wrong with such a view is brought out most clearly perhaps when Merleau-Ponty draws an analogy between the Moscow Trials and the purges in post-war France of those who had collaborated with the German occupation: "By confronting the collaborator before he was in the wrong historically and he who resisted before history proved him right, and both again after history has proved the one wrong and the other right, the Moscow Trials reveal the subjective struggle to the death which characterizes contemporary history."[31]

But what does being "in the wrong [or right] historically" mean here? Though he rejects the accusation that he is making a vulgar Hegelian equation of moral rightness with practical success, Merleau-Ponty comes dangerously close to saying that the collaborators were proved wrong and the resisters proved right because Germany lost the war. But that can't possibly be right. Surely we don't admire those who fought in the French resistance just—or indeed at all—because they happened to choose the winning side?

Similarly it seems to me that Trotsky's true greatness emerged not when he organized the October insurrection or led the Red Army but when in the 1930s, virtually alone and at a terrible personal price to his family and himself, he defiantly defended the revolutionary tradition against Stalin. His own response to the Moscow Trials was summed up in these words: "History has to be taken as she is; and when she allows herself such extraordinary and filthy outrages, one must fight her back with one's fists."[32] Merleau-Ponty seems to regard this stance as turning socialist revolution into a kind of Kantian idea of pure reason bearing no relation to social reality: but I think it would be better to say that Trotsky's situation is one where the only hope of influencing the future—in that sense of being vindicated by history—lies (as Benjamin would put it) in rubbing history against the grain, in defying the way things are going in the present.

Merleau-Ponty tacitly acknowledges the point in the following passage:

> What we reproach the collaborators for is surely not a mistake in reading [history] any more than what we honor in the Resistance is simply coolness of judgment and clairvoyance. On the contrary, what one admires is that they took sides against the probable and that they were devoted and enthusiastic enough to allow reasons to speak to them that only came afterward. The glory of those who resisted—like the dishonor of the collaborators—presupposes both the contingency of politics, without which no one would be to blame in politics, and the rationality of history, without which there would only be madmen.[33]

But the final sentence quoted undermines the concession made in the rest of the passage. Is it really the case that it is because the future is uncertain that blameworthy actions are performed in politics? Hitler failed to anticipate events correctly when he opened a second front against the U.S.S.R. in June 1941: Is that the reason why we condemn him? The question has only to be posed to answer itself: it is, if anything a saving grace of Hitler that he so grossly miscalculated and thus helped to engineer his own destruction and that of his regime, albeit at an appalling human cost.

Trotsky by comparison offers a much more restrained consequentialism. He insists on what he calls the "dialectical interdependence of ends and means":

> That is permissible . . . which *really* leads to the liberation of humanity. Since this end can be achieved only through revolution, the liberating morality of the proletariat of necessity is endowed with a revolutionary

character. It reconcilably counteracts not only religious dogma but all kinds of idealistic fetishes, these philosophical gendarmes of the ruling class. It deduces a rule for conduct from the laws of development of society, thus primarily from the class struggle, this law of all laws.

. . . Permissible and obligatory are those and only those means . . . which unite the revolutionary proletariat, fill their hearts with irreconcilable hostility to oppression, teach them contempt for official morality and its democratic echoers, imbue them with consciousness of their own historic mission, raise their courage and spirit of self-sacrifice in the struggle. Precisely from this it flows that not all means are permissible. When we say that the end justifies the means, then for us the conclusion follows that the great revolutionary end spurns those base means and ways which set one part of the working class against other parts, or attempt to make the masses happy without their participation or lower the faith of the masses in themselves and their organization, replacing it with worship of the "leaders."[34]

Trotsky goes on somewhat to spoil his argument when he says, "Dialectical materialism does not know dualism of means and end. The end flows naturally from the historical movement. Organically the means are subordinated to the end."[35] As Dewey points out in his response to Trotsky, this involves the Hegelian "belief that human ends are interwoven into the very texture and structure of existence."[36] This slide into the naturalistic fallacy, which is reflected also in the idea that ethical norms can be deduced from "the laws of development of society," should not, however, be allowed to obscure the fact that Trotsky's main point here is that not all means are justified by the goal of liberating humanity. He goes on to illustrate this by arguing that individual terror—the assassination of individual leaders and officials, even when the person targeted is as wicked as Stalin—is not an acceptable method of struggle because it involves substituting personal heroism for mass action: "The liberation of the workers can only come through the workers themselves."[37]

Trotsky, like other classical Marxists, here shows himself to subscribe to a confused and erroneous meta-ethics, one that both denies moral principles any universal validity and seeks to infer the principles on which his own ethical judgments rely from the structure of the world.[38] This does not alter the substantive point he makes here concerning the ethics of political action, that the means chosen condition the end actually achieved. He approvingly quotes this passage from Lassalle's play *Franz von Sickingen*:

> Do not only show the goal, show the path as well.
> For so closely interwoven with one another are path and goal
> That a change by one means a change in the other,
> And a different path gives rise to a different goal.[39]

Dewey argues that Trotsky fails to distinguish between two senses of the term "end"—(1) "the actual objective consequences" of certain actions, and (2) the "*end-in-view*" with which they are performed, "an *idea* of the final consequences, in case the idea is formed *on the ground of the means that are judged to be most likely to produce the end.*" The second point is thus "itself a means for directing action" while the first is the "actual outcome" of action.[40] Dewey goes on to accuse Trotsky of dogmatically deducing class struggle as the privileged means of achieving human liberation from the Marxist theory of history. Whatever we think of this criticism, it is clear that the distinction Dewey draws is in fact implicit in Trotsky's own text. Thus Trotsky argues that we may sympathize with the reasons someone has for, say, assassinating a leading Stalinist official: "However, not the question of subjective motives but that of objective efficacy has for us the decisive significance. Are the given means really capable of leading to the goal? In relation to individual terror, both theory and experience bear witness that such is not the case."[41]

In any case, the distinction between actual consequences and end-in-view is critical to a proper assessment of Leninism. Contrary to the claims of both Cold War liberals and Stalinist apologists, it is plain that the Stalinist system as it took shape at the end of the 1920s was radically different from the end-in-view of Lenin or indeed any other leading Bolshevik (including Stalin himself) at the time of the October Revolution. It is equally undeniable that the methods used by the Bolsheviks in order to take power and—perhaps even more important—to retain power during the Civil War of 1918–21 materially contributed to the formation of the Stalinist system as it took shape during the 1930s. The critical questions concern both whether such an outcome flowed inevitably from use of these methods and what alternatives were available to the Bolsheviks and indeed other Russian radicals (Mensheviks, Social Revolutionaries, and Anarchists) in the rapidly deteriorating situation after the February Revolution.

Finding the answers to these questions is a complex and difficult matter since, apart from anything else, it requires a resort to counterfactual history, with all the hazards this involves. The debate over these issues began almost as soon as the fall of the Provisional Government: it has recently been renewed by Arno Mayer's major comparative study of the French and Russian Terrors.[42] My own view, for what this is worth, is that Stalinism represented a break with Leninism rather than its completion, and that its emergence was not inevitable but was a contingent outcome of the circumstances in which the Bolsheviks found themselves, particularly as a result of the final defeat of the German Revolution in October 1923.[43]

My aim here is not to rehearse old debates but rather to observe that decisionism is not particularly helpful in trying to assess these issues. Stalin, after all, might well have sought to justify his actions by the "end-in-view" of human liberation. He might even, in the watches of the night when he sought to justify his deeds to himself, have met Žižek's requirement for being "authentic in the sense of fully assuming the consequences of his choices, that is, of being fully aware of what it actually means to take power and to exert it." He might well have defended the destruction of the peasantry, the Terror, and the Gulag Archipelago as "unpleasant" acts necessary to save the revolution.[44]

It is precisely here that critical judgment is required in order to determine whether the Bolshevik end-in-view corresponded to the actual consequences of Stalin's actions. It is, moreover, hard to see how any adequate conception of the end-in-view can avoid an appeal to some general normative principles in order to characterize how that end realizes or contributes toward the good for human beings. Here, then, we reach the limits of the kind of consequentialism defended by Trotsky. The effect is not necessarily to reinstate a Kantian deontological conception of ethics. On the contrary, the cases considered indicate how ethical considerations and political calculations are inextricably interwoven when crucial judgments are undertaken: in particular, discussion of the moral validity of any resort to violence is typically inseparable from an assessment of its political efficacy.[45] Indeed Trotsky himself goes beyond his official consequentialism both by the stress he lays on the interdependence of ends and means and the model his resistance to Stalinism in the 1930s offers. These conjure up the image of a political practice that, while not deduced from a universal norm, bears an intrinsic connection to the good that it seeks to realize. Trotsky's defiance of history implies not the renunciation of this world demanded by Weber of consistent revolutionaries but rather the recognition that their actions may only help produce the desired consequences only in the long term and more by the example they offer than by any direct causal role they play.[46]

By contrast, Žižek's decisionism seems to focus attention on the intentions with which actions are performed. The authentic political act is one that is taken when fully aware of the meaning of power. Does this mean that, provided the actor has the right state of mind, the consequences of his or her actions are beyond criticism? Žižek surely cannot intend to authorize such an inference. It would have the effect, for example, of absolving the NATO bombing campaign against Serbia provided it were undertaken by a conservative acting lucidly in the spirit of Carl Schmitt, who (whatever liberal-humanist rationales about preventing massacres and expulsions he used publicly) recognized the ungrounded nature of his decision as an assertion of imperial power. But to avoid such an implication requires acknowledging that an ethics of political action requires both the careful assessment of consequences and an appeal to universal normative principles.

Interestingly, Weber comes to a similar conclusion. Having asserted, as we have seen, that the ethics of conviction and of responsibility are mutually incompatible, he then goes on to contradict himself toward the end of "Politics as a Vocation":

> It is immensely moving when a mature person (whether old or young) who feels with his whole soul the responsibility he bears for the real consequences of his actions, and who acts on the basis of an ethics of responsibility, says at some point, "Here I stand, I can do no other." That is something that is genuinely human and profoundly moving. For it must be *possible* for *each* of us to find ourselves in such a situation if we are not inwardly dead. In this respect, the ethics of conviction and the ethics of responsibility are not absolute opposites. They are complemen-

tary to one another, and only in combination do they produce the true human being who is *capable* of having a vocation for politics.[47]

This passage is saturated with a decisionist, indeed almost romantic, rhetoric symptomatic of what Anderson calls Weber's "vulcanism," his portrayal of the authentic actor as somehow synthesizing passion and detachment.[48] But it is still possible to extract a substantive point from this peculiar discursive context, namely that political action unavoidably brings together the calculation of consequences and the invocation of norms. In challenging the liberal humanitarian rhetoric that has provided such a convenient cover for contemporary imperial designs it is important to insist on the ineliminable role played by the realistic analysis of context and consequences in a serious politics of the Left; but, equally, when seeking to motivate the critique of global capitalism implicit in such a challenge, it is essential that universal ethical principles are articulated and defended.[49]

Leninism Today

This essay has largely been devoted to a kind of meta-discussion of what Lenin's theory and practice reveal about the nature of political action. But it may be worthwhile, in conclusion, to return to the question I asked at the beginning of this essay: What relevance does Lenin have to the Left at the beginning of the twenty-first century?[50] Let me offer a summary answer in the form of three points:

1. *The importance of strategic analysis of capitalism.* Lenin was by no means the greatest Marxist economic thinker. His essay on imperialism was avowedly a secondary popularization drawing on the more original contributions made notably by the Marxists Hilferding and Bukharin and the liberal Hobson. But what Lenin showed more effectively than any other Marxist was the importance of theoretical analysis of capitalism in strategically situating political actors. For all its weaknesses *Imperialism* provided a means of reorienting the revolutionary Left in the unanticipated situation produced by the outbreak of the First World War and the collapse of the Second International by seeking the causes of this crisis in the maturation of a new stage of capitalist development in which economic competition and

geopolitical rivalries were tending to merge together and outlining a new set of political tasks based on the development of an anti-imperialist alliance between the working class in the advanced countries and national liberation movements in the colonies.

The Left needs such strategic analysis today. It needs to go beyond the critique, however valid, of the apologetic theories of globalization put forward by avowed neoliberals and their allies among the defenders of the Third Way to develop a proper understanding of the phase of development capitalism is currently undergoing. To this extent Michael Hardt's and Tony Negri's fine book, *Empire*, has an importance independent of how far one agrees or disagrees with their analysis in that it addresses the distinctive features of contemporary capitalism. Without the kind of understanding *Empire* seeks to develop we are flying blind.

2. *The specificity and centrality of politics.* "Politics is the most concentrated expression of economics," Lenin wrote.[51] It is in the structures of the state and the struggles around it that all the contradictions of class society are concentrated and fused. Strategic analysis is driven by this insight and therefore seeks to trace the implications of all the heterogeneous determinations that, for example, produced the February Revolution for the struggle for political power.[52]

Can this stance survive the weakening of the nation-state, which most commentators believe has been caused by economic globalization? I believe that it has. The exercise of state power was critical in promoting globalization in the first place, and it remains one of the main means through which capitalist economic interests that are still largely nationally constituted are asserted. A complex political arena is emerging in which the international capitalist institutions that were developed to provide forums where the conflicts among these interests can be articulated and regulated are becoming the object of pressure and protest by transnational campaigns such as the anti-capitalist movement that emerged in Seattle.[53] As this movement develops it will have to make strategic judgments about where to focus its efforts in order to hit the system where it is most vulnerable. Hardt and Negri argue that the Leninist idea of the weakest link is no longer appropriate in the global capitalist "Empire," which is vulnerable at every point.[54] But unless it is literally true that the power of capital and of those it exploits are uniformly distributed across the world, some attempt to develop a set of priorities for propaganda and agitation seems simply unavoidable.

3. *The necessity of political organization.* This final point is closely connected to the preceding one. The necessity of concentrating proletarian energies to meet the equivalent concentration of capitalist power in the state was one of the main motivations for Lenin's conception of the revolutionary party. As I noted at the start of this essay, many in the anti-capitalist movement dispute the necessity of such centralization, whatever may have been necessary in the past. For Naomi Klein, for example, the dispersal of campaigning energies serves to confuse the corporate establishment and keep it on the defensive. But, quite aside from the dangers of confusion and exhaustion that such a strategy risks, any effective radical movement requires some means of fitting together specific grievances into some more comprehensive picture of what is wrong and of how to remedy it and some systematic means of translating this vision into reality.

In modern times, the political party is the institutional form that has emerged to play this programmatic and strategic role. Before one gives way to the fashionable idea that this form is obsolete, one should consider the fate of mass movements that failed to make creative use of this form—for example, the anti–Vietnam War movement, the failure of whose vast mass mobilizations to end the war immediately tended to provoke a cycle of trailing the electoral campaigns of liberal Democrats and resorting to destructive terrorist campaigns.[55] Of course, Lenin advocated a much more definite conception of political organization than this very general idea of a party (though the Bolsheviks' practice was considerably more flexible and context specific than it is usually portrayed).[56] But the problem of the party—of a socialist political organization that generalizes and gives focus to all the myriad grievances produced by capitalist society—is an inalienable part of his legacy to the contemporary Left.

Notes

1 O. Figes, *A People's Tragedy* (London: Jonathan Cape, 1996). To take the most obvious examples: *The Development of Capitalism in Russia* was published in 1899, not 1893 (p. 146); Lenin only broke with the idea that the Russian Revolution would

have to go through a bourgeois stage in April 1917 and not, as Figes asserts, after the 1905 Revolution (p. 211); and the Treaty of Brest-Litovsk did not represent Lenin's adoption of the doctrine of "Socialism in One Country" (p. 550): even Robert Service's very critical biography (see below) makes it clear that Lenin remained committed to the goal of international socialist revolution till his death.

2   R. Service, *Lenin: A Biography* (London: Macmillan, 2000), 195–96.

3   Ibid., 363–64.

4   Naomi Klein gives a relatively balanced and judicious defense of decentralized forms of organizing in "The Vision Thing," *The Nation*, 10 July 2000.

5   Compare S. Žižek, *The Ticklish Subject* (London: Verso, 1999), 236, 377. A similar assessment of Leninism is developed elsewhere in Žižek's published writings. See, for example, "When the Party Commits Suicide," *New Left Review* 1: 238 (1999), 26–47; and "Georg Lukács as the Philosopher of Leninism," postface to G. Lukács, *A Defence of History and Class Consciousness* (London: Verso, 2000).

6   Max Weber, *Political Writings*, ed. P. Lassman and Ronald Speirs (Cambridge: Cambridge University Press, 1994), 359–60.

7   P. Anderson, "Max Weber and Ernest Gellner: Science, Politics, Enchantment," in *A Zone of Engagement* (London: Verso, 1992), 182–97—an excellent close and critical reading of "Politics as a Vocation" and its companion "Science as a Vocation."

8   Weber, *Political Writings*, 367, 365.

9   Letter of 4 August 1908, quoted in W. Hennis, *Max Weber* (London: Allen and Unwin, 1988), 246 n. 45 (translation modified).

10   Weber, *Political Writings*, 360.

11   Ibid., 367.

12   For further discussion of the role of reason in Weber's thought, see J. Habermas, *The Theory of Communicative Action*, vol. 1 (London: Heinemann, 1984); and A. Callinicos, *Social Theory* (Cambridge: Polity Press, 1999), chapter 7.

13   P. Anderson, "Max Weber and Ernest Gellner," 189.

14   R. Service, *Lenin*, 410–11.

15   Three such biographies are T. Cliff, *Lenin*, 4 vols. (London: Pluto Press, 1975–79); M. Liebman, *Leninism under Lenin* (London: Jonathan Cape, 1975); and N. Harding, *Lenin's Political Thought*, 2 vols. (London: Macmillan, 1977, 1981).

16   V. I. Lenin, "Our Revolution (Apropos of N. Sukhanov's Notes) (1923)," in *Selected Works* (London: Lawrence and Wishart, 1969), 698. What Napoleon in fact said was something rather different: "On s'engage *partout* et après on voit"; see H. Delbrück, *History of the Art of War* (Westport, Conn.: Greenwood Press, 1985), 4:409 (emphasis added).

17   V. I. Lenin, *Between the Two Revolutions* (Moscow: Progress Publishers, 1971), 11.

18   Ibid., 13, 16.

19   L. Althusser, *For Marx* (London: Allen Lane, 1969), chapter 3.

20   V. I. Lenin, *What Is to Be Done?*, in *Collected Works* (Moscow: Progress Publishers, 1961), 5:502.

21   Lenin, *Between the Two Revolutions*, 18.

22 Ibid., 506. See more generally A. Rabinowitch, *The Bolsheviks Come to Power* (London: New Left, 1976).

23 See, for example, M. Lewin, *Lenin's Last Struggle* (London: Pluto Press, 1974).

24 See also my discussion of decisionism in a review article of Žižek's *The Ticklish Subject* (London: Verso, 2000) in *Historical Materialism* 8 (2001): 373–403.

25 For a useful general survey, see S. Lukes, *Marxism and Morality* (Oxford: Oxford University Press, 1986).

26 L. D. Trotsky et al., *Their Morals and Ours* (New York: Merit Publishers, 1973), 48.

27 Lukes, *Marxism and Morality*, 137.

28 M. Merleau-Ponty, *Humanism and Terror* (Boston: Beacon Press, 1969), 31.

29 Ibid., 90; see, generally, chapter 1, "Bukharin and the Ambiguity of History," and chapter 2, "Trotsky's Rationalism." What makes this argument more than simple Stalinist apologetics is, first, the difference between Merleau-Ponty's left-Hegelian philosophy of history and orthodox Marxism-Leninism, second, his rejection of the prosecution's charges that Bukharin's and his co-defendants' alleged treason was intentional, and, third, the recognition of the discrepancy between the Stalinist system and the classical Marxist conception of revolution.

30 For a recent study of the terror based on archival sources made available under Gorbachev and Yeltsin, see J. A. Getty and O. A. Naumov, *The Road to Terror* (New Haven, Conn.: Yale University Press, 1999).

31 Merleau-Ponty, *Humanism and Terror*, 41.

32 Letter to Angelica Balabanoff, 3 February 1937, quoted in I. Deutscher, *The Prophet Outcast* (Oxford: Oxford University Press, 1970), 363. Perhaps the most eloquent record of the personal price Trotsky and his family paid for this stance (though it dates from just before the Moscow Trials) is *Trotsky's Diary in Exile 1935* (London: Faber and Faber, 1956), in which he reports the very moving dream about Lenin that Fredric Jameson discusses in his essay in this book.

33 Merleau-Ponty, *Humanism and Terror*, 40–41.

34 Trotsky et al., *Their Morals and Ours*, 48–49.

35 Ibid., 49.

36 Ibid., 73.

37 Ibid., 51.

38 The best discussion of these questions remains N. Geras, "The Controversy about Marx and Justice," reprinted in A. Callinicos, *Marxist Theory* (Oxford: Oxford University Press, 1989).

39 Trotsky et al., *Their Morals and Ours*, 49–50.

40 Ibid., 71.

41 Ibid., 50.

42 A. J. Mayer, *The Furies: Violence and Terror in the French and Russian Revolutions* (Princeton, N.J.: Princeton University Press, 2000).

43 See T. Cliff, *State Capitalism in Russia*, rev. ed. (London: Bookmarks, 1988); A. Callinicos, *The Revenge of History* (Cambridge: Polity Press, 1991); and J. Rees, "In Defence of October," *International Socialism* 2(53) (1991).

44 The ideological problems caused Stalin by his betrayal of Bolshevism is one of the main themes of Moshe Lewin's important essay "Stalin in the Mirror of the Other," in *Stalinism and Nazism*, ed. I. Kershaw and M. Lewin (Cambridge: Cambridge University Press, 1997).

45 For an illustration of this general point, see A. Callinicos, "The Ideology of Humanitarian Intervention," in *Masters of the Universe*, ed. T. Ali (London: Verso, 2000).

46 Trotsky's concern with influencing future generations is clear from, for example, *Diary in Exile*, 46–47. In formulating the thought that the text to this note expresses I am indebted to Matt Matravers and Susan Mendus for suggestive comments they made on an earlier version of this essay at the Political Theory Workshop at the University of York. Any resonances that this thought has with the conception of practice developed by Alasdair MacIntyre in *After Virtue* (London: Duckworth, 1981) is probably not an accident: MacIntyre was once a Trotskyist, and the final pages of that book still engage explicitly with Trotsky.

47 Weber, *Political Writings*, 367–68. Merleau-Ponty, in an admittedly overindulgent reading of "Politics as a Vocation" that largely ignores the nationalist and decisionist elements highlighted by Anderson, treats Lenin and Trotsky as exemplars of this kind of reconciliation of the two ethics; see *Adventures of the Dialectic* (London: Heinemann, 1974), 28–29.

48 Anderson, "Max Weber and Ernest Gellner," 190–91.

49 For a discussion of some of the issues raised by the latter requirement, see A. Callinicos, *Equality* (Cambridge: Polity Press, 2000). Philosophically, the claims made in the text are, depending on the level at which they are taken, either trivial or tremendously difficult to work into a satisfactory theory. For a suggestive exploration of the terrain that addressing the second alternative opens up, see J. McDowell, *Mind and World*, expanded ed. (Cambridge, Mass.: Harvard University Press, 1996).

50 See also C. Bambery, "Leninism in the 21st Century," *Socialist Review* (January 2001) (from whom I stole the title of this paper); A. Callinicos, "In Defence of Leninism," *Socialist Review* (January 1984); and Daniel Bensaïd's excellent contribution to this volume.

51 Lenin, "The Trade Unions, the Present Situation and Trotsky's Mistakes," *Collected Works*, 32.

52 In my view, this point informs the illuminating comparison Trotsky draws between Lenin and the left-Menshevik leader Martov in P. Pomper, ed., *Trotsky's Notebooks, 1933-1935* (New York: Columbia University Press, 1986), 94–96.

53 For more on this, see A. Callinicos, *Against the Third Way* (Cambridge: Polity Press, 2001), especially chapters 3 and 4.

54 See, for example, M. Hardt and A. Negri, *Empire* (Cambridge, Mass.: Harvard University Press, 2000), 59.

55 See T. Wells, *The War Within* (New York: Henry Holt, 1996).

56 See especially Cliff, *Lenin*, vol. 1.

3

Lenin in the

Terry Eagleton | **Postmodern Age**

It is not Leninism that a postmodern age admires. What it values is a truth that is corrigible, provisional, unstable, rather than the inalienable possession of a vanguard perched authoritatively above the people. It is not enthused by the notion that middle-class intellectuals are there to tell the laboring masses what to do, or by the view that knowledge is a matter of eternal scientific verities rather than the fruit of historical practice. It is alarmed by the prospect of culture being obediently harnessed to the ends of the party. It is suspicious of teleologies, of historical epochs laid out end to end like so many dominoes, and it turns instead to time, which is looped and staggered, fractured and multilayered. It is allergic to political purity and metaphysical breaks, favoring the hybrid and ambiguous over the glare of absolute certainty. It resists the crude reductions of economism. Its preferred model of power is not centralized but multiple, diffuse, and all-pervasive. It is skeptical of a narrowly class-based politics, hankering instead for one that is alert to ethnic difference and the wretched of the earth.

What a postmodern age admires, in short, is . . . Leninism. For all this is true of Leninism too.

To many of its critics, Leninism seems an offense against democracy. Is it not odiously patronizing for a small band of politically motivated individuals to claim access to some assured truth that is hidden from the rest of us, by which our conduct is to be rigorously guided? Are decent, ordinary folk really to alter their behavior because a few eccentric dogmatists—feminists, for example, or ethnic activists—lay noisy claim to something called "the truth"? Indeed, some of these moral and epistemological absolutists not only lay claim to "the truth" but have the impudence to insist that they are *certain* that their outlandish dogmas are correct—that white supremacism or homophobia, genocide or sexual oppression are "wrong." They do not seem to regard these opinions as polyvalent, undecidable, eminently deconstructable, as they do everyone else's. Moreover, far from being content to keep these certainties to themselves, to cultivate them as a private hobby or harmless pastime, they are constantly trying to impose them through law, politics, propaganda, and the like on ordinary, non-doctrinaire sexists and supremacists who want nothing more than to be left alone in decent privacy to get on with their sexist or racist practices.

It is not done these days to speak as Lenin does in *What Is to Be Done?* of raising the masses to the level of the intelligentsia, even if it might be no bad thing to persuade your average Texan redneck to think like Angela Davis or Noam Chomsky. Are the anti-Leninists really against the suggestion? The early Lenin writes notoriously of the working class as being able by its own efforts to achieve no more than trade union consciousness, a case he was later to revise in the light of historical events; but it is not beyond argument that without a fresh kind of politico-intellectual input, the movement that cut its teeth in Seattle might achieve no more than anti-capitalist consciousness. And that, precious though it is, is not exactly everything. We have not, in our time, moved from socialism to apathy or reaction, whatever the pessimists may consider. We have moved instead from socialism to anti-capitalism. That is hardly much of a shift at all, and one which is in any case entirely understandable in the light of recently actually existing socialism; but it is, even so, a backsliding.

You can attain anti-capitalist consciousness simply by looking around the world with a modicum of intelligence and moral decency, but you cannot attain a knowledge of global trade mechanisms or the institutions of workers' power in this way. The distinction between spontaneous and acquired political consciousness, whatever historical disasters it may have contributed to, is itself a valid and necessary one. It is not a matter of the percipient vanguard versus the dim-witted masses, but of an epistemological distinction between types of knowledge that are the same for everyone. This, however, is not a particularly valued difference for a pseudo-populist culture that increasingly suspects specialist knowledge itself as elitist, and you knowing something that I do not as privileged. This is not a surprising reaction to a society where knowledge has itself become one of the most prized commodities, a source of rigid ranking and intense competitiveness; but you do not counteract that by a democracy of ignorance. The steel-hard English vanguardist in the 1970s who piously informed me that he derived his theory from his practice was no doubt convinced that he had arrived at his preference for Luxemburg's theory of imperialism over Hilferding's by selling socialist newspapers outside Marks and Spencer every Saturday morning. A naïve historicism of knowledge is no answer to a suave theoreticism of it.

There is a paradox in the very idea of revolution that makes the notion of a vanguard so unpalatable. Revolutions are passionate, turbulent, earth-shaking affairs full of wrath and exuberance, and to imagine that they need experts or professionals sounds to some like needing an expert at sneezing or a professional soul-mate. It is just the same with literary theory. People see the need for specialists in plant science or political economy, but if "literary theory" sounds like an oxymoron it is because literature itself is so untheoretical, so much the locus of values and feelings common to us all. Yet both literature and revolution are of course art forms as well, and revolution in particular is an immensely complex practical operation, which from some angles is more like brain surgery than beer drinking. Anyone can revolt, but not everyone can carry through a successful revolution. If one rejects the Maoist fantasy that brain surgery is carried out by the people with a spot of help from the odd medic, the need for those with revolutionary phronesis, those who are especially good at this art as others are good at basketball, becomes clear. There will always be such types, and in a successful revolution they are likely to come to the fore. The question of a vanguard cannot be this, which is surely beyond doubt, but whether, for example, such figures are produced spontaneously by the masses or whether they must already be in business as a well-disciplined unit to whom, at moments of political crisis, the masses will spontaneously turn. Or whether such experts need to be middle-class, professional intellectuals, custodians of the ultimate truth of history or potentially effective government leaders.

One of the signal advantages of what one might call vulgar anti-Leninism—of the belief that it is *ipso facto* authoritarian for you to tell anyone else what to do, or elitist to be apprised of an assured truth of which others are currently ignorant—is that nobody can tell you what to do either. And this is certainly one of the supremely privileged effects of this humbly self-effacing attitude. Those who inform me in their hectoringly self-righteous fashion that I really ought to release the five famished slaves I currently have chained up in my basement, and whose ribs I can hear rattling from where I sit, are simply trying to impose their cut-and-dried dogmas from above on my spontaneous conduct. By virtue of what "hierarchist" access to some foundational "truth" can they justify such appalling arrogance? Are they not aware that it takes all kinds to make a world, that (as the English working class says) it would be a funny world if we all thought the same, that vital diversity and not dreary homogeneity is the *summum bonum*, and that the more differences flourish, among them no doubt rabid free-market beliefs, slaves-in-the-basement practices, and the like, the more we can resist the centripetal tyranny of consensus? Am I supposed to be sunk in so-called false consciousness, an elitist conception if ever there was one, just because I find myself continually eyeing up people I meet at sherry parties with a view to how they might look chained to my basement wall? Why is everyone out to deny the validity of my experience with their smug certainties? Why are they so patronizingly eager to dismiss me as "mystified" just because I spend my weekends dressing up in Nazi uniform and stomping around my room?

It is curious how intellectuals, when expressing their customary liberal distaste for telling ordinary people what to do, assume with typical narcissism that it is middle-class intellectuals like themselves who are at issue here. They do not seem to imagine that the intellectual in question might be a Communist bus driver and the "ordinary" person a banker. Yet "intellectual" for Marxism is of course just such a designation. The distinction between intellectual and nonintellectual is not homologous with that between middle-class and working-class. Indeed, the form that was traditionally seen as suspending this distinction was known as the party. Intellectuals in general are specific functionaries within social life, and revolutionary intellectuals are functionaries within a political movement. They need to be neither geniuses nor genteel. Those who regarded Louis Althusser's brand of Marxism as elitist because they imagined academic Theory delivering austerely scientific lectures to a befuddled proletarian Ideology seemed to assume that working people cannot be theoreticians and intellectuals cannot be ideological. There may be other reasons for objecting to the Althusserian model, but this particular one revealed more about the spontaneous prejudices of the critic than of the author.

"Intellectual," then, designates a social or political location, like "hairdresser," "chief executive" or "commissar," not a social rank or origin. It is true that most Marxist intellectuals, like Lenin himself, have been middle-class in origin, but this is largely on account of the cultural and educational deprivation of the working class under capitalism. It is a confirmation of the socialist critique, not an embarrassment for it. Those who consider it elitist for you to have access to forms of technical knowledge that are useful to me, but to which I have no access myself, still see knowledge primarily in terms of personal endowments or hierarchies, rather than in terms of the social division of labor, class conditions, specialized techniques, social locations, and the like and thus fall back into the very liberal humanism they usually upbraid. They also tend to fall prey to the very universalism of which they are suspicious, since what seems objectionable to the anti-Leninist is the idea that someone should be in possession of a total knowledge of which I am deprived. But there is no reason why someone who can tell me about the laws of capitalist production may not also have something to learn from me in return. There are several kinds of vanguard, some of whom have, say, medical knowledge rather than political knowledge out ahead of the rest of us.

Even less is "intellectual" an esoteric synonym for "very intelligent." This is why right-wing philistines feel the need to speak of "so-called" or "soi-disant" intellectuals, meaning "You're not really very clever at all," even though to describe oneself as an intellectual is not to claim that one is. Not all intellectuals are intelligent, and not all of the intelligent are intellectuals. Some years ago at Ruskin College, the establishment for working-class students in Oxford, an Oxford don began the lecture he had been invited to deliver with the faux self-deprecating remark, *de rigueur* in certain cavalier English circles, that he really knew very little about the subject on which he was about to hold forth. A gruff Glaswegian voice bawled from the back of the hall: "You're paid to know!" That student had grasped the meaning of the term "intellectual," as the don had not. He had recognized that the lecturer's remark, far from being some seductive disowning of authority, was as obtuse as a motor mechanic's claim not to be able to identify a gear box. We like our motor mechanics, brain surgeons, and aeronautical engineers to speak with authority, rather than to lower themselves chummily to our level. Elites are superior to the masses in their very being, motor mechanics because they have specialized knowledge that we do not.

Leninism, to be sure, involves a great deal more than telling other people what you judge to be the truth. But the stereotyping and travestying of it has been such—and absolutely no political current has been so mercilessly caricatured in our time, largely by those piously opposed to stereotyping—that it requires a gargantuan effort simply to surmount such vulgar prejudices as these before moving on to more substantive matters. It is well-nigh impossible to discuss the concept of political vanguardism, for example, in a cultural climate that can perceive no difference between the terms "vanguard" and "elite." It is true that for movements like romanticism, the wires between these two conceptions become notably tangled. But you do not have to support uncritically the classical Leninist doctrine of the vanguard to point out that it has nothing to do with being socially or spiritually superior to the bovine masses.

For one thing, elites are self-perpetuating whereas vanguards are self-abolishing. Vanguards arise in conditions of uneven cultural and political development. They are an effect of heterogeneity—of situations in which a certain group of men and women are able because of their material circumstances, not necessarily because of their superior talents, to grasp "in advance" certain realities that have not yet become generally apparent. They may be able to do this because of their more privileged cultural position, or for exactly the opposite reason—because of their dearly won experience as targets of oppression and fighters against it. It is that experience from which the more fortunate among us have then to learn. It is strange that many among those who reject the notion of vanguardism are devotees of the African National Congress or cheer on those who do the Internet organizing for the anti-capitalist campaign. Those who suspect authority as oppressive in itself, and their name today is legion, forget about the authority that springs from hardearned experience and whose voice is accordingly compelling. There is nothing in the least wrong with authority, provided it is of an emancipatory kind. Once that experience has been generalized and acted upon, the avant-garde can wither away, its task completed. Vanguards, to be sure, can petrify into elites, which is no doubt one rather inadequate way of describing the transition from Leninism to Stalinism; but this happens under specific historical conditions, not by some metaphysical fatality. Those who object to Leninism because it is blind to the contingent, aleatory nature of history should not be too implacably deterministic in their view of such matters. The diggers, suffragettes, futurists, and surrealists were vanguards of a kind, but they were not inexorably transformed into elites.

It is important to appreciate the self-evident truth that revolutions are unusual, aberrant affairs. They do not happen every day, and revolutionary movements are not to be seen as microcosms of everyday life, let alone as foretastes of utopia. They should, in fact, try to prefigure in their conduct and relationships some of the values of the society they are striving for, a dimension notably lacking in a ruthlessly instrumental Bolshevism. But they are no more images of utopia than are rescue teams at mining disasters, which require chains of command and forms of discipline we would find objectionable if we woke up to them every day. Instrumentalism, for all its appalling dangers, has a point. The more you see revolutionary movements as instrumental, abnormal, strictly temporary, the less likely it is that their necessary emphasis on struggle, conflict, austere self-denial, and the like will be mistaken for the shape of a political future characterized by freedom, prosperity, and peace. This may well mean that those most active in such movements are, Moses-like, the least likely to enter the promised land they themselves have helped to create. As Brecht puts it in his poem "To Those Born Afterwards": "Oh we who tried to create the conditions for friendship / Could not ourselves be friendly." Or as a socialist in Raymond Williams's novel *Second Generation* remarks, "We'd be the worst people, the worst possible people, in any good society. And we're like this because we've exposed ourselves and we've hardened." What marks out Williams's thought on this question is that he regards this conflict between the struggle for socialism and socialism itself not just as a regrettable necessity that history will find it in its heart to forgive, but as tragic.

Those members of the Citizen Army and Irish Volunteers who fought with James Connolly against the British imperial state in the Dublin

Post Office in 1916 constituted a vanguard. But this was not because they were middle-class intellectuals—on the contrary, they were mostly Dublin working men and women—or because they had some innate faculty of superior insight into human affairs, or because they were in serene possession of the scientific laws of history. They were a vanguard because of their *relational* situation—because, like the revolutionary cultural avant-gardes in contrast with the modernist coteries, they saw themselves not as a timeless elite but as the shock troops or front line of a mass movement. There can be no vanguard in and for itself, as coteries are by definition in and for themselves. And a vanguard would not be in business unless it trusted profoundly in the capacities of ordinary people, as elites by definition disdain them. Semiotically speaking, the relation between vanguard and army is metonymic rather than metaphorical. To see it as the latter would be the heresy of substitutionism. It is true that the vanguard can also become a floating signifier, as the Bolshevik party soon found itself hanging in space over a marginal, depleted referent known as the Russian proletariat. But the Leninist conception of the vanguard is very far from the putschism or Blanquism for which it is commonly mistaken and which Lenin himself always rejected.

History, as it happens, was to prove the Irish Volunteers right. In two or three years time, the pathetic clutch of patriots who had stormed the Dublin Post Office, and who as they were led off to prison were jeered at by the plain people of Dublin as cranks and dreamers, had grown into the mass-based Irish Republican Army. The plain people of Dublin had abandoned their jeering and joined up to fashion the first anti-colonial revolution of the twentieth century. They had learned the lesson that a crank is a small instrument that makes revolutions. And that they did so was partly because the Volunteers and the Citizen Army did not stay at home in 1916 for fear of being thought elitist and hierarchical.

Postmodern thought is in general enthusiastic about margins and minorities, but not about this particular species of them. Since its commitment to minorities is as hostile to majoritarian thought as elitism is, it does not have much time for minorities that build constructive relations to majorities. Given its universalist dogma that all majorities are oppressive, this could only mean appropriation.

The idea that the vanguard dispenses some timeless truth to the masses is especially ironic in the case of Leninism. For Lenin was the great virtuoso of political modernism, the practitioner of an innovative art form known as revolutionary socialist politics for which there were as few established paradigms or prototypes as there were for expressionism or suprematism. It is not for nothing that Tom Stoppard's brilliantly empty play *Travesties* puts Lenin in the company of James Joyce and the Dadaists. When Jean-François Lyotard writes of a knowledge or practice that has no existing model, a disturbance of the order of reason by a power manifested in the promulgation of new rules for understanding,[1] the kind of experimental or paralogical science that he has in mind is not far from the discourse of the Finland Station. It is a familiar truth that almost all of Lenin's major theoretical positions are political interventions that transform received theoretical norms in the act of applying them. Thus, to take an obvious example, the apparently narrow insistence on the party of *What Is to Be Done?* is to be seen in the light of the conditions of illegality at the time, as well as part of a critique of economism; and Lenin himself was to write in 1905 that workers should be welcomed into the party by the hundreds of thousands. From here on until just after the revolution, his writings are marked by a confidence in the creative capacities of the masses and in the soviets that express it: "Comrades, working people!," he writes in 1917, "Remember that now you yourselves are at the helm of the state. No one will help you if you yourselves do not unite and take into your hands all affairs of the state. . . . Get on with the job yourselves; begin right at the bottom, do not wait for anyone."[2] Not long after, however, as workers' self-government scarcely survived a few weeks of post-revolutionary fervor, and as the Bolshevik party tightened its grip on political life, it was to be a different story.

Ironically, even the doggedly reflectionist epistemology of *Materialism and Empirio-Criticism*, a work in which one can hear the occasional gurgling of a man well out of his depth, is itself an interventionist stance against the ultra-leftist Bogdanovites, *Proletkultists*, and neo-Kantian reactionaries. Theoretical knowledge is in all these cases a performative act, not just because of some epistemological preference, as it might be in a modern-day postgraduate seminar, but because a revolutionary history is likely to throw the usually concealed affinities between thought and practice into abnormally high relief. Like hanging, it concentrates the mind wonderfully, and not just the mind: Walter Benjamin once remarked that his prose style might have been less cryptic had there been a German revolution. We have perhaps been a little slow to appreciate the modernist dimension of this political practice, which is not at all bereft of rules, guidelines, or received truths as in some banal libertarian wisdom, but part of whose fidelity to tradition, as with all effective art, consists in allowing such procedures to intimate to you when you should bend or go beyond them. And since there are no rules for determining this, we are speaking of a full-blooded innovatory art. Lenin himself speaks in his work on imperialism of 1917 as "a novel and unprecedented interlacing of democratic and proletarian revolutions." Where this art form is precisely not postmodern is in its refusal to follow Lyotard's implacable antithesis between innovation and consensus, one bred by an age for which the notion of revolutionary consensus can only be an oxymoron.

Lenin, however, practiced a popular avant-gardism just as devotedly as his fellow exile in Zurich, James Joyce, a man who penned some of the most avant-garde prose of the century while describing himself as having a mind like a grocer. Joyce is subversively commonplace, outrageously banal, shockingly quotidian; and the Bolshevik revolution was one of the few other early-twentieth-century examples of this mind-shaking conjuncture of the experimental and the everyday. If, in a bizarre modernist logic, a seedy Dublin Jew can play Odysseus, then in Russia the proletariat can stand in for an absent bourgeoisie and spearhead its revolution itself. It is a case of modernist irony and paradox, as when Lenin remarks in *Two Tactics of Social Democracy* that the Russian working class is suffering from an insufficient dose of capitalism.

It was also, like Yeats, Joyce, Stravinsky, Eliot, or Benjamin, a typically modernist constellation of the very old and the very new, of the archaic and the avant-garde, one which grasped history as a stack of nonsynchronous time-streams rather than as a unified stratum through which one might slice a neat cross-section. "In a revolutionary break in the life of society," writes Trotsky, "there is no simultaneousness and no symmetry of process either in the ideology of society, or in its economic structure."[3] What we have instead is that folding of one narrative inside another, which was to become known as permanent revolution. If a skepticism of historical progress could persuade some modernist art to throw linear narrative to the winds, so, ironically, could the possibility of revolutionary breakthrough in political life. What could be more exemplary of the Ibsenite tension-cum-collusion between past and nature, this time, however, as comedy rather than tragedy, than a nation that combined a brutal autocracy with a minority, unskilled yet militant working class; hungry cities and an enlightened, disaffected intelligentsia who were rootless enough to make common cause with the people, along with an army of politically ambiguous peasants; rapid industrialization and major influxes of foreign capital with a weak indigenous bourgeoisie; and an imposing lineage of high culture with a drastically impoverished civil society? In a similar brand of retrograde radicalism, the nation contained a proletariat that was unskilled and culturally backward but for the same reason untainted by the ideological complicity of a more affluent labor force. The difference between this situation and some straight teleology is rather like that between George Eliot's *Middlemarch*, with its evolutionary narrative and liberal trust in progress, and Joseph Conrad's *Nostromo*, which orchestrates a number of different histories—imperial, liberal-progressive, popular, proletarian—in the context of a mythical Latin American state, and whose narrative is accordingly fractured and recursive, resistant to any simple chronological reading.

If these lags and overlappings provided some of the conditions for political revolution, they are also, as Perry Anderson has argued, the classic conditions for modernism.[4] The result, as Walter Benjamin observes in his essay on Moscow, is "a complete interpenetration of technological and primitive modes of life,"[5] as in both cases linear temporality is, so to speak, exploded from within, the great classical historicisms are unmasked as discredited, *chronos* becomes *kairos*, and the flow of empty homogeneous history is suddenly brimmed full of what Benjamin called "the time of the Now." A ripe moment of the time of bourgeois revolution becomes the strait gate through which the proletariat and peasantry will enter, the *Jeztzeit* in which different histories—absolutist, bourgeois-democratic, proletarian, rural petty-bourgeois, national, cosmopolitan—are looped and braided into a new constellation. Like Benjamin's *angelus novus*, the revolution is blown into the future with its eyes turned mournfully to the garbage of the past. And just as revolutionary time in general is neither self-identical nor purely diffuse, so is the time of both modernism and the Bolshevik experiment, as in the one case national cultures are contemptuously abandoned for some hybrid, polyglot, cosmopolitan capital in which the new *lingua franca* or global *argot* is art itself, while in the latter case the powers released by the national revolution begin to warp the global space of capitalism and fashion unpredictable new internationalist conjunctures, blasting the national revolution out of the temporal continuum of the nation itself into another space altogether. There is a modernist, topsy-turvy logic at work here, in the so-called weakest link theory for which loss is gain, the old is the new, weakness becomes power, and the margin shifts to the center. Like the expatriate modernist artist, the revolution was ectopic as well as untimely, pitched on the narrow ground between Europe and Asia, city and country, past and present, the First World and the Third World, and thus a kind of in-betweenness, an event that, as Lenin himself remarked, had not broken out where it should have. Similarly, one might claim that modernism "should have" broken out in the world metropolis of Britain, but it did so instead in the stagnant backwaters of colonial Ireland.

There is quite enough suspicion of classical teleology in all this to catch the eye of even the most inveterate postmodern anti-Marxist, just as there is a stress on the provisional, pragmatic nature of theory that ought to delight his or her heart. Between the St. Petersburg Soviet of Workers' Deputies and the "April Theses," history is moving so fast beneath its protagonists' feet that theory has to hobble remarkably hard to keep abreast of practice, which is not quite the political situation with which we ourselves are most familiar. What we get is accordingly a kind of theorizing on the hoof, as doctrines are overtaken and overturned by events and performatives turn overnight into constatives. Lenin himself, who quoted Napoleon's "On s'engage et puis on voit," speaks in *What Is to Be Done?* of the party lagging behind the spontaneous practice of the workers. It took Marx, Lenin, and Luxemburg rather longer to enthuse over the idea of soviets than many of those soviets' working-class architects, just as it took the leaders of 1917 a surprisingly long time to realize quite what they had done, catch up in the mind with what they had created in reality, begin to talk of "socialist" rather than "democratic" revolution, or conclude that nationalization might be a good idea. As late as 1921, Lenin was dismissive of the whole idea of a national economic plan and seemed to some old-church Bolsheviks to be ready to go to any length to encourage the merchant and private farmer.

Without revolutionary theory there is no revolutionary movement, to be sure, which at one level means no more than that you can't have a women's movement without the idea of feminism. But at the same time, according to Lenin, there is no adequate theory without revolutionary practice. Correct revolutionary theory, he insisted, assumes final shape only in close connection with the practical activity of a mass revolutionary movement. For most of Lenin's critics today, living in an age of leftist political pluralism, that revolutionary practice is too narrowly, reductively class based; but this again is for the most part a convenient straw target. A contradictory, conflict-ridden alliance of middle-class intellectuals, soldiers, workers, and peasants spearheading what remains in part a liberal-bourgeois revolution sounds more like a riddle than a reduction. Lenin was a pitiless purist when it came to the party, purging and expelling with unshakeable zeal. But he was not a purist when it came to the actual business of political revolution, a point evident enough in his defense of Dublin 1916 on the grounds that whoever lives in hopes of a pure revolution will never see one.

Meanwhile, those today for whom class is embarrassingly *passé*—a group that includes rather more academics than grape-pickers—and for whom destiny lies now with postcolonialism and sexual politics should remember not only that postcolonial struggle is class politics (unless, of course, you conveniently confine it to questions of identity, culture, difference, and the like), but that, as Robert Young has recently reminded us, this whole project of interrelating various forms of struggle was to begin with almost exclusively a Marxist one, hatched and hotly debated in the successive Socialist Internationals. "Communism," Young writes, "was the first, and only, political program to recognize the interrelation of these different forms of domination and exploitation and the necessity of abolishing all of them as the fundamental basis for the successful realization of the liberation of each."[6] The uprising that was to topple the tsar began with demonstrations on International Women's Day in 1917, and the Bolsheviks made equality for women an urgent political priority. In general, the Communist movement opposed separate organizations for women; but it regarded women's liberation and working-class freedom as indissociably linked, and its commitment to female equality was in Young's words "unmatched by any other political party then or since."[7] It was equally convinced of the relations between class conflict and anti-colonial struggle. Lenin himself famously defended the right to national self-determination, rejecting the case that nationalism was a purely bourgeois phenomenon. It was he who placed colonial revolution at the forefront of the policies of the new Soviet government and who had argued from the outset, not least in the teeth of economism, that Communists must be champions of every protest against tyranny, becoming the focal-point for the victimized among students, oppressed religious sects, schoolteachers, and the like.

If Leninism stubbornly refuses to conform to its postmodern stereotype in this respect, so it does where culture is concerned. Like the postmodernists, Lenin greatly valued culture, though not quite in their sense of the term. Whereas they tend to think of electronic music, he was thinking of electric cables. But just as the postmodern concept of culture is often closer to economics than it is to politics, so in a way was Lenin's. Indeed, he saw culture as a key element in the making of the Russian Revolution, as well as the single most vital factor that threatened it. "The whole difficulty of the Russian revolution," he writes in 1918, "is that it was much easier for the Russian revolutionary working class to start than it is for the West European classes, but it is much more difficult for us to continue."[8] This is a comment on culture, not politics. It was the weakness of culture in Russia, in the sense of the paucity of civil society, the lack of an elaborate ruling-class hegemony, as well as of a "civilized" and hence incorporated working class, that helped to make the revolution possible; ironically, the Russian working class was ideologically stronger just because it was culturally weaker. But it was the relative absence of culture, in the alternative sense of science, knowledge, literacy, technology, and know-how, which made it so hard to sustain. The non-events that helped to bring the revolution to birth also threaten to scupper it.

It is here, in the cultural realm, that Lenin's thought is least avant-garde—not because of his admiration for Tolstoy and furtive enjoyment of classical music, but because unlike the political revolution there was indeed a given model here to conform to, the developed technology and productive forces of the West. "We must take the entire culture that capitalism left behind and build socialism with it," he writes. "We must take all its science, technology, knowledge and art."[9] It is as though it is enough for the proletariat to appropriate this whole lineage, not to submit it to criticism in the style of, say, *Proletkult*, for socialism to be established. The contradiction of the revolution is thus an arresting one: it is the very backwardness and devastation of Russian society, the drastic depths of the problems it confronts, that forces one into a nonrevolutionary, "continuist" position as far as Western capitalist civilization goes; whereas the whole notion of cultural transformation—the equivalent in everyday life of modernism in the aesthetic realm or revolution in the political one—appears an idle distraction in a famished, illiterate, civically inexperienced nation. It is because of the depth of social need that the revolution cannot penetrate to the depths of the self.

Here, then, is the Lenin who, along with Vladimir the vanguardist, is least palatable to today's Left: the champion of Western industry and Enlightenment, the man for whom science and ideology are politically neutral, the Eurocentric admirer of technical experts and Fordist techniques. And it is certainly true that he would have benefited from thinking as adventurously in this field as he did politically. But it was dire material constraint as well as personal conviction that prevented him from making this leap and that thus poses a relevant question to those radicals today whose enemy is as much modernity as capitalism: To what extent is avant-garde thought about culture and identity dependent on material prosperity—which is to say, on the very modernity that it claims to repudiate? Modernity is in this respect a little like celebrity: it is those who have it who claim to despise it.

Lenin's most audaciously avant-garde text is surely *The State and Revolution*—avant-garde not only in the sense of being poised at a political cutting-edge, but in the more technical sense of promoting the politics of form. Its thesis, derived from Marx's reflections on the Paris Commune, that socialist power must involve a passage not simply from one class to another, but from one modality of power to another, belongs to the avant-gardist climate that prompted Walter Benjamin to insist in his essay "The Author as Producer" that genuine revolutionary art transforms the cultural institutions themselves, rather than pumping a new kind of content down old channels. If Lenin's view of culture and technology has the continuist stress of Lukácsian realism, his conception of soviets is more akin to Brecht's collective theatrical experiments, which are out to transform the power relations between stage, text, actors, and audience, to revolutionize the very concept of theater and not just its content, to dismantle the whole theatrical apparatus rather than to use it to communicate a new message in the manner of leftist-naturalist drama. We will know that a successful revolution has happened when, looking back over a lengthy stretch of time, we recognize that there are now only the faintest, most formal family resemblances between our own conceptions of power and those of the prerevolutionary era, rather as we might just about bemusedly recognize some bizarre antique ceremony as a version of what we now call hockey.

It is worth noting the contrast between this transformed vision of power and the neo-Nietzschean pan-powerism of a Michel Foucault. The Foucauldian, one might naïvely imagine, ought to welcome this decentralized, grass-roots version of power, which has certain affinities with their own diffusionist vision. But, of course, for them there is really nothing to choose between the soviet and the centralized state, since their own argument moves at a quasi-metaphysical level quite indifferent to such sublunary distinctions. If power is everywhere anyway, as protean and quicksilver as the Will-to-power itself, how can it not be just as cramped and disciplined by soviets as by autocracies? This flamboyantly subversive conception of power can thus provide no practical political guidance whatsoever, since any political agenda must secretly be as much a betrayal of it as a verbal formulation is a betrayal of the proliferating differences of the world.

Just as Lenin did not simply "transplant" Marxism to a situation it had scarcely foreseen, so can there be no question of simply transplanting Leninism itself into a transnational world. In the end, the Bolsheviks were simply too fearful to trust the working class as they might have done, and their relentless vanguardism helped to destroy soviet democracy and lay the ground for Stalinism. If it is "metaphysical" to posit sheer continuities (say, between Lenin and Stalin), it is equally metaphysical, as some Trotskyists need reminding, to posit a mysterious abyss between them. Even so, the grotesque travesty that passes for the post-Marxist, postmodern version of Leninism cannot be allowed to escape without challenge. Lenin may have been too continuist in his approach to Western civilization, but the obverse of this one-sidedness was his recognition that you cannot have socialism without a reasonable degree of prosperity. And his cherishing of that truth, ironically, then allows us an appropriate critical perspective on the regime that followed from his own revolution, which was to march its people into modernity at gunpoint. If Lenin, the mighty opponent of capitalism, was also too one-sided about Western capitalism, today's post-Marxists commit just the opposite error. They forget that socialism, that "avant-garde" negation of the capitalist mode of production, must at the same time soberly acknowledge its debt to the great revolutionary bourgeois tradition, along with its material developments, rather than merely write it off in a fit of moralistic self-righteousness. Without such continuism there is no negation. Whatever his failings, Lenin stands as a perpetual reminder that only those who enjoy the benefits of modernity can afford to be so scornful about it.

Notes

1 Jean-François Lyotard, *The Postmodern Condition* (Manchester: Manchester University Press, 1984), 61.
2 V. I. Lenin, "To the Population," in *Collected Works* (Moscow: Progress Publishers, 1972), 26:297.
3 Leon Trotsky, *The Permanent Revolution* (New York: Merit Publishers, 1969), 132.
4 Perry Anderson, "Modernity and Revolution," in *A Zone of Engagement* (London: Verso, 1992).
5 Walter Benjamin, *One-Way Street and Other Essays* (London: New Left, 1979), 190.
6 Robert J. C. Young, *Postcolonialism: A Historical Introduction* (Oxford: Blackwell, 2001), 142.
7 Ibid., 143.
8 Lenin, "Fourth Conference of Trade Unions and Factory Committees of Moscow, June 27–July 2, 1918: Report on the Current Situation," in *Collected Works*, 27:464.
9 Lenin, "Achievements and Difficulties of the Soviet Government," in *Collected Works*, 29:70.

4

Lenin and

Fredric Jameson

Revisionism

On the night of June 25, 1935, Trotsky had a dream:

> Last night, or rather early this morning, I dreamed I had a conversation
> with Lenin. Judging by the surroundings, it was on a ship, on the third-
> class deck. Lenin was lying in a bunk; I was either standing or sitting
> near him, I am not sure which. He was questioning me anxiously about
> my illness. "You seem to have accumulated nervous fatigue, you must
> rest . . ." I answered that I had always recovered from fatigue quickly,
> thanks to my native *Schwungkraft*, but that this time the trouble seemed
> to lie in some deeper processes . . . "then you should seriously (he em-
> phasized the word) consult the doctors (several names). . . ." I answered
> that I already had many consultations and began to tell him about my
> trip to Berlin; but looking at Lenin I recalled that he was dead. I immedi-
> ately tried to drive away this thought, so as to finish the conversation.
> When I had finished telling him about my therapeutic trip to Berlin in
> 1926, I wanted to add, "This was after your death"; but I checked myself
> and said, "After you fell ill. . . ."[1]

This "singularly moving dream," as he puts it, is analyzed by Lacan in
his Sixth Seminar (on "desire and its interpretation") in the lecture of
January 7, 1959. Readers of Lacan will recognize its affinity with other
narratives of which Lacan was particularly fascinated, most notably
Freud's own dream about his father ("he was dead, but he didn't know
it"). And indeed the situation in question accumulates a number of

Lacanian motifs: the big Other, barred, castrated, dead; God as dead (without knowing it); the unconscious as the place of this nonknowledge of death, very much like that noumenon that for Kant is the subject (the soul) and that we can never know directly. I will rapidly summarize Lacan's observations: Lenin's nonknowledge in the dream is the projection of Trotsky's own nonknowledge, not only of his own death (he is beginning to feel the weight of illness and age, the diminution of his extraordinary energies), but also of the very meaning of his dream. He has also projected onto Lenin the fact and experience of pain itself, the pain of Lenin's last illness, the "suffering of existence" (as Lacan calls it elsewhere), which emerges when desire ceases to conceal it. In the dream Lenin, the dead father, is also the shield against this existential dread, a perilous footbridge over the abyss, as Lacan puts it: "the substitution of the father for the absolute Master, death."

Lenin does not know he is dead: this will be our text and our mystery. He doesn't know that the immense social experiment he singlehandedly brought into being (and which we call Soviet Communism) has come to an end. He remains full of energy, although dead, and the vituperation expended on him by the living—that he was the originator of the Stalinist terror, that he was an aggressive personality full of hatred, an authoritarian in love with power and totalitarianism, even (worst of all) the rediscoverer of the market in his NEP—none of those insults manage to confer a death, or even a second death, upon him. How is it, how can it be, that he still thinks he is alive? And what is our own position here—which would be that of Trotsky in the dream, no doubt—what is our own nonknowledge, what is the death from which Lenin shields us? Or, to put all of this in a different terminology (that of Jean-François Lyotard), if we know what "the desire called Marx" is all about, can we then go on to grapple with "the desire called Lenin"?

The premise is that Lenin still means something: but that something, I want to argue, is not precisely socialism or communism. Lenin's relationship to the latter is on the order of absolute belief, and since it never gets questioned, we will also find no new thinking about it in his work: Marx is a big Other, the big Other.

Then what about something that everyone agrees to have been his most original idea: What about the party and the party structure? Is this still what Lenin means to us? It is, to be sure, except for the fact that no one nowadays wishes to raise the question or to mention the unmentionable term "party." The word seems to carry with it layers of material and associations from which the current mentality recoils with acute displeasure: first, the authoritarianism and sectarianism of Lenin's first party form; then the murderous violence of the Stalin era (trained as much, to be sure, on the original Bolshevik party members as on the latter's opponents and critics); and finally, the corruption of Brezhnev's party, held out to us as a horrible object lesson in what happens when some party or "new class" becomes comfortably encrusted in its power and privileges. These offer so many reasons for repressing the problematic of the party altogether, or at least for turning away from it in the quite reasonable conviction that new times and new historical situations demand new thoughts about political organization and action. It is to be sure, but my impression is that most often the appeal to historical change is little more than an excuse for avoiding these problems altogether: in a period whose political atmosphere is largely anarchistic (in the technical sense of the term), it is unpleasant to think about organization, let alone institutions. This is indeed at least one of the reasons for the success of the market idea: it promises social order without institutions, claiming not to be one itself. Then, in another way, what I am calling Lenin's sectarianism perhaps sends its own image back in a wholly unwanted and undesirable way (its own bad smell, as Sartre puts it) to a Left that (at least in the United States) has traditionally been utterly given over to the logic of sectarianism as well as fission and proliferation.

I will say more about the party later on. But perhaps at this point I can raise some conceptual problems that offer a different and a defamiliarizing approach to the matter. Let me put it this way: Is the problem of the party a philosophical problem? Is the party itself a philosophical concept that can be thought or even posed within the framework of traditional philosophy? This is not a question that can be answered in the traditional terms of some Leninist "philosophy," which has generally, and even in Althusser, involved the problem of materialism. I'm not very interested in that metaphysical question; nor will I take up the newer assertion of Lenin's Hegelianism (about which more later on). Meanwhile Badiou's stimulating book, which sees the party as a combination of an expressive and an instrumental function,[2] certainly succeeds in philosophizing the party, as the "organization of politics, the organization of the future anterior";[3] but it does not raise my topic, which I prefer to leave in the form and status of an unanswered question, namely, what kind of philosophical concept does the problem or the idea of the party constitute, if any?

Yet, it will be observed, there is such a thing as political philosophy, a recognized branch of traditional philosophy as such, which includes Hobbes, Locke, and Rousseau and accommodates certain modern thinkers, Carl Schmitt in one way, Rawls perhaps in another. Presumably, in a problematic that raises the question of the state and civil society, of freedom and rights, even of political representation as such, there might be found some neglected corner in which Lenin's reflections on the party could be offered storage space. Still, with the signal exception of Schmitt, this collection of philosophers does not seem unduly preoccupied with the philosophical status of political philosophy as such and rarely seeks to found or to ground it. Questions about representation and constitutions meanwhile quickly slide down into some empirical realm in which they rejoin the Leninist party as some purely instrumental and historical set of recipes. Or to put it the other way round, can one not raise the same question about those issues and equally pose the question of the status of constitutions and parliaments, for example, as properly philosophical concepts? Even in Hegel, who was so intensely preoccupied by the interrelationship of his various subsystems, we find little more than a grounding of political and state forms in something like a deduction from human nature, or, in other words, in an ontology quite different from the dialectical one of the *Logic*. These questions no doubt convey some of my own doubts and suspicions about political philosophy in general; and I'll come back to those later on as well.

Finally, there is a more naïve and impressionistic way of talking about all of this, which does, I think, have its value and remain suggestive. This is the feeling we all have, and which we sometimes express like this, in the form of a kind of amazement and admiration, namely, that Lenin is always thinking politically. There is not a word that Lenin writes, not a speech that he gives, not an essay or a report that he drafts that is not political in this sense—even more, that is not driven by the same kind of political impulse.[4] This can of course strike others as obsessional and repulsive, inhuman: this anxiety before politics mobilizes the nobler word "reductive" for such single-minded and unblinking attention. But is this reduction of everything to politics, to thinking politically, "reductive"? What is reduced, what is left out or repressed? Is it not extraordinary to witness what happens when all of reality is grasped through the Absolute of this focus or optic? Or to contemplate this unique concentration of human energy? Better still, proceeding by the negative, can such absolute reduction be considered a desire? And if so, a desire for what, a desire called what? Or is this truly the in-strumental in its most nightmarish ultimate form, the transformation of everything into a means, the translation of everyone into agency or counteragency (Schmitt's friend or foe)? What possible end could justify this omnipotence of political thinking, or, as I prefer, of thinking politi-cally? So I slowly make my way back to my initial question: Is thinking politically incompatible with philosophical thought? What could justify its centrality and its new status, which might be comparable to the role of the cogito in other philosophical systems? Does thinking politically offer a resource of certainty and a test for doubt around which some utterly new philosophical system or stance might be organized? It will at any rate have become clear that whatever thinking politically is, it has little enough to do with the traditional conceptions of politics or politi-cal theory, little enough also with that untranslatable distinction that has had its fortune in France in the last years, namely, the distinction between *le politique* and *la politique*. May we then venture to say that in that sense Lenin has nothing to do with politics if it means any of those traditional or contemporary things?

But now we need to confront another alternative, a traditionally in-fluential one, even if it has suffered the same opprobrium in recent years as the problem of the party. This alternative to the political is the economic, by which I must first and foremost mean the economic in the Marxian sense, that is, Marxist economics, a field and a category that immediately raises philosophical questions in its own right, and most notably the question as to whether Marxist economics is an economics at all in the traditional sense. Surely the critique of political economy leads out of political economy altogether, a departure that has at least the merit of barring those tempting paths that lead down into the flat-lands of bourgeois economics and positivism. If so many people are trying to feel their way back to political economy today it is in order to locate that other path that can lead out of it in the other direction of Marxism, which is henceforth how I will more simply identify Marxist economics as such in everything that is distinctive about it.

Marxism in this sense—neither an economic ontology nor a purely negative critique or deconstruction—is presided over by two gener- alities, two universal and abstract names, whose philosophical status we also need to worry about: capitalism and socialism. Capitalism is that machine whose dynamism and perpetual expansion results from the unresolvable contradictions it carries within it and which define its essence; socialism is that sketch or possibility of collective or coopera- tive production, some of whose traits can already be glimpsed within our own (capitalist) system. Are either of these "systems" philosophical concepts? Certainly philosophers have over and over again attempted to translate them into more respectable—if paradoxical—philosophi- cal concepts, such as the one and the many, translations that, however stimulating, always seem to lead us back into the most sterile ideo- logical judgments and classifications, not least because, like any binary pair, the one and the many keep changing places. For Marxists, it is capitalism that is the one (whether in the form of the state or the sys- tem), while for the others it is socialism that is the bad totalitarian one, and the market that is somehow a more democratic space of plural- ism and difference. The problem is that neither concept, if that is what they both are, is empirical; both designate the empty yet indispensable place of the universal. As a thinker Lenin begins to approach all of this through his late Hegelian moment and his return to the greater *Logic*, as Kevin Anderson and others have so luminously demonstrated.[5] But at that point we are far enough from economics in the Marxian sense (even though we are fairly close to Marx's *Capital*, in the dialectical one).

Is Lenin an economic thinker? Certainly, there are wonderful utopian passages in *The State and Revolution*; everyone agrees that *The Devel- opment of Capitalism in Russia* is a pioneering classic of socioeconomic analysis; and *Imperialism* certainly underscores one of the fundamental contradictions of capitalism, if only one. Nor is it to be doubted that the external situation of the revolution in wartime Russia and then even more during the Civil War is such that meditations on socialism as such could never have been in the very forefront of Lenin's agenda.

But I would also like to point to a deeper structural issue. It has always been my feeling that the peculiarity of Marxism as a thought system (or better still, like psychoanalysis, as a unique "combination-of-theory-and practice")—but also its originality—lies in the way in which in it two complete Spinozan modes overlay each other and coexist: the one is that of capitalist economics, the other that of social class and class struggle. These are in one sense the same; and yet different vocabularies govern each in such a way that they are not interrelated within some meta-language but constantly demand translation—I would even want to say transcoding—from the one language into the other. If this is so, then Lenin's dominant code is clearly that of class and class struggle, and only much more rarely that of economics.

But I also want to insist on the priority, within Marxism, of economics as some ultimately determining instance. I know that this is not a fashionable position (even though, in the era of the worldwide sway of the market it may come once again to have its attractiveness). It should be clear, by the way, that when I use the words economics and economic they have nothing to do with that purely trade-union consciousness and politics Lenin designated by the term economism long ago and in another situation (even though the phenomenon called economism is certainly still very much with us). To be sure, the term *economics* is no more satisfactory to characterize Marxism than sexuality is to characterize Freudian psychoanalysis: the latter is not an erotics, not a form of sexual therapy, and when psychoanalysis is described in terms of some sexual, ultimately determining instance, it is a very generalizing and impressionistic characterization indeed. Still, whenever Freud sensed a movement of his disciples toward a formulation calculated to dilute the sheer empirical scandal of the sexual and generalize libido out into the more nonspecific and metaphysical areas of power or spirituality or the existential—such are, for example, the well-known moments of Adler, Jung, and Rank—he draws back theoretically with some sharp and one may even say instinctual sense of the focus and boundaries of his object as originally constituted: and these are indeed the most admirable and heroic moments in Freud, the ones in which he most stubbornly keeps faith with his own discoveries and insights. Thus one cannot say positively that sexuality is the center of Freudianism, but one can say that any retreat from the fact of sexuality opens up a kind of revisionism that Freud himself was always quick and alert to criticize and to denounce.[6] (Does this mean that Freud's late concept of the death instinct is *his* NEP?)

Something like this is what I would have wanted to argue for the centrality of economics in Marxism: this is clearly not an economics in any traditional sense, yet all the attempts to substitute another thematics for the economic, or even to propose additional and parallel thematics—such as those of power, or the political in any of its traditional senses—undo everything that made up the originality and also the force of Marxism as such. The substitution of the political for the economic was of course the standard move of all the bourgeois attacks on Marxism—to shift the debate from capitalism to freedom, from economic exploitation to political representation. But since the various leftist movements of the 1960s, since Foucault on the one hand and the innumerable revivals of anarchism on the other, Marxists have been relatively unvigilant—whether for tactical reasons or out of theoretical naïveté—about such crucial substitutions and surrenders. Then too—beginning, I believe, with Poulantzas, and in the light of all the well-publicized abuses in the Soviet Union—the conviction became increasingly widespread that the crucial weakness of Marxism was that it structurally lacked a dimension of political (and juridical) theory; that it needed to be augmented with some new doctrines of socialist politics and socialist legality. I think this was a great mistake, and that the very force and originality of Marxism was always that it did not have a political dimension of this kind, and that it was a completely different thought system or unity-of-theory-and-practice altogether. The rhetoric of power, then, in whatever form, is always to be considered a fundamental form of revisionism. I should add that the unpopular opinion I am expressing may be more reasonable today than it might have been in previous decades (those of the Cold War or Third World liberation) decades. For now it is clear that everything is economic again, and this even in the most vulgar Marxist senses. In globalization, in its external dynamics as well as its internal or national effects, it should be clearer once again to what degree even things that looked like purely political or power issues have become transparent enough to glimpse the economic interests at work behind them.

But now we have a problem, for I have asserted that Marxism is based on the structural priority of economics over politics, at the same

time that I have conceded that Lenin was to be considered a fundamentally political thinker rather than a theoretician of economics, let alone
of socialism. Does this mean that Lenin is not a representative Marxist
thinker? Or does it explain why a hyphenated Leninism needed to be
added to Marxism in order properly to identify the new doctrine and
to suggest that Lenin in fact had something unique and different, supplementary, to add to Marx?

The solution to the paradox lies, I think, in the introduction of a
third term, one in which it would be tempting to say that these two
alternatives, the political and the economic, somehow come together
and become indistinguishable. And I think that that formulation is
right, but in the temporal sense, in that of Badiou's Event, rather than
in any structural fashion. This term, which is the very center of Lenin's
thinking and action, is, as you will perhaps already have guessed, the
term "revolution." This is also not a popular concept nowadays, and
it is even more of an embarrassment than any of the other traditional
slogans I have mentioned. That revolution can be a truly philosophical
concept far more readily than notions like the party or capitalism I
think could be demonstrated throughout the philosophical tradition,
even though we may wish to wait further for some fully developed philosophy of revolution for our own time.

If I dared to sketch in my own requirements for such a philosophy
to come, I would insist on two distinct dimensions that are somehow
united and identified, however fleetingly, in the moment of revolution.
One is that of the Event, about which one must say that it achieves
some absolute polarization. (Schmitt's definition of politics is thus in
reality merely a distorted apprehension of revolution as such.) And this
polarization constitutes the one moment in which the dichotomous
definition of class is concretely realized.

Revolution is also that unique phenomenon in which the collective
dimension of human life comes to the surface as a central structure,
the moment in which a collective ontology can at least be seized otherwise than in some adjunct to individual existence or in those euphoric
moments of the manifestation or the strike, all of which are in fact so
many allegories of the collective, just as the party or the assembly are
its allegories. (I will return to this crucial notion of the allegorical in a
moment.)

But all these features still tend to summon up archaic images, which foreground violence, about which it is crucial to say and repeat that in the revolutionary situation, violence first comes from the Right, from reaction, and that violence from the Left is a reaction against this re-action. Still, none of the images of the punctual seizures of power—the great peasant revolts (about which Guha has taught us that they are very far from being spontaneous[7]), the French Revolution, the desperate revolt of the Luddites (which Kirkpatrick Sale has in so timely a fashion restored to the properly revolutionary tradition[8]), Lenin's putsch in October, finally, or the triumphant floodtide of the Chinese or the Cuban Revolutions—seem very appropriate or reassuring when we come to the postmodern age, the age of globalization.

This is why, at this point, we must insist that revolution has another face or dimension, equally essential, which is that of process itself (as opposed to Event). Revolution is then seen from that angle, the whole lengthy, complex, contradictory process of systemic transformation, a process menaced at every turn by forgetfulness, exhaustion, the retreat into individual ontology, the desperate invention of "moral incentives," and above all the urgency of collective pedagogy, of the point by point cartographic charting of the ways in which so many individual events and crises are themselves components of an immense historical dialectic, invisible and absent as an empirical perception at every one of those points, but whose overall movement alone gives them their meaning. It is precisely this unity of the absent and the present, of the universal and the particular, unity indeed of the global and the local so often insisted on today—it is this dialectical unity that I call allegorical, and which demands at every step a collective awareness of the way in which revolution is being played out symbolically and actually in each of its existential episodes.

Now perhaps it will be clearer why the true meaning of Lenin is neither political nor economic, but rather both fused together in that Event-as-process and process-as-Event we call revolution. The true meaning of Lenin is the perpetual injunction to keep the revolution alive, to keep it alive as a possibility even before it has happened, to keep it alive as process at all those moments when it is threatened by defeat or worse yet, by routinization, compromise, or forgetfulness. He didn't know he was dead: this is also the meaning of the idea of Lenin for us; it is the keeping alive of the idea of revolution as such in a time when this word and idea have become a virtually biblical stumbling block or scandal.

Those who have wished to do away with it have found it necessary to perform a very enlightening preliminary operation: they have had first to undermine and discredit the notion of totality, or, as it is more often called today, the notion of system as such. For if there is nothing like a system, in which everything is interrelated, then it is clear that it is both unnecessary and improper to evoke systemic change. But here contemporary politics, and in particular the fortunes of social democracy, have the decisive lessons for us. I speak as one who is very far from endorsing Lenin's sectarianism as a practical political strategy, his intransigent refusal of the compromisers and the social democrats (in our modern sense). Today, speaking at least from the perspective of the United States, but also, I venture to say, from that of the Europe of the European Union countries, the most urgent task seems to me the defense of the welfare state and of those regulations and entitlements that have been characterized as barriers to a completely free market and its prosperities. The welfare state is of course the great postwar achievement of social democracy, even though in continental Europe it knows longer and older traditions. But it seems to me important to defend it, or better still, to give social democracy and the so-called Third Way, a chance to defend it, not because such a defense has any prospects of succeeding, but rather very precisely because from the Marxian perspective it is bound to fail. We must support social democracy because its inevitable failure constitutes the basic lesson, the fundamental pedagogy, of a genuine Left. And I hasten to add here that social democracy has already failed, all over the world: something one witnesses most dramatically and paradoxically in the Eastern countries about which it is generally only said that in them Communism failed. But their rich and privileged historical experience is much more complex and instructive than that: for if one can say of them that they experienced the failure of Stalinist Communism, one must also add that they then experienced the failure of orthodox capitalist free-market neoliberalism, and that they are now in the process of experiencing the failure of social democracy itself. The lesson is this, and it is a lesson about system: one cannot change anything without changing everything. Such is the lesson of system, and at the same time, if you have followed my argument, the lesson of revolution. As for the lesson about strategy, the lesson of *What Is to Be Done?*, I hope I have suggested an important differentiation between strategy and tactics in these remarks: one need not, in other words, slavishly imitate Lenin's divisive, aggressive, sectarian recommendations for tactics to grasp the ongoing value of a strategy that consists in tirelessly underscoring the difference between systemic and piecemeal goals, the age-old differentiation (and how far back in history does it go after all?) between revolution and reform.

He didn't know he was dead. I want to conclude these remarks with a different kind of problem, one absolutely related to Lenin's revolutionary meaning, as you will agree, but whose relationship to that meaning remains a puzzle and a problem. The problem is philosophical, I continue to think, but how it is philosophical is part of the problem itself. Maybe I can quickly encapsulate it with the word charisma (itself a part, the tip end so to speak, of the fuzzy ideological notion of totalitarianism, which means repression on the one hand and dependence on the leader on the other). Every revolutionary experience or experiment we know about has also been named for a leader and has equally often been bound up with the personal fate of that leader, however biologically. We must feel something scandalous about this: it is for one thing allegorically improper for a collective movement to be represented by a single named human individual. There is something anthropomorphic about this phenomenon, in the bad sense in which over so many decades of modern or contemporary thought we have been taught an alert suspicion not only about individualism and the mirage of the centered subject but about anthropomorphism in general and the humanisms it inevitably brings with it. Why should a political movement, which has its own autonomous systemic program, be dependent on the fate and the name of a single individual, to the point of being threatened with dissolution when that individual disappears? The most recent explanation, that of the phenomenon of the generation we have suddenly discovered miraculously at work in history, is not a particularly satisfying one (and indeed requires some historical explanation—as a theory and a historical experience—in its own right).

The individual seems to signify unity, ran the explanation from Hobbes to Hegel; and there certainly would seem to be much empirical truth to the function of such an individual in holding an immense collective together, and in damming up that tide of sectarianism and fission, secession, that menaces revolutionary movements like a flaw in human nature. Charisma is, however, an utterly useless pseudo-concept or pseudo-psychological figment: it simply names the problem to be solved and the phenomenon to be explained. Lenin was in any case, we are told, far from being a charismatic speaker like many, but not all, of the other favorite great dictators. There is a weight of legend that gets elaborated later on, but what is its function? There is the matter of legitimation and violence or terror, but what is legitimation in the first place?

Is all of this to be explained psychoanalytically, whether in terms of the father or the big Other of transference?[9] Lacan's "four discourses" would seem to offer a less simplistic framework for analysis, positing a variety of relationships to the "subject supposed to know." They include, alongside the seemingly fundamental "discourse of the Master," that of the university, that of the hysteric, and that of the analyst, which significantly does not coincide with that of the Master, despite Lacan's own apparent occupation of both these positions. But the very coquetry and Zen-like character of Lacan's own pronouncements may be taken as a deliberate strategy to avoid or evade the position of the Master itself, which can never coincide with the illusion of the "subject supposed to know," that is to say of Absolute Knowledge. Indeed, in that sense, perhaps the discourse of the Master only exists for other people; and indeed those other people may be identified in the discourse of the university, which posits all truths as signed and which crystallizes around the private property of proper names (identifying itself as Lacanian, Deleuzian, Spinozist, Leninist, Gramscian, or whatever). The discourse of the hysteric then wishes to cut through all this to "sincerity" and to desire as such, which the subject desperately seeks to act out and to satisfy (when not, indeed, to identify it in the first place). There remains the discourse of the analyst, which scans the rhythms of enunciation in order to hear the desire at work in its pulsations: and this is surely the position of the great political leader as such, who listens for collective desire and crystallizes its presence in his political manifestos and "slogans."[10] I do think, however, in passing, of Elizabeth Roudinesco's remark, in her history of the politics of the Lacanian movement itself, that the latter's political structure offered the unique spectacle of an absolute monarchy combined with an equally absolute anarchist democracy at the base.[11] It is an interesting (and Maoist) model, whose results, however, seem to have been as catastrophic as the sequels to most of the revolutionary movements one can think of.

I myself imagined a different one, which is so grotesque as to merit mentioning it in passing. Tito was still alive then, and it occurred to me that there was a place, in revolutionary theory, for something like a concept of socialist monarchy. The latter would begin as an absolute one, and would then, in the course of things, be phased down into something exceedingly limited like a constitutional monarchy in which the named and charismatic leader has reduced himself to a mere figurehead. However desirable, that does not seem to have happened very often either, if at all. And so I much appreciate Slavoj Žižek's return to the allegedly conservative Hegel, in which the place of the monarch, indispensable and yet external to the system, is a merely formal point without content[12]: this would be something like paying its tribute to anthropomorphism while placing it as it were under erasure. Is this the way to deal with Lenin, dead without knowing it?

Shall I end with a question, or with a proposition? If the former, it is done; if the latter, one would only want to observe that if one wants to imitate Lenin, one must do something different. *Imperialism* represented Lenin's attempt to theorize the partial emergence of a world market: with globalization the latter has come into view far more completely or at least tendentially completely, and as with the dialectic of quality and quantity it has modified the situation Lenin described beyond all recognition. The dialectic of globalization, the seeming impossibility of delinking—this is our "determinate contradiction" to which our political thought remains shackled.

Notes

1 Trotsky, *Diary in Exile 1935* (Cambridge, Mass.: Harvard University Press, 1976), 145–46.

2 A. Badiou, *Peut-on penser la politique?* (Paris: Seuil, 1985), 107–8.

3 Ibid., 109.

4 See, for example, S. Žižek's stimulating selection from Lenin's 1917 texts in *Revolution at the Gates* (London: Verso, 2002).

5 K. Anderson, *Lenin, Hegel and Western Marxism* (Urbana: University of Illinois

Press, 1995). Lenin's original notes on the Logic are to be found in his *Philosophical Notebooks*, in *Collected Works*, vol. 38 (Moscow: Progress Publishers, 1972).

6   The equivalent would of course be Lenin's "April Theses": see Žižek, *Revolution at the Gates*, 56–61; and for the astonishment of his Bolshevik co-conspirators at his call for immediate revolution in October, A. Rabinowitch, *The Bolsheviks Come to Power* (New York: Norton, 1976), 178ff.

7   R. Guha, *Elementary Aspects of Peasant Insurgency in Colonial India* (Delhi: Oxford, 1983).

8   Kirkpatrick Sale, *Rebels against the Future* (Reading, Mass.: Addison-Wesley, 1995).

9   J. Lacan, *Le Séminaire*, Livre XVII: *L'Envers de la psychanalyse* (Paris: Seuil, 1991), 9–91.

10   See indeed "On Slogans," in Žižek, *Revolution at the Gates*, 62–68.

11   E. Roudinesco, *Jacques Lacan* (Paris: Fayard, 1993), 411–13.

12   S. Žižek, *For They Know Not What They Do* (London: Verso, 1991), 81–84.

5

A Leninist Gesture Today:

Against the Populist

Slavoj Žižek　**Temptation**

The fate of Jože Jurančič, an old Slovene Communist revolutionary, stands out as a perfect metaphor for the twists of Stalinism. In 1943, when Italy capitulated, Jurančič led a rebellion of Yugoslav prisoners in a concentration camp on the Adriatic island of Rab: under his leadership, 2,000 starved prisoners single-handedly disarmed 2,200 Italian soldiers. After the war, he was arrested and put in a prison on the nearby small Goli Otok ("naked island"), a notorious Communist concentration camp. While there, he was mobilized in 1953, together with other prisoners, to build a monument to celebrate the tenth anniversary of the 1943 rebellion on Rab—in short, as a prisoner of Communists, Jurančič was building a monument *to himself*, to the rebellion led by him. If poetic (not justice but, rather) injustice means anything, this was it: is the fate of this revolutionary not the fate of the entire people under the Stalinist dictatorship, of the millions who, first, heroically overthrew the *ancien régime* in the revolution, and, then, enslaved to the new rules, were forced to build monuments to their own revolutionary past? This revolutionary is thus effectively a "universal singular," an individual whose fate stands for the fate of all.[1]

The proper task is thus to think the *tragedy* of the October Revolution: to perceive its greatness, its unique emancipatory potential, and, simultaneously, the *historical necessity* of its Stalinist outcome. One should oppose both temptations: the Trotskyist notion that Stalinism was ultimately a contingent deviation, as well as the notion that the

Communist project is, in its very core, totalitarian. In the third volume of his supreme biography of Trotsky, Isaac Deutscher makes a perspicuous observation about the forced collectivization of the late 1920s: ". . . having failed to work outwards and to expand and being compressed within the Soviet Union, that dynamic force turned inwards and began once again to reshape violently the structure of Soviet society. Forcible industrialization and collectivization were now substitutes for the spread of revolution, and the liquidation of the Russian kulaks was the *Ersatz* for the overthrow of the bourgeois rule abroad."[2]

Apropos Napoleon, Marx once wrote that the Napoleonic wars were a kind of export of revolutionary activity: since, with Thermidor, the revolutionary agitation was stifled, the only way to give an outlet to it was to displace it toward the outside, to rechannel it into war against other states. Is the collectivization of the late 1920s not the same gesture turned around? When the Russian Revolution (which, with Lenin, explicitly conceived itself as the first step of a pan-European revolution, as a process that can only survive and accomplish itself through an all-European revolutionary explosion) remained alone, constrained to one country, the energy had to be released in a thrust inward. It is in this direction that one should qualify the standard Trotskyist designation of Stalinism as the Napoleonic Thermidor of the October Revolution: the "Napoleonic" moment was rather the attempt, at the end of the Civil War in 1920, to export revolution with military means; the attempt failed with the defeat of the Red Army in Poland; if anyone, it was Tukhachevsky who effectively was a potential Bolshevik Napoleon.

The twists of contemporary politics render palpable a kind of Hegelian dialectical law: a fundamental historical task that "naturally" expresses the orientation of one political bloc can only be accomplished by the opposite bloc. In Argentina a decade ago, it was Menem, elected on a populist platform, who pursued tight monetary politics and the IMF's agenda of privatizations much more radically than his "liberal" market-oriented radical opponents. In France in 1960, it was the conservative de Gaulle (and not the Socialists) who broke the Gordian knot by giving full independence to Algeria. It was the conservative Nixon who established diplomatic relations between the United States and China. It was the "hawkish" Begin who concluded the Camp David Treaty with Egypt. Or, further back in Argentinian history, in the 1830s and 1840s, the heyday of the struggle between "barbarian" Federalists (representatives of provincial cattle owners) and "civilized" Unitarians (merchants and so forth from Buenos Aires who were interested in a strong central state), it was Juan Manuel Rosas, the Federalist populist dictator, who established a centralist system of government that was much stronger than Unitarians dared to dream of. The same logic was at work in the crisis of the Soviet Union of the second half of the 1920s: in 1927, the ruling coalition of Stalinists and Bukharinists, pursuing the policy of appeasement of the private farmers, was ferociously attacking the united leftist opposition of Trotskyists and Zinovievists who called for accelerated industrialization and fights against rich peasants (higher taxes, collectivization). One can imagine the surprise of the Left Opposition when, in 1928, Stalin enforced a sudden "leftist" turn, imposing a politics of fast industrialization and brutal collectivization of land, not only stealing their program but even realizing it in a much more brutal way than they had dared to imagine—their criticism of Stalin as a Thermidorian right-winger all of a sudden became meaningless. It is no wonder that many Trotskyists recanted and joined the Stalinists, who, at the very moment of the ruthless extermination of the Trotskyist faction, realized their program. Communist parties knew how to apply "the rule which permitted the Roman Church to endure for two thousand years: condemn those whose politics one takes over, canonize those from whom one does not take anything."[3] And, incidentally, there was the same tragic-comic misunderstanding in Yugoslavia in the early 1970s: after the large student demonstrations, during which calls for democracy were heard, along with accusations that the ruling Communists pursued the politics that favored the new "rich" technocrats, the Communist counterattack that stifled all opposition was legitimized, among others, by the idea that Communists had heard the message of the student protests and were meeting their demands. Therein resides the tragedy of the leftist-Communist opposition, which pursued the oxymoron of the anti-market "radical" economic politics combined with calls for direct and true democracy.

So where do we stand today with regard to these dilemmas? Let us begin with one of the few political events proper: the French and Dutch "No" to the project of European constitution, which confronts us with a new version of this strange dialectical law. The French and Dutch

"No" was a clear-cut case of what in the "French theory" is referred to as a *floating signifier*: a "No" of confused, inconsistent, overdetermined meanings, a kind of container in which the defense of workers' rights coexists with racism, in which the blind reaction to a perceived threat and fear of change coexist with vague utopian hopes. We are told that the "No" was really a "No" to many other things: to Anglo-Saxon neoliberalism, to Chirac and the present French government, to the influx of the immigrant workers from Poland who lower the wages of the French workers, and so forth. The real struggle is going on now: the struggle for the *meaning* of this "No"—who will appropriate it? Who—if anyone—will translate it into a coherent alternate political vision?

If there is a predominant reading of the "No," it is a new variation on the old Clinton motto, "It's the economy, stupid!": the "No" was supposedly a reaction to Europe's economic lethargy—to falling behind with regard to other newly emerging blocks of economic power, to its economic, social, and ideologico-political inertia—*but*, paradoxically, it was an inappropriate reaction, a reaction *on behalf of* this very inertia of privileged Europeans, of those who want to stick to old welfare state privileges. It was the reaction of "old Europe," triggered by the fear of any true change, the refusal of the uncertainties of the Brave New World of globalist modernization.[4] It is no wonder that the reaction of the "official" Europe was one of near panic at the dangerous "irrational" racist and isolationist passions that sustained the "No," at a parochial rejection of openness and liberal multiculturalism. One is used to hearing complaints about the growing apathy among the voters, about the decline of popular participation in politics, so worried liberals talk all the time about the need to mobilize people in the guise of civil society initiatives, to engage them more in a political process. However, when people awaken from their apolitical slumber it is as a rule in the guise of a rightist populist revolt—no wonder many enlightened technocratic liberals now wonder whether the foregoing "apathy" had not been a blessing in disguise.

One should be attentive here to how even those elements that appear as pure rightist racism are effectively a displaced version of workers' protests. Of course there is racism in demanding the end of immigration of foreign workers who pose a threat to "our jobs." However, one should bear in mind the simple fact that the influx of immigrant workers from post-Communist countries is not the consequence of some multiculturalist tolerance—it effectively *is* part of the strategy of capital to hold in check the workers' demands. This is why, in the United States, Bush did more for the legalization of the status of Mexican illegal immigrants than the Democrats caught in trade union pressures. So, ironically, rightist, racist populism is today the best argument that the class struggle, far from being obsolete, goes on. The lesson the Left should learn from it is that one should not commit the error symmetrical to that of the populist, racist mystification of displacement of hatred onto foreigners. One should not throw the baby out with the bath water, that is, to merely oppose populist anti-immigrant racism on behalf of multiculturalist openness, obliterating its displaced class content; benevolent as it wants to be, the mere insistence on multiculturalist openness is the most perfidious form of anti-workers' class struggle.

Typical here is the reaction of German mainstream politicians to the formation of the new Linkspartei for the 2005 elections, a coalition of the East German PDS and the leftist dissidents of the SPD—Joschka Fischer himself reached one of the lowest points in his career when he called Oskar Lafontaine "a German Haider" (because Lafontaine protested the importation of cheap East European labor to lower the wages of German workers). It is symptomatic of the exaggerated and panicky way the political (and even cultural) establishment reacted when Lafontaine referred to "foreign workers," or when the secretary of the SPD called the financial speculators "locusts"—as if we were witnessing a full neo-Nazi revival. This total political blindness, this loss of the very capacity to distinguish Left and Right, betrays a panic at politicization as such. The automatic dismissal of entertaining any thoughts outside the established postpolitical coordinates as "populist demagoguery" is the hitherto purest proof that we effectively live under a new *Denkverbot*. (The tragedy, of course, is that the Linkspartei effectively *is* a pure protest party with no global viable program of change.)

Populism: From the Antinomies of the Concept

The French-Dutch "No" thus presents us with the latest adventure in the story of populism. For the enlightened liberal-technocratic elite, populism is inherently proto-Fascist, the demise of political reason, a revolt in the guise of the outburst of blind utopian passions. The easiest reply to this distrust would have been to claim that populism is inherently neutral, that it is a kind of transcendental-formal political *dispositif* that can be incorporated into different political engagements. This option was elaborated in detail by Ernesto Laclau.[5]

For Laclau, in a nice case of self-reference, the very logic of hegemonic articulation applies also to the conceptual opposition between populism and politics: populism is the Lacanian *objet a* of politics, the particular figure that stands for the universal dimension of the political, which is why it is "the royal road" to understanding the political. Hegel provided a term for this overlapping of the universal with part of its own particular content: oppositional determination, or *gegensäetzliche Bestimmung*, is the point at which the universal genus encounters itself among its particular species. Populism is not a specific political movement but the political at its purest: the "inflection" of the social space that can affect any political content. Its elements are purely formal, transcendental, not ontic: populism occurs when a series of particular "democratic" demands (for better social security, health services, lower taxes, against war, and so forth) is enchained in a series of equivalences, and this enchainment produces the "people" as the universal political subject. What characterizes populism is not the ontic content of these demands but the mere formal fact that, through their enchainment, the "people" emerges as a political subject, and all different particular struggles and antagonisms appear as parts of a global antagonistic struggle between "us" (the people) and "them." Again, the content of "us" and "them" is not prescribed in advance but is, precisely, the stake of the struggle for hegemony: even ideological elements such as brutal racism and anti-Semitism can be enchained in a populist series of equivalences, in the way "them" is constructed.

It is clear now why Laclau prefers populism to class struggle: populism provides a neutral transcendental matrix of an open struggle whose content and stakes are themselves defined by the contingent struggle for hegemony, while "class struggle" presupposes a particular social group (the working class) as a privileged political agent. This privilege is not itself the outcome of hegemonic struggle but is grounded in the objective social position of this group—the ideologico-political struggle is thus ultimately reduced to an epiphenomenon of "objective" social processes, powers, and their conflicts. For Laclau, on the contrary, the fact that some particular struggle is elevated into the "universal equiva-lent" of all struggles is not a predetermined fact but is itself the result of the contingent political struggle for hegemony. In some constella-tion, this struggle can be the workers' struggle, in another constella-tion, the patriotic anti-colonialist struggle, in yet another constellation the anti-racist struggle for cultural tolerance. There is nothing in the inherent positive qualities of some particular struggle that predestines it for such a hegemonic role of the "general equivalent" of all struggles. The struggle for hegemony thus not only presupposes an irreducible gap between the universal form and the multiplicity of particular con-tents but also the contingent process by means of which one among these contents is "transubstantiated" into the immediate embodiment of the universal dimension. In Laclau's own example, Poland of the 1980s, the particular demands of Solidarnosc were elevated into the embodiment of the people's global rejection of the Communist regime, so that all different versions of the anti-Communist opposition (from the conservative-nationalist opposition through the liberal-democratic opposition and cultural dissidence to leftist workers' opposition) recog-nized themselves in the empty signifier "Solidarnosc."

This is how Laclau tries to distinguish his position both from gradu-alism (which reduces the very dimension of the political so that all that remains is the gradual realization of particular "democratic" demands within the differential social space) and from the opposite idea of a total revolution that would bring about a fully self-reconciled society. What both extremes miss is the struggle for hegemony in which a particular demand is "elevated to the dignity of the Thing," that is, it comes to stand for the universality of the "people." The field of politics is thus caught in an irreducible tension between "empty" and "floating" sig-nifiers: some particular signifiers start to function as "empty," directly embodying the universal dimension, incorporating into the chain of equivalences, which they totalize, a large number of "floating" signi-fiers.[6] Laclau mobilizes this gap between the "ontological" need for a populist protest vote (conditioned by the fact that the hegemonic power discourse cannot incorporate a series of popular demands) and the con-tingent ontic content to which this vote gets attached to explain the supposed shift of many French voters who, till the 1970s, supported the Communist Party to the rightist populism of the Front National.[7]

The elegance of this solution is that it dispenses us with the boring topic of the alleged "deeper (totalitarian, of course) solidarity" between the extreme Right and the "extreme" Left.

Although Laclau's theory of populism stands out as one of today's great (and, unfortunately for social theory, rare) examples of true conceptual stringency, one should note a couple of problematic features. The first one concerns his very definition of populism: the series of formal conditions he enumerates are not sufficient to justify calling a phenomenon "populist." A thing to be added is the way the populist discourse displaces the antagonism and constructs the enemy. In populism, the enemy is externalized or reified into a positive ontological entity (even if this entity is spectral), whose annihilation would restore balance and justice. Symmetrically, our own—the populist political agent's—identity is also perceived as preexisting the enemy's onslaught. Let us take Laclau's own precise analysis of why one should count Chartism as populism: "Its dominant leitmotiv is to situate the evils of society not in something that is inherent in the economic system, but quite the opposite: in the abuse of power by parasitic and speculative groups which have control of political power—'old corruption,' in Cobbett's words. . . . It was for this reason that the feature most strongly picked out in the ruling class was its idleness and parasitism."[8]

In other words, for a populist, the cause of the troubles is ultimately never the system as such, but the intruder who corrupted it (for example, financial speculators, not capitalists as such); the cause is not a fatal flaw inscribed into the structure as such, but an element that doesn't play its role within the structure properly. For a Marxist, on the contrary (like for a Freudian), the pathological (deviating misbehavior of some elements) is the symptom of the normal, an indicator of what is wrong in the very structure that is threatened with "pathological" outbursts. For Marx, economic crises are the key to understanding the "normal" functioning of capitalism; for Freud, pathological phenomena such as hysterical outbursts provide the key to the constitution (and hidden antagonisms that sustain the functioning) of a "normal" subject. This is also why Fascism definitely is a populism. Its figure of the Jew is the equivalential point of the series of (heterogeneous, inconsistent even) threats experienced by individuals: the Jew is simultaneously too intellectual, dirty, sexually voracious, hard-working, financially exploitative, and so forth. Here we encounter another key feature of populism not mentioned by Laclau. Not only is—as he is right to emphasize—the populist Master-Signifier for the enemy empty, vague, imprecise, and so on: ". . . to say that the oligarchy is responsible for the frustration of social demands is not to state something which can possibly be read out of the social demands themselves; it is provided from *outside* those social demands, by a discourse on which they can be inscribed. . . . It is here that the moment of emptiness necessarily arises, following the establishment of equivalential bonds. *Ergo*, 'vagueness' and 'imprecision,' but these do not result from any kind of marginal or primitive situation; they are inscribed in the very nature of the political."[9]

In populism proper, this "abstract" character is furthermore always supplemented by the *pseudo-concreteness* of the figure that is selected as *the* enemy, the singular agent behind all the threats to the people. One can buy today laptops with the keyboard artificially imitating the resistance to the fingers of the old typewriter, as well as the typewriter sound of the letter hitting the paper—what better example of the recent need for pseudo-concreteness? Today, when not only social relations but also technology are getting more and more nontransparent (who can visualize what is going on inside a PC?), there is a great need to re-create an artificial concreteness in order to enable individuals to relate to their complex environs as to a meaningful life-world. In computer programming, this was the step accomplished by Apple, which developed the pseudo-concreteness of icons. Guy Debord's old formula about the "society of spectacle" is thus getting a new twist: images are created in order to fill in the gap that separates the new artificial universe from our old life-world surroundings, that is, to "domesticate" this new universe. And is the pseudo-concrete populist figure of the "Jew," which condenses the vast multitude of anonymous forces that determine us, not analogous to a computer board that imitates the old typewriter board? The Jew as the enemy definitely emerges from outside the social demands that experience themselves as frustrated.

This supplement to Laclau's definition of populism in no way implies any kind of regress to the ontic level. We remain at the formal-ontological level and, while accepting Laclau's thesis that populism is a certain formal political logic that is not bounded by any content, we only supplement it with the characteristic (no less transcendental than its other features) of reifying antagonism into a positive entity. As such, populism by definition contains a minimum, an elementary form, of ideological mystification. That is why, although it is effectively a formal frame or matrix of political logic that can be given different political twists (reactionary-nationalist, progressive-nationalist, and so on), nonetheless, insofar as in its very notion it displaces the immanent social antagonism into the antagonism between the unified "people" and its external enemy, it harbors "in the last instance" a long-term proto-Fascist tendency.[10]

This is also why it is problematic to count any kind of Communist movement as a version of populism. Against the "populization" of Communism, one should remain faithful to the Leninist conception of politics as the art of intervening in the conjunctures that are themselves posited as specific modes of concentration of the "main" contradiction (antagonism). It is this persisting reference to the "main" contradiction that distinguishes the truly "radical" politics from all populisms.

After evoking the possibility that the point of shared identification that holds together a crowd can shift from the person of the leader to an impersonal idea, Freud states: "This abstraction, again, may be more or less completely embodied in the figure of what we may call a secondary leader, and interesting varieties would arise from the relation between the idea and the leader."[11] Does this not hold especially for the Stalinist leader who, in contrast to the Fascist leader, is a "secondary leader," the embodiment-instrument of the Communist idea? This is the reason Communist movements and regimes cannot be categorized as populist.

Linked to this are some further weaknesses of Laclau's analysis. The smallest unit of his analysis of populism is the category of "social demand" (in the double meaning of the term: a request and a claim). The strategic reason for choosing this term is clear: the subject of demand is constituted through raising this demand. The "people" thus constitutes itself through equivalential chains of demands; the "people" is the performative result of raising these demands, not a preexisting group. However, the term "demand" involves a whole theatrical scene in which a subject is addressing her demand to an Other presupposed to be able to meet it. Does the proper revolutionary or emancipatory political act not move beyond this horizon of demands? The revolutionary subject no longer operates at the level of demanding something from those in power—she wants to destroy them. Furthermore, Laclau calls such an elementary demand, prior to its eventual enchainment into a series of equivalences, "democratic." As he explains it, he resorts to this slightly idiosyncratic use to signal a demand that still functions *within* the sociopolitical system, that is, a demand that is met as a particular demand, so that it is not frustrated and, because of this frustration, forced to inscribe itself into an antagonistic series of equivalences. Although he emphasizes how, in a "normal" institutionalized political space, there are, of course, multiple conflicts, which are dealt with one by one, without setting in motion any transversal alliances or antagonisms, Laclau is well aware that chains of equivalences can also form themselves within an institutionalized democratic space. Recall how, in the United Kingdom under John Major's Conservative leadership in the early 1990s, the figure of the "unemployed single mother" was elevated into the universal symbol of what was wrong with the old welfare state system—all "social evils" were somehow reduced to this figure (if there is a state budget crisis it is because too much money is spent on supporting these mothers and their children; if there is juvenile delinquency it is because single mothers do not exert enough authority to provide the proper educational discipline; and so forth).

What Laclau neglected to emphasize is not only the uniqueness of democracy with regard to his basic conceptual opposition between the logic of differences (society as a global regulated system) and the logic of equivalences (the social space as split into two antagonistic camps that equalize their inner differences), but also the full inner entwinement of these two logics. The first thing to note here is how, only in a democratic political system, the antagonistic logic of equivalences is inscribed into the very political edifice as its basic structural feature. It seems that Chantal Mouffe's work[12] is here more pertinent in its heroic attempt to bring together democracy and the spirit of agonistic struggle, rejecting both extremes: on the one side, the celebration of heroic struggle-confrontation that suspends democracy and its rules (Nietzsche, Heidegger, Schmitt); on the other side, the evacuation of true struggle out of the democratic space, so that all that remains is anemic rule-regulated competition (Habermas). Here, Mouffe is right to point out how violence returns with a vengeance in the exclusion of those that do not fit the rules of unconstrained communication. However, the main threat to democracy in today's democratic countries resides in none of these two extremes, but in the death of the political through the commodification of politics. What is at stake here is not primarily the way politicians are packaged and sold as merchandise at elections. A much deeper problem is that elections themselves are conceived along the lines of buying a commodity (power, in this case): they involve a competition among different merchandise-parties, and our votes are like money that we give to buy the government we want. What gets lost in such a view of politics as another service we buy is politics as a shared public debate of issues and decisions that concern us all.

Democracy, it may seem, thus not only can include antagonism, it is the only political form that solicits and presupposes it, that *institutionalizes* it. What other political systems perceive as a threat (the lack of a "natural" pretender to power), democracy elevates into a "normal" positive condition of its functioning: the place of power is empty, there is no natural claimant for it, *polemos* or struggle is irreducible, and every positive government must be fought out, gained through *polemos*. This why Laclau's critical remark about Lefort misses the point: "For Lefort, the *place* of power in democracies is empty. For me, the question poses itself differently: it is a question of *producing* emptiness out of the operation of hegemonic logic. For me, emptiness is a type of identity, not a structural location."[13] The two emptinesses are simply not comparable. The emptiness of the "people" is the emptiness of the hegemonic signifier that totalizes the chain of equivalences, that is, whose particular content is "transubstantiated" into an embodiment of the social whole, while the emptiness of the place of power is a distance that makes every empirical bearer of power "deficient," contingent, and temporary.

The further feature neglected by Laclau is the fundamental paradox of authoritarian Fascism, which almost symmetrically inverts what Mouffe calls the "democratic paradox": if the wager of (institutionalized) democracy is to integrate the antagonistic struggle itself into the institutional, differential space, transforming it into regulated agonism, Fascism proceeds in the opposite direction. While Fascism, in its mode of activity, brings the antagonistic logic to its extreme (talking about the "struggle to death" between itself and its enemies, and always maintaining—if not realizing—a minimum of an extra-institutional threat of violence, of a "direct pressure of the people" bypassing the complex legal-institutional channels), it posits as its political goal precisely the opposite, an extremely ordered hierarchic social body (no wonder Fascism always relies on organicist-corporatist metaphors). This contrast can be nicely rendered in the terms of the Lacanian opposition between the "subject of enunciation" and the "subject of the enunciated (content)": while democracy admits antagonistic struggle as its goal (in Lacanese: as its enunciated, its content), its procedure is regulated-systemic; Fascism, on the contrary, tries to impose the goal of hierarchically structured harmony through the means of an unbridled antagonism.

The conclusion to be drawn is that populism (the way we supplemented Laclau's definition of it) is not the only mode of existence of the excess of antagonism over the institutional-democratic frame of regulated agonistic struggle: neither the (now defunct) Communist revolutionary organizations nor also the wide phenomena of noninstitutionalized social and political protest, from the student movements in the 1968 period to later anti-war protests and the more recent anti-globalization movement, can be properly called populist. Exemplary here is the case of the anti-segregation movement in the United States of the late 1950s and early 1960s, epitomized by the name of Martin Luther King. Although it endeavored to articulate a demand that was not properly met within the existing democratic institutions, it cannot be called populist in any meaningful sense of the term—the way it led the struggle and constituted its opponent was simply not populist. (A more general remark should be made here about the single-issue popular movements [for example, the "tax revolts" in the United States]: although they function in a populist way, mobilizing the people around a demand that is not met by the democratic institutions, they do *not* seem to rely on a complex chain of equivalences, but remain focused on one singular demand.)

. . . to the Deadlock of Political Engagements

Although, for Laclau, rhetorics is operative in the very heart of the ideologico-political process, in establishing the hegemonic articulation, he does sometimes succumb to the temptation of reducing the troubles of today's Left to a "mere rhetorical" failure, as in the following passage:

> The Right and the Left are not fighting at the same level. On the one hand, there is an attempt by the Right to articulate various problems that people have into some kind of political imaginary, and on the other hand, there is a retreat by the Left into a purely moral discourse which doesn't enter into the hegemonic game. . . . The main difficulty of the Left is that the fight today does not take place at that level of the political imaginary. And it relies on a rationalist discourse about rights, conceived in a purely abstract way without entering that hegemonic field, and without that engagement there is no possibility of a progressive political alternative.[14]

So the main problem of the Left is its inability to propose a passionate global vision of change . . . but is it really that simple? Is the solution for the Left to abandon the "purely moral" rationalist discourse and to propose a more engaged vision addressing the political imaginary, a vision that could compete with the neoconservative projects and also with the past leftist visions? Is this diagnosis not similar to the proverbial answer of a doctor to the worried patient: "What you need is a good doctor's advice!"? What about asking the elementary question: *What, concretely, would that new leftist vision be with regard to its content?* Is not the decline of the traditional Left, its retreat into the moral rationalist discourse that no longer enters the hegemonic game, conditioned by the great changes in global economy in the last decades? So where *is* a better leftist global solution to our present predicament? Whatever one says against the Third Way, it at least tried to propose a vision that does take into account these changes. It is no wonder that, as we approach concrete political analysis, confusion starts to reign—in a recent interview, Ernesto Laclau made a weird accusation against me, imputing me that I

> claimed that the problem with the United States is that it acts as a global power and does not think as a global power, but only in the terms of its own interests. The solution is then that it should think and act as a global power, that it should assume its role of world policeman. For somebody like Žižek, who comes from the Hegelian tradition, to say

this means that the United States tends to be the universal class. . . . The function that Hegel attributes to State and Marx to proletariat, Žižek now attributes to the highpoint of American imperialism. There is no basis for thinking that things will be in this way. I do not believe that any progressive cause, in any part of the world, could think in these terms.[15]

I quote this passage not to dwell on its ridiculously malicious interpretive twist: of course I never pleaded for the United States to be the universal class. When I stated that the United States "acts globally and thinks locally," my point was not that it should both think and act globally; it was simply that this gap between universality and particularity is *structurally necessary*, which is why the United States is in the long term digging its own grave. Incidentally, *therein* resides my Hegelianism: the motor of the historico-dialectical process is precisely the *gap* between acting and thinking. People do not do what they think they are doing: while thought is formally universal, the act as such is particularizing, which is why, for Hegel precisely, there is no self-transparent historical subject; all acting social subjects are always and by definition caught in the "cunning of reason," and they fulfill their role through the very failure to accomplish their intended task. Consequently, the gap we are dealing with here is also not simply the gap between the universal form of thought and the particular interests that "effectively" sustain our acts legitimized by the universal thought: the true Hegelian insight is that the very universal form as such, in its opposition to the particular content that it excludes, particularizes itself, turns into its opposite, so there is no need to look for some particular "pathological" content that smears the pure universality.

The reason I quote this passage is to make a precise theoretical point about the status of the universality: we are dealing here with two opposed logics of universality to be strictly distinguished. On the one hand, there is the state bureaucracy as the universal class of a society (or, in a larger scope, the United States as the world's policeman, the universal enforcer and guarantor of human rights and democracy), the direct agent of the global order; on the other hand, there is the "surnumerary" universality, the universality embodied in the element that sticks out of the existing order, which, while internal to it, has no proper place within it (what Jacques Rancière calls the "part of no-part"). Not only are the two not the same,[16] but the struggle is ultimately *the struggle between these two universalities*, not simply between the particular elements of the universality: it is not just about which particular content will "hegemonize" the empty form of universality, but rather it is a struggle between two exclusive *forms* of universality themselves.

This is why Laclau misses the point when he opposes the "working class" and the "people" along the axis of conceptual content versus the effect of radical nomination:[17] the "working class" designates a preexisting social group, characterized by its substantial content, while the "people" emerges as a unified agent through the very act of nomination—there is nothing in the heterogeneity of demands that predisposes them to be unified in the "people." However, Marx distinguishes between the "working class" and the "proletariat": the "working class" effectively is a particular social group, while the "proletariat" designates a subjective position. And Lenin follows Marx here in his "nonorganic" conception of the party as differentiated from the class, with "class" itself conceived as a highly heterogeneous and contradictory entity, as well as in his deep sensibility for the specificity of the political dimension among different social practices.

This is why Laclau's critical debate about Marx's differentiation of "proletariat" and "*lumpenproletariat*" also misses the point: the distinction is not the one between an objective social group and a nongroup, a remainder-excess with no proper place within the social structure, but a distinction between two modes of this remainder-excess, which generate two different subjective positions. The implication of Marx's analysis is that, paradoxically, although the "*lumpenproletariat*" seems more radically "displaced" with regard to the social body than the "proletariat," it effectively fits into the social edifice much more smoothly. To refer to the Kantian distinction between negative and infinite judgment, the *lumpenproletariat* is not truly a nongroup (the immanent negation of a group, a group that is a nongroup), but it is not a group, and its exclusion from all strata not only consolidates the identity of other groups but makes it a free-floating element that can be used by any stratum or class. It can be the radicalizing "carnivalesque" element of workers' struggle, pushing them from compromising moderate strategies to an open confrontation, or the element that is used by the ruling class to degenerate from within the opposition to its rule (the long tradition of the criminal mob serving those in power). The working class, on the contrary, is a group that is in itself, *as a group* within the social edifice, a non-group, that is, whose position is in itself "contradictory": the working class is a productive force, which society and those in power need in order to reproduce themselves and their rule, but for which, nonetheless, they cannot find a "proper place."

This brings us to Laclau's basic reproach to the Marxian "critique of political economy" (CPE): it is a positive "ontic" science that delimits a part of substantial social reality, so that any direct grounding of emancipatory politics in the CPE (or, in other words, any privilege given to class struggle) reduces the political to an epiphenomenon embedded in substantial reality. Such a view misses what Derrida called the "spectral" dimension of Marx's CPE: far from offering the ontology of a determinate social domain, the CPE demonstrates how this ontology is always supplemented by "hauntology," science of ghosts—what Marx calls the "metaphysical subtleties and theological niceties" of the universe of commodities. This strange "spirit/ghost" resides in the very heart of economic reality, which is why, with the CPE, the circle of Marx's critique is closed. Marx's initial thesis, in his early works, was that the critique of religion is the starting point of every critique. From here he proceeded to the critique of state and politics, and, finally, to the CPE, which gives us insight into the most basic mechanism of social reproduction. However, at this final point, the movement becomes circular and returns to its starting point, that is, what we discover in the very heart of this "hard economic reality" is again the theological dimension. When Marx describes the mad self-enhancing circulation of capital, whose solipsistic path of self-fecundation reaches its apogee in today's meta-reflexive speculations on futures, it is far too simplistic to claim that the specter of this self-engendering monster that pursues its path while disregarding any human or environmental concern is an ideological abstraction, and that one should never forget that, behind this abstraction, there are real people and natural objects on whose productive capacities and resources capital's circulation is based and on which it feeds itself like a gigantic parasite. The problem is that this "abstraction" is not only in our (financial speculator's) misperception of social reality, but that it is "real" in the precise sense of determining the structure of the very material social processes: the fate of whole strata of the population and sometimes of whole countries can be decided by the "solipsistic" speculative dance of capital, which pursues its goal of profitability in a blessed indifference with regard to how its movement will affect social reality. Therein resides the fundamental systemic violence of capitalism, which is much more uncanny than the direct precapitalist socio-ideological violence: this violence is no longer attributable to concrete individuals and their "evil" intentions but is purely "objective," systemic, anonymous. Here we encounter the Lacanian difference between reality and the Real: "reality" is the social reality of the actual people involved in interaction and in the productive processes, while the Real is the inexorable "abstract" spectral logic of capital that determines what goes on in social reality.

Furthermore, let us not forget what the very term CPE indicates: the economy is in itself political, so that one cannot reduce political struggle to a mere epiphenomenon or secondary effect of a more basic economic social process. This is what "class struggle" is for Marx: the presence of the political in the very heart of the economy, which is why it is significant that the manuscript of *Capital III* breaks precisely when Marx would have to deal directly with class struggle. This break is not simply a lack, the signal of a failure, but, rather, the signal that the line of thought bends back into itself, turns to a dimension that was always already here. The "political" class struggle permeates the entire analysis from the very beginning: the categories of political economy (say, the "value" of the commodity "labor power," or the rate of profit) are not objective socioeconomic data, but data that always signal the outcome of a "political" struggle. And, once again, is Lenin's highly political understanding of the economic questions after the seizure of power, contrary to Stalin's rehabilitation of the "law of value under socialism," not a decisive step forward in that direction? (Incidentally, in dealing with the Real, Laclau seems to oscillate between the formal notion of the Real as antagonism and the more "empirical" notion of the Real as that which cannot be reduced to a formal opposition: "the opposition A-B will never fully become A—not A. The 'B-ness' of the B will be ultimately non-dialectizable. The 'people' will always be something more than the pure opposite of power. There is a Real of the 'people' which resists symbolic integration."[18])

The crucial question, of course, is this: What, exactly, is the character of this excess of "people" over being the "pure opposite of power," that is, *what* in "people" resists symbolic integration? Is it simply the wealth of its (empirical or other) determinations? If this is the case, then we are *not* dealing with a Real that resists symbolic integration, because the Real, in this case, is precisely the antagonism A—non-A, so that "that which is in B more than non-A" is not the Real in B but B's symbolic determinations.

"Capitalism" is thus not merely a category that delimits a positive social sphere, but a formal, transcendental matrix that structures the entire social space—literally, a *mode* of production. Its strength resides in its very weakness: it is pushed into a constant dynamic, into a kind of permanent emergency state, in order to avoid confronting its basic antagonism, its structural imbalance. As such, it is ontologically "open": it reproduces itself through its permanent self-overcoming; it is as it were indebted to its own future, borrowing from it and forever postponing the day of reckoning.

"Was Will Europa?"

The general conclusion is that, although the topic of populism is emerging as crucial in today's political scenery, it cannot be used as the ground for the renewal of the emancipatory politics. The first thing to note is that today's populism is different from the traditional version. What distinguishes it is the opponent against which it mobilizes the people: the rise of post-politics, the growing reduction of politics proper to the rational administration of the conflicting interests. In the highly developed countries of the United States and western Europe, at least, "populism" is emerging as the inherent shadowy double of institutionalized post-politics: one is almost tempted to say as its *supplement* in the Derridean sense, as the arena in which political demands that do not fit into the institutionalized space can be articulated. In this sense, there is a constitutive mystification that pertains to populism: its basic gesture is to refuse to confront the complexity of the situation, to reduce it to a clear struggle with a pseudo-concrete enemy figure (from the Brussels bureaucracy to illegal immigrants). "Populism" is thus by definition a negative phenomenon, a phenomenon grounded in a refusal, even an implicit admission of impotence. We all know the old joke about a guy looking for his lost key under the street light: when asked where he lost it, he admits that it was in a dark corner; so why is he looking for it here, under the light? Because the visibility is much better here. There is always something of this trick in populism. So not only is populism not the area within which today's emancipatory projects should inscribe themselves—one should even go a step further and propose that the main task of today's emancipatory politics, its life-and-death problem, is to find a form of political mobilization that, while (like populism) critical of institutionalized politics, *avoids* the populist temptation.

Where, then, does all of this leave us with regard to Europe's imbroglio? The French voters were not given a clear symmetrical choice, since the very terms of the choice privileged the "Yes": the elite proposed to the people a choice that was effectively no choice at all—people were called to ratify the inevitable, the result of enlightened expertise. The media and the political elite presented the choice as one between knowledge and ignorance, between expertise and ideology, between post-political administration and old political passions of the Left and the Right.[19] The "No" was thus dismissed as a short-sighted reaction that was unaware of its own consequences: a murky reaction of fear in the face of the emerging new postindustrial global order, an instinct to stick to and protect the comfortable welfare state traditions, a gesture of refusal lacking any positive alternative program. No wonder the only political parties whose official stance was "No" were the parties at the opposite extreme of the political spectrum, Le Pen's Front National on the Right and the Communists and Trotskyists on the Left.

However, even if there is an element of truth in all this, the very fact that the "No" was not sustained by a coherent alternative political vision is the strongest possible condemnation of the political and mediatic elite: it is a monument to their inability to articulate, to translate into a political vision, the people's longings and dissatisfactions. Instead, in their reaction to the "No," they treated the people as retarded pupils who did not get the lesson of the experts: their self-criticism was the one of the teacher who admits that he failed to educate his pupils properly. What the advocates of this "communication" thesis (the French and Dutch "No" means that the enlightened elite failed to communicate properly with the masses) fail to see is that, on the contrary, the "No" in question was a perfect example of communication in which, as Lacan put it, the speaker gets from the addressee its own message in its inverted, that is true, form: the enlightened European bureaucrats got back from their voters the shallowness of their own message to them in its true form. The project of European Union that was rejected by France and the Netherlands stood for a kind of cheap trick, as if Europe can redeem itself and beat its competitors by simply combining the best of both worlds: by beating the United States, China, and Japan in scientific-technological modernization through keeping alive its cultural traditions. One should insist here that if Europe is to redeem itself it should, on the contrary, be ready to take the risk of *losing* (in the sense of radically questioning) *both*: to dispel the fetish of scientific-technological progress *and* to get rid of relying on the superiority of its cultural heritage.

So, although the choice was not the choice between two political options, it was also not the choice between the enlightened vision of a modern Europe, ready to fit into the new global order, versus old confused political passions. When commentators described the "No" as a message of confused fear, they were wrong. The main fear we are dealing with here is the fear the "No" itself provoked in the new European political elite, the fear that people will no longer so easily buy their post-political vision. For all others, the "No" is a message and expression of hope: hope that *politics* is still alive and possible, that the debate about what the new Europe shall and should be is still open. This is why we, on the Left, should reject the sneering insinuation by the liberals that, in our "No," we find ourselves with strange neo-Fascist bedfellows. What the new populist Right and the Left share is just one thing: the awareness that *politics* proper is still alive.

There *was* a positive choice in the "No": the choice of the choice itself, the rejection of the blackmail by the new elite that offers us only the choice to confirm their expert knowledge or to display one's "irrational" immaturity. The "No" is the positive decision to start a properly *political* debate about what kind of Europe we really want. Late in his life, Freud asked the famous question "Was will das Weib?," "What does the woman want?," admitting his perplexity when faced with the enigma of the feminine sexuality. Does the imbroglio with the European constitution not bear witness to the same puzzlement: which Europe do we want?

Every crisis is in itself an instigation for a new beginning, every collapse of short-term strategic and pragmatic measures (for financial reorganization of the Union, and so on) a blessing in disguise, an opportunity to rethink the very foundations. What we need is a retrieval-through-repetition (*Wieder-Holung*): through a critical confrontation with the entire European tradition, we should repeat the question "What is Europe?," or, rather, "What does it mean for us to be Europeans?," and thus formulate a new inception. The task is difficult, it compels us to take a great risk of stepping into the unknown—yet its only alternative is slow decay, the gradual transformation of Europe into what Greece was for the mature Roman Empire, a destination for nostalgic cultural tourism with no effective relevance.[20]

And—a further point apropos of which we should risk the hypothesis that Heidegger was right, although not in the sense he meant it— what if democracy is not the answer to this predicament? In his *Notes Towards a Definition of Culture*, the great conservative T. S. Eliot remarked that there are moments when the only choice is the one between sectarianism and nonbelief, when the only way to keep a religion alive is to perform a sectarian split from its main corpse. This is our only chance today: only by means of a "sectarian split" from the standard European legacy, by cutting ourselves off from the decaying corpse of the old Europe, can we keep the renewed European legacy alive. Such a split should render problematic the very premises that we tend to accept as our destiny, as nonnegotiable data of our predicament—the phenomenon usually designated as the global new world order and the need, through "modernization," to accommodate ourselves to it. To put it bluntly, if the emerging new world order is the nonnegotiable frame for all of us, then Europe is lost, so the *only* solution for Europe is to take the risk and *break* this spell of our destiny. *Nothing* should be accepted as inviolable in this new foundation, neither the need for economic "modernization" nor the most sacred liberal and democratic fetishes.

This is the space for repeating the Leninist gesture today. In the summer of 1921, in order to strengthen the links between peasants and the Soviet government, Lenin convoked a small group composed of Bonch-Bruevich, the commissar of agriculture Ossinski, and a couple of others, in order to elaborate a proposal to freely give land to old proto-

Communist Christian sects (they had 3–4 million members in Russia at that time). On October 5, a proclamation was printed and addressed to "Members of the Sect of Old Believers" (who, from the seventeenth century, were persecuted by the tsarist regime), inviting them to install themselves on abandoned land and to live there according to their mores. This appeal directly quotes *Apostles*: "Nobody should say that what he owns belongs to him only; all should be hold in common. . . ." Lenin's goal was not only pragmatic (to produce more food); he also wanted to explore the Communist potentials of the precapitalist forms of common property (which already Marx, in his letter to Vera Zassulitch, saw as a potential base for Communist production). Old Believers then effectively founded a model *sovkhoz* in Lesnaya Polyana near Moscow, whose activity was closely followed by Lenin.[21] The Left should display the same openness today, even with regard to the most "sectarian" fundamentalists.

Notes

1   What this means is that precisely on account of the unbearable horror of Stalinism, any direct moralistic portrayal of Stalinism as evil misses its target—it is only through what Kierkegaard called "indirect communication," by way of practicing a kind of irony, that one can render its horror.

2   Isaac Deutscher, *The Prophet Outcast* (London: Verso, 2003), 88.

3   Jean-Claude Milner, *Le périple structural* (Paris: Seuil, 2002), 213.

4   Many pro-European commentators favorably contrasted the readiness to bear financial sacrifices of the new Eastern European members of the Union to the egotistic intransigent behavior of the United Kingdom, France, Germany, and some other old members. However, one should also bear in mind the hypocrisy of Slovenia and other new Eastern members: they behaved as the latest members of an exclusive club, wanting to be the last to be allowed to enter. While accusing France of racism, they themselves opposed the entry of Turkey.

5   See Ernesto Laclau, *On Populist Reason* (London: Verso, 2005).

6   This distinction is homologous to that between "thin" and "thick" morality (see Michael Walzer, *Thick and Thin* [Notre Dame, Ind.: University of Notre Dame Press, 1994]). Walzer gives the example of the big demonstration in the streets of Prague in 1989 that toppled the Communist regime. Most of the banners read simply "Truth," "Justice," or "Freedom," general slogans even the ruling Communists had to agree with. The catch was, of course, in the underlying web of "thick" (specific, determinate) demands (freedom of the press, multiparty elections, and so forth) that indicated what the people *meant* by the simple general slogans. In short, the struggle was not simply for freedom and justice, but for the meaning of these words.

7 Laclau, *On Populist Reason*, 88.

8 Ibid., 90.

9 Ibid., 98–99.

10 Many people sympathetic to Hugo Chavez's regime in Venezuela like to oppose Chavez's flamboyant and sometimes clownish *caudillo* style toward the vast popular movement of the self-organization of the poor and dispossessed that surprisingly brought him back to power after he was deposed in a coup backed by the United States. The error of this view is to think that one can have the second without the first: the popular movement *needs* the identificatory figure of a charismatic leader. The limitation of Chavez lies elsewhere, in the very factor that enables him to play his role: oil money. It is as if oil is always a mixed blessing, if not an outright curse. Because of this supply, he can go on making populist gestures without paying the full price for them, without really inventing something new at the socioeconomic level. Money makes it possible to practice inconsistent politics (populist anti-capitalist measures *and* leaving the capitalist edifice basically untouched), of not acting but postponing the act, the radical change. (In spite of his anti-U.S. rhetoric, Chavez takes great care that Venezuelan contracts with the United States are regularly met—he is effectively a "Fidel with oil.")

11 Sigmund Freud, *Group Psychology and the Analysis of the Ego*, in *The Standard Edition of the Complete Psychological Works of Freud* (New York: W. W. Norton, 1975) 18:100.

12 See, especially, Chantal Mouffe, *The Democratic Paradox* (London: Verso, 2000).

13 Laclau, *On Populist Reason*, 166.

14 Ernesto Laclau, as quoted in Mary Zournazi, ed., *Hope* (London: Lawrence and Wishart, 2002), 145.

15 Ernesto Laclau, "Las manos en la masa," *Radar*, 5 June 2005, 20. My translation.

16 The best anecdotal example of what is wrong with the first mode of universality is the story, from World War I, about a working-class English soldier on leave from the front, who was enraged by encountering an upper-class youth calmly leading his life of exquisite "Britishness" (tea rituals, and so on) and not perturbed by the war at all. When he explodes against the youth, asking "How can you just sit here and enjoy it while we are sacrificing our blood to defend our way of life?," the youth calmly responds, "But I *am* the way of life you are defending there in the trenches!"

17 Laclau, *On Populist Reason*, 183.

18 Ibid., 152.

19 The limitation of post-politics is best exemplified not only by the success of rightist populism, but by the U.K. elections of 2005. In spite of the growing unpopularity of Tony Blair (he is regularly voted the most unpopular person in the United Kingdom), there is no way for this discontent with Blair to find a politically effective expression; such a frustration can only foment dangerous extra-parliamentary explosions.

20 In March 2005, the Pentagon released the summary of a top-secret document, which sketches America's agenda for global military domination. It calls for a more "pro-active" approach to warfare, beyond the weaker notion of "preemptive" and defensive actions. It focuses on four core tasks: to build partnerships with failing states to

defeat internal terrorist threats; to defend the homeland, including offensive strikes against terrorist groups planning attacks; to influence the choices of countries at a strategic crossroads, such as China and Russia; and to prevent the acquisition of weapons of mass destruction by hostile states and terrorist groups. Will Europe accept this, will it be satisfied to take on the role of anemic Greece under the domination of the powerful Roman Empire?

21 See Jean-Jacques Marie, *Lénine 1870–1924* (Paris: Editions Balland, 2004), 392–93. I thank Sebastian Budgen for drawing my attention to this unexpected activity of Lenin.

PART II | **Lenin in philosophy**

6

Lenin and the

Savas Michael-Matsas   **Path of Dialectics**

1.

"Il faut continuer, je ne peux pas continuer, je vais continuer" — You must continue, I cannot continue, I will continue. These are the last words by Samuel Beckett in *The Unnamable*.[1] They are also our words. What to continue? How to continue? The all-pervading philistinism of the rulers triumphantly proclaims that nothing emancipatory exists any more; everything that remains will continue its humiliating existence forever. So, why continue?

The end of the twentieth century appears to vindicate the impasse, to annihilate every gain of the liberation achieved since 1917, signifying its complete destruction. The collapse of the post-revolutionary bureaucratized regimes, which did everything possible to distort and betray in the most horrendous ways the principles upon which they were founded, likewise threatens to bury under their rubble what was also the exact opposite of their tyranny, the revolutionary expectation of a Communist perspective. The flag of surrender is raised upon the ruins: *emancipate yourselves from emancipation*. This is the order of the day.

But the world is hideous and insupportable as never before. We must continue. But from this perspective at least, we cannot continue. "We cannot stand this world that we don't have the will to deny."[2] This is the nightmare of contemporary nihilism, "the nihilism of the last man," as Nietzsche described it. A century later, this disease of nihilism is not solely European in scope but global. It declares the end of metaphysics, of all systems, of all ideologies, of the "great meta-narratives," of revolutions, of Communism, even of history itself. In a typical chiliastic and ludicrous manner, not only by the likes of Fukuyama and company, it even gives an exact date for the End: 1989.

This new fashionable eschatology presents itself as the tomb of all eschatologies, keeping their fallacy and rejecting everything emancipatory in their kernel. The collapse of all certainty is dogmatically considered as the highest certainty. The most vulgar market metaphysics is raised as the doctrine of the end of all metaphysics.

On the left and on the right they rush to give answers—the already known. But the main question is *to find how to pose the right questions*. Taking Lenin as our cue, the first thing to learn is precisely this: *boldly, without preconceptions and prejudices, without being trapped by previous examples, focusing on the object itself, to enter the dialectical realm of questioning, searching to find the new, most tormenting, not yet known questions, which emerge in every dramatic turning point of history and cognition.*

Here, in the turning points, in the void created by the rupture of historical continuity, the painful inner dialogue is heard: "You must continue, I cannot continue, I will continue."

2.

This inner dialogue had shaken Lenin himself, as never before, in those days of torment in 1914 that look so much like our days, when the body of Europe was torn apart by antagonisms and nationalistic fever, when the "Great War" was exploding among the different imperialist powers, and when the historical opponent of imperialism, the official "socialist camp" at that time would also self-destruct.

For Lenin the shock was terrible. When he heard the news about the vote in support of the kaiser's war budget by the SPD, or of Plekhanov's support of the tsarist government's war effort, he simply could not believe it. Lenin was never the unemotional icon of steel portrayed by Stalinists. The shock puts in relief his human, all too human, qualities. Furthermore, without this initial, desperate denial of what was real, without the moment of temporary powerlessness, without the terrible moment of recognition of the impossibility of continuing, while you know at the same time that you must continue, it is impossible to appreciate the tension and the impulse necessary for the leap that establishes continuity.

Beckett recounts the truth. Lenin, by means of his own path, encounters this truth.[3] Continuity is not growth, extension, and repetition of the same. It is a *contradiction* that by its own sharpening and culmination finds the path to its transcendence leading into another, new contradiction. *Continuity is the fruit of its necessity as well as of the impossibility to be established.*

3.

A contradiction cannot be resolved automatically or smoothly. Its objective nature always implies the real threat of a catastrophe. It demands probing and grasping its specific logic, and from there emerges the elaboration of a strategy of overcoming it in practice. It is precisely here that Lenin is incomparably relevant today.

Lenin was not immobilized by the first shocking impression, nor did he rush into making immediate, hasty political answers and conclusions. He turned instead to the fundamental questions that needed to be asked. Often erroneously seen as a pragmatist, his response here could not have been further from this. After the declaration of war and the collapse of the Second International, while the conflagration in the battlefields escalated, he plunged into a systematic study of philosophy, most notably of Hegel's *The Science of Logic*, in the Berne Library from September 1914 to May 1915.

Only after this cycle of profound philosophical work was completed did Lenin then go on to write, from the second half of May to the first half of June 1915, his pamphlet "The Collapse of the Second International" and begin the elaboration of an analysis of imperialism. These major works were in turn followed by other crucially significant theoretical and practical studies leading to the change of strategy in the "April Theses" of 1917, the libertarian *The State and Revolution*, and the final assault on the Winter Palace. But the point of departure should not be forgotten. The preparation for the "assault to heaven" began in the silence of the Berne Library, over the open books of Hegel.

The new epoch of crisis, into which humanity and the international workers' movement had entered as a result of the eruption of the "Great War," decomposed and recomposed all social relations and functions, both material as well as mental. The crisis was not restricted to the productive-economic structure; it involved all levels of reality. It became a crisis of civilization, a crisis of all objective, historically developed forms of social consciousness, of all given conceptions of the world, of all forms and ways of representation. It was an epistemological crisis that involved not just the privileged classes and the intellectuals tied to them but the popular classes as well, first of all the working class, its political leadership, and its own organic intellectuals.

The ultimate capitulation of social democracy to capitalism, to the imperialist state and its war aims, had been prepared well in advance by the acceptance of a theoretical horizon adapted to the limits of the capitalist world itself and its fetishist illusions.

Only a theoretical approach that challenged the limits of bourgeois society, its worldview or, rather, the fragments of it, could transcend the epistemological crisis in its entirety; that is to say, only then could such an approach go beyond a vague "crisis consciousness" (Andras Gedö),[4] and give a conscious expression to the interests of the working class, a sense of real direction to a new praxis of revolutionary transformation. From this vantage point, Lenin's turn to questions of dialectical method and epistemology, as it is recorded in his *Philosophical Notebooks* of 1914-15, constitutes the first decisive step of an entire strategy to overcome the crisis of leadership of the working class that erupted with the beginnings of the war.

4.

The collapse of the Social Democratic International from top to bottom, to its very foundations, revealed that something terribly destructive had taken place in its theoretical-methodological foundations, not solely in its actual politics. This demanded an exhaustive fundamental re-examination of Marxism in contradistinction with the official conception of Marxism as it was institutionalized by the "popes" and "cardinals" of "Marxist orthodoxy" such as Kautsky and Plekhanov. But the radical break needed to go one stage further. It was not content with asking anew what the foundations of Marxism were. More than this, it needed to search for a philosophical answer as to what a foundation itself actually represents.

The "orthodox Marxism" of the Second International was characterized above all by its indifference, if not by an open rejection, of the need for a philosophical foundation of Marxism. Above all, the origins of Marxian dialectics in the Hegelian dialectic, even the very notion of dialectics as such, were considered as Hegelian, and therefore unusable, harmful remnants to be rejected. This was not only the position of Bernstein's revisionism or of those openly embracing positivism and neo-Kantianism; it was similarly the doctrine of the "Pope of orthodoxy" himself, Karl Kautsky, who stressed in no ambiguous terms that he "regard[ed] Marxism not as a philosophical doctrine but as an empirical science, as a special understanding of society." Plekhanov also, who, in contradistinction to other theoreticians of the Second International, did pay attention to philosophy, and who wrote one thousand pages or more on philosophy and dialectics, simply could not penetrate beyond the surface. As Lenin himself remarked, when it came to Hegelian logic, the connections it led to, its thought (that is, dialectics proper, as philosophical science), there was nothing at all (274). It was on this theoretical soil that the evils of dogmatic petrifaction, bureaucratic opportunism, apologetics of current tactics, worship of the accomplished fact in the form of mechanical determinism, economism, and gradualism flourished.

Elsewhere, while it is true that Austro-Marxism, particularly that of Max Adler, had an insight into the connection between ascending reformism and this anti-philosophical, anti-dialectical attitude, and while it did make an attempt to establish a critical stand against this degeneration by a philosophical return to Kant, this attempt too almost completely bypassed the vital transition from Hegel to Marx. The transformation of social objectivity into a formal transcendental condition of politics was counterposed to the mechanical objectivism of Bernstein and Kautsky. But the only real consequence of this was the obscuring of the relationship between subject and object, theory and practice in a neo-Kantian way, thus itself leading politically to centrism, to paralysis, and finally to capitulation to reformism.

The road, or rather, the tortuous path opened and followed by Lenin, however, was totally different. As already stressed, he did not restrict himself, as Plekhanov did, to identifying the foundations of Marxism. He reopened the question about what a foundation and a founding act are.

Is a foundation a static, axiomatic, already given principle, as it was for the theoreticians of the Second International? Or is it the outcome of a dialectical transcendence (*Aufhebung*)? Is it permanently static or dynamically renewable? Is it a category intervening as a middle term between the object of cognition, the "edifice" as a whole, and the reasoning subject, separating rather than connecting object and subject? Or is it reflection, the self-penetration of Being into itself, to the innermost point that can be reached at any particular historical moment, passing through and transcending the limits existing until then? Is a foundation the reduction into an ultimate abstract identity or the "unity of the identity and difference, the truth of what difference and identity have turned out to be . . . essence put explicitly as a totality?" [5] But, I hear some of you object, isn't this the language of Hegel, the scandal of all scandals!

Lenin returned to Hegel in 1914 not to be enclosed into his system but to transcend it, to turn Hegel upside down, materialistically, as the famous dictum says. The materialist reversal of Hegel, the transcending of his dialectics on materialist lines, is *the self-genesis and founding act of Marxism*. It is not an act performed once and for all by Marx, a century and a half ago, or by Lenin in 1914. It is an open, active, permanent process until the full realization of philosophy into a radically transformed world. The foundation, the ground, is located always at the depths of the present.

5.

One needs to return to Hegel, then, so as to continue this task of his materialist reversal. But let us be clear about one thing. It has nothing in common with the often repeated "return to the roots," "return to Marx," or even "back to Lenin," as if it were a ritual of purification of the virginity of the sources, an alignment with what existed before everything went wrong.

Lenin in his *Philosophical Notebooks* distinguishes between a motion without repetition, without a return to the point of departure, and dialectical motion, "motion precisely with a return to the point of departure" (343). The return is expressed in an "identity of opposites," not in a simple alignment with the initial situation, not by establishing an abstract identity with it, without opposition, not by a restoration of the *status quo ante*. A return to the unity of opposites is a process where, under certain conditions, the opposites "are identical, becoming transformed into one another" (109). As Lenin goes on to note, "the movement of cognition to the object can always only proceed dialectically." It is necessary to go back so as better to leap forward. "Converging and diverging lines: circles which touch one another. *Knottenpunkte* = the practice of mankind and of human history" (277–78).

In this sense, then, practice is the "criterion of the coincidence of one of the infinite aspects of the real," the criterion of the return to the point of departure of cognition on a higher level of the spiral motion. Such returns are *Knottenpunkte*, nodal points, turnings of the spiral and they "represent a unity of contradictions, when Being and not-Being, as vanishing moments, coincide for a moment, in the given moments of the movement (of technique, of history, etc.)" (278). Lenin's return to the point of departure of Marxism—Hegel's materialist reversal—on a new level, in the nodal point of 1914, constitutes a unity of contradictions that includes and transcends developments in the class struggle and in theory from the point of departure of the spiral to its new curve.

Thus, return has the character that Hegel's friend from their student years, the great poet and dialectical thinker Hölderlin, had given to what he called a "reversal back to the native land" (*vaterlandische Umkehr*) in his remarks on Sophocles's tragedies *Oedipus* and *Antigone*. It is a reversal interconnected with every radical turn in historical time, when nothing could be equated with the initial condition,[6] "because the reversal back to the native land is the reversal of all ways of representation and of all forms."[7] The return to the point of departure of Marxism demands the revolutionizing of all the historically developed forms of Marxism, without losing their truth content. It is the innovative act of self-refoundation, a veritable renaissance.

6.

A renaissance is not identical with but is the opposite of regression. In our case it can never be a regression into the uterus—the absolute idealism of Hegel.

The Hegelian system constitutes a limit. As Gadamer pointed out, even the most different or diametrically opposed thinkers, from Marx and Kierkegaard to Heidegger, agree that "the two thousand year tradition which shaped Western philosophy came to an end in Hegel's system and in its sudden collapse in the middle of the nineteenth century."[8] The task is not to restore the building that has collapsed. For Marx and for Lenin the questions that need to be posed of this task must go beyond the limit. It involves the transcending of Hegel by a radically new relationship of philosophy with the world, of theory and practice, in the framework of a revolutionary process where philosophy becomes world and the world becomes philosophy, to use the expression by Marx in his preparatory notes on the philosophy of Epicurus.

Hegel is for Marxism the equivalent of the Red Sea in the exodus from the land of slavery. You have to pass through it, through its opening, which reveals the solid sea bed in its materiality (materialist reversal), marching with all the oppressed in the long march of liberation. *There is always the danger of being drowned in it, together with the oppressors, when the opening begins to close.*

Absolute idealism has to be destroyed *from within*, by the means offered by Hegel's dialectical logic itself but purified of its mysticism, and re-elaborated on a materialist basis. It is of course a huge undertaking that has not yet been completed. Lenin recognizes both the magnitude as well as the incomplete character of the task: "Hegel's logic cannot be *applied* in its given form, it cannot be *taken* as given. One must *separate out* from it the logical (epistemological) nuances, after purifying them from *Ideenmystik*: that still is a big job" (264, emphasis in the original).

7.

Lenin took on this "big job" and he never stopped the undertaking right up until the moment of his death.

A materialist reading of Hegel, such as Lenin performed, is not reduced into a simple interchange of terms by restoring matter in motion. Nor does it give primacy to consciousness, or reposition Nature in the hegemonic site occupied by the Idea. The reversal of Hegelian dialectics, the return to its material point of departure, has to be itself dialectical, that is, through the merger of contradictions and their transcendence into new unities of contradictions. The dialectical return is always an Odyssey, as Lenin's *Philosophical Notebooks* clearly show.

The *Notebooks*, when they are not totally disregarded as casual notes "destined not to be published," are usually seen as little more than an anthology of disparate quotations on dialectics where every eclectic can choose and pick what he or she likes as an ornament for his or her discourse. But this completely underestimates their significance. The *Philosophical Notebooks* of 1914–15 should instead be studied as a *single, organic, developing, open totality*, which passes through different moments and transitions. Only in this way can the logic of Lenin's research, the logical unfolding of his readings, the interconnection of different transitions of his thinking, become visible.

The materialist exploration of the "Hegelian lost continent" compelled Lenin to move in convergent and divergent circles in all the historical breadth of philosophy, focusing on some crucial nodal points (*Knottenpunkte*) such as Hegel's works and on the contribution of Leibniz, as well as on ancient philosophy, particularly Heraclitus and Aristotle. Without an examination of these circles and nodal points, the entire Leninist effort to reverse Hegel materialistically is obscured. For this reason it is absolutely necessary to proceed to a mapping of the entire philosophical circumnavigation of Lenin's *Notebooks*.

8.

In September 1914, Lenin commenced his study of Hegel's *The Science of Logic*. Hegel was not unknown to him (despite the widespread legend). He was his companion from his first steps as a revolutionary Marxist. Nadezhda Krupskaya writes in her memoirs that the young Lenin, exiled in Sushenskaye, was already studying Hegel, particularly the *Phenomenology of Mind*.[9]

In 1914, his attention was attracted and focused on Hegel's great work of *Logic*. It is not accidental. As he notes in his *Notebooks*, quoting and commenting on Hegel, "a natural-historical description of the phenomena of thought" is not sufficient. There must also be "correspondence with truth." And Lenin adds: "*Not* psychology, *not* the phenomenology of the mind *but* logic = the question of truth" (175). In the margins he then goes on to write: "In this conception, logic coincides with the *theory of knowledge*. This is in general a very important question"; it represents "the general laws of *movement of the world* and *of thought*." By transcending the rigid metaphysical separation of ontology, logic, and theory of knowledge that Hegel was the first to investigate, but on an idealist basis, Lenin tries to let it stand on materialist ground. Dialectics as the logic and theory of knowledge of Marxism becomes the new theoretical horizon after the end of metaphysics. Logic ceases to be a system of formal rules and of forms of thought. For Hegel and Lenin, "Logic is the science not of external forms of thought but of the laws of development 'of all material, natural and spiritual things' i.e., of the development of the entire concrete content of the world and of its cognition, i.e., the sum-total, the conclusion of the *History* of knowledge of the world" (92–93, emphasis in the original).

In his *The Science of Logic* Hegel himself excavates the subterranean tunnels for the exit from the idealist prison, although of course he himself does not follow them. He reaches, without transcending it, the extreme limit, beyond which absolute idealism is self-negated and transformed into its opposite, *materialist* dialectics.

In the last chapter of *The Science of Logic* (and in the last paragraphs, 575–577, of the *Encyclopedia*) logic itself disappears in what it grounds: the logical (*das Logische*) as the universal interconnection of nature and mind.

Lenin finds that the last page of the great *Logic* comes extremely close to (dialectical) materialism. He concludes: "The sum total, the last word and essence of Hegel's logic is the *dialectical method*—this is extremely noteworthy. And one thing more: in this *most idealistic* of Hegel's works, there is the *least* idealism and the *most materialism*. 'Contradictory,' but a fact!" (233, emphasis in the original).

For the "Marxists" who came after Marx, this fundamental book remained sealed. But Lenin was adamant: "It is impossible completely to understand Marx's *Capital*, and especially its first chapter, without having thoroughly studied and understood the *whole* of Hegel's *Logic*." And he adds with bitterness and regret: "Consequently, half a century later none of the Marxists understood Marx!!" (180, emphasis in the original). The same happens, with some exceptions and many adventures, 135 years later. In this sense, how can we speak about an "end of Marxism"? What "Marxism" has ended?

9.

The systematic critical reading of *The Science of Logic* (supplemented by readings of relevant sections of the *Encyclopedia*) was completed by Lenin in three months, in December 1914. It is noteworthy that between September and November 1914, that is, when Lenin was probably in the middle of his study of the crucial second book, *Essence of Science of Logic*, the reading and notes on the book by Feuerbach on Leibniz are also interposed. This particular attention paid by Lenin to Leibniz has been more or less completely disregarded.[10] From a point on the periphery of the primary circle of study of Hegel's works a supplementary circle is opened, moving in the opposite direction, the pre-Hegelian dialectics, and then converging to meet again the primary circle of Hegelian studies. This renewed interest for Leibniz was not an accidental digression produced by the chance reading of Feuerbach's book. The main points on which Lenin's study is focused are important for the elaboration of a dialectical conception of the *historical development* of nature and of society counterposed to the mechanical materialist conception of the Second International.

Noting how Marx himself valued Leibniz, Lenin stresses the fact that with the thinker of *Monadology* the Cartesian view of matter as a dead mass moved from outside is overcome. For Leibniz corporeal substance "has within it an active force, a never resting principle of activity" (378). "Ergo," Lenin writes, "Leibniz through theology arrived at the principle of the inseparable (and universal, absolute) connection of matter and motion" (377).

Without any concession to idealism and clericalism, to the "Lassallean features" in Leibniz of an accommodation to state power, Lenin has the insight that contained in this philosophy there is the possibility of a deeper, qualitative, dynamic conception of matter, one that is opposed to mechanical materialism and closer to the discoveries of contemporary non-Newtonian physics (380). The qualitative dynamism of matter in motion that Marx finds in Bacon and, particularly, in Jacob Boehme,[11] is precisely what Lenin sees in Leibniz. As the Leninist aphorism says "intelligent idealism is [always] closer to intelligent materialism than stupid [vulgar] materialism" (274).

10.

It is at this point that another "detour" in Lenin's philosophical readings should be noted. In the turning point, when he completes the reading of the great *Logic* at the end of 1914 and begins to study Hegel's
History of Philosophy and then his *Philosophy of History*, in other words
when he was well advanced and was navigating in the middle of the
Hegelian ocean, Lenin reads and keeps notes on various books related
to the revolution in natural and biological sciences. These "natural scientific" readings, in the middle of his Hegelian studies,[12] demonstrate
that Lenin never left the line of research that he followed in 1908 in
Materialism and Empirio-Criticism relating to the revolution in natural
sciences, the collapse of the classical natural scientific picture of the
world, and its philosophical implications for the confrontation between
materialism and idealism.

The 1914–15 *Philosophical Notebooks* undoubtedly represent a qualitative leap in the philosophical thought of Lenin. There is, nevertheless,
within the overall discontinuity, a degree of continuity with his previous
philosophical battles, particularly with that against Machism in 1908.
The commonly repeated notion of some kind of separation between a
dialectical Lenin in 1914 and a "mechanical materialist" Lenin in 1908
(put forward, for example, by Raya Dunayevskaya, the Yugoslav Praxis
School, or Michael Löwy) is misplaced. The fact that Stalinism reduced
Materialism and Empirio-Criticism to a vulgar platitude in its own Vulgate does not justify its condemnation into oblivion. It was the great
anti-Stalinist Soviet philosopher, E. V. Ilyenkov, who first proposed a
path-breaking, nonconformist interpretation here with his (censored!)
posthumous book, *Leninist Dialectics and the Metaphysics of Positivism* (originally published in Russian in 1980, and followed two years
later by an English translation). Such a thought-provoking analysis and
interpretation deserves to restore the objective value of Lenin's early
work.

11.

During the first months of 1915, Lenin turns away from *The Science
of Logic* in another direction, apparently remote from it but actually
deeper into it: toward ancient Greek dialectics. The materialist reversal

of speculative dialectics, the return to its point of departure, involves a return to its native land, the ancient Greek *polis*.

Lenin, initially in 1915, during his studies of Hegel's *History of Philosophy* concentrates almost exclusively on the section related to ancient Greek philosophy. He quite quickly leaves behind the Hegelian *Philosophy of History* because, as he himself writes, "it is here in this field, in this science that Marx and Engels made the greatest leap forward" (312). He then reads Heraclitus, courtesy of the book by Lassalle on the Ionian pioneer of dialectics. Finally, perceiving the tension between the Heraclitean ideas and Aristotle's thought, Lenin carefully studies the latter's magnum opus Μετά τα Φυσικά (Metaphysics). It is here that the big arc, originally opened with the study of *The Science of Logic*, is finally closed. It is only after the completion of his reading of Aristotelian metaphysics that Lenin writes the summing up of the results of his philosophical wanderings, the brief but extremely dense essay, "On the Question of Dialectics."

What Lenin rediscovers thanks to the ancient Greeks is the freshness of dialectics that was lost, the original robustness of its concepts, "the naïveté, profundity, the flowing transitions" (342) of its movements. He does not look at antiquity for answers to problems of modernity. On the contrary, what we have to learn from the Greeks, Lenin writes, is "precisely modes of framing questions, as it were *tentative* systems, a naïve discordance of views, excellently reflected in Aristotle" (367, emphasis in the original). In our times of distress, when everything provokes perplexity but not the stimulus of surprise, the dialecticians of antiquity teach us the "naïve" (that is, the nonpretentious) questioning about everything, the art of being surprised when faced with the natural historical universe.

Lenin attacks scholasticism and clericalism precisely because it "took what was dead in Aristotle, but not what was *living*; the *inquiries*, the searchings, the labyrinth, in which man lost his way" (366, emphasis in the original). He then goes on to explain where and how Aristotle was lost in the labyrinth: "In Aristotle, objective logic is *everywhere confused* with subjective logic and, moreover, in such a way that everywhere objective logic is visible. There is no doubt as to the objectivity of cognition" (366, emphasis in the original). Later, commenting on sections 1040b–1041a in the *Metaphysics*, he adds: "Delightful! There are no doubts of the reality of the external world. The man gets into a muddle precisely over the dialectics of the universal and the particular, of concept and sensation, etc., of essence and phenomenon, etc." (367). Aristotle's logic is not, for Lenin, a fossilized *Organon* but "an inquiry, a searching, an approach to the logic of Hegel" that "*everywhere*, at every step, raises *precisely* the question *of dialectics*" (366, emphasis in the original).

The Russian revolutionary develops a kind of counterpoint of ancient and Hegelian dialectics. The ultimate aim of his return to ancient philosophy is precisely to assist the materialist reversal of Hegel and provide fresh impetus to Marxism's self-constitution.

The same approach is adopted in Lenin's reading of Lassalle's book on Heraclitus. He finds there not just a source of invaluable material from the father of ancient dialectics that was then difficult to reach, but also the example par excellence of how to *avoid* rereading Hegel, the constant rehash of the German idealist's works, without any attempt to go beyond their limits. The political result in Lassalle's case was the idealization of the State, the submission to its power, the infamous Lassallean version of "state socialism" or rather anti-socialism.

The huge difference of attitude on the interrelated questions of Hegelian dialectics and the state between Marx and Lassalle is extremely important for Lenin as he sees it to be reproduced in his confrontation with Plekhanov and the Second International. On the one side, there is the materialist transcendence of speculative dialectics and socialism by means of the withering away of the state; and on the other, opposite side, there is the disregarding of dialectics as the logic and theory of knowledge, and the submission to the state in the name of socialism.

12.

Lenin excavates the idealist embankment built up by Lassalle and discovers underneath the buried precious metal of Heraclitean *Logos*, and in the famous fragment 30 by Heraclitus he sees "a very good exposition of the principles of dialectical materialism" (347): Κόσμον τόνδε, τον αυτόν απάντων, ούτε τις θεών ούτε ανθρώπων εποίησεν, αλλ' ην αεί και έστιν και έσται πυρ αείζωον, απτόμενον μέτρα και αποσβεννύμενον μέτρα (The world, an entity out of everything, was created by none of the gods or men, but was, is, and will be eternally living fire, regularly becoming ignited and regularly becoming extinguished.)

Lenin's tremendous enthusiasm for fragment 30 (he quotes it twice) (344 and 347) can be clearly understood if we keep in mind that it expresses and deepens a fundamental idea noted previously in his reading of Hegel's *History of Philosophy*: the need to combine the "universal principle of the *unity of the world*, nature, motion, matter etc." with "the universal principle of development" (254). This is not "the principle of development" as it was understood and generally accepted in the nineteenth and twentieth centuries in a "superficial, not thought out, accidental, philistine 'agreement' . . . an agreement of *such a kind* as stifles and vulgarizes the truth." Nor is it one that sees development as "a simple, universal and eternal *growth, enlargement.*" Instead, it is a principle of development that focuses on "the arising and passing away of everything, as mutual transitions" (253–54, emphasis in the original), as eternally living fire, πυρ αείζωον.

Here can be found the essence of the rupture with the evolutionism of the past and current centuries, of the break with the reformist fetishism of an eternal gradual progress.

13.

Far from being randomly taken notes, the *Philosophical Notebooks* as a whole combine the method of research and the method of exposition according to the distinction made by Marx.[13] The research methodically assimilates and conquers the immense philosophical material, analyzes the different forms of its development, and discovers their inner connection. From time to time, Lenin presents an exposition or synthesis of the results of research. Three such major expositions or syntheses merit our attention:

a) the *Elements of Dialectics* (220–22) near the end of the *Conspectus of Hegel's Science of Logic*;
b) the *Plan of Hegel's Dialectics (Logic)* (315–18); and, above all,
c) the essay "On the Question of Dialectics" (357–61).

The method of exposition is determined by the necessity of the point of departure. This is respectively:

a) the "objectivity of consideration" in the *Elements of Dialectics*;

b) the "abstract *Sein* [Being]" in the *Plan of Hegel's Dialectics*; and

c) the "splitting of a single whole" in the essay "On the Question of Dialectics."

It is in the last text that the findings of the research are then fully synthesized and the radical theoretical rupture from the "orthodox Marxism" of the Second International is consummated.

Lenin's approach to dialectics does not have any closed totality as a point of departure but the "splitting of a single whole" and the discovery of its contradictory tendencies and aspects. Only through this penetration in the interior of the object is the latter revealed as an open totality. Development is not simply "increase or decrease" that is produced by an external source of motion. It is contradiction, a unity of opposites having within itself, in its inner strife, the driving force of its self-movement.

In short, dialectics is not a sum of didactic examples. It is the discovery of the new. In other words, it "is the theory of knowledge of (Hegel and) Marxism." This is "the *essence* of the matter to which Plekhanov, not to speak of other Marxists, paid no attention" (360, emphasis in the original).

Lenin counterposes dialectics to subjectivism, skepticism, and sophistry, and underlies the crucial dialectical categories: relative/absolute, individual/universal, logical/historical. While he reveals the epistemological roots of the practices of his opponents in the class struggle, he carefully safeguards the specificity of philosophy. For Lenin, unlike Louis Althusser, philosophy is *not* the class struggle in theory. Only under certain conditions, an epistemological weakness, particularly separation of the part from the whole and transformation of the relative into an absolute, does it lead "into the quagmire . . . where it is *anchored* by the class interests of the ruling classes" (361, emphasis in the original).

14.

Lenin never turned his own important findings into a new kind of absolute truth. In the *Notebooks* he sketches three research programs for the further development of dialectics.

First, "continuation of the work of Hegel and Marx must consist in the *dialectical* elaboration of the history of human thought, science and technique" (147, emphasis in the original). Second, there needs to be a further elaboration of the logic of Marx's *Capital* (317). And third, there are a number of "fields of knowledge from which the theory of knowledge and dialectics should be built," the history of philosophy, the Greeks, the history of the separate sciences, of the mental development, of the child, of the mental development of animals, psychology, neurophysiology, and the study of language (351).

15.

Ninety-two years later, these programs of research, in the main part, remain unrealized. Lenin himself did not abandon them in May 1915. Dialectics imbues all his theoretical and practical work up to the 1917 October Revolution and beyond, until his last dramatic struggle against the emerging bureaucracy in the isolated and devastated first workers' state prior to his death. The delay of the socialist revolution in the West and the betrayals of Social Democracy left the young Soviet state in the grip of a bureaucracy that grew into a monstrous cancer.

The twilight of revolution brought the twilight of the science of revolution — dialectics. Social Democracy had long since rejected dialectics; Stalinism would go on to prostitute it, transforming it into a custodian of bureaucratic rule under the code name "DiaMat," an arbitrary machine of apologetics where even the law of negation of negation was forbidden by Stalin's diktat! Of the old Bolsheviks, very few found the courage to challenge this trend. The most notable exception, of course, was Leon Trotsky, who, from his imposed exile, still firmly insisted on calling for the necessity of a new return to a materialist reading of Hegel.

If we bring matters up to the contemporary era, what is most striking is how the collapse of Stalinism threatens to bury under its ruins all the theoretical legacy of Marxism, above all its dialectical method. There can surely be no greater shameful irony in the current period of explosion of all contradictions, in such a period of violent convulsions and sharp discontinuities marking the post–Cold War world, than the one that witnesses the mainstream on the Left claiming that Social Democracy, together with its conception of gradual, peaceful evolution, is somehow confirmed!

Dialectics, "the study of contradiction in the very essence of objects" (251–52), is the necessary path for the way out of today's vague "crisis consciousness" to historical consciousness and the much needed practical-critical activity to change the world. Perhaps more than anything else dialectics is the study of transition. Without it, there is no theory of an epoch like ours, which is transitional *par excellence*; above all, what is most lacking is a theory of transition in crisis. If we are to escape the blocked historical transition in which we exist now, we can only achieve it by a revolutionary transcendence of the impasse.

The Odyssey must start again, and it must not be the kind of Odyssey that it was for Bernstein and his companions; one without adventure, where a "movement" without zigzags, dangers, catastrophes, and fantastic discoveries of new worlds is "everything" and the aim of socialism, our Ithaca, "is nothing."

"By the rivers of Babylon, there we sat and wept." [14] But we should never forget Jerusalem, Ithaca, or the aim that is the real essence of our wanderings: a worldwide classless society, Communism.

We must continue. We cannot continue as before. But *we will continue.*

Notes

1   Samuel Beckett, *L' Innommable* (Paris: Minuit, 1953), 262.

2   F. Nietzsche, *La Volonté de Puissance* (Paris: Aubier-Montaigne, 1969), 3:111.

3   V. I. Lenin, *Philosophical Notebooks*, in *Collected Works* (Moscow: Progress Publishers, 1972), 38:358. Other references in this chapter to Lenin's *Philosophical Notebooks* are subsequently cited parenthetically in the text by page number.

4   A. Gedö, *Crisis Consciousness in Contemporary Philosophy* (Minneapolis: Marxist Educational Press, 1982).

5   Hegel, *Logic, Part One of the Encyclopaedia of the Philosophical Sciences*, trans. W. Wallace (Oxford: Clarendon Press, 1975), 175 § 121.

6   F. Hölderlin, *Remarques sur Œdipe-Antigone* (Paris: UGE 10/18, 1965), 65.

7   Ibid., 83.

8   H. G. Gadamer, *Hegel's Dialectic* (New Haven, Conn.: Yale University Press, 1976), 100.

9   Krupskaya, *Memoirs of Lenin*, cited in E. V. Ilyenkov, *Leninist Dialectics and the Metaphysics of Positivism* (London: New Park, 1982), 10.

10 Among the few exceptions is Hans Heinz Hölz, *Entretiens avec Georg Lukács* (Paris: Maspero, 1969), 20–21. Lukács himself recognizes the fact that Leibniz was neglected by Marxists.

11 Karl Marx and Friedrich Engels, *The Holy Family*, in *Collected Works* (Moscow: Progress Publishers, 1975), 4:128.

12 See Lenin, *Philosophical Notebooks*, notes on J. Perrin, *Treatise on Physical Chemistry*, 38:325, P. Volkmann, *Epistemological Foundations of the Natural Sciences*, 38:328, Max Verworn, *The Hypothesis of Biogenesis*, 38:329, Fr. Dannemann, *How Our Picture of the World Arises?*, 38:331, Ludwig Darmstaedter, *Handbook of the History of the Natural Sciences and Technique*, 38:333, Arthur Erich Haas, *The Spirit of Hellenism in Modern Physics*, 38:335, Theodor Lipps, *Natural Science and World Outlook*, 38:336.

13 Karl Marx, *Capital* (Moscow: Progress Publishers, 1986), 1:28.

14 Psalm 137:1.

7

The Rediscovery and Persistence of the Dialectic in Philosophy and in World Politics

Kevin B. Anderson

Today, evoking Lenin's name in any affirmative sense usually sounds naïve, if not jarring, even on the Left. Again and again since 1980, it has been said that Lenin laid the ground for Stalin's barbaric totalitarian system, that not only his actions, but also his political ideas, were authoritarian, crude, even violent. Again and again, it has been suggested that if one wishes to return to Marx, one needs to do so by creating a *cordon sanitaire* around Lenin and Bolshevism. Again and again, Lenin's name, if it is invoked at all, is mentioned as an example of how one can court disaster by getting caught up in "utopian" thinking.

I would argue that the proponents of such notions are themselves guilty of naïve and self-contradictory thinking, not to speak of arrogance. First, they fail to take account of some of the notable positive achievements of the Russian Revolution in its early years. Second, they fail to note Lenin's major original contributions to political thought. Third, they also forget the many important thinkers, still widely respected and referred to today, who themselves appreciated and were deeply indebted to Lenin. To remember these and similar points is in no way to avoid the needed critique of many aspects of Lenin's life and work. Remembering these kinds of issues is rather the precondition for any serious (rather than caricaturing) critique of Lenin and his legacy.

Since this chapter will stress Lenin's theoretical achievements, I would like to state at the outset that I also see some serious weaknesses in Lenin's thought. First, his espousal of the leading role of the vanguard party, a concept that cannot be found in Marx, has burdened us for too long with a poor model of revolutionary organization.[1] Second, many of Lenin's actions after 1917, especially the establishment of the one-party state and the undermining of the workers' soviets, were no model of revolutionary democracy.[2] Third, although I will argue below that Lenin made a significant contribution to dialectical thinking, his work on this issue was uneven, as seen in his crude and mechanistic *Materialism and Empirio-Criticism* (1908).[3] These things said, one could still appreciate the many attractive features of this great revolutionary leader without in any way self-identifying as a Leninist, which in the dominant discourse usually means an adherence to his elitist concept of the vanguard party.

I would like to begin by citing a statement on Lenin by a well-known thinker whose whole image is that of a humanistic, even liberal leftist, whose life and thought, it would be assumed by many, were far removed from Lenin and Bolshevism. I refer to Erich Fromm, the noted Frank-furt school psychologist. It may surprise the reader to learn that, in the late 1950s, Fromm wrote of Lenin as someone who was imbued with "an uncompromising sense of truth, penetrating to the very essence of reality, and never taken in by the deceptive surface; of an unquenchable courage and integrity; of deep concern and devotion to man and his future; unselfish and with little vanity or lust for power." Fromm also contrasted Lenin to "the vengeful killer Stalin" and the "opportunistic conservative Stalin." Additionally, Fromm deplored "the general habit of considering Stalinism . . . as identical with, or at least as a continua-tion of revolutionary Marxism."[4]

This statement from the noted author whose books include *Socialist Humanism, Escape from Freedom, The Art of Loving,* and many other works in humanistic psychology, a man who supported both the peace movements and the Eastern European dissident movements of the 1960s, should give us pause. Fromm was certainly aware of the destructiveness of the Russian Civil War of 1918–21 and the authoritarian measures that Lenin took during those years, but, unlike most of today's com-mentators on Lenin and Russia, he also saw the grandeur of the vision of 1917. To Fromm and much of his generation, this was a revolution that had helped to end the carnage of World War I, that had brought to power a pro-working-class government, that had freed Jews and other minorities from tsarism, Europe's most intolerant political system, and that had also inspired great revolutionaries such as Rosa Luxemburg to attempt the radical transformation of Germany, an attempt that failed when she was brutally murdered by precursors of Nazism in 1919.

Lenin, Hegel, and "Western Marxism": The Subterranean Relationship

None of Fromm's Frankfurt school colleagues, even those usually considered further to the left such as Herbert Marcuse, ever voiced openly such sentiments about Lenin. Instead, the Frankfurt school philosophers, when they mentioned Lenin at all, tended to disparage him as crude and vulgar (Theodor Adorno) or to view him a little less disparagingly but nonetheless as a precursor of Stalin, who was in fundamental continuity with him (Marcuse). Marcuse and Adorno never discussed Lenin's 1914–15 Hegel notebooks.[5] This is extremely surprising, given the fact that both of them wrote extensively on the relationship of Marxism to Hegel throughout their careers. Nonetheless, this silence on their part cannot alter the fact that they as well as the so-called Western Marxists of the 1920s—Georg Lukács, Antonio Gramsci, and Karl Korsch—were in important ways indebted to Lenin and the Russian Revolution, not least for the new impulse 1917 gave to the rediscovery of the dialectical core of Marxism.

Standard accounts of the history of Western Marxism and critical theory leave out or minimize two important facts. First, at a general level, there is the fact that Lenin wrote his most serious work on Hegel, the notebooks of 1914–15, nearly a decade before Lukács published *History and Class Consciousness* in 1923. And while Lenin's Hegel notebooks were not published until 1932 in German, some of his other post-1914 writings on Hegel and dialectics had begun to appear in German by the early 1920s. Thus, Lenin helped pave the way for Lukács.

West German critical Marxists of the 1960s almost never mentioned this fact, even though the same people tended to extol Lukács and Korsch. The dismissal of Lenin was true not only of Jürgen Habermas and of his students, but also of those then considered further to the left, such as Oskar Negt.[6] A rare exception was Iring Fetscher's long essay on Marxism and Hegel that was published in 1960, in which Lenin's writings on dialectics were considered quite seriously.[7] However, this aspect of Fetscher's writings had little impact. Its appearance did not mitigate the virulent rejection of Lenin by Rudi Dutschke and other leaders of the West German New Left.[8] Even the Berlin-based journal *Das Argument*, which was known for its more "orthodox" Marxism, tended to discuss Rosa Luxemburg but not Lenin.

Second, in addition to Fromm's essay, there is considerable specific evidence of Lenin's influence on Western or critical Marxism. For example, even though he violently repudiated Lenin later on, Korsch's *Marxism and Philosophy*, first published in 1923, the same year as *History and Class Consciousness*, carried as its epigraph the following statement by Lenin written in 1922: "We must organize a systematic study of the Hegelian dialectic from a materialist standpoint."[9] Yet even so acute a philosopher as Maurice Merleau-Ponty viewed Korsch's book as a founding text of Western Marxism, which he contrasted to "Leninist orthodoxy."[10]

In contrast, the Marxist philosopher Ernst Bloch, a contemporary of Lukács, Korsch, Marcuse, and Adorno, tied the revival of Hegel in the twentieth century directly to Lenin. He noted that there was nothing inherent in the German tradition that would necessarily have revived Hegel, because, he wrote, "Hegel was never so pushed aside as in Germany after 1850."[11] During the closing years of the nineteenth century and the first years of the twentieth, Hegel was still being discussed somewhat in Italy, France, and the English-speaking world. However, Bloch suggested, the real revival came only after 1917:

> The shock before the walls of the Kremlin did more than catch up to the shock of the Hegelian left; the dialectic had become, instead of a forgotten folly, a living scandal. . . . Nonetheless, it was no longer Hegel who was forgotten, but rather the chic ignorance of enlightened positivism. . . . Lenin renewed authentic Marxism not least by a return to the "core" of the Hegelian dialectic ("contradiction as the source of all movement and life") and through Hegelian logic itself: "It is impossible fully to grasp Marx's *Capital*, and especially its first chapter, if you have not studied through and understood the whole of Hegel's *Logic*. Consequently, none of the Marxists for the past half-century has understood Marx!!" (LCW 38:180).[12] In this way, it was precisely orthodox Marxism, as restored by Lenin, that presupposed knowledge of Hegel, as against a vulgar, schematic, and traditionless Marxism, which, like a shot out of a pistol, isolated Marx from Hegel, thus isolating itself from Marx.[13]

Surely, it was in a similar vein that Lukács wrote in "What Is Orthodox Marxism?," the opening chapter of *History and Class Consciousness*: "Orthodox Marxism, therefore, does not imply the uncritical acceptance of the results of Marx's investigations. It is not the 'belief' in
this or that thesis, nor the exegesis of a 'sacred' book. On the contrary,
orthodoxy refers exclusively to method. It is the scientific conviction
that dialectical materialism is the road to truth and that its methods can
be developed, expanded and deepened only along the lines laid down by
its founders."[14]

These connections between Lenin and the Hegelian Marxism of the
1920s have usually been passed over by scholars of critical theory.

In this chapter, I want to concentrate on three points. First, Lenin's
intellectual crisis in 1914, under the impact of World War I and the
betrayal of socialism, led to a profound rethinking of his earlier categories. I will argue that his recovery of Hegel in his notebooks of 1914–
15 and after made an important contribution to the dialectical perspective in Marxism. Second, Lenin's use of the new dialectical concepts
he had developed out of his reading of Hegel led him to formulate
some strikingly perceptive and radical perspectives on world politics.
This was especially true of his analysis of colonialism and imperialism,
on the one hand, and of the anti-imperialist national liberation movements—from India to Ireland and from China to the Middle East—on
the other. Third, I examine how Lenin's new perspectives on Hegel
and the dialectic affected later Marxist thinkers. While these points are
often omitted in studies of Lenin's life and thought,[15] I believe that they
are significant for an understanding of Lenin in his own time. I also believe that they are among those aspects of his thought that are the most
relevant for today.

Lenin, Hegel, and the Dialectic

By the 1890s, many of the dominant thinkers of Central European
Marxism had moved toward forms of neo-Kantianism or even positivism. None of the major figures, including Engels, seemed very interested
in Hegel. Thus, when the sixtieth anniversary of Hegel's death came
around in 1891, it was a Russian, Georgii Plekhanov, who wrote the
article commemorating the founder of modern dialectics in *Die Neue*

Zeit, at the time the world's leading journal of Marxist thought. Unfortunately, Plekhanov, who in this article coined the somewhat dubious term "dialectical materialism," also developed there an evolutionist and crudely materialist version of the dialectic. He saw no fundamental difference between the Marxian dialectic and Darwinian evolutionism, even though Marx had referred in *Capital*, vol. 1, to Darwin's perspective as an example of "the weakness of the abstract materialism of natural science, a materialism which excludes the historical process."[16]

Until 1914, Lenin followed Plekhanov not so much politically—for Plekhanov was often on the right wing of Russian social democracy—as philosophically. This is obvious in Lenin's mechanistic book *Materialism and Empirio-Criticism* (1908). This book had two fundamental limitations from a dialectical perspective. First, it put forth a crude reflection theory in which Marxist materialism was "a copy, an approximate copy, of objective reality" (LCW 14:182). Second, Lenin dismissed all forms of idealism as "nothing but an embellished ghost story" (LCW 14:165).

Let us follow these two strands of Lenin's thought, theory as a photocopy of reality and the utter rejection of idealism, during his intellectual crisis of 1914, when he really began to study Hegel. The transformation of these two points will show Lenin's originality after 1914. As is well known, in the political sphere, Lenin was at this time breaking with the Marxism of the Second International. He was calling for a new international, for turning the imperialist war into a civil war, even for revolutionary defeatism. He and a few others, such as Luxemburg, Liebknecht, and Trotsky, were among the important figures who took a firm stance against a war that was eventually to result in some ten million deaths. Luxemburg, for example, was sent to jail for her principled opposition to the war.

From Switzerland, where he sought refuge in the fall of 1914, Lenin began for the first time to think of himself not only as a leader of Russian Marxism, but also as a crucial figure in the effort to rebuild international Marxism on the ruins of the old, discredited Second International. Thus, Lenin began his philosophical rethinking not in a period of calm when there was little to occupy him in the political sphere, but in a turbulent time that demanded a reorganization of his fundamental principles. He, too, had followed the very leaders of the Second Interna-

tional who had now betrayed socialism and the working classes, help-
ing to send them into the slaughter in the trenches.

Lenin carried out his most intensive study of Hegel in the first months
of the war, from September 1914 through January 1915. Major changes
in his philosophical outlook took place as he began to summarize, outline, and comment upon Hegel's massive *The Science of Logic*. Lenin
studied this work intensively, copying out whole passages in German,
interspersed with his own comments, the latter most often in Russian.

First, there was the move away from crude materialism and toward
a critical appropriation of Hegel's idealist dialectic. As with Engels,
Lenin felt an affinity for the fluidity and flexibility of Hegelian thought:
"Hegel analyzes concepts that usually appear dead and he shows that
there is movement in them" (LCW 38:110). But soon he was moving
toward something else, beyond the Engelsian dichotomy of "two great
camps [*Lager*]" in philosophy, idealism, and materialism:[17] "The idea
of the transformation of the ideal into the real is profound! Very important for history. But also in the personal life of man it is evident that
there is much truth in this. Against vulgar materialism. Nota bene. The
difference of the ideal from the material is also not unconditional, not
boundless"(LCW 38:114).

Here he had introduced for the first time a new category, "vulgar materialism." Further on in his notes he wrote that Plekhanov had never
analyzed *The Science of Logic*, in Lenin's eyes Hegel's most fundamental
work, and he bluntly labeled Plekhanov not a dialectical materialist but
a "vulgar materialist" (LCW 38:179). At a more general level, it should
of course be noted that such remarks on Lenin's part are far closer to
what is usually termed critical Marxism than to what is usually considered to be orthodox Leninism.

In addition, and this would later present problems for Marxist-
Leninist students of Spinoza such as Louis Althusser, Lenin seemed
to agree with Hegel's critique of Spinoza's deterministic system. Spinoza's philosophy, wrote Hegel, lacked a free and conscious subject,
instead making thought, as Lenin put it, into a mere "attribute of substance" (LCW 38:168). Throughout the notes on *The Science of Logic*,
Lenin seemed to be trying to avoid the one-sidedness of crudely materialist perspectives, to wit: "It is absurd . . . to reject the objectivity of
notions [concepts]" (LCW 38:178). Part of this involved how one should

approach the critique of neo-Kantianism. Seeming to criticize his own earlier writings such as *Materialism and Empirio-Criticism*, as well as those of others such as Plekhanov, Lenin wrote, "At the beginning of the twentieth century, Marxists criticized the Kantians and Humists more in a Feuerbachian (and Büchnerian) than a Hegelian manner" (LCW 38:179). Something rather remarkable had occurred here. For the first time since the young Marx, a major figure in the Marxian tradition had suggested that a problem be approached in "a Hegelian manner," without the need to refer immediately to qualifiers about materialism. In fact, Lenin was tacking in the opposite direction, away from vulgar materialism, which, in his view, had developed a materialist but un-Hegelian, and therefore undialectical, critique of neo-Kantian idealism.

This led directly to Lenin's well-known aphorism, already cited earlier in this chapter: "Aphorism: It is impossible fully to grasp Marx's *Capital*, and especially its first chapter, if you have not studied through and understood the whole of Hegel's *Logic*. Consequently, none of the Marxists for the past half-century has understood Marx!!" (LCW 38:180).

Elsewhere, Lenin referred to Hegel's dialectic as "the inner pulsation of self-movement and vitality." Gradually, he came to reject his earlier rejection of idealism. The key now was to appropriate critically Hegel's dialectical idealism and to connect it to Marxist materialism. As against Engels's notion of two camps, idealism and materialism, Lenin was coming close to a position suggesting some type of dialectical unity between idealism and materialism. Unknown to Lenin, something similar had been espoused in 1844 by the young Marx, who wrote of "a consistent naturalism or humanism" that was "distinguished from both idealism and materialism, and at the same time constitutes their unifying truth."[18]

Second, I would like to look at Lenin's increasing rejection of crude reflection theory, another point of rupture with his perspectives of 1908. The most explicit evidence for this move is a statement near the end of Lenin's Hegel notebooks: "Man's cognition not only reflects the objective world, but creates it" (LCW 38:212). This is an example of an active, critical, revolutionary appropriation of Hegel's idealism. Here the cognition embodied in revolutionary theory is not only the reflection of material conditions. It is also a reaching beyond those conditions, toward the creation of a new world, one free of the dehumanized social relations of capitalism. Nor does the side materialism or reflection get priority "in the last analysis" here. If anything, the flow of the sentence leads in the opposite direction, moving us from the limitations of a reflection theory to the notion that ideas, concepts can "create" the objective world.

Leszek Kolakowski, despite his strongly critical view of Lenin, conceded that these notes on Hegel go beyond the orthodox Engelsian position that reduced the dialectic to a focus on fluid versus static forms. In his *Main Currents of Marxism*, Kolakowski writes that the Hegel notebooks "suggest an interpretation of Hegelianism that is less simplified than Engels's. The dialectic is not merely an assertion that 'everything changes,' but an attempt to interpret human knowledge as a perpetual interplay between subject and object, in which the 'absolute primacy' of either loses its sharpness."[19]

National Liberation Movements: A New Dialectical Opposition in the Era of Imperialism

As is well known, Lenin's "Imperialism, the Highest Stage of Capitalism" (1916) was one of his major theoretical works. Few, however, have examined its relationship to his writings on national liberation and anti-imperialist movements. Fewer still have explored the relationship of that book to his Hegel notebooks completed the previous year. That is what I will explore below.

Today there is a tendency on the Left to dismiss all forms of nationalism as reactionary. This is curious, since a generation ago, the tendency was often in the opposition direction, toward an uncritical support of all forms of Third World national liberation movements, from South Africa to Palestine and from Vietnam to Cuba. Lenin's writings, especially those after 1915, put forth a position that is far from uncritical of national movements. At the same time, however, he was the first major political theorist, Marxist or non-Marxist, to grasp the importance that anti-imperialist national movements would have for global politics in the twentieth century.

As mentioned earlier, up to 1914, Lenin had considered himself a

Russian Marxist leader rather than one of the leaders of international Marxism. In this sense, his trajectory is very different from that of Luxemburg, who had become a prominent fixture at international socialist gatherings during the years before World War I. Lenin's wartime activities and writings constituted his stepping out onto the world stage of revolutionary politics in at least four major ways. First, as we have seen, his Hegel notebooks were part of an evident attempt on his part to reconstitute Marxist theory after the betrayal of 1914. Second, his book *Imperialism* (1916) never mentioned Russia but concentrated instead on the leading capitalist nations, Britain, France, Germany, and the United States. It was only after the crisis of 1914 that Lenin decided to enter this debate, which had engaged world Marxism since around 1910, with important contributions by Luxemburg, Karl Kautsky, and Rudolf Hilferding, among others. Nor did his related writings after 1915 on anti-imperialist national liberation movements concentrate narrowly on nationalities within the Russian Empire; instead, they focus as much or more on Ireland, China, India, and the Middle East. Third, his *The State and Revolution* (1917) hardly mentioned Russian developments at all. It was a theoretical treatise that attacked the main line of German Social Democratic theory and practice since the death of Engels in 1895, a clear bid on his part to lay down a theoretical marker for world, not Russian Marxism. Fourth, his attempts to found a new International from 1914 onward, finally achieved in 1919, illustrate this shift at a more practical level. It is true that his young Bolshevik colleague, Nikolai Bukharin, also wrote treatises on imperialism and the state shortly before Lenin did so. In yet another of the innumerable attempts to underplay the originality of Lenin's thought and to portray him as mainly an organization man, key differences between Lenin and Bukharin have also been obscured, especially in the studies of Lenin by Tony Cliff and Neil Harding, who have argued at length that in both *Imperialism* and *The State and Revolution* Lenin was mainly following out points previously developed by Bukharin.[20]

When Lenin began to develop the notion that anti-imperialist liberation movements would be a major force of opposition to capitalism in its imperialist stage, his position met with strong opposition. Bukharin's argument that the centralization of world capital produced by the war would make nationalism obsolete had far more support among the revolutionary Left.[21] That is why Lenin continued to be in the minority until after 1917 concerning what were then termed the national and colonial questions, even among those Marxists who had broken with the Second International. This can easily be seen in the polemics against his position, not only by Luxemburg and Bukharin, but also by Karl Radek and others.[22]

In his 1916–17 writings on imperialism and nationalism, written from exile, Lenin referred especially to the Irish uprising of Easter 1916, as well as to China, Iran, Turkey, and India. The Irish case, because it involved the war's only major anti-imperialist national uprising, the Easter Rebellion of 1916, touched off fierce polemics in which Lenin elaborated his own perspectives at some length. Lenin hailed the rebellion, also bringing in the issue of dialectics: "The dialectics of history are such that small nations, powerless as an *independent* factor in the struggle against imperialism, play a part as one of the ferments, one of the bacilli, which help the *real* anti-imperialist force, the socialist proletariat, to make its appearance on the scene" (LCW 22:357).

On the right wing of Russian socialism, Plekhanov had hailed the collapse of the Easter Rebellion, while Radek, a former colleague of Luxemburg's who was now working with Lenin, dismissed it as a "putsch": "This movement, called 'Sinn Fein,' was a purely urban petty-bourgeois movement, and although it caused considerable commotion, it had little social backing."[23] Trotsky took a position midway between Radek's and Lenin's, downplaying the significance of the revolt but seeing some potential for the movement if it were to overcome its nationalism. He was not very prescient when he wrote that, given the development of world capitalism, "the historical basis for a national revolution has disappeared even in backward Ireland." Thus, Trotsky concluded, "the experiment of an Irish national rebellion" exemplified "outworn hopes and methods of the past."[24] This debate has not received the attention it deserves, in part because the texts cited above by Radek and Trotsky were translated into Western languages only belatedly. The several lengthy studies of Lenin published since 1970, mainly by British scholars, either do not mention Lenin and Ireland at all, or give the topic short shrift.[25]

Again and again, Lenin wrote of the hundreds of millions of people oppressed by global imperialism and of their yearning for liberation. He saw a profound difference between the emancipatory national movements inside oppressed nations and the chauvinist nationalism of dominant nations. National liberation was the dialectical opposite of global imperialism, whereas the nationalism of the great powers of Europe, the United States, and Japan promoted and underpinned imperialism.

Those who minimize Lenin's theoretical contribution, or view him as a mere tactician, should consider his prescience on these issues. Over three decades before India won its independence and more than four decades before the African liberation movements came to the fore in the early 1960s, he was already theorizing anti-imperialist national movements as a major factor in global politics.

In a 1916 critique of what he evidently regarded as Bukharin's formalistic rejection of all forms of nationalism, Lenin accused his young Bolshevik colleague of wanting to "paint . . . the future in monotonous gray": "The social revolution can come only in the form of an epoch in which are combined civil war by the proletariat against the bourgeoisie in the advanced countries and a whole series of democratic and revolutionary movements, including the national liberation movements in the underdeveloped, backward, oppressed nations" (LCW 23:70).

In one of his very last writings, the "Notes on Sukhanov" (1923), Lenin attacked those who sought to enclose the particularity of non-European developments within an abstract universal:

> They call themselves Marxists, but their conception of Marxism is impossibly pedantic. They have completely failed to understand what is decisive in Marxism, namely, its revolutionary dialectics. They have even absolutely failed to understand Marx's plain statements that in times of revolution the utmost flexibility is demanded. . . . Up to now they have seen capitalism and bourgeois democracy in Western Europe follow a definite path of development, and cannot conceive that this path can be taken as a model only mutatis mutandis, only with certain amendments. . . . For instance, it does not even occur to them that because Russia stands on the borderline between the civilized countries and the countries which this war has for the first time definitely brought into the orbit of civilization—all the oriental, non-European countries—she could and was, indeed, bound to reveal certain distinguishing features. . . . (LCW 33:476–77, emphasis added)

As Lenin underlined above, all of this was tied to the lack of a dialectical standpoint.

In this sense, his Hegel studies and his writings on national liberation were of a piece. A year earlier, in 1922, Lenin had called for the study of Hegelian dialectics in Soviet Russia, linking this study to the awakening of oppressed and colonized nations:

> The contributors to *Under the Banner of Marxism* must arrange for the systematic study of Hegelian dialectics from a materialist standpoint, i.e., the dialectics which Marx applied practically in his *Capital* and in his historical and political works, and applied so successfully that now every day of the awakening to life and struggle of the new classes in the East (Japan, India, and China)—i.e. the hundreds of millions of human beings who form the greater part of the world population and whose historical passivity and historical torpor have hitherto conditioned the stagnation and decay of many advanced European countries—every day of the awakening to life of new peoples and new classes serves as a fresh confirmation of Marxism. (LCW 33:234)

As seen above, it was only the first part of this statement—but significantly, not the part on anti-imperialist movements in Asia—that the Western Marxist Korsch included as the epigraph to his *Marxism and Philosophy*. In this way, Korsch walled off the discussion of Hegel and dialectics, making that a "Western" issue. He left aside what he evidently disagreed with even in 1923, Lenin's embrace of the new "Eastern" liberation movements. This type of separation would impoverish many post-Lenin discussions of dialectics in the West.

The International Impact of Lenin's Writings on National Liberation: New Voices from India, Iran, and Black America

The new spirit introduced by Lenin into Marxism can easily be seen in the debates at the 1920 Second Congress of the Communist International. Lenin's "Draft Theses on the National and Colonial Questions" referred not only to geographically separate nations such as Ireland and the Ukraine, but also to national minorities such as "the Negroes in America" (LCW 31:144). Grigorii Zinoviev was one of the few Bolsheviks who during World War I shared many of Lenin's positions on national liberation. However, just after the Second Congress opened, Zinoviev allowed himself, while speaking before an audience drawn in large part from predominantly Muslim societies during the Baku Congress of the Peoples of the East, to call for a "holy war, in the first place against British imperialism."[26] Lenin's 1920 theses called instead for "the struggle against Pan-Islamism" (LCW 31:144). However, he emphasized the notion "that all Communist Parties should render direct aid to the revolutionary movements among the dependent and under-privileged nations (for example Ireland, the American Negroes, etc.) and in the colonies" (LCW 31:148).

The Second Congress held an especially serious and wide-ranging debate on imperialism and national liberation. In addition to Lenin's theses, supplementary ones were presented by the well-known Indian Marxist M. N. Roy, who agreed with Lenin in arguing that "the break-up of the colonial empire, together with proletarian revolution in the home country, will overthrow the capitalist system in Europe."[27] Other parts of Roy's speech showed some disagreement with Lenin, however. For example, Roy attacked "the narrow circle of bourgeois-democratic nationalists" (223), acknowledging more tentatively than Lenin that "revolutionary nationalism will play a part" (224).

The important Iranian Marxist thinker Avetis Sultanzadeh,[28] whose position was somewhat closer to Lenin's, advocated the intertwining of anti-imperialist movements with the labor movement inside the developed capitalist lands:

> The Second International studied the colonial question at most of its congresses. It drew up elegant resolutions, which, however, were never put into effect. Often these questions were debated and positions adopted without the participation of representatives of the backward countries. What is more, when the Russian and British hangmen suppressed the First Persian Revolution[29] and the Persian social democrats turned for help to the European proletariat, then represented by the Second International, they were not even granted the right to put a resolution on this matter to a vote. (238)

With a sense of political realism all too rare at such congresses, Sultanzadeh also noted: "It is true that the capitalist drive in the colonies awakens the revolutionary spirit. But it is just as true that the capitalist exploitation of the colonies creates a counter-revolutionary spirit among the labor aristocracy in the metropolitan countries" (238). However, the 1917 Revolution had created a different situation, he concluded: "The thunder of revolution in the West shook the Orient to the roots, giving strength to revolutionaries in Persia and Turkey" (239).

The U.S. journalist John Reed reported on white racist violence and black resistance during the race riots of 1919: "The first of these outbreaks happened in the national capital, Washington, where petty government officeholders came back from the war to find their places taken by Negroes. Most of these officeholders were southerners anyway. They organized nighttime attacks on the Negro part of town in order to terrorize the Negroes into giving up their jobs. Much to everyone's astonishment, the Negroes poured into the streets fully armed, and a battle raged . . ." (226–27).

After describing similar events in Chicago and elsewhere, Reed concluded: "In all of these fights, Negroes showed for the first time in history that they were armed, well organized, and absolutely unafraid of the whites. The effect of the Negro resistance was, first, belated government intervention and, second, the opening of the American Federation of Labor unions to Negro workers" (227).

Not since Marx's day had an American Marxist thundered like this on racial issues.

By the Fourth Congress of the Communist International in 1924, where the noted black writer Claude McKay participated as a U.S. delegate, there was for the first time an entire session devoted to "the Negro question." Where Reed had critiqued the attitudes of white workers, McKay's attack on racism hit closer to home, targeting the racial attitudes of U.S. Socialists and Communists themselves:

> The reformist bourgeoisie have been carrying on the battle against discrimination and racial prejudice in America. The Socialists and Communists have fought very shy of it because there is a great element of prejudice among the Socialists and Communists of America. They are not willing to face the Negro question. In associating with the comrades of America, I have found demonstrations of prejudice on the various occasions when the white and black comrades had to get together; and this is the greatest obstacle that the Communists of America have got to overcome—the fact that they first have got to emancipate themselves

from the ideas they entertained toward Negroes before they can be able to reach the Negroes with any kind of radical propaganda.

McKay also spoke of how publicizing Marx's position on slavery and racism had shaken up African American opinion:

> In 1918, when the Third International published its Manifesto and included that part referring to the exploited colonies there were several groups of Negro radicals in America that sent this propaganda among their people. When in 1920 the American government started to investigate and to suppress radical propaganda among the Negroes, the small radical Negro groups in America retaliated by publishing the fact that the Socialists stood for the emancipation of the Negroes, and that reformist America could do nothing for them. Then, I think, for the first time in American history, the American Negroes found that Karl Marx had been interested in their emancipation, and had fought valiantly for it.[30]

While McKay advocated unity between workers across racial lines, he also called upon predominantly white labor and socialist organizations to take stronger stands in support of the black movement as a whole. This unprecedented session also resulted in a book manuscript by McKay, *The Negroes in America*, commissioned by the Comintern, as well as public dialogue between McKay and Trotsky in the Russian press.[31]

While Trotsky never made a very significant contribution to dialectics, by the late 1930s he came much closer to Lenin's position on national liberation. One example of this is his remarkable 1939 conversation with the Caribbean Marxist thinker C. L. R. James, then a Trotskyist. During their discussion of the setting up of a non-Stalinist organization of black radicals, a white Trotskyist stated, "I cannot see how the Negro bourgeoisie can help the Negro proletariat fight for its economic development." James replied, "In our movement some of us are petty bourgeois. If a bourgeois Negro is excluded from a university because of his color, this organization will probably mobilize the masses to fight for the rights of the bourgeois Negro student." Trotsky then replied, "I believe that the first question is the attitude of the [Trotskyist] Socialist Workers Party toward the Negroes. It is very disquieting to find that until now the party has done almost nothing in this field. It has not published a book, a pamphlet, leaflets, nor even any articles in the *New International*. . . . Our party is not safe from degeneration. . . ." Trotsky seemed to be very open to new forms of anti-racist organizing. Given the color bar, he added, the Trotskyist party might under certain conditions support a black versus a white member of the Democratic Party: "We consider that the Negro's candidacy as opposed to the white's candidacy, even if both are of the same party, is an important factor in the struggle of the Negroes for their equality; and in this case we can critically support them." [32]

Another instance of Trotsky's new thinking on national liberation was his changing position on Jewish nationalism after Hitler had come to power and after Stalin had resorted to anti-Semitic innuendo during the purge trials of the 1930s. In a 1937 interview with a Jewish newspaper, Trotsky recounted his changed position:

> During my youth I rather leaned toward the prognosis that the Jews of different countries would be assimilated and that the Jewish question would thus disappear in a quasi-automatic fashion. The historical development of the last quarter of a century has not confirmed this perspective. Decaying capitalism has everywhere swung over to an exacerbated nationalism, one part of which is anti-Semitism. The Jewish question has loomed largest in the most highly developed capitalist country of Europe, in Germany. On the other hand the Jews of different countries have created their press and developed the Yiddish language as an instrument of modern culture. One must therefore reckon with the fact that the Jewish nation will maintain itself for an entire epoch to come. [33]

Today the issues of race, ethnicity, and imperialism take a different form, but despite the near demise of direct colonial rule, the patterns of exploitation and oppression between the wealthy capitalist nations and the peoples of Africa, Asia, the Middle East, and Latin America still exist. Along with these patterns came liberation movements by those oppressed by imperialism, as well as movements by those inside the imperialist countries who were in solidarity with them, one of the most notable examples being the struggle against the apartheid system in South Africa. A generation earlier, *national* resistance movements to fascism had developed, from China to Yugoslavia and from France to Poland. Many of these movements have inspired theoretical studies that have drawn from Lenin's writings. In different ways, for example, C. L. R. James and Raya Dunayevskaya used Lenin's concepts to analyze the African liberation movements of the 1950s and 1960s, even though Lenin had not written directly on Africa very much.[34]

One of the differences today is that, alongside the continued domination they face from globalized capitalism, formerly colonized or occupied nations, once they are independent, can themselves become oppressors of national minorities within and without their borders. Here Lenin's focus on whether a specific form of nationalism tended toward reactionary or emancipatory politics becomes actual. His notion of reactionary nationalism was not limited to that of great powers such as Britain or the United States. As seen above, he also had condemned pan-Islamism even though it strongly opposed British imperialism in the Middle East. In addition, he attacked pan-Slavism throughout his life, which he linked to Russian imperialism and the repression of ethnic minorities. Using his writings as part of their foundation, over the past decade several writers have mapped out a strong opposition to genocidal Serbian nationalism in the Balkans, while at the same time critically supporting the more emancipatory national movements of the Kosovars and especially the Bosnians in the former Yugoslavia.[35] Another example of the complexity of this issue is the Zapatista movement in Mexico, which has represented indigenous communities left out of the 1910 Revolution, while also winning mass support across Mexico, as well as significant support from the international movement against globalization.

Lenin's Impact on Later Debates over the Dialectic: From Henri Lefebvre to Raya Dunayevskaya

As against the Frankfurt school philosophers, two strands of twentieth-century Marxism outside Germany did appropriate Lenin's writings on Hegel in a manner that made them central to their overall understanding of dialectics. These were of Henri Lefebvre in France and of C. L. R. James and especially Raya Dunayevskaya in the United States. Each developed new forms of Hegelian Marxism, in part through a discussion of Lenin and Hegel.

Few outside France are aware that Lefebvre, together with Norbert

Guterman, published an independent, scholarly edition of Lenin's Hegel notebooks in French in 1938. (Five years earlier, they had also published a translation of Marx's "Critique of the Hegelian Dialectic" of 1844.) Issued by Éditions Gallimard, still today France's most prestigious publisher, their volume on Lenin, *Cahiers sur la dialectique d'Hegel*, helped to make Lenin's writings on Hegel prominent among the French intellectual public in a unique way. Elsewhere, especially in Germany and the English-speaking world, discussion of Lenin's writings on Hegel tended more often to be limited to a narrower circle of either partisans of Lenin or the usually anti-Lenin academic specialists. Lefebvre and Guterman's substantial 130-page introduction barely mentioned *Materialism and Empirio-Criticism* in an oblique reference to the progress Lenin's thought had made since from 1908 to 1914. Their introduction broke new ground by attacking those who wished to use Hegel's method but not his system.[36] Instead, they argued that the "content of Hegel" needed to be appropriated. In a bow to Communist Party orthodoxy, however, they failed to mention that this had been Engels's position.

Lefebvre's subsequent writings on Lenin and Hegel were even more circumspect. This was true of his *Logique formelle, logique dialectique* (1947), as well as his major study, *La Pensée de Lenine* (1957). In fact, it was only after he had finally been expelled from the French Communist Party that Lefebvre finally stated openly what had been at stake all along. In his 1959 autobiography, *La Somme et le reste*, Lefebvre wrote of Lenin: "He did not read or study Hegel seriously until 1914–15. Also, if one considers it objectively, one notices a great difference in tone and content between the Hegel Notebooks and *Materialism and Empirio-Criticism*. Lenin's thought becomes supple, alive . . . in a word, dialectical. Lenin did not truly understand the dialectic until 1914, after the collapse of the International." Lefebvre adds in a footnote: "Here we see the significance of the profound reticence of the Stalinists toward the Notebooks, who for a long time put them aside in favor of *Materialism and Empirio-Criticism*."[37]

This rather late acknowledgment of the core issues, which Lefebvre published not in any of his major books or essays on Lenin, but as a passing statement in a very long autobiography, left the door open to the anti-dialectical, anti-Hegelian, proto-Maoist[38] interpretations of

Louis Althusser and his school in the 1960s and 1970s, as seen especially in Althusser's *Lenin and Philosophy*. The title essay of that book, first delivered as a public lecture in 1968, concentrated on *Materialism and Empirio-Criticism* and Lenin's economic writings, never mentioning the Hegel notebooks. After Jean Hyppolite publicly called this to his attention, Althusser finally wrote an article specifically on the Hegel notebooks. There and elsewhere in his comments on Lenin and Hegel, Althusser was often evasive, attributing critiques of Hegel to Lenin by splicing together texts that actually stated the opposite. In response to Lenin's well-known statement, cited earlier, that one needed to study Hegel's *Logic* to grasp fully Marx's *Capital*, Althusser subjected Lenin's words to a virtual "deconstruction," at the end of which he informed the reader rather peremptorily: "it is impossible to understand Hegel without having thoroughly studied and understood *Capital*."[39] In attempting to elide Hegel from Lenin's thought, Althusser was carrying out a crucial part of his overall project of erasing Hegel from Marxism. Clearly, any notion of a return to Hegel by Lenin constituted a grave threat to Althusserianism, which had proclaimed that Marx had gotten rid of most of his Hegelianism by 1846. For, if Lenin had really returned to Hegel in 1914, it would be much harder for Marxists to "drive the shade of Hegel . . . back into the night," as Althusser had proposed in 1962.[40]

In the United States, C. L. R. James and Raya Dunayevskaya began to write on Lenin and Hegel during the 1940s. In 1948, James wrote some informal reflections on Lenin and Hegel that he later published.[41] Dunayevskaya had translated the whole of Lenin's Hegel notebooks by 1949 but was unable to find a publisher. This was very likely due to positivist opposition to Hegel, which was quite common at the time in the United States, even among prominent leftist philosophers such as Sidney Hook. Unlike Lefebvre, James and Dunayevskaya were members of the Trotskyist movement. Using Lenin's Hegel notebooks as an important part of their philosophical foundation, they took several positions that moved them some distance from orthodox Trotskyism. First, they developed a theory of state capitalism to describe Stalin's Russia. Second, they critiqued Lenin's concept of the vanguard party as elitist and anti-dialectical. Third, they called for a systematic study of dialectics based on Hegel, Marx, and Lenin, drawing a separation between Lenin's 1908 philosophical stance and that after 1914. Fourth, they posed the notion that African Americans were an independent and potentially revolutionary oppositional force to American capitalism.

In the 1950s and 1960s, after she and James had moved in different directions, Dunayevskaya developed these somewhat unformed concepts as part of what she called Marxist humanism. No Marxist thinker, before or since, has delved as deeply or as creatively into Lenin's Hegel notebooks, appropriating them critically as ground for a contemporary dialectics of revolution. For example, Dunayevskaya pioneered the linking together of Lenin's perspectives on dialectics and on national liberation that I put forth above. She also published the first English translation of major parts of Marx's 1844 Manuscripts and Lenin's Hegel notebooks, each as an appendix to her *Marxism and Freedom* (1958). In her *Philosophy and Revolution* (1973), Dunayevskaya took up Lenin's return to Hegel alongside that of Marx as part of a discussion entitled "Why Hegel? Why Now?": "Lenin certainly didn't mean that all students of *Capital* must first labor through the two volumes of *The Science of Logic*. What was crucial was Lenin's break with old concepts, which is nowhere more sharply expressed than in his commentary that 'Cognition not only reflects the world, but creates it.' . . . Lenin had gained from Hegel a totally new understanding of the *unity* of materialism and idealism. It was this new understanding that subsequently permeated Lenin's post-1915 writings."[42]

At the same time, Dunayevskaya developed several cogent critiques of Lenin's appropriation of Hegel. First, she argued that he had left an ambiguous legacy by not having referred more openly to his new thinking on Hegel and dialectics:

> The emphasis that Lenin put on "dialectic proper, as a philosophic science" separated him from all other post-Marx Marxists, not only up to the Russian Revolution but also after the conquest of power. . . . What was most manifest of what he had gained from the 1914–15 Hegel studies was that the Hegelian dialectic needs to be studied "in and for itself." . . . That Lenin kept his direct encounter with the Hegelian dialectic—his Abstract of Hegel's *The Science of Logic*—to himself, however, shows the depth of the economist mire into which the whole Second International, and not just the German Social-Democracy, had sunk; revolutionaries stood on the same ground![43]

To Dunayevskaya, all of this was compounded by the fact that Lenin had allowed *Materialism and Empirio-Criticism* to be reprinted in Russian in 1920. For the record, it should be noted that he did not have it translated into other languages, as he had done with *Imperialism* and *The State and Revolution*. In 1927, however, the increasingly Stalinist apparatus published *Materialism and Empirio-Criticism* widely in foreign translations, and the international Communist Parties made good use of its crude attacks on idealism to call intellectuals to account, among them Lefebvre.

In her second critique of Lenin on dialectics, Dunayevskaya argued that, at crucial junctures, Lenin had overplayed the practical, activist side of dialectics, here minimizing the theoretical side. This was seen especially in his discussion of the section on the idea of the good, near the end of *The Science of Logic*.

Third, Dunayevskaya argued that at several points Lenin interpreted Hegel in too narrowly materialist a fashion, especially in his discussion of the last pages of *The Science of Logic*, on the Absolute Idea. It was true that Lenin had broken partially with Engels's notion in *Ludwig Feuerbach and the End of Classical German Philosophy* (1886) that Hegel's Absolute Idea embodied a non-dialectical and abstractly idealist notion of the end of history. To Engels, the Absolute Idea was an especially prominent example of Hegel's "system," which had to be rejected in favor of Hegel's dialectical "method." In *Ludwig Feuerbach*, written long after his youthful enthusiasm for Hegel, Engels cited no textual evidence for these conclusions, probably because little could have been found. Lenin, during his careful study of the last chapter of *The Science of Logic*, took a different tack, arguing that the Absolute Idea chapter contained not so much idealism as materialism and could thus be appropriated by Marxism. Nonetheless, Dunayevskaya argued that Lenin, while going deeper than Engels, had made two crucial errors. Lenin gave very little weight to the core Hegelian concept of negativity, instead focusing on contradiction. Here he paid the price for not having been familiar with Marx's crucial discussion of the dialectics of negativity in the 1844 Manuscripts, a text that in 1914–15 lay forgotten in the archives of the Second International. Dunayevskaya also argued that Lenin had interpreted Hegel's Absolute Idea in too narrowly a materialist fashion. To be sure, he seized upon the fact that, in the closing paragraphs of the last chapter in *The Science of Logic*, Hegel had written of a transition from logic to nature. Here, Lenin wrote, Hegel "stretches a hand to materialism" (LCW 38:234). However, as Dunayevskaya pointed out, Lenin ignored what followed immediately after this in Hegel, for Hegel now developed another transition, this one from logic to spirit or mind [*Geist*].

Fourth and finally, Dunayevskaya argued that while it was Lenin's great achievement to have reinterpreted world politics dialectically around the contradiction between imperialism and national liberation, he had failed to reinterpret dialectically the elitist concept of the vanguard party, which, although modified greatly under the impact of the spontaneous creativity from below during the revolution, nonetheless remained essentially unchanged from *What Is to Be Done?* (1902). She pointed instead to the need to develop a new concept of organization, one rooted in what she termed the dialectics of organization and philosophy.[44] It would have to be grounded not only in Hegel, but also in Marx's extensive but ignored work within organizations, as well as his writings on organizational issues, from the Communist League of the 1840s, to the First International of the 1860s, to the *Critique of the Gotha Program* (1875).

Conclusion

All of these dimensions of Lenin's encounter with Hegel in 1914–15 are an important part of the legacy of Marxism, as are issues flowing from them. To skip over them is to ignore some of the richness of that tradition. The fact that the Russian Revolution was transformed under Stalin and his successors into its opposite, a totalitarian state capitalist society, is all the more reason to face squarely the deeply contradictory nature of the history of twentieth-century Marxism. That is why efforts to return to Marx without also coming to terms with Lenin and his generation have important limitations. This is true even of the best-known recent attempt to recover Marx for today, Jacques Derrida's *Specters of Marx* (1993).

I have outlined three major achievements of Lenin with regard to dialectics and national liberation. First, he opened up the issue of the dialectic proper as the ground for revolutionary Marxism as opposed to reformist Marxism, thus paving the way for subsequent authors such as Lukács. Second, his dialectical analysis of imperialism and national liberation constituted a prescient analysis of the importance of anti-imperialist movements for the twentieth century and beyond. By widening the orthodox Marxian notion of the revolutionary subject, he helped pave the way for later attempts to widen this still further, to embrace not only, as Lenin had begun to do, national and ethnic liberation movements, but also those of women, ecologists, gays and lesbians, and youth. However, unlike contemporary identity politics, Lenin also pointed us toward a form of dialectical unity of these various particular forms of resistance. Third, his work on Hegel and dialectics had a direct impact on a number of creative strands within Hegelian Marxist thought, especially in France and the United States.

All of these points show not only the importance of Lenin's rediscovery of the dialectic, but also the persistence of the dialectic within revolutionary thought and activity. It is a heritage that we ignore at our peril. Still, we need to appropriate it most critically if we are not to repeat the wrong turns of the last century, which have left us with a crisis in Marxian and radical thought far deeper than the one faced by Lenin in 1914.

Notes

I would like to thank Shannon Linehan, Heinz Osterle, and Albert Resis for helpful comments on earlier versions of this essay.

1   On this point, see especially Raya Dunayevskaya, *Marxism and Freedom: From 1776 until Today* (New York: Bookman, 1958).

2   See Samuel Farber, *Before Stalinism: The Rise and Fall of Soviet Democracy* (New York: Verso, 1990).

3   For a serious critique of Lenin's *Materialism and Empirio-Criticism*, see Maurice Merleau-Ponty, *Adventures of the Dialectic*, trans. Joseph Bien (Evanston, Ill.: Northwestern University Press, 1973; orig. French edition 1955).

4   Fromm made these comments in an unpublished review of *Trotsky's Diary in Exile* (Cambridge, Mass.: Harvard University Press, 1958). Fromm's comments cited here concerned not only Lenin, but also Trotsky, Marx, and Engels. For the full text, see Kevin B. Anderson, "A Recently Discovered Article by Erich Fromm on Trotsky and the Russian Revolution," *Science and Society* 66:2 (summer 2002): 266–73.

5   See Herbert Marcuse, *Reason and Revolution* (New York: Oxford, 1941), a pathbreaking Marxist study of Hegel and social theory. While Marcuse referred very briefly to one of Lenin's discussions on dialectics (314, 401), he did not mention the

Hegel notebooks at all. Later, in his *Soviet Marxism* (New York: Columbia University Press, 1958), Marcuse made no reference at all to Lenin and Hegel in his chapter on dialectics, while presenting the transition from Lenin to Stalin as an example of "the dialectical law of the turn from quantity to quality" (74).

6   See Oskar Negt, ed., *Kontroversen über dialektischen und mechanistischen Materialismus* (Frankfurt: Suhrkamp Verlag, 1969).

7   See Iring Fetscher, "The Relationship of Marxism to Hegel" (orig. 1960) in his *Marx and Marxism* trans. John Hargreaves (New York: Herder and Herder, 1971). For more detailed discussion of this and many other issues in this chapter, see my *Lenin, Hegel, and Western Marxism: A Critical Study* (Urbana: University of Illinois Press, 1995).

8   See Rudi Dutschke, *Versuch, Lenin auf die Füsse zu Stellen* (Berlin: Verlag Klaus Wagenbach, 1974); and Bernd Rabehl, *Marx und Lenin* (Frankfurt: Verlag für das Studium der Arbeiterbewegung, 1973).

9   Karl Korsch, *Marxism and Philosophy*, trans. Fred Halliday (London: New Left Books, 1970), 29; Lenin, "On the Significance of Militant Materialism," *Collected Works* (Moscow: Progress Publishers, 1961) 33:233, hereafter cited parenthetically in the chapter text as LCW followed by the volume number and the page number.

10   Merleau-Ponty, *Adventures of the Dialectic*, 64.

11   As Friedrich Nietzsche wrote in "Schopenhauer as Educator" (1874), earlier there had been "a fine bumper crop of Hegelian corn standing in the fields. But now that harvest has been ruined by the hail and all the ricks stand empty," cited in Donald N. Levine, *Visions of the Sociological Tradition* (Chicago: University of Chicago Press, 1995), 193.

12   Here and elsewhere, while I refer to the standard English edition of Lenin's Hegel notebooks in volume 38 of his *Collected Works*, in most cases I am actually using the more precise translation by the Hegelian Marxist Raya Dunayevskaya, published as an appendix to the first edition of her *Marxism and Freedom* in 1958.

13   Ernst Bloch, *Subjekt-Objekt: Erläuterungen zu Hegel* (Frankfurt: Suhrkamp Verlag, 1962), 382–83.

14   Georg Lukács, *History and Class Consciousness: Studies in Marxist Dialectics*, trans. Rodney Livingston (Cambridge, Mass.: MIT Press, 1971), 1.

15   Despite their many contributions in other areas, the lengthy studies of Lenin published in English in the past three decades have tended to ignore or minimize the importance of the 1914–15 Hegel notebooks. Tony Cliff's four-volume *Lenin* (London: Pluto Press, 1974–79) devotes one sentence to them. Neil Harding's two-volume *Lenin's Political Thought* (New York: St. Martin's, 1978, 1981) does not mention them at all. Robert Service's three-volume *Lenin: A Political Life* (Bloomington, Ind.: Indiana University Press, 1985, 1991, 1996) takes them up in a couple of pages but stresses that their importance has been overrated. Harding's later *Leninism* (Durham, N.C.: Duke University Press, 1996) devotes a chapter to Lenin's philosophy but dismisses even the Hegel notebooks as dogmatic. Service's more recent *Lenin: A Biography* (Cambridge, Mass.: Harvard University Press, 2000) represents a backward

step on the issue of Lenin and Hegel, since in this book he devotes greater attention to Lenin's very brief notes on Aristotle from the same period than to the Hegel notebooks. Such a nearly total avoidance of the issue of Lenin and Hegel has not been the case in France. There, ever since Lefebvre's discussions in the 1930s (I take these up later in this chapter), it has been impossible to ignore the issue of Lenin's debt to Hegel. See, for example, Marcel Liebman, *Leninism under Lenin*, trans. Brian Pearce (London: Jonathan Cape, 1975, orig. French edition 1973), as well as the more philosophical considerations by Michael Löwy, *Dialectique et révolution* (Paris: Éditions Anthropos, 1973). I treat Louis Althusser's writings below.

16 Marx, *Capital*, trans. Ben Fowkes (London: New Left Books, 1976), 1:494.

17 As is well known, Engels used this somewhat martial metaphor—as with the English word "camp," the German *Lager* can refer to a military encampment—in his *Ludwig Feuerbach and the End of Classical German Philosophy*, in Marx and Engels, *Collected Works* (Moscow: Progress Publishers, 1990), 26:366.

18 Marx, "Critique of the Hegelian Dialectic" (1844), in Erich Fromm, *Marx's Concept of Man* (New York: Frederick Ungar, 1961), 181. The 1844 Manuscripts, which the Second International (and Engels) had ignored, were not published until after Lenin's death, as part of the work around the first *Marx-Engels Gesamtausgabe* (MEGA). The first MEGA (MEGA² is proceeding today) commenced in the early 1920s with Lenin's strong support. It was discontinued under Stalin, who had its main editor, David Riazanov, executed.

19 Leszek Kolakowski, *The Golden Age*, vol. 2 of *Main Currents of Marxism* (New York: Oxford University Press, 1978), 464. Kolakowski is not the only non-Leninist philosopher to have appreciated the Hegel notebooks. See, for example, Louis Dupré's more probing study, *Marx's Social Critique of Culture* (New Haven, Conn.: Yale University Press, 1983).

20 For alternative views, see Raya Dunayevskaya, "Hegelian Leninism," in *Towards a New Marxism*, ed. Bart Grahl and Paul Piccone, 159–75 (St. Louis: Telos Press, 1973), as well as my "Lenin, Bukharin, and the Marxian Concepts of Dialectic and Imperialism: A Study in Contrasts," *Journal of Political and Military Sociology* 15:1 (1987): 197–212.

21 This was another result of Second International Marxism. By the late 1890s, Kautsky and Viktor Adler had distanced themselves from Marx's and Engels's strong support for the Polish and Irish independence movements. The leftist revolutionary Luxemburg had long rejected all forms of nationalism as bourgeois but had the intellectual honesty to make her disagreement with Marx and Engels explicit.

22 I leave aside here a third strand of this debate, Otto Bauer's theory of national and cultural autonomy.

23 See Karl Radek, "Their Song Is Played Out," in *Lenin's Struggle for a Revolutionary International*, ed. John Riddell (New York: Monad Press, 1984), 375.

24 Leon Trotsky, "Lessons of the Events, in Dublin," in *Lenin's Struggle for a Revolutionary International*, ed. John Riddell (New York: Monad Press, 1984), 372–73.

25 The following works fail to mention Lenin's writings on the Irish uprising: Service's

Lenin: A Biography (2000), a 500-page study otherwise notable for its discussion of ethnicity; Cliff's *Lenin* (1974–79), a work that goes into enormous detail on political issues and debates; Harding's *Lenin's Political Thought* (1978, 1981); and Harding's *Leninism* (1996), even though the latter has a chapter entitled "Nationalism and Internationalism." Service's earlier *Lenin: A Political Life* (1985, 1991, 1996) devotes a few lines to Ireland in 1916. On this issue, Liebman's *Leninism under Lenin* (1973) is not very helpful either, since it hardly mentions the whole issue of imperialism and national liberation.

26   See John Riddell, ed., *To See the Dawn: Baku, 1920—First Congress of the Peoples of the East* (New York: Pathfinder Press, 1993), 78.

27   See John Riddell, ed., *Workers of the World and Oppressed Peoples Unite! Proceedings and Documents of the Second Congress, 1920,* 2 vols. (New York: Pathfinder Press, 1991), 219. Further page references are given directly in the text.

28   Sultanzadeh perished in Stalin's purges, and Iran's fawningly pro-Soviet Tudeh (Communist) Party expunged even his name from its official history.

29   For a study of this often forgotten and surprisingly secular upheaval, see Janet Afary, *The Iranian Constitutional Revolution, 1906-11: Grassroots Democracy, Social Democracy, and the Origins of Feminism* (New York: Columbia University Press, 1996).

30   Fourth Congress of the Communist International. *Abridged Report of Meetings Held at Petrograd and Moscow, Nov. 7-Dec. 3, 1924* (London: Communist Party of Great Britain, n.d.), 260–61.

31   Claude McKay, *The Negroes in America*, ed. Alan L. McLeod, trans. Robert J. Winter (Port Washington, N.Y.: Kennikat Press, 1979). The American Communist Party was evidently so uninterested in his book that the English text seems to have been lost. For this 1979 publication, it had to be retranslated into English from a Russian version, also unpublished, that had been discovered by chance in the Slavic Division of the New York Public Library. For one of the few Marxist discussions of the importance of McKay's intervention at the 1924 Congress, see Raya Dunayevskaya, *American Civilization on Trial* (Detroit: News and Letters, 1963).

32   See Leon Trotsky, *Leon Trotsky on Black Nationalism and Self-Determination* (New York: Merit Publishers, 1967), 42, 48.

33   Leon Trotsky, *On the Jewish Question* (New York: Pathfinder Press, 1970), 20. See also Enzo Traverso, *The Marxists and the Jewish Question: The History of a Debate, 1843-1943*, trans. Bernard Gibbons (Atlantic Highlands, N.J.: Humanities Press International, 1994).

34   See, for example, C. L. R. James, *Nkrumah and the Ghana Revolution* (London: Allison and Busby, 1977), and Raya Dunayevskaya, *Nationalism, Communism, Marxist Humanism, and the Afro-Asian Revolutions* (Chicago: News and Letters, 1984, orig. 1959).

35   See especially Peter Hudis, "Kosova: Achilles Heel of the Left," in *The Kosova Reader*, ed. Danny Postel (Cybereditions: forthcoming), a book that includes a contribution by Slavoj Žižek. See also the contributions of Hudis and others, including the present writer, to *Bosnia-Herzegovina: Achilles Heel of "Western" Civilization* (Chi-

cago: News and Letters, 1996) and *Kosova: Writings from News and Letters, 1998-99* (Chicago: News and Letters, 2000) as well as Joanne Landy, "Self-Determination and Diplomacy," *New Politics* 27 (summer 1999): 27–33.

36 For background on Lefebvre in this period, see especially Fred Bud Burkhard, *French Marxism between the Wars: Henri Lefebvre and the "Philosophies"* (Amherst, N.Y.: Prometheus Books, 1999).

37 Henri Lefebvre, *La Somme et la reste* (Paris: La Nef, 1959), 85.

38 On Althusser's philosophical affinity to Maoism, see Gregory Elliott, *Althusser: The Detour of Theory* (London: Verso, 1987).

39 Louis Althusser, *Lenin and Philosophy, and Other Essays*, trans. Ben Brewster (New York: Monthly Review, 1971), 112. I go into much more detail on this point in my *Lenin, Hegel, and Western Marxism*.

40 Louis Althusser, *For Marx*, trans. Ben Brewster (New York: Vintage, 1970), 116. (The essay in question was first published in French in 1962.)

41 C. L. R. James, *Notes on Dialectics: Hegel-Marx-Lenin* (Westport, Conn.: Lawrence Hill, 1980).

42 Raya Dunayevskaya, *Philosophy and Revolution: From Hegel to Sartre and from Marx to Mao* (New York: Delacorte, 1973), 103.

43 Raya Dunayevskaya, *Rosa Luxemburg, Women's Liberation, and Marx's Philosophy of Revolution* (Urbana: University of Illinois Press, 1991, orig. 1982), 116.

44 See Raya Dunayevskaya, *The Power of Negativity: Selected Writings on the Dialectic in Hegel and Marx*, ed. Peter Hudis and Kevin B. Anderson (Lanham, Md.: Lexington Books, 2002).

8

"Leaps! Leaps! Leaps!"

Daniel Bensaïd

Hannah Arendt was worried that politics might disappear completely from the world. The century had seen such disasters that the question of whether "politics still has any meaning at all" had become unavoidable. The issues at stake in these fears were eminently practical: "The lack of meaning in which the whole of politics has ended up is confirmed by the dead end into which specific political questions are flocking."[1]

For her, the form taken by this feared disappearance of politics was totalitarianism. Today we are confronted with a different form of the danger: totalitarianism, the human face of market tyranny. Here politics finds itself crushed between the order of financial markets—which is made to seem natural—and the moralizing prescriptions of ventriloquist capitalism. The end of politics and the end of history then coincide in the infernal repetition of the eternity of the commodity, in which echo the toneless voices of Fukuyama and Furet. According to them, "the idea of *another* society has become almost impossible to conceive of, and no one in the world today is offering any advice on the subject. Here we are, condemned to live in the world as it is."[2] This is worse than melancholy—it is despair, as Blanqui might have said, this eternity of mankind through the Dow Jones and the FT 100.

Hannah Arendt thought she could set a date on the beginning and end of politics: inaugurated by Plato and Aristotle, it found "its definitive end in the theories of Marx."[3] Announcing the end of philosophy, Marx is also, by some jest of the dialectic, said to have pronounced that of politics. This fails to recognize Marx's politics as the only one that is conceivable in the face of capitalized violence and the fetishisms of modernity. The state is not valid for everything, he wrote in his early writings, standing up clearly against the presumptuous exaggeration of the political factor, which makes the bureaucratic state into the embodiment of the abstract universal. Rather than a one-sided passion for the social, Marx's effort is directed toward the emergence of a politics of the oppressed starting from the constitution of nonstate political bodies that prepare the way for the necessary withering away of the state as a separate body.

The vital, urgent question is that of politics from below, politics for those who are excluded and cut off from the state politics of the ruling class. We have to solve the puzzle of proletarian revolutions and their repeated tragedies: How do we spurn the dust and win the prize? How can a class that is physically and morally stunted in its daily life by the involuntary servitude of forced labor transform itself into the universal subject of human emancipation? Marx's answers on this point derive from a sociological gamble—industrial development leads to the numerical growth and the concentration of the working classes, which in turn leads to progress in their organization and consciousness. The logic of capital itself is thus said to lead to "the constitution of the proletarians into a ruling class." Engels's preface to the 1890 edition of the *Communist Manifesto* confirms this assumption: "For the ultimate triumph of the ideas set forth in the *Manifesto* Marx relied solely and exclusively upon the intellectual development of the working class as it necessarily had to ensue from united action and discussion."[4] The illusion according to which the winning of universal suffrage would allow the English proletariat, which was a majority in society, to adjust political representation to social reality derives from this gamble. In the same spirit, in his 1896 commentary on the *Manifesto*, Antonio Labriola expressed the view, "The desired union of communists and proletarians is henceforth an accomplished fact."[5] The political emancipation of the proletariat flowed necessarily from its social development.

The convulsive history of the last century shows that we cannot so easily escape from the haunted world of the commodity, from its bloodthirsty gods and from their "box of repetitions." Lenin's untimely relevance results necessarily from this observation. If politics today still has a chance of averting the double danger of a naturalization of the economy and a fatalization of history, this chance requires a new Leninist act in the conditions of imperial globalization. Lenin's political thought is that of politics as strategy, of favorable moments and weak links.

The "homogeneous and empty," to use Walter Benjamin's terms, time of mechanical progress, without crises or breaks, is a nonpolitical time. The idea maintained by Kautsky of a "passive accumulation of forces" belongs to this view of time. A primitive version of calm force, this "socialism outside of time" and at the speed of a tortoise dissolves the uncertainty of the political struggle into the proclaimed laws of historical evolution.

Lenin, in contrast, thought of politics as a time full of struggle, a time of crises and collapses. For him the specificity of politics is expressed in the concept of a revolutionary crisis, which is not the logical continuation of a social movement, but a general crisis of the reciprocal relations between all the classes in society. The crisis is then defined as a national crisis. It acts to lay bare the battle lines, which have been obscured by the mystical phantasmagoria of the commodity. Then alone, and not by virtue of some inevitable historical ripening, can the proletariat be transformed and "become what it is."

The revolutionary crisis and political struggle are thus closely linked. For Lenin, the knowledge that the working class can have of itself is indissolubly linked to a precise knowledge of the reciprocal relations of all the classes in contemporary society, a knowledge which is not only theoretical, we should rather say which is less theoretical than founded on the experience of politics. It is through the test of practical politics that this knowledge of the reciprocal relations between classes is acquired. To paraphrase Lenin, this makes "our revolution" into a "revolution of the whole people."

This approach is the complete opposite of a crude workerism, which reduces the political to the social. Lenin categorically refuses to mix the question of classes with that of parties. The class struggle is not reduced to the antagonism between the worker and his boss. It confronts the proletariat with the capitalist class as such on the level of the process of capitalist production as a whole, which is the object of study in volume 3 of *Capital*. This, moreover, is why it is perfectly logical for Marx's unfinished chapter on class to come precisely at this point and not in volume 1 on the process of production or volume 2 on the process of circulation. As a political party, revolutionary Social Democracy thus represented for Lenin the working class, not just in its relations with a group of employers, but also with all the classes of contemporary society and with the state as an organized force.

The time of the propitious moment in Leninist strategy is no longer that of the electoral Penelopes and Danaïdes, whose work is constantly undone again, but that which gives a rhythm to struggle and which is suspended by crisis—the time of the opportune moment and of the singular conjuncture, where necessity and contingency, act and process, history and event are knotted together. We should not imagine revolution itself in the form of a singular act: the revolution will be a rapid succession of more or less violent explosions, alternating with phases of more or less deep calm. That is why, according to Lenin, the essential activity of the party, the essential focus of its activity, must be possible and necessary work both in the periods of the most violent explosion and in those of calm, that is, a work of unified political agitation.

Revolutions have their own tempo, marked by accelerations and slow-downs. They also have their own geometry, where the straight line is broken in bifurcation and sudden turns. The party thus appears in a new light. For Lenin, it is no longer the result of a cumulative experience, nor the modest teacher with the task of raising proletarians from the darkness of ignorance to the illumination of reason. It becomes a strategic operator, a sort of gearbox and point man of the class struggle. As Walter Benjamin very clearly recognized, the strategic time of politics is not the homogeneous and empty time of classical mechanics, but a broken time, full of knots and wombs pregnant with events.

Without any doubt there is, in the formation of Lenin's thought, an interplay of continuities and breaks. The major breaks (which are not epistemological breaks) can be placed in 1902, around *What Is to Be Done?* and *One Step Forward, Two Steps Back*, or again in 1914–16, when it was necessary to rethink imperialism and the state amid the twilight of the war and by taking up again the thread of Hegelian logic. At the same time, from *The Development of Capitalism in Russia*, a foundational work, Lenin will establish the framework that will allow him subsequently to make theoretical corrections and strategic adjustments.

The confrontations in the course of which Bolshevism was defined are an expression of this revolution in the revolution. From the polemics of *What Is to Be Done?* and *One Step Forward, Two Steps Back*, the classic texts essentially preserve the idea of a centralized vanguard with military discipline. The real point is elsewhere. Lenin is fighting against the confusion, which he describes as disorganizing, between the party and the class. The making of a distinction between them has its context in the great controversies then running through the socialist movement, especially in Russia. This is in opposition to the populist, economist, and Menshevik currents, which sometimes converge to defend pure socialism. The apparent intransigence of this formal orthodoxy in fact expresses the idea that the democratic revolution must be a necessary stage on the road of historic evolution. While waiting to be strengthened and to achieve the social and electoral majority, the nascent working-class movement was supposed to leave the leading role to the bourgeoisie and be satisfied with acting in support of capitalist modernization. This confidence in the direction of history, where everything would come in due time to those who wait, underlies the orthodox positions of Kautsky in the Second International: we must patiently advance along the roads to power until power falls like a ripe fruit.

For Lenin, in contrast, it is the goal that orientates the movement; strategy takes precedence over tactics, politics over history. That is why it is necessary to demarcate oneself before uniting, and, in order to unite, "to utilize every manifestation of discontent, and to gather and turn to the best account every protest, however small." In other words, it means to conceive the political struggle as "far more extensive and complex than the economic struggle of the workers against the employers and the government."[6] Thus when *Rabocheye Dyelo* deduces the political objectives from economic struggle, Lenin criticizes it for lowering the level of the many-sided political activity of the proletariat. It is an illusion to imagine that the "labour movement pure and simple" is capable by itself of elaborating an independent ideology. The merely spontaneous development of the working-class movement on the contrary leads to "its subordination to bourgeois ideology"[7] For the ruling ideology is not a question of the manipulation of consciousness, but the objective result of the fetishism of commodities. Its iron grip and enforced servitude can only be escaped through the revolutionary crisis and the political struggle of parties. This is indeed the Leninist answer to the unsolved puzzle of Marx.

For Lenin everything leads to the conception of politics as the invasion whereby that which was absent becomes present: the division into classes is certainly, in the last resort, the most profound basis for political groupings, but this last resort is established only by political struggle. Thus, communism literally erupts from all points of social life: decidedly it blossoms everywhere. If one of the outlets is blocked with particular care, then the contagion will find another, sometimes the most unexpected. That is why we cannot know which spark will ignite the fire.

From whence comes the slogan that, according to Tucholsky, sums up Leninist politics: "Be ready!" Be ready for the improbable, for the unexpected, for what happens. If Lenin could describe politics as "concentrated economics," this concentration means a qualitative change on the basis of which politics cannot fail to "take precedence over economics," "Bukharin's insistence on combining the political *and* the economic approach," in contrast, "has landed him in theoretical *eclecticism*."[8] Likewise, in his 1921 polemic against the Workers' Opposition, Lenin criticizes this "disreputable" name,[9] which once again reduces politics to the social and which claims that the management of the national economy should be directly incumbent on the "producers organized in trade and industrial unions," which would come down to reducing the class struggle to a confrontation of sectional interests without synthesis.

Politics, on the contrary, has its own language, grammar, and syntax. It has its latencies and its slips. On the political stage, the transfigured class struggle has its fullest, most rigorous and best defined expression in the struggle of parties. Deriving from a specific register, which is not reducible to its immediate determinations, political discourse is more closely related to algebra than to arithmetic. Its necessity is of a different order, much more complex, than that of social demands directly linked to the relationship of exploitation. For contrary to what vulgar Marxists imagine, politics does not tamely follow economics. The ideal of the revolutionary militant is not the trade unionist with a narrow horizon, but the tribune of the people, which fans the embers of subversion in all spheres of society.

Leninism, or rather Stalinized Leninism, built up as a state orthodoxy, is often made responsible for bureaucratic despotism. The notion
of the vanguard party, separate from the class, is thus believed to have
contained the germ of the substitution of the apparatus for the real
social movement and of all the circles of bureaucratic hell. However
unfair it may be, this accusation raises a real difficulty. If politics is not
identical with the social, the representation of the one by the other necessarily becomes problematic—on what can its legitimacy be based?

For Lenin, the temptation very much exists of resolving the contradiction by supposing a tendency for representatives to adequately represent their constituents, culminating in the withering away of the
political state. The contradictions in representation do not allow for
any exclusive agent, and being constantly called into question in the
plurality of constitutive forms, they are eliminated at the same time.
This aspect of the question risks covering up another, which is no less
important, inasmuch as Lenin does not seem to recognize the full extent of his innovation. Thinking that he was paraphrasing a canonical text by Kautsky, he distorted it significantly as follows. Kautsky
wrote that "science" comes to the proletarians "from outside the class
struggle, borne by 'the bourgeois intelligentsia.'" By an extraordinary
verbal shift, Lenin translates this so that "class political consciousness"
(rather than "science"!) comes "from outside the economic struggle"[10]
(rather than from outside the class struggle, which is political as much
as social!), borne no longer by the intellectuals as a social category, but
by the party as an agent that specifically structures the political field.
The difference is pretty substantial.

Such a constant insistence on the language of politics, where social
reality is manifested through a permanent interplay of displacements
and condensations, should logically result in a way of thought based
on plurality and representation. If the party is not the class, the same
class should be represented politically by several parties expressing its
differences and contradictions. The representation of the social in the
political should then become the object of an institutional and juridical
elaboration. Lenin does not go so far. A detailed study, which would go
beyond the dimensions of an essay like this, of his positions on the national question, on the trade union question in 1921, and on democracy
throughout 1917 would enable us to verify it.[11]

Thus he subjects representation to rules inspired by the Paris Commune, aiming to limit political professionalization: elected representatives to be paid a wage equal to that of a skilled worker, constant vigilance about favors and privileges for office holders, the responsibility of those elected to those who elected them. Contrary to a persistent myth, he did not advocate binding mandates. This was the case in the party: the powers of delegates must not be limited by binding mandates; in the exercise of their powers they should be completely free and independent.

As for plurality, Lenin constantly affirmed that "the struggle of shades of opinion" in the party is inevitable and necessary, so long as it takes place within limits "approved by common agreement." He maintained "that it is necessary to include in the party rules guarantees of minority rights, so that the dissatisfactions, irritations and conflicts that will constantly and unavoidably arise may be diverted from the accustomed philistine channels of rows and squabbling into the still unaccustomed channels of a constitutional and dignified struggle for one's convictions. As one of these essential guarantees, we propose that the minority be allowed one or more writers' groups, with the right to be represented at congresses and with complete 'freedom of speech.'"[12]

If politics is a matter of choice and decision, it implies an organized plurality. This is a question of principles of organization. As for the system of organization, it may vary according to concrete circumstances, on the condition that it does not lose the guiding thread of principle in the labyrinth of opportunities. Then even the notorious discipline in action seems less sacrosanct than the golden myth of Leninism would have it. We know how Zinoviev and Kamenev were guilty of indiscipline by publicly opposing the insurrection, yet they were not permanently removed from their responsibilities. Lenin himself, in extreme circumstances, did not hesitate to demand a personal right to disobey the party. Thus he considered resigning his responsibilities in order to resume "freedom to campaign among the *rank and file* of the party."[13]

His own logic led him to envisage plurality and representation in a country with no parliamentary or democratic traditions. But Lenin did not go all the way. There are (at least) two reasons for that. The first is that he had inherited from the French Revolution the illusion that once the oppressor has been removed, the homogenization of the people (or of the class) is only a matter of time: contradictions among the people can now come only from the other (the foreigner) or from treason. The second is that the distinction between politics and the social is not a guarantee against a fatal inversion: instead of leading to the socialization of the political, the dictatorship may mean the bureaucratic statification of the social.

In *The State and Revolution* parties do indeed lose their function in favor of a direct democracy, which is not supposed to be entirely a separate state. But, contrary to initial hopes, the statification of society was victorious over the socialization of state functions. Absorbed in the main dangers of military encirclement and capitalist restoration, the revolutionaries did not see growing beneath their feet the no less important danger of bureaucratic counter-revolution. Paradoxically, Lenin's weaknesses are linked as much, or even more, to his libertarian inclinations as to his authoritarian temptations, as if a secret link united the two.

The revolutionary crisis appears as the critical moment of the possible resolution, where theory becomes strategy. History in general and more particularly the history of revolutions is always richer in its content, more varied, more many-sided, more alive, more ingenious than is conceived by the best parties, the most conscious vanguards of the most advanced classes. And that is understandable since the best vanguards express the consciousness, the will, and the passion of tens of thousands of men, while the revolution is one of the moments of special exaltation and tension of all human faculties—the work of the consciousness, the will, the imagination, the passion of hundreds of thousands of men spurred on by the harshest class struggle. Hence two practical conclusions of great importance: first, that the revolutionary class must, in order to carry out its task, be able to take possession of all forms and all aspects of social activity without the slightest exception; secondly, the revolutionary class must be ready to replace one form by another rapidly and without warning.

From this Lenin deduces the need to respond to unexpected events where often the hidden truth of social relations is suddenly revealed: "We do not and cannot know which spark . . . will kindle the conflagration, in the sense of raising up the masses; we must, therefore, with our new and communist principles, set to work to stir up all and sundry, even the oldest, mustiest and seemingly hopeless spheres, for otherwise we shall not be able to cope with our tasks, shall not be comprehensively prepared, shall not be in possession of all the weapons." [14]

Stir up all spheres! Be on the watch for the most unpredictable solutions! Remain ready for the sudden change of forms! Know how to employ all weapons!

These are the maxims of a politics conceived as the art of unexpected events and of the effective possibilities of a determinate conjuncture.

This revolution in politics brings us back to the notion of revolutionary crisis systematized in "The Collapse of the Second International." It is defined by an interaction between several variable elements in a situation: when those above can no longer govern as they did before; when those below will not tolerate being oppressed as they were before; and when this double impossibility is expressed by a sudden effervescence of the masses. Adopting these criteria, Trotsky stresses in his *History of the Russian Revolution* "that these premises condition each other is obvious. The more decisively and confidently the proletariat acts, the better will it succeed in bringing after it the intermediate layer, the more isolated will be the ruling class, and the more acute its demoralization. And, on the other hand, a demoralization of the rulers will pour water into the mill of the revolutionary class." [15] But the crisis does not guarantee the conditions of its own resolution. That is why Lenin makes the intervention of a revolutionary party into the decisive factor in a critical situation: "It is not every revolutionary situation that gives rise to a revolution; revolution arises only out of a situation in which the above-mentioned objective changes are accompanied by a subjective change, namely, the ability of the revolutionary *class* to take revolutionary mass action *strong* enough to break (or dislocate) the old government, which never, not even in a period of crisis, 'falls,' if it is not toppled over." [16] The crisis can be resolved only by defeat at the hands of a reaction that will often be murderous or by the intervention of a resolute subject.

This was very much the interpretation of Leninism in Lukács's *History and Class Consciousness*. Already at the Fifth Congress of the Communist International this earned him the anathema of the Thermidorian Bolshevizers. Lukács in fact insisted on the fact that "*Only the consciousness of the proletariat can point to the way that leads out of the impasse of capitalism. As long as this consciousness is lacking, the* crisis remains permanent, it goes back to its starting-point, repeats the cycle. . . ." Lukács states that

> the difference between the period in which the decisive battles are fought and the foregoing period does not lie in the extent and the intensity of the battles themselves. These quantitative changes are merely symptomatic of the fundamental differences in quality which distinguish these struggles from earlier ones. . . . Now, however, the process by which the proletariat becomes independent and "organizes itself into a class" is repeated and intensified until the time when the final crisis of capitalism has been reached, the time when the decision comes more and more within the grasp of the proletariat.[17]

This is echoed in the 1930s when Trotsky, facing Nazism and Stalinist reaction, produced a formulation equating the crisis of humanity with the crisis of revolutionary leadership.

Strategy is "a calculation of mass, speed and time," wrote Chateaubriand. For Sun Tzu, the art of war was already the art of change and of speed. This art required acquiring "the speed of the hare" and "coming to a decision immediately," for it is proven that the most famous victory could have turned to defeat "if battle had been joined a day earlier or a few hours later." The rule of conduct derived from this is valid for politicians as well as soldiers: "Never let any opportunity slip, when you find it favorable. The five elements are not everywhere, nor are they equally pure; the four seasons do not follow each other in the same fashion every year; the rising and setting of the sun are not always at the same point on the horizon. Some days are long and others short. The moon waxes and wanes and is not always equally bright. An army that is well led and well disciplined aptly imitates all these variations."[18]

The notion of revolutionary crisis takes up this lesson of strategy and politicizes it. In certain exceptional circumstances the balance of forces reaches a critical point. Any disruption of the rhythms produces effects of conflict. It upsets and disturbs. It can also produce a gap in time, to be filled with an invention, with a creation. This happens, individually and socially, only by passing through a crisis." Through such a gap or moment can arise the unaccomplished fact, which contradicts the fatality of the accomplished fact.

In 1905 Lenin comes together with Sun Tzu in his praise of speed. It is necessary, he says, "to begin on time," to act "immediately." "Form immediately, in all places, combat groups." We must indeed be able to grasp in flight those "fleeting moments" of which Hegel speaks and which constitute an excellent definition of the dialectic. For the revolution in Russia is not the organic result of a bourgeois revolution extended into a proletarian revolution, but an "intertwining" of two revolutions. Whether the probable disaster can be avoided depends on an acute sense of conjuncture. The art of the slogan is an art of the favorable moment. A particular instruction that was valid yesterday may not be so today but may be valid again tomorrow. "The slogan 'All Power to the Soviets!' . . . was possible in April, May, June and up to July 5–9 [1917] . . . This slogan is no longer correct." "At this moment and this moment alone, perhaps for a few days at most, or for a week or two, such a government could survive."[19]

A few days! A week! On 29 September 1917 Lenin wrote to the hesitating central committee: "The crisis has matured."[20] Waiting was becoming a crime. On 1 October he urged them to *take power at once,* to *resort to insurrection at once.*[21] A few days later he tried again: "I am writing these lines on 8 October. . . . The success of both the Russian and the world revolution depends on two or three days' fighting."[22] He still insisted: "I am writing these lines on the evening of the 24th. The situation is critical in the extreme. In fact it is now absolutely clear that to delay the uprising would be fatal. . . . Everything now hangs by a thread." So it is necessary to act "this very evening, this very night."[23]

"Breaks in gradualness" noted Lenin in the margins of Hegel's *The Science of Logic* at the beginning of the war. And he stressed, "Gradualness explains nothing without leaps. Leaps! Leaps! Leaps!"[24]

Three brief remarks will conclude this discussion on the relevance of Lenin today. His strategic thought defines a state of being available to act in relation to whatever event may arise. But this event is not the absolute Event, coming from nowhere, which some people have mentioned with reference to 11 September. It is situated in conditions of historically determined possibility. That is what distinguishes it from the religious miracle. Thus the revolutionary crisis of 1917 and its resolution by insurrection become strategically thinkable in the framework traced by *The Development of Capitalism in Russia*. This dialectical relation between necessity and contingency, structure and break, history and event, lays the basis for the possibility of a politics organized in duration, whereas the arbitrarily voluntarist gamble on the sudden explosion of an event may allow us to resist the mood of the times, but it generally leads to a stance of aesthetic resistance rather than militant commitment to patiently modify the course of things.

For Lenin—as for Trotsky—the revolutionary crisis is formed and begins in the national arena, which at the time constitutes the framework of the struggle for hegemony and goes on to take its place in the context of the world revolution. The crisis in which dual power arises is therefore not reduced to an economic crisis or an immediate conflict between wage labor and capital in the process of production. The Leninist question—who will come out on top?—is that of political leadership: Which class will be capable of resolving the contradictions that are stifling society, capable of imposing an alternative logic to that of the accumulation of capital, capable of transcending the existing relations of production and opening up a new field of possibilities? The revolutionary crisis is therefore not a simple social crisis but also a national crisis: in Russia as in Germany, in Spain as in China. The question today is doubtless more complex to the extent that capitalist globalization has reinforced the overlapping of national, continental, and world spaces. A revolutionary crisis in a major country would immediately have an international dimension and would require responses in terms that are both national and continental, or even directly global on questions such as energy, ecology, armaments policy, movement of migrants, and so forth. It nonetheless remains an illusion to believe that we can evade this difficulty by eliminating the question of the conquest of political power (on the pretext that power today is divorced from territory and scattered everywhere and nowhere) in favor of a rhetoric of counterpowers. Economic, military, and cultural powers are perhaps more widely scattered, but they are also more concentrated than ever. You can pretend to ignore power, but it will not ignore you. You can act superior by refusing to take it, but from Catalonia 1937 to Chiapas, via Chile, experience shows right up to this very day that it will not hesitate to take you in the most brutal fashion. In a word, a strategy of counterpower only has any meaning in the perspective of dual power and its resolution. Who will come out on top?

Finally, detractors often identify Leninism and Lenin himself with a historical form of the political party, which is said to have died along with the collapse of the bureaucratic party-states. In this hasty judgment there is a lot of historical ignorance and political frivolity, which can be only partially explained by the traumatism of Stalinist practices. The experience of the past century poses the question of bureaucratization as a social phenomenon, rather than the question of the form of vanguard party inherited from *What Is to Be Done?* Mass organizations (not only political ones, but equally trade unions and associations) are far from being the least bureaucratic: in France the cases of the CFDT, of the Socialist Party, of the allegedly renovated Communist Party, and of the Greens are absolutely eloquent on this point. But at the same time—as we have mentioned—in the Leninist distinction of party and class there are some fertile trails for thinking about the relations between social movements and political representation. Likewise in the superficially disparaged principles of democratic centralism, detractors stress primarily the bureaucratic hypercentralism exemplified in sinister fashion by the Stalinist parties. But a certain degree of centralization, far from being opposed to democracy, is the essential condition for it to exist—because the delimitation of the party is a means of resisting the decomposing effects of the dominant ideology, and also of aiming at a certain equality between members, counter to the inequalities that are inevitably generated by social relations and by the division of labor. Today we can see very well how the weakening of these principles, far from favoring a higher form of democracy, leads to co-option by the media and the legitimization by a plebiscite of leaders who are even less controlled by the rank and file. Moreover, the democracy in a revolutionary party aims to produce decisions that are assumed collectively in order to act on the balance of forces. When the superficial detractors of Leninism claim to have freed themselves from a stifling discipline, they are in fact emptying discussion of all its relevance, reducing it to a forum of opinions that does not commit anybody: after an exchange of free speech without any common decision, everyone can leave as they came and no shared practice makes it possible to test the validity of the opposing positions under consideration. Finally, the stress laid—in particular by recycled bureaucrats from the former Communist parties—on the crisis of the party form often enables them to avoid talking about the crisis of the programmatic content and justifies the absence of strategic preoccupation.

A politics without parties (whatever name—movement, organization,

league, party—that they are given) ends up in most cases as a politics
without politics: either an aimless tailism toward the spontaneity of social movements, or the worst form of elitist individualist vanguardism,
or finally a repression of the political in favor of the aesthetic or the
ethical.

Notes

This essay was originally published in *International Socialism Journal* 95 (Summer
2002) and in D. Bensaïd, *Un monde à changer* (Paris: Editions Textuel, 2003).

1 H. Arendt, *Was ist Politik?* (Munich: M. Piper Verlag, 1993), 28, 31.

2 F. Furet, *The Passing of an Illusion* (Chicago: University of Chicago Press, 1999),
   502.

3 Arendt, *Was ist Politik?*, 146.

4 K. Marx and F. Engels, "Preface to the Fourth German Edition of the *Manifesto of
   the Communist Party*," *Collected Works* (London: Lawrence and Wishart, 1975ff.),
   27:59.

5 Antonio Labriola, *Essais sur la conception matérialiste de l'histoire* (Paris: Gordon and
   Breach, 1970), 46.

6 V. I. Lenin, "What Is to Be Done?" *Collected Works* (Moscow: Progress Publishers,
   1960), 5:430, 452. All subsequent references in this chapter to the *Collected Works*
   refer to this edition.

7 "What Is to Be Done?," *Collected Works* 5:382, 384.

8 "Once Again on the Trade Unions," 25 January 1921, *Collected Works* 32:83, 84.

9 "Summing-Up Speech on the report of the CC of the RCP(B) March 9, 1921," *Collected Works* 32:195, 198.

10 V. I. Lenin, "What Is to Be Done?" *Collected Works* 5:383, 422.

11 Thus in the 1915 debate on ultra-imperialism, Lenin perceives the danger of a new
    economism whereby the maturity of the capitalist relations of production on the
    world scale would be a prelude to a final collapse of the system. We again find this
    concern to avoid any reduction of the political to the economic or the social in the
    debates of the early 1920s on the characterization of the Soviet state. To those who
    speak of a workers' state, Lenin replies that "the whole point is that it is not quite a
    workers' state." His formulation is then more descriptive and complex than a socio-
    logical characterization: it is a workers' and peasants' state "with a bureaucratic
    twist to it," and "there you have the reality of the transition" (Lenin, "The Trade
    Unions, the Present Situation and Trotsky's Mistakes," *Collected Works* 32:24).
    Finally, in the debate on the trade unions, Lenin again defends an original position:
    because they are not an organ of political power, the unions must not be transformed
    into "coercive state organizations."

12 Lenin, "What We are Working For," *Collected Works* 7:450.

13 Lenin, "The Crisis has Matured," *Collected Works* 26:84.

14 Lenin, "'Left-Wing' Communism—An Infantile Disorder," *Collected Works* 31:99.

15 L. Trotsky, *The History of the Russian Revolution* (London: Pluto, 1997), 1024.

16 Lenin, "The Collapse of the Second International," *Collected Works* 21:214.

17 G. Lukács, *History and Class Consciousness* (London: Merlin Press, 1971), 76, 313. Emphasis in original.

18 On this topic see H. Lefebvre, *Eléments de rythmanalyse* (Paris: Syllepse, 1996).

19 Lenin, "The Political Situation," 10 July 1917, *Collected Works* 25:177.

20 Lenin, "The Crisis has Matured," *Collected Works* 26:82.

21 Lenin, "Letter to the Central Committee, the Moscow and Petrograd Committees and the Bolshevik Members of the Petrograd and Moscow Soviets," *Collected Works* 26:140–41.

22 Lenin, "Advice of an Onlooker," *Collected Works* 26:179–81.

23 Lenin, "Letter to Central Committee Members," *Collected Works* 26:234.

24 Lenin, "Conspectus of Hegel's Book *The Science of Logic*," *Collected Works* 38:123.

Lenin as Reader of Hegel: Hypotheses for a Reading of Lenin's Notebooks on Hegel's *The Science of Logic*

Stathis Kouvelakis

The First World War was not simply an eruption of massacres on a massive scale at the heart of the imperialist countries. After a century of relative internal peace, it brought at the same time the collapse of its historical opponent, the European workers' movement, essentially organized in the Second International. The term "disaster" is quite apposite for this, though Alain Badiou uses it to refer to the final refutation of a certain form of emancipatory politics following the more recent collapse of the so-called communist regimes of Eastern Europe.[1] If we consider that this second disaster struck at precisely the political truth that was born in response to the earlier one, under the name of "October 1917" or equally "Lenin," it is then the loop of the "short twentieth century" that was closed by this repetition of disaster. Paradoxically, therefore, it is not such a bad moment to go back to the beginning, the moment at which, in the mud and blood that drowned Europe in the summer of 1914, this century first arose.

The Disaster

Dragged into the whirlpool of the conflict, both European and non-European[2] societies had their first experience of total war. The whole of society, combatants and noncombatants alike, economics and politics, state and civil society (trade unions, churches, media) fully participated in a general mobilization absolutely unprecedented in world history.

The *traumatic* dimension of the event had no common measure with any previous armed confrontation. It was the general feeling of the end of a whole "civilization" that emerged from the monstrous butchery of the trenches—a real industry of massacre, highly technologized and practiced both on the battlefield and beyond it (bombing of civilians, displacement of populations, targeted destruction of zones outside the front). The industry of mass murder was closely interwoven with mechanisms for controlling social life and populations directly or indirectly exposed to the conflict. This apocalyptic atmosphere, the echo of which resonates loudly in the entire culture of the immediate postwar period (born in the war itself were Dada, then surrealism and the other avant-gardes of the 1920s and 1930s), pervaded all contemporary life. We can get an idea of this today by reading Rosa Luxemburg's "Junius Pamphlet,"[3] one of the most extraordinary in all socialist literature, in which each page attests to the unprecedented character of the barbarism under way.

The dimension of a brutalization of all social relations, terrifying as it was and still seems, should not, however, conceal the large-scale *innovations* that this conflict bore within it. Indeed, it is well known that every war is a genuine laboratory for the "modernization" of social relations,[4] but the total and totalitarian character of this one gave the process a scale that was previously unknown. With the large-scale establishment of concentration camps; with policies of the deportation of populations and cleansing of territories (previously reserved for the colonies: the world conflict precisely made it possible to import into the metropolises the kind of violence that had up till then been practiced on the imperial periphery); with the forms of planning and state control of the economy, including the integration of the trade unions into the war economy (which took on the appearance of complete capitalist rationalization, theorized as such by Rathenau); with recourse to female labor in industry (with all the consequences of this, combined with the absence of men at the front, at the level of the family structure, and male domination in social life); with the forms of conditioning practiced on a large scale on the combatants and on public opinion by an impressive mechanism of control of information and the development of new means of distribution (radio, cinema); and without forgetting, of course, the governments of the *union sacrée*, which ensured the participation of workers' parties at the summit of the state and went together with forms of planning and consensus at the economic level— not a single aspect of collective and individual life was left untouched by this experience, a genuinely radical one.

Nothing would ever be the same as it was before, and first of all for the workers' movement. The collapse of the Second International, its total impotence in the face of the outbreak of imperialist conflict, in fact only revealed deep-rooted tendencies, existing well before the First World War, toward an "integration" of the organizations of this movement (and a large part of its social base) into the compromises that supported the social and political order of the metropolitan countries (especially in its imperialist dimension). The "collapse," in Lenin's term, was thus that of the entire political practice of the workers' and socialist movement, which was now forced to radical reconsiderations: "The world war has changed the conditions of our struggle and has radically changed ourselves as well" wrote Luxemburg, going on to appeal for an "unsparing self-criticism" as "life and breath for the proletarian movement."[5]

Lenin, though being far from the least well-armed (even if in a certain sense he still did not realize this), was none the less among those struck by the disaster in the most immediate manner. His incredulity in the face of the unanimous vote of war credits by the German Social Democrats, and more generally in the face of the collapse of the International and its orthodox "Kautskyan" center, as well as the slow and rare character of his initial interventions after August 1914, say a great deal. They comment not so much on a (supposed) lack of lucidity (even if it is true that his earlier desire for "orthodoxy"—not shared by Luxemburg—contributed to the illusion retrospectively revealed by the disaster), but far more so on the genuinely unprecedented character of what was happening.

This setback to political intervention was still more clearly signaled by the evolution of his position toward the attitude of revolutionary socialists in the face of the war. At the moment when war broke out, and the "horror" of the collapse of the International was the hardest thing of all to bear, the Bolshevik leader launched an "emergency" slogan that was still in the tradition of the "anti-war culture" of the defunct International. This was the democratic (Jacobin-Kantian) slogan of "transformation of all European states into a republican United States of Europe," a transformation that implied the overthrow of the German, Austro-Hungarian, and Romanov dynasties among others.[6] Soon after (in 1915) this position was abandoned, owing to its problematic economic content (capable of being interpreted as supporting a possible unified European imperialism) and Lenin's categorical rejection of any Eurocentric conception of the revolution. It was a rejection that undoubtedly betokened a very pessimistic appreciation of the state of the European workers' movement: "The time has passed for ever when the cause of democracy and socialism was directly tied to Europe."[7] His concomitant assertion of "revolutionary defeatism," this line representing a radical innovation for the culture of the international workers' movement, thus appeared indissociable from his reflection on the devastating consequences of the political implosion of August 1914. More precisely, it appeared indissociable from the unusual occupation that Lenin devoted himself to in the months that followed these events.

Lenin's Solitude

It was precisely in this context of generalized apocalypse that, attending to the most urgent tasks first (and as is generally the case, this always means for a while recourse to the old remedies, the real innovation being still to come), Lenin withdrew into the calm of a Berne library to plunge into his reading of Hegel. This moment was indeed in a very concrete sense that moment in which Lenin's political isolation, indeed the isolation of the minority of the workers' movement that set itself against the imperialist war, was at its greatest. This taking distance, this solitude, which is often to be found at moments of sudden change, not only among thinkers but also among men of action, is an absolutely necessary moment of the process of events itself: the caesura of the initial event (the war) is silently echoed in their taking distance, a silence from which the new initiative, the opening to the new, will resurge. It is only in the light of this *novum* that the process can retroactively appear as necessary, the self-criticism of thought interacting with the self-criticism of things themselves, which it recognizes as its own, without anything managing to reduce the share of contingency in this encounter, its complete lack of any advance guarantee.

The frequency of these moments of solitude in Lenin's life,[8] a life made up of long exiles and almost permanent struggle against the current, is in this sense indicative of its highly eventful tenor. This is why, far from disappearing, they reappear and establish themselves at the very heart of the most decisive period, that stretching from the start of the First World War to October 1917. Such moments include, for example, almost a year of so-called philosophical reading, chiefly devoted to Hegel, after August 1914; an enormous documentation on imperialism (eight hundred pages of notes and the famous booklet); and a tough theoretical work on the question of the state, culminating in the so-called Blue Notebook and the writing of *The State and Revolution* in the enforced retreat in nearby Finland, which he was "unable to complete," as in a writer's dream, owing to the meeting of discourse and reality in the October Revolution itself. Everything thus happened as if, in his stubbornness, Lenin managed to immobilize—or rather capture by turning it in a certain sense back on itself, creating this space around him—a historical time that did not cease its vertiginous acceleration.

The most competent biographies of Lenin have indeed stressed this fact. "Perhaps the most puzzling and inexplicable period of Lenin's life, from the standpoint of those . . . who would have us believe that he was pre-eminently an instinctive practical politician, are his activities in the turbulent months following the downfall of the autocracy in February 1917 . . . instead of devoting his time to political wheeler-dealing to achieve immediate tactical advantage to his party in Russia, he concentrated his energies on an almost academic, exhaustive study of Marx and Engels on the question of the state with a view to outlining the long-term strategic objectives of the global socialist revolution."[9] It is the other side of this solitude that is noted here: not a contemplative retreat, nor even a temporary halt to gather one's strength before moving again into action, but a distancing, a necessary removal from immediacy in order to radically rethink (from the roots) the conditions for action. To put it another way: if in order to grasp the conjuncture and trace the line of intervention it is necessary to replay and reconstitute one's theoretical bearings (Marxism not as a dogma but a "guide to action," in a favorite adage of Lenin's), then in the face of disaster it is a question of returning to the very basis, a theoretical refoundation of Marxism.

This is what undoubtedly explains not only the exceptional intensity of Lenin's theoretical intervention throughout the period opened by the First World War, but also its genuinely refounding significance and, as we shall see, its self-criticism: the systematic return to the texts of Marx and Engels was combined from the start with an enormous effort of theoretical updating and analysis of the new conditions raised by the imperialist total war. The impressive accumulation of empirical documentation went together with a re-examination of the very status of Marxism in the face of an orthodoxy that had irremediably shattered. The break involved in this situation was continued as a theoretical one: the crisis, even the disaster, could then in its very unpredictability be the basis of a new beginning and become absolutely constructive. It was in this effort, too, that Lenin found himself alone, as comparison with the best minds of the revolutionary movement, including Luxemburg, Trotsky, and Bukharin, readily confirms. It was not by chance that *none* of these figures, eminent thinkers and leaders of the international workers' movement as they were, went back to Hegel in this crucial period, or more generally to the so-called philosophical and theoretical aspects of Marxism.

The Breakthrough

Lenin thus began the new period with a reading of Hegel, to think through to the limit the break with the Second International, the "bankruptcy" of which had been sounded by the war. The writers who peopled his solitude, Hegel above all, thus became the object of a particular type of reading, indissociable from the political issues at stake in philosophy. If, as he himself admitted in his initial "emergency" reaction (in a text that was published only posthumously), "to the socialist it is not the horrors of war that are the hardest to endure—we are always for *'santa guerra di tutti gli oppressi per la conquista delle* loro *patrie!'* [a holy war of all the oppressed, for the conquest of their *own* fatherland]—but the horrors of the treachery shown by the leaders of present-day socialism, the horrors of the collapse of the present-day International," [10] this confessed "difficulty" served as a motor for a process of internal criticism and self-criticism that was already under way. The choice of Hegel—unique, and in appearance at least, highly improbable—and of

The Science of Logic in particular as his privileged and almost exclusive terrain for the decisive period from August to December 1914,[11] the period of this break, has itself to be understood as an *encounter* between several series of relatively heterogeneous determinations, which is only given the aspect of unity and convergence by its retrospective effect. Even if, concerning this itinerary, the task invoked several years ago by Michael Löwy in a pioneering text still remains to be completed ("it will one day be necessary to reconstitute precisely the itinerary that led Lenin from the traumatism of August 1914 to Hegel's *Logic*"),[12] we shall put forward here some hypotheses (four in particular) to try and reconstitute some aspects of this. More particularly, we shall put forth those that follow from the double intuition formulated by Löwy in the same text: Was the return to Hegel a "simple desire to return to the sources of Marxist thought, or a lucid intuition that the methodological Achilles' heel of Second International Marxism was its incomprehension of dialectics?"[13] Undoubtedly the answer is *both*, though it must immediately be made clear that the procedure of a "return to sources" has nothing "simple" about it, but actually offers the surest indication of the radical import of Lenin's action.

I.

This action should be understood first of all as an almost instinctive *reaction* to the devalorization or rather repression of Hegel and dialectics that was the distinctive sign of Second International Marxism in general, and particularly of Plekhanov, its Russian representative in philosophical questions, whose prestige was considerable throughout the International (with a small qualification that will be developed below). We need simply recall at this point how, basing itself mainly on the writings of the late Engels, themselves already simplified, the official doctrine of the Second International, from Mehring via Plekhanov to Kautsky, consisted in a variant of scientistic evolutionism and determinism with materialist pretensions, combined with a political quietism that, with the exception of Labriola, was challenged within the International only by the "revisionists" of right and left, from Bernstein to Sorel and Karl Liebknecht, almost always on the basis of neo-Kantian positions. In reality, this matrix fully participated in the typical intellectual climate of the time, that of late-nineteenth-century positivism imbued with the belief in progress, the mission of science, and of European civilization at the apogee of its colonial expansion. It is hardly an exaggeration to say that in its Russian variant, coming from a country with a very belated modernization and still dominated by the obscurantist forces of the *ancien régime*, these features were considerably reinforced. Plekhanov openly inscribed Marx in the line of the materialism of D'Holbach and Helvétius,[14] and in the continuity of a Russian Feuerbachian tradition, more particularly that of Chernychevsky, he proclaimed Feuerbach the great conqueror of Hegelian idealism, whose work Marx had essentially only continued.

That is true, we might say, but a similar reaction had already brought Lenin to the terrain of philosophy: that is, *Materialism and Empirio-Criticism*, a reaction to the defeated revolution of 1905 on the philosophical *Kampfplatz*.[15] But it is precisely the comparison between the two actions that is eloquent: from one end to the other in the work of 1908, in his confrontation between the "materialism" he professes and the empirio-criticism that he attacks, Lenin constantly appeals to Plekhanov as the unchallenged philosophical authority at that point (precisely up to the "crisis" opened up by the defeat of 1905) for all Russian Social Democrats. It was, indeed, Plekhanov who, whatever his differences with Kautsky, was his structural homologue in Russia, the unquestioned source of the speculative and even metaphysical scaffolding of the orthodoxy that irredeemably shattered in August 1914.

Six years later, it was Hegel, the *bête noire* of any "materialism," to whom Lenin turned, above all, to his dialectic—such an encumbrance, since it was this, the very apex of Hegelian idealism, that Marx claimed in the well-known formula to have "turned upside down" and "placed on its feet." It was a dialectic on which Plekhanov (and he was far from being an exception), the very specialist on philosophical questions of the Second International, had practically nothing at all to say in the thousands of pages of history and philosophical polemic that he wrote, as Lenin would note a few months after his own work on the *Logic*.[16] The little he did write, moreover, shows to what extent his intellectual universe, that of an entire epoch or nearly so, had become foreign to the tradition of German idealism. In his article "For the Sixtieth Anniversary of Hegel's Death,"[17] the only one that *Neue Zeit* published for this occasion (which already says much on the state of philosophical discussion within German Social Democracy), Plekhanov treated Hegel's views on world history, the philosophy of right, religion, and so forth in the manner of an encyclopedia article. The "historical influence of the geographical environment"[18] found some favor in his eyes—he undoubtedly detected here a "germ of materialism"—while the question of dialectics was literally dispatched in less than a page,[19] providing the opportunity to introduce the two or three quotations from Marx that were always invoked on this subject. The object of this repression was not exactly Hegel as such (in a certain sense, Hegel had been far less repressed among the Russian intelligentsia, Plekhanov included, than elsewhere in Europe), but rather the question of the dialectic in Hegel, the "essence of the matter," as Lenin said in settling his philosophical accounts with Plekhanov soon after his reading of the *Logic*.[20]

2.

My second hypothesis on the return to Hegel in this extreme conjuncture refers to Lenin's specific conception of philosophical intervention. What we should note here is effectively the other side of an almost inverted image: his *public* intervention in the philosophical *mêlée* opened up by the crisis of 1908 versus his *private*, almost secret quest, in the most arduous paths of metaphysics, under the impulse of the disaster of 1914. If it does indeed seem that the two were separated by an "abyss," [*abime*] as Henri Lefebvre termed it, and that the continuist arguments typical of a certain Leninism[21] can sustain neither a reading of the texts themselves nor a minimal perception of the conjunctures, it still remains that Lenin effectively retained something of his previous descent into the arena of philosophy. That is to say, in such conjunctures of "crisis," the specificity of which lay in the forms assumed by the resonance of the crisis in the revolutionary subject itself ("a terrible debacle has struck Social-Democracy"), the philosophical battle can assume first importance, since the theoretical issues at stake in it directly affect the status of political practice.

In the conjuncture of the "disaster" of the summer of 1914, this syllogism in a certain sense worked the other way around: the implosion of all Social Democratic politics changed everything in the domain of theory. Orthodoxy, in the emblematic figure of the Kautsky-Plekhanov duumvirate, collapsed along with the vote for war credits and the rallying to the *union sacrée*. To think through this bankruptcy, and destroy theoretically the matrix of the Second International, it was necessary to start by destroying the metaphysics that presided over the technics of the workers' organization.[22] And the weak link of Social Democratic metaphysics was Hegel. Not just any Hegel, and in particular not the Hegel that for a while interested Plekhanov; not the Hegel of the most immediate, external, political writings, but rather the speculative heart of the system, the dialectical method presented in *The Science of Logic*.

Lenin perfectly understood, in other words, that the real issue at stake in Hegel's system was not to be found in the most directly political or historical texts, but rather in the most abstract ones, the most metaphysical and most idealist. He thus broke in an irrevocable manner with the way of dealing with philosophical questions inherited from the late Engels and consecrated by the entire Second International, including his own "former philosophical consciousness": the division of philosophy into two opposing camps, materialism and idealism, each basically external to the other and expressing the interests of antagonistic classes. All the same — and as we shall see this raises certain further questions, we can even say that it is precisely here that the *punctum dolens* of the Hegel notebooks is to be found — if the distinction between materialism and idealism is grasped afresh in dialectical terms, and thus in a certain sense relativized, it is not for all that rejected, but rather (as we shall see) reformulated, reopened, or more exactly radicalized in the sense of a new materialism. To put it differently: leaving the stream of orthodoxy, Lenin did not change his philosophical camp, he did not become an idealist any more than he adhered to one of the philosophical revisionisms on offer, let alone invent his own. What he always categorically rejected was precisely this, a third way, middle or conciliatory, between materialism and idealism or beyond their opposition.[23] A posture of this kind would amount, moreover, to retaining the very terms of the theoretical mechanism that needed to be rejected *en bloc*. Lenin "simply" attempted — but this is indeed the nub of the difficulty — to *read Hegel as a materialist* and *in this way* open the way to a new beginning, a genuine refoundation, of Marxism itself.

3.

In the face of disaster, Lenin thus sought to return to the constitutive moment, the actual text of Marx. Even though it was written on commission, his text for the Granat encyclopedia[24] plays a revealing role in this respect. Straddling the moment of the disaster, it remains faithful, for the greater part of its exposition, to the Engels-Kautsky orthodoxy (particularly in its reprise of the canonical definitions of materialism). It is distinguished, however, by the place it gives to "philosophical" questions, which appear at the start of the presentation, something unusual in itself (especially in the context of a pedagogical text), as well as by the existence of a separate section titled "dialectics." Even if, here too, the text rehearses the typical formulae of orthodoxy, especially the primacy of evolution and development in nature and society, invoking in support of this (in the purest Plekhanov style) the "modern development of chemistry and biology" and even "the electrical theory of nature," it is none the less marked by a desire to distance itself from "vulgar" materialism, which was a rather suspect formulation, we should recall, in the eyes of the Second International, for which any materialism served well enough. Lenin did not hesitate to call this "metaphysics in the sense of anti-dialectics," an accusation that would scarcely be conceivable with Plekhanov, for whom the old materialism was at most simply "inconsistent," insufficiently materialist, and insufficiently faithful to the monism of "matter," to determinism by the socionatural "environment," or at the very most, "one-sided."[25]

In this same text, Lenin is equally concerned to distinguish, with an insistence very far from ordinary, between "evolution" according to Marx and the "current idea of evolution," the Marxian idea being one of evolution "by leaps, catastrophes, revolutions" (the key word here is surely "catastrophe");[26] he insists on the "dialectic" as the "revolutionary aspect of Hegel's philosophy," avoiding the customary distinction between Hegel's method and his system. His reference to the "Theses on Feuerbach," partial and distorted as this is, even so strikes a different tone from the orthodox commentators, and Plekhanov in particular. It is particularly significant that Lenin ended the section on "philosophical materialism" with a reference to the notion of "revolutionary practical activity"[27] that had been rigorously dismissed by the determinist evolutionism of orthodoxy.[28]

Lenin thus became aware of the need to return to the Feuerbach-Hegel nexus in order to tackle the question of Marxism at its foundations, to radically disembarrass it of the vulgate orthodoxy, what Marx called "the standpoint of old materialism" (the tenth thesis on Feuerbach). It should thus be no surprise that while this encyclopedia article was already in preparation for the publisher, and he had begun his reading of *The Science of Logic*, he inquired as to the possibility of changing parts of the article, especially that on dialectics.

4.

A further element arose, however, in the configuration of this moment of refoundation. In the theoretical radicalism that his solitude made possible, Lenin found himself inevitably faced with the need for a reconstruction in relation to the *national* revolutionary tradition, the famous "heritage" (a term customarily used by the opposition intelligentsia) of the founding figures of the Russian Enlightenment, and revolutionary democracy. It was a heritage that Lenin always proudly claimed, even as he was rejecting its confiscation by the populist current *of his time*, and asserting the legitimacy and necessity of a critical reconsideration of it. To put it another way, it was precisely the solitude of his reading in Berne that enabled Lenin to enter into a *free* dialogue, in a sense via the intermediary of Hegel, with these great ancestors, and especially the founding figure of Herzen.

This reference from one founding action to another, reactivated by a relationship reconstructed in the present and fully assumed as such, should be understood in a double sense: Herzen was above all the link connecting the Russian revolutionary heritage with the great current of the European revolutions of 1848. Brought up on Hegelianism, more precisely the Young Hegelians[29] (an "out of phase" phenomenon characteristic of a "late-comer" country: when Hegel reached Russia, it was both precociously and belatedly, already the Hegel of the Young Hegelian movement), and marked more particularly by a revolutionary reading under the impulse of Bakunin and Heine, whom he met in his Paris exile, Herzen was incontestably the first to raise the question of what was later to be known as "Russian non-contemporaneity."[30] Reformulating the "German" theme of a reversal of belatedness (extreme in the Russian case) as a possible "advance" (over other European countries)—no longer in the euphoric context of the years before 1848, but in that of defeat and despair—he traced the outlines of a "Russian road" as a singular way of access to the universal. Russia, protected by the very fact of its belatedness from the combined effects of the crushing of the democratic revolution *and* capitalist development, with its communitarian social forms still alive in its rural immensity, could thus open the way to an emancipation still more advanced than that initiated by the French Revolution of 1789 and glimpsed concretely in 1793–94, of which the bloody defeat in 1848 had sounded the bell for the rest of the continent swept by the wave of reaction. In solitude and defeat, in the void created by the counter-revolution everywhere triumphant, Herzen *discovered*, in his own terms, a new way forward, a historical possibility that was previously unheard of: "my discoveries made me giddy, an abyss opened before my eyes, and I felt the ground give way under my feet."[31]

This possibility of a radical historical opening went together in a sense, as we have seen, with the historical role of Herzen in the Russian reception of Hegel before 1848.[32] In the 1840s, against the previous generation of the Moscow intelligentsia molded by Schelling, he defended Hegel's *Logic*. Fed on Saint-Simonism even before setting himself to study philosophy and a reader of A. Cieszkowski, whose idea of a "philosophy of action" inspired him before he had started to read Hegel, he followed closely, along with other Russian intellectuals (in particular Belinski) the development of the Hegelian Left by way of the two leading reviews edited by Arnold Ruge (the *Hallische Jahrbücher*, which became the *Deutsche Jahrbücher* after Ruge's expulsion from Saxony). Persuaded of the revolutionary role of philosophy and its capacity to intervene actively in political actuality, Herzen set his sights on the proletariat as the central actor in the coming revolution as early as 1842 (before turning away from it under the effect of the massacres of June 1848 and the generalized defeat). It was Herzen who particularly coined the expression "algebra of revolution" to denote the Hegelian dialectic, a formula that Plekhanov liked to repeat and which he undoubtedly transmitted to Lenin, though the former often transformed it into an "algebra of *evolution*."[33]

A radical Young Hegelian therefore even before being a Hegelian, Herzen introduced into the bastion of European despotism the entire

Young Hegelian problematic, Feuerbach included. The consequences of this action were genuinely incalculable for generations of the Russian radical intelligentsia. They explain why, in the climate of generalized reaction that succeeded the defeats of the 1848 revolutions, and of which the repression of Hegel served as a rallying point on a European scale (starting with Germany, where he was treated as a "dead dog" as Marx famously wrote in the preface to *Capital*), the spirit of the '48ers survived precisely on this European periphery, in the heart of tsarist Russia.[34]

After the debacle, Herzen turned more particularly to the study of the sciences[35] and wrote his *Letters on the Study of Nature*, bathed in a climate of naturalist finalism, in which Hegelian *Naturphilosophie* vied for place with a pantheism of a Feuerbachian register and even overt shades of Schelling. The issue at stake, however, was clearly political: in fact, Herzen offered an account that based the possibility of human action and its transformative effects in a broad account of natural processes grasped in their inner finality and reflecting mediations. Here too his work played a founding role, and we can say that Russian materialism, which located itself in the continuity of these *Letters* and accentuated their Feuerbachian aspect, also shared its constitutive ambiguity. Chernychevsky, whose considerable impact on Lenin is well known, was here an emblematic case, in the same way as Plekhanov, who devoted a number of essays to him, including a work carefully annotated by Lenin in 1910–11.[36] The reference to Herzen thus leads in a number of ways to the Hegel-Feuerbach theoretical nexus, mediated by the exceptional tradition of the Russian reception of the two thinkers. And it was indeed in these terms, those of the relationship of materialism to revolution, that Lenin, while still within the framework of orthodoxy, summed up Herzen's achievement in his 1912 article "In Memory of Herzen." We find here the Lenin of before the disaster, who though recalling Herzen's "assimilation of Hegelian dialectic" as condensed in the formula "algebra of revolution," immediately went on to praise the publisher of *Kolokol*, in the strictest Plekhanovite orthodoxy, of "going beyond Hegel, following Feuerbach toward materialism."[37] This occurred despite the fact that, shortly before writing this text, the marginal notes that Lenin made on Plekhanov's work on Chernychevsky show how he was aware of the basically *contemplative* character of this materialism, even going so far as to detect traces of this in Plekhanov himself.[38] The fact remains that throughout the discussion of the road to revolution in Russia, Hegel and his intellectual successors were implicitly present right from the start.

Lenin's path to Hegel thus leads us back to three other paths, each with their distinct modalities, but also with an inner necessity. Independently of one another, but broadly stemming from the same theoretical trunk, Herzen and Marx had to resolve the same political enigma, which was nothing other than that of the non-contemporaneity of their respective social formations, the reversal of their tardiness into advance, the initiative that would transform the very terms of this "too early" and "too late" to posit the specific actuality of the revolutionary process in a determinate conjuncture. But this, as Lenin would discover in his turn, was nothing more than the dialectic.

Textures

We have thus now arrived at the actual text of Lenin's notebooks on Hegel's *Logic*. Before tackling what Lenin found in this reading of Hegel, it is necessary to dwell for a moment on what the majority of commentators mention only in passing, when they do not reduce it to a mere limitation of the text or a shortfall from the philological norms that a philosophical commentary should fulfill. We should therefore start by saying that Lenin's notebooks on Hegel's *The Science of Logic* do not really exist! They share this status with a number of other mythic texts in the Marxist tradition, and beyond,[39] that is, of being manuscripts written for private use, or at least not intended for publication in the state in which we know them. In these eminent cases, the very form of their publication *always* constitutes a theoretical issue in itself, and even a directly political one, particularly for texts in the Marxist tradition, and these notebooks on Hegel in particular. Should they be included—and thus diluted, as some would say—in a mass of other notes and materials from very diverse periods, as the early Soviet editions had it? Should they be separated out to give them their due prominence, as in the pioneering effort of Lefebvre and Guterman?[40] Or should one adopt an intermediate solution as the Soviet editions did from a certain date (1955), and in their wake, those of the international Communist movement?

There is still more involved in these questions of form: the notebooks on Hegel's *Logic* are a very strange text, unique even in the Marxist tradition. As a set of notes and a collection of extracts from Hegel's works, they appear as an incredible *collage*, a text that is constitutionally fragmented and heterogeneous, being made up of several levels that are constantly intertwined and function as a number of relatively autonomous texts, subtexts, and intertexts. Each of them permanently refers to the others, and in particular to an absent (sub)text, that is, everything that is *not* recopied from *The Science of Logic*. The radically broken up and incomplete (or rather incompletable) aspect of the text, its *montage effect*, in the sense of synthetic cubism or the cinema of Vertov, is still further accentuated by the linguistic babble that is its distinctive mark: extracts from Hegel, generally in German but sometimes translated into Russian, mingle with annotations referring to these extracts, which are generally in Russian but also—and some of the most striking—in French or German, as well as sometimes even odd phrases in English. Without even speaking of their form as such, Lenin's marginal annotations resort to all kinds of schemas, abbreviations, tables, and diagrams, readily mixing the quasi-scholarly summary with a highly elaborate commentary, and the whole with a consummate use of aphorism. We find here a Lenin who does not hesitate to resort to irony or even insult.

The hypothesis that I will risk advancing here is that this very improbable construction of the Hegel notebooks, their material texture as an object, is necessarily related to the status explicitly claimed by their author, that of an attempted *materialist* reading of a canonical text of classical German philosophy. To put it another way, it is their very form, or rather their total absence of pre-established form, their completely experimental dimension, through which the Hegel notebooks are the expression of this paradox that is the emergence of something like "materialism" in philosophy (but, it must undoubtedly be said, in its lacunae, its internal gaps).

Before returning to this question of materialism, we have to sketch an initial presentation of the lines of force around which this extremely disparate material is organized. What was it that interested Lenin in *The Science of Logic*, what were the points at which his radical and solitary act of theoretical recommencement was to cross paths with, and even bump into, the text of Hegel? It seems possible to distinguish at least three, all placed under the sign of the dialectic as logic of contradiction, which enabled them to communicate with the notes devoted to the other philosophical literature that Lenin devoured around the same period.[41] They signal lines of rupture with both orthodoxy and with his own former philosophical consciousness.

I

The dialectic not as a "method" external to its object, or dissociable from Hegel's "system" (in the formulations of the late Engels),[42] but as the very positing of the immanence and self-movement of things grasped by thought, a thought traversed by the same movement and returning on itself. Since each thing is at once itself and its other, its unity breaks up, it divides by reflecting itself into itself and becomes other by tearing itself away from this moment of difference itself, canceling it in a certain fashion by the assertion of its "absolute" identity in the very movement of its self-mediation.

2

This self-movement must itself be understood not in the trivial sense of a "flux," the course of things, and all sorts of hydraulic metaphors dear to orthodoxy, but rather as a unity of opposites, contradictions internal to things themselves, and the unfurling of this contradiction in the strictest immanence. Thus the positing of extremes and the ascent to extremes, the transition from one extreme to the other in the very movement that opposes them, the sudden reversal of situations. The assertion of the creative power of *division*, the work of the negative, eliminates any evolutionist vision of "transition," and in particular of "leaps" as an acceleration of "evolution" or of "opposites" as mere complementary terms within a totality.

3

Self-movement is *transformative activity* and the grasping of this activity in its processual character, as revolutionary practice. This third point is the most delicate. It directly touches the questions of the materialist reading to which Lenin submitted Hegel's text. To put the matter very schematically, Lenin sought to draw support from the "active/subjective side" of the Hegelian concept, which he directly tied to the appreciation made of the "active/subjective side" of idealism in general in the "Theses on Feuerbach."[43] But he categorically rejected, in the name of materialism, the abolition of objectivity in the self-movement of categories, the omnipotence of a thought capable, in its internal unfurling, of setting itself up as a superior instance able to digest reality itself. In order to avoid any ontological temptation in the mode of exposition of the categories, Lenin reintroduced into this new attempt a piece of his former mechanism of philosophical intervention, the theory of "reflection" from *Materialism and Empirio-Criticism*. This was indeed even a central piece, equipped with all the guarantees of Engelsian and Plekhanovite orthodoxy that furnished the target of the *Philosophical Notebooks*. This non-contemporaneity of problematics at the very heart of Lenin's reading of the *Logic* has historically been the focus of all the difficulties in interpreting Lenin's effort, alternatively rejected due to an implied distrust of Hegelian categories, or on the contrary praised as a fundamental continuity with the "materialism" of 1908.

It is at this point that we have to introduce the hypothesis that will order the indications that follow. Undeniably, the notebooks that Lenin kept during his reading of the *Logic* were his logbook of an experience that was at the same time a discovery of and a resistance to Hegel. There is nothing illogical in this sense, in seeing the presence of the category of "reflection"—posited at the start as a touchstone of the "materialist reading" that Lenin proposed to conduct—as an element of "primary materialism," a residue of Plekhanovite orthodoxy that Lenin actually bent himself to transcend, in sum the very index of the limit of Lenin's reading of Hegel, or in other words, of his break with the orthodoxy of the Second International.

The terms of the question have been clearly formulated by Slavoj Žižek:

> The problem with Lenin's "theory of reflection" lies in its implicit idealism: its compulsive insistence on the independent existence of material reality outside consciousness is to be read as a symptomatic displacement, destined to conceal the fact that consciousness itself is implicitly

posed as external to the reality it "reflects." . . . Only a consciousness observing the reality from the outside world would see the whole of reality "the way it really is" . . . , just as a mirror can reflect an object perfectly only if it is external to it. . . . The point is not that there is an independent reality out there, outside myself; the point is that I myself am "out here," part of that reality.[44]

To put this in the language of Hegel's *Logic*, what Lenin did not see, in this argument, is that this initial externality of being and consciousness is transcended and thus abolished by the subjective activity that the concept precisely denotes. And the "reflection" or rather *Reflexion* (the German term has rather the sense of "consideration") can then be understood not as a copy of external reality but as the moment of mediation, of the negative: the movement that, in the multiplicity of its moments, exhibits the reciprocal presupposition of externality and internality, and the immanence of the former within the latter, now genuinely posited as interior, an essential internal mediation: not something other than being, but being itself revealed, at rock bottom, in the reflecting movement of its own depth.

We know, however, that what interested Lenin above all in *The Science of Logic* was precisely the economy of the "subjective logic" (the "doctrine of the notion") as a way of grasping the rationality of practice, labor, and the activity of knowledge as modalities of the transformation of the real. The decisive point on which we have to insist is that it was by the very act of resisting Hegel that Lenin transformed his own categories and thus transformed himself. This is precisely how the genuine function of the extraordinary "collage" of the Hegel notebooks should be grasped: as a thought experiment that introduces "vulgar materialism," in the manner of a scandalous parataxis, into the very heart of the "Summa Theologica" of idealism, rather in the way that Adorno, especially in his aesthetic writings, asserted—by very direct references to class and "orthodox" reminders of the primacy of the object—the omnipresence of the social totality (repressive and even nightmare-like) in the very texture of the elements that seek to break it.[45] If this is the case, then the persistence of elements of "vulgar materialism" in the Hegel notebooks must itself be understood as the trace of the unprecedented violence that the eruption of imperialist war had brought into the very midst of the most "abstract" mechanism of the modern philosophical enterprise, the pure science of thought, or science of pure thought, that Hegel sought to achieve in his *Logic*.

The notion of "reflection," therefore, we must stress from the start, was not abandoned, but as we shall see, was itself "dialecticized" in a mechanism with a double action: to let the true content of Hegel's logic emerge in order to reconstruct the Hegel-Marx relationship, which had been massively repressed by orthodoxy, and to restore at the same stroke the properly revolutionary impulse of Marxism itself, its dialectical heart. In this process, "reflection" becomes something quite different from the initial assertion (in the opening pages of Lenin's notebook on the *Logic*) of the externality of matter to consciousness, or the irreducibility of nature to spirit. To anticipate a little here, the result that Lenin arrived at is that the genuine "materialist reversal" of Hegel did not lie, as the late Engels thought, and Plekhanov and other temple guardians of the Second International repeated ad nauseam, in asserting the primacy of being over thought, but rather in understanding the subjective activity displayed in the "logic of the notion" as the "reflection," idealist and thus inverted, of revolutionary practice, which transforms reality by revealing in it the result of the subject's intervention. And it is here that Hegel was infinitely closer to materialism than the orthodox "materialists" (or the pre-Marxist earlier versions of materialism), since he was closer to the *new* materialism, that of Marx, which asserted the primacy not of "matter" but of the activity of *material transformation* as revolutionary practice. The promise of a "materialist reading of Hegel" was thus kept, but in a manner far removed from that which its author initially envisaged.

Bearings

In his notes on the first book of the *Logic*, the doctrine of Being, Lenin set down his reading protocol in a box that starts with the exclamation "Nonsense about the Absolute," and continues as follows: "I am in general trying to read Hegel materialistically: Hegel is materialism which has been stood on its head (according to Engels)—that is to say, I cast aside for the most part God, the Absolute, the pure Idea, etc."[46] At the end of his reading of this work, after having devoted dozens of pages of notes to precisely what he was going to "cast aside" (that is, Book Three on subjective logic and its third section on "the Idea," the bulk of these notes being on the third and last chapter of this, the "Absolute Idea," though this occupies less than a third of this section), Lenin wrote these famous concluding remarks: "It is noteworthy that the whole chapter on the 'Absolute Ideas' scarcely says a word about God . . . and apart from that—*this NB*—it contains almost nothing that is specifically *idealism*, but has for its main subject the *dialectical method*. The sum-total, the last word and essence of Hegel's logic is the *dialectical method*—this is extremely noteworthy. And one thing more: in this *most idealistic* of Hegel's works there is the *least* idealism and the *most materialism*. 'Contradictory,' but a fact!"[47] It is this genuine reversal of perspective that gives the measure of the distance he had traveled.[48] The transformation of the category of "reflection" thus effected will serve us as an indicator signaling the results reached at each of the steps crossed.

Soon after announcing the protocol of a "materialist reading of Hegel" as already mentioned, Lenin gives an initial definition of reflection: coextensive with the "dialectic" itself, it exists inasmuch as it "reflects the material process in all its aspects and in its unity," thus becoming a "correct reflection of the eternal development of the world."[49] There is thus on the one hand the material world and its "eternal development," and on the other hand the "reflection" of this world and its development in the "multiform and universal flexibility" of specifically dialectical categories—a flexibility "that extends to the unity of opposites," Lenin adds. In concluding his notes on the first part of the doctrine of Essence, Lenin—shaken by the development devoted to the category of "*Reflexion*"—tries for a last time to find in this modality of recourse to "reflection" the confirmation of a "materialist reversal of Hegel."[50] This confirmation is closely bound up with the conception of the dialectic as a "*picture* of the world." And it is the metaphor of Heraclitean inspiration of the river and its drops, and of concepts as so many "registrations" of "individual aspects of the movement" and their components, that serves him as illustration.[51] This metaphor finds its place in the context of the "eternal development of the world," to resume the formulation already cited, that is, of a flux or fundamental movement *external to the observer*, who only contemplates it from the

bank. It is a movement of this kind that is involved in the initial definition of "reflection," that of the world assimilated to a "great whole,"
from which history and human practice appear strangely absent.

Up to this point, we are still in strict continuity with the late Engels,
especially his text on Ludwig Feuerbach, which was canonized by
the orthodoxy of the Second International: making a distinction between Hegel's "system," which is idealist and conservative, and his
"method"—that is, the dialectic—which is critical and revolutionary,
and like science made up of "general and universal laws of motion" and
development, of both nature and human action. These laws in turn are
simply the reflection of the real movement, objective in the mind of the
thinker, and not the other way round as Hegel believed, the Absolute
Idea for him alienating itself and debasing itself into nature. "Put back
on its feet" in this way, the dialectic of concepts is the conscious reflection of the dialectical movement of the real and objective world.[52]

For Lenin, however, things soon start to get more complicated, very
seriously so, when the doctrine of Essence is reached. True, his fairly
brief notes on the doctrine of Being ended with the well-known excla-
mations on the "leaps"[53] and their necessity, thus a certain distancing
from the gradualism that orthodoxy inescapably associated with its
conception of the great organically linked totality of the universe in perpetual motion. His remarks on Hegel's prefaces to the work had equally
led him to sense the difficulty of dissociating "system" and "method,"
inasmuch as logic, according to Hegel, required forms that are "*gehalt-
volle Formen*, forms of living, real content, inseparably connected with
the content."[54] But it is only with his reading of the doctrine of Essence
that Lenin started to take the measure of the unsatisfactory character,
indeed naïve and cobbled together, of his "materialist" dualisms, and
to penetrate into the level of immanence that unfurls in the categories
of Hegelian logic.

As a "reflection into itself," essence is identified with the reflecting
movement internal to being itself. Outward appearance is only the reflection of the essence in itself, not something other than being, but
being posited in externality and as externality in order to recognize
that this movement of positing of itself proceeds from itself, from its
own internality. This "return on itself" does not mean that externality
is mere projection or reduplication of internality, it is rather already

there, presupposed and inscribed in the internality itself, and enabling the totality to engage the movement of its own determination. Returning to the metaphor of the river, Lenin understands that if it is possible to distinguish between the "foam" and the "deep currents," then "*even the foam* is an expression of essence!"[55] To put it another way, the essence's appearance, the "reflection," is not so much an illusion to be reduced (by bringing it back to the true material being of which it is only the imitation) as the projected image of an external movement. It is the initial moment of a process of self-determination leading to the unfurling of the real as effectivity (*Wirklichkeit*). Hence the problems of terminology that Lenin considers for the proper translation of the term "*Reflexion.*"[56] Hence too his enthusiasm, just after reading the pages devoted to the three forms of reflecting movement (forms that he elsewhere found "expounded very obscurely"[57]), when he discovers the true level of immanence that the Hegelian "movement" reveals. Not the flux, the flow of the universe observed from a position outside, but rather self-movement (*Selbstbewegung*): "Movement and 'self-movement' (this NB! Arbitrary [independent], spontaneous, internally necessary movement) . . . who would believe that this is the core of 'Hegelianism,' of abstract and abstrusen . . . Hegelianism? This core had to be discovered, understood, *hinüberretten*, laid bare, refined, which is precisely what Marx and Engels did."[58]

If this is the case, then the concept of "law" must be stripped of its "simplification" and "fetishization":[59] this is the object of Lenin's remarks on the following section of the doctrine of Essence, which is devoted to the "phenomenon." Lenin understands completely the anti-relativist and anti-subjectivist sense of Hegel's analysis of *Erscheinung*, the phenomenon as reprise of being in its essential consistency, unity of appearance and essence (where neo-Kantian subjectivism stubbornly dissociated these). As the initial expression of essence as ground, the concept of law is in effect located at the level of the phenomenon. For Hegel, law is "the Reflection of Appearance into identity with itself," immediately present in the appearance as its "quiescent reflection." Lenin approves: "This is a remarkably materialistic and remarkably appropriate (with the word *ruhige*) determination. Law takes the quiescent—and therefore law, every law, is narrow, incomplete, approximate."[60]

To be sure, we can see this as simply a reprise of the theory of "reflection," approximate but ever more "faithful" copy, "close" to "objective" and "material" reality.[61] But this perception of the fundamentally *limited* character of external laws represents a considerable shift in relation to the cardinal thesis of orthodoxy, which Lenin had so insisted on in *Materialism and Empirio-Criticism*, positing "the necessity of nature" as "primary" and "human will and mind" as "secondary": "The latter must *necessarily* and *inevitably adapt themselves* to the former."[62] It was from this ontology that Lenin deduced the necessity for "social consciousness and class consciousness in all capitalist countries" to "adapt" to the "objective logic of economic evolution," a logic reflected in the "laws of historical development."[63] In his reprise of the Hegelian conception of laws in the Hegel notebooks, however, there is already an initial grasp of the pre-inscription of subjectivity, the activity of knowledge, at the very heart of objectivity, in the internal movement of the essence:

> Law is relation. This NB for the Machists and other agnostics, and for the Kantians, etc. Relation of essences or between essences.
>
> The beginning of everything can be regarded as inner—passive—and at the same time as outer. But what is interesting here is not that, but something else: Hegel's criterion of dialectics that has accidentally slipped in: "in all natural, scientific and intellectual development" here we have a grain of profound truth in the mystical integument of Hegelianism![64]

It is only subsequent to this, in the notes devoted to "subjective logic," that Lenin realizes how this criterion did not escape Hegel "by oversight," but represents this "active side" of "sensuous human activity," "developed in a one-sided manner by idealism" (rather than materialism), which Marx refers to in the first of the "Theses on Feuerbach." He then reformulates the process of knowledge not as a rapprochement to the concrete, but on the contrary, as a process of *growing* abstraction (including among its results the natural laws as "scientific abstraction"), a process that opens out to *practice*, and, grasped as a whole, to the knowledge of truth.[65] He has no hesitation now in identifying "the true sense, the significance and the role of logic for Hegel" with the revelation of the power of thought as *abstraction*, in the *distance* therefore that separates it from the object. It is a distance that properly speaking is not a distance from anything, devoid of any proper thickness; this is what "reflection" now denotes, assimilated to the work of thought (the "formation of abstraction concepts and the operations made with them") as a *process* revealing the objectivity of subjective knowledge as an integral part of the self-exfoliation of the world.[66]

Aphorisms

It is this proposition that led Lenin to formulate three of the most famous "aphorisms" (the term he himself uses) that figure in the Hegel notebooks: the first of these assimilates Plekhanov—and through him, implicitly, the metaphysics of the Second International as a whole—to "vulgar materialism," as his critique of Kant and "agnosticism" remains an extrinsic critique, below the work of (self-)rectification of categories reached by Hegel in his own critique of Kant. The second aphorism, this time *explicitly*, focuses on the "Marxists . . . at the beginning of the twentieth century" for having criticized the "Kantians and Humists more in the manner of Feuerbach (and Büchner) than of Hegel."[67] It is undoubtedly here that we should see Lenin as crossing a definite threshold on his route. Plekhanov, the unchallenged philosophical authority of Russian Social Democracy in all its tendencies and the inventor of "dialectical materialism," the official metaphysics of the Second International, was irrevocably deposed. And the root of his "vulgar materialism" is indicated: it lies in his incomprehension of the dialectic, which brings him back below the level reached by Hegel in his immanent critique of Kant, this having become the new reference model of intervention in philosophy.[68]

By replacing Hegel with Feuerbach (an action that Lenin fully approved of before 1914),[69] Plekhanov had in fact regressed to the level of "vulgar materialism." His "monism," which he had presented as the foundation of a finished materialist philosophy, was thus located below Marx's materialism.

Lenin made this realization the pivot of a real settling of accounts with his own "former philosophical consciousness," generalizing its scope to the whole set of Second International Marxists. He included himself in that generalization, since he refers explicitly on two occasions to the philosophical battle of the previous decade (against "contemporary Kantianism and Machism," the critique conducted by "Marxists" "at the start of the twentieth century . . . of Kantians and Humeans"), a battle in which, with *Materialism and Empirio-Criticism*, he was one of the main protagonists. In an important manuscript written soon after these reading notes on *The Science of Logic*, Lenin even went so far as to distance himself from the late Engels, whom he reproaches, just like Plekhanov, of flattening the dialectic to a "sum-total of examples," in the interest of "popularization."[70]

Lenin's third "aphorism" enabled him to explore a previously unknown track, completely inconceivable in the intellectual horizon of "orthodoxy," that of a study of Hegel's *Logic* as an indispensable key to the understanding of *Capital* (and "in particular its first chapter"), which led him to the famous conclusion that "Consequently, half a century later none of the Marxists understood Marx!"[71] The question of the Hegel-Marx relationship thus leaves the terrain of formalism and generalities on the "dialectical method" and "gnoseology" to relocate at the heart of fundamental discoveries stored in the theory of the capitalist mode of production. Lenin, as has already been emphasized elsewhere,[72] was not only the first Marxist of the twentieth century to open this workshop on reading *Capital*, and more particularly on its mode of exposition, in the light of the Hegelian *Logic*. He himself offers some indications in this sense, scattered throughout the Hegel notebooks and subsequently resumed in a more compact fashion in a text of 1915 devoted to the "plan of the dialectic (logic) of Hegel." He identifies here the object of the famous first chapter of *Capital*, the commodity, with the moment of Being, and the value/price couple as that of Essence and Appearance.[73] These intuitions, fragmentary and barely sketched out (though they have been abundantly discussed in the Marxist tradition) are certainly debatable, yet they should not lead us to forget the essential point: that through these collages of quotations and notes taken in a Berne library, something began that would mark the twentieth century as a whole.

Praxis

Let us return to the shift in the category of "reflection." Lenin was now in a position to define it as a *processus*, grasped in the immanence of the real in movement: "Knowledge is the reflection of nature by man. But this is not a simple, not an immediate, not a complete reflection, but the process of a series of abstractions, the formation and development of concepts, laws, etc., and these concepts, laws, etc. (thought, science = "the logical Idea") *embrace* conditionally, approximately, the universal law-governed character of eternally moving and developing nature."[74] The idea of knowledge as an active process, historically unfurling, starts to emerge, but it is only when he moves on to Hegel's analysis of labor in the following section ("objectivity"), as activity oriented toward a goal, with finality (*zweckmässig*), that Lenin manages to re-elaborate a more satisfactory notion of practice, enabling him to return to the reflection-*processus*. In his analysis of the labor process as a syllogism Hegel had stressed the importance of mediation, the instrument or tool as a means of transcending the external and limited character of the subjective purpose by the manifestation of its rational content. In this aspect of the analysis, which in a certain manner is immediately and familiarly "materialist" ("the plough is more honourable than are those immediate enjoyments which are procured by it, and serve as Ends," writes Hegel[75]), Lenin sees the "germs of historical materialism" and goes so far as to posit "historical materialism as one of the applications and developments of the ideas of genius—seeds existing in embryo in Hegel."[76]

This aspect of things is well known, but the essential point is in a certain sense absent here. The conclusion that Lenin goes on to draw from this analysis of rational or teleological activity (oriented to a purpose) is double. At first, he grasps the significance of Hegel's analysis of human activity as mediation toward the "truth," the absolute identity of concept and object, an objective truth that includes and recognizes in itself the work of subjectivity. It is in this way, therefore (and not simply by the rehabilitation of the tool, which is after all only an initial form of mediatization of the rationality of the subjective purpose) that Hegel is seen as being "very close to" historical materialism, defined in terms of the second thesis on Feuerbach as the primacy of practice: "the view that man by his *practice* proves the objective correctness of his ideas, concepts, knowledge, science";[77] the "correctness" is immanent in these practices, which produce their own criteria of validity.

By the same token, the "materialist inversion" of Hegel acquires a different meaning: it is no longer the relationship between nature and spirit, thought and Being, or matter and the Idea that is at issue here, but the relation, the "identity," between logic and practical activity. It is here that the "very deep, purely materialist content" of Hegel's propositions has to be sought. The "materialist reversal" consists then in asserting the *primacy of practice*, which produces the very axioms of logic itself (by the repetition, "a thousand million times," of different logical figures in human activity). Lenin formulates this idea in a more precise fashion in his copious notes on the final section of the *Logic* (the Idea): "For Hegel *action*, practice, is a *logical 'syllogism,'* a figure of logic. And that is true! Not, of course, in the sense that the figure of logic has its other being in the practice of man (= absolute idealism), but vice versa: man's practice, repeating itself a thousand million times, becomes consolidated in man's consciousness by figures of logic."[78] He thus rejects any ontological pretension of the *Logic*, not in an external, "vulgar" sense, but starting from its identity with practice and turning it back on itself, grasping it on the basis of the process character of praxis, of which it represents a moment of externalization.

The conditions are then fulfilled for a final return to the notion of "reflection": the *processus* of knowledge that it denotes can now be understood as an activity of material transformation of the world, in which logical categories "fix" the conceptual matrix: "the human notion 'definitively' catches this objective truth of cognition, seizes and masters it, only when the notion becomes 'being-for-itself' in the sense of practice. That is, the practice of man and of mankind is the test, the criterion of the objectivity of cognition." "Is that Hegel's idea?," Lenin immediately wonders, sensing the importance of the question, before ending this note with the significant words "it is necessary to return to this."[79] His response comes a few lines further on, in the commentary devoted to the transition from chapter 2 ("The Idea of Cognition") to the following chapter ("The Absolute Idea"). These for-mulations unquestionably represent the ultimate expression of Lenin's break with orthodoxy: "undoubtedly, in Hegel practice serves as a link in the analysis of the process of cognition, and indeed as the transition to objective ('absolute,' according to Hegel) truth. Marx, consequently, clearly sides with Hegel in introducing the criterion of practice into the theory of knowledge: see the Theses on Feuerbach." And, giving the *coup de grâce* to the "vulgar" conception of reflection as gradual adaptation of consciousness to an impassive objective reality, he immediately adds in the margin: "Man's consciousness not only reflects the objective world, but creates it."[80]

Not only, but also: in fact, if knowledge is indeed practical, Lenin does not forget the reminder in the "Theses on Feuerbach" of its character as *material* transformation: if, "in contradistinction to materialism" "the *active* side was developed abstractly by idealism," idealism "of course does not know real (*wirklich*), sensuous (*sinnlich*) activity as such."[81] The reprise of the category of "reflection" in the Hegel notebooks functions here as a reminder of "sensuousness," a typically Feuerbachian category that Marx recycled in his theses, transforming it here into a sensuousness that breaks with contemplation (still a characteristic of Feuerbach, as of all previous materialism). The material character of "effective" (*wirklich*) transformative activity is thus denoted, at grips with an external world that resists it. "Translating" a Hegelian phrase in materialist fashion, Lenin writes in this sense that "the activity of the end is not directed against itself . . . but aims, by destroying definite (sides, features, phenomena) of the *external* world, at *giving itself reality in the form of external actuality.* . . ."[82] Although this formulation was certainly cobbled together and revised some pages later (see the passage below, where Lenin recognizes that human activity actually removes the "features of externality" from the world), it investigates the services expected of this exercise.

Knowledge is therefore a moment (and just one moment) of practice: it is the transformation of the world according to the modalities specific to this. The metaphor of reflection as an "objective picture of the world" returns, but is reversed here in the dimension of practice: "The activity of man, who has constructed an objective picture of the world for himself, *changes* external actuality, abolishes its determinateness (= alters some sides or other, qualities, of it), and thus removes from it the features of Semblance, externality and nullity, and makes it as being in and for itself (= objectively true)."[83] There is no longer a "picture" in any real sense; it dissolves as it were under our eyes and is abolished in the material activity of its fabrication. Or rather, as the pictorial revolution of Manet had already announced in a practical way,[84] it is the picture itself that becomes the means of knowledge and intervention for the appearances and significations of the world, and in this sense, a process of transformation, of testing, of this same world by the specific materiality of the techniques applied by the painter.

The Real Materialist Reversal

Lenin was now ready to tackle Hegel's final chapter on the "Absolute Idea," for this, as he noted immediately, is nothing more than "the unity of the theoretical idea (of knowledge) *and of practice*—this NB— and this unity *precisely in the theory of knowledge.*" [85] The unity of theory and practice in theory itself, that was the standpoint of the "absolute method." "What remains to be considered is no longer *Inhalt*, but . . . 'the universal element of its form—that is, the *method.*'" [86] Universality has thus to be sought on the side of *form* and not content. What Lenin glimpsed here, despite the limits of his understanding of certain essential points of Hegel (above all the quadruple character of the dialectical process, that is, the fact that negation has to be counted "twice," related to itself as "absolute" negation, pure difference that disappears in the result[87]), was the self-referential character of the Absolute, the fact that, as against what Engels wrote in "Ludwig Feuerbach," [88] the Absolute Idea is not "a dogmatic content" (identifiable with "Hegel's system" as the ultimate end of knowledge), persisting impassively, but rather the process itself taken to its point of self-reference, at which it is now itself one of its own moments. This is the dazzling moment of the reversal of perspective, at which we understand that "within" the theory itself, there is always already the unity of theory and practice (a thesis that Gramsci was to develop in an extraordinary manner), that the question of the unity of "form" and "content" is itself a question of form, of "absolute" form outside of which no content subsists.

To grasp the dialectic as "absolute method" is thus not to render a sum of categories "flexible" or fluid, in a constant attempt to embrace a process that overflows them: it is to "localize the motive forces of their movement *in the immanence of their own contradiction.*" [89] This is why, at the end of the day, the chapter on the "Absolute Idea," in Lenin's final remark, "scarcely says a word about God . . . [and] contains almost nothing that is specifically idealism." There is in fact no need for an "Absolute Idea" in the sense of ultimate Truth or Meaning beyond the world, for this world *is* already in itself, reduced to the movement of its self-mediation, the truth that is sought beyond it. This chapter thus retrospectively supplies the meaning of *The Science of Logic* as a whole: "in this most *idealistic* of Hegel's works there is the *least* idealism and the *most materialism*,"[90] The paradox of the "transition from idealism to materialism" does not consist in "removing" the idealism, but, on the contrary, of "adding more." If "Marx agrees with Hegel," in Lenin's formulation, it is in absolutizing the absolute idealism itself.

To put it another way, the materialist reversal is to be understood as an *event* of which idealism proves to be the bearer. It is not a transition (gradual or sudden) to an opposite camp, defined in exteriority, like the movement from one army to another, but the result of an internal transformation triggered by the eruption of the antagonism actually within the philosophical "battleground," and in the very materiality of the written form: as the insurrection of the Silesian weavers was the trigger for Marx's Paris manuscripts, so was the First World War for Lenin's *Philosophical Notebooks*, and the rise of fascism for Gramsci's *Quaderni*. It is not by chance that in each of these cases we find ourselves faced with texts that deny the very notion of a "work"—fragmentary and incomplete in the extreme, the extremity of the situations of which they bear, or indeed are, the mark, and in which their vocation is to disappear in the effects that they contribute to producing.

As absolute method, the dialectic is thus nothing but the sum of its results. It is good dialectical logic that Lenin did not write another book, or even a philosophical text, in any way comparable to *Materialism and Empirio-Criticism*. This is tantamount to saying that the new position that Lenin attained with his reading of Hegel is to be sought nowhere else than in his political and theoretical intervention in the years that followed the First World War. Without repeating the demonstrations that others have already given,[91] I shall confine myself to what seems to me the irreducible core. This lies in the two theses that seal the sequence of the years 1914–17.

The first is the thesis of the transformation of the imperialist war into a civil war, in its double dimension of struggle for national liberation in the colonies and by the oppressed peoples, and anti-capitalist revolution within the metropolises. A real dialectical reversal, this thesis assumes the understanding of the war as an antagonistic *processus* and not a classic inter-state conflict, in which the question is to "turn" the eruption of the masses in the "total war" into an armed insurrection, to reverse in other words the power of the masses channeled into the industry of massacre by turning it against the enemy within, the colonial power or dominant bourgeoisie.

The second is the thesis of the transformation of the "bourgeois-democratic" revolution into a proletarian revolution, as formulated in the "Letters from Afar" and the "April Theses," which lead on to the initiative of October 1917. Here again, the question is to place oneself in the immanence of the contradictions of the revolutionary process, in a determinate situation, thus diametrically opposed both to the "stages" vision of Social Democratic orthodoxy (which Lenin shared at the start of the war) and to abstract (or abstractly correct) views as to the inability of the Russian bourgeoisie to resolve the tasks of a democratic revolution. The reversal of the democratic revolution into a proletarian revolution was in no way an organic development or a linear radicalization, a passage from the horizon of the "minimum program" to that of the "maximum program," but a vital decision in the face of "imminent catastrophe." It was in this turning the immediate demands of the masses, democratic and not directly socialist (peace, land, workers' and people's control), against the "bourgeois democratic" framework that concretely resolved the situation of dual power: by a mass initiative under proletarian leadership aiming at the conquest of political power, that is, breaking the existing state apparatus and replacing it with a contradictory state, the bearer of a tendency to its own demise. As Slavoj Žižek has forcefully emphasized, the transition from the moment of "February" to that of "October" was in no way a transition from one "stage" to another, a symptom of "maximalism" or a voluntarist leap above the "immaturity" of conditions, but rather a radical questioning of the very notion of "stage," a reversal of the fundamental coordinates that define the very criteria of the "maturity" of a situation.[92]

In the event that bears the name of Lenin, the *Philosophical Notebooks* themselves, private manuscripts published five years after his death, are this "vanishing mediator"[93] that passes away into the trajectory that led Lenin, in Michael Löwy's judicious formulation, "from Hegel's *Logic* to the Finland Station," from the disaster of the summer of 1914 to its reversal in the "great initiative" of October, the threshold of the first victorious revolution of the new century.

Notes

1   Cf. Alain Badiou, *D'un désastre obscur* (La Tour d'Aigues: Éditions de l'Aube, 1991).

2   A fundamental dimension of the conflict, never to be forgotten in relation to Lenin and October, involves the "imperial" reality of the forces involved and the mobilization of the colonized peoples in the conflict. The character of the October Revolution as the first revolution of anti-colonial emancipation followed directly from this.

3   Rosa Luxemburg, *The Crisis of Social-Democracy* (abridged English translation), in *The Rosa Luxemburg Reader*, ed. P. Hudis and K. B. Anderson (New York: Monthly Review Press, 2004), 312–41.

4   This was particularly the object of many demonstrations by Engels, especially in the chapters of *Anti-Dühring* that were rewritten and published as *The Role of Force in History*. It is also true of a number of other writings, a selection of which is translated in French as Marx and Engels, *Écrits militaires* (Paris: Cahiers de l'Herne, 1970).

5   Luxemburg, *The Crisis of Social-Democracy*, 314 and 316.

6   Cf. Lenin's texts "Tasks of the Revolutionary Social-Democracy in the European War" and "The War and Russian Social-Democracy," in Lenin, *Collected Works* (Moscow: Progress Publishers, 1960), 21:18 and 23 respectively.

7   None the less, when the revolutionary offensive in Europe reached its apogee four years later, Lenin wrote, "Not only in the East-European but also in the West-European countries . . . the movement in favor of Soviets is spreading farther and farther" (Lenin, "First Congress of the Communist International," *Collected Works*, 28:476), and asserted "the firm conviction that in the West-European states the revolution is advancing more quickly and will yield great victories" (ibid., 472).

8   This emblematic opposition between Lenin and Martov was already noted by Trotsky in the *Iskra* period: "Lenin was the political guide of *Iskra*, but as a publicist Martov was its head. He wrote easily and unceasingly, exactly as he spoke. Lenin passed much time in the library of the British Museum, where he was busy with theoretical studies" (L. Trotsky, *Lenin* [London: Harrap, 1925], 47–48).

9   N. Harding, cited in Kevin Anderson, *Lenin, Hegel and Western Marxism* (Chicago: University of Illinois Press, 1995), 150–51.

10   Lenin, "The European War and International Socialism," in *Collected Works*, 21:20. Emphasis in original.

11   Cf. the quantitative estimates of the table recapitulating the period 1914–17 in Anderson, *Lenin, Hegel and Western Marxism*, 109.

12   Michael Löwy, "De la Grande Logique de Hegel à la gare finlandaise de Petrograd," in *Dialectique et révolution* (Paris: Anthropos, 1973), 137.

13   Ibid.

14   D'Holbach, Helvétius, and Marx were the three sections of Plekhanov's *Essays in the History of Materialism* (London: John Lane, 1934).

15   Lenin's analyses of 1905 as a "dress rehearsal" involve either a prospective or retrospective illusion, sometimes indeed both.

16 Cf. this note of 1916, in the margin of Hegel's *Lectures on the History of Philosophy*: "Plekhanov wrote on philosophy (dialectics) about 1,000 pages (Beltov + against Bogdanov + against the Kantians + fundamental questions, etc., etc.). Among them, *about* the large *Logic, in connection with* it, *its* thought (i.e., dialectics *proper*, as philosophical science) nil!" (Lenin, Hegel notebooks, in *Collected Works*, 38:274). Emphasis in original.

17 Cf. G. Plekhanov, *Philosophical Works* (Moscow: Foreign Languages Publishing House, 1977), 1:407–32.

18 Ibid., 421. See also Plekhanov, "The Fundamental Questions of Marxism," in *Philosophical Works*, 1:142–45.

19 G. Plekhanov, *Philosophical Works*, 1:427.

20 "Dialectics *is* the theory of knowledge of (Hegel and) Marxism. This is the 'aspect' of the matter (it is not 'an aspect' but the *essence* of the matter) to which Plekhanov, not to speak of other Marxists, paid no attention" (Lenin, *Philosophical Notebooks*, in *Collected Works*, 38:360). Emphasis in original.

21 The arguments were formulated chiefly by Althusser and his followers, but not exclusively so. Cf., for example, Ludovico Geymonat, or Guy Planty-Bonjour, *Hegel et la pensée philosophique en Russie 1830-1917* (The Hague: Martinus Nijhoff, 1974), not forgetting of course, on a quite different level, the vulgate of *diamat*.

22 I use here the strong formulations of Costanzo Preve's work *Il Convitato di pietra*: *Saggio sul marxismo et sul nihilismo* (Milan: Vangelista, 1991).

23 It is a disagreement on this point that spoils the reading, however rich and systematic, of Lenin's "Notebooks" by Kevin Anderson (*Lenin, Hegel and Western Marxism*), a disciple of Raya Dunayevskaya. Legitimate as far as it goes (as the rejection of an argument from authority), Anderson's approach nevertheless reproduces a misinterpretation of the status of Lenin's reading (which was not a philosophical discourse on Hegel) and incessantly reproaches him with being too "materialist" and "selective" in his reading of the *Logic*, as well as too oriented toward "action" and insufficiently "humanist" — in other words, being Lenin and not Dunayevskaya.

24 Lenin, "Karl Marx (A Brief Biographical Sketch with an Exposition of Marxism)," in *Collected Works*, 21:43–91.

25 Cf. respectively Plekhanov, "The Fundamental Questions of Marxism," 136 (Feuerbach was not a materialist in history), and *Essays in the History of Materialism*.

26 Plekhanov was prolix enough on the existence of "leaps" in the course of "evolution" (cf. "The Fundamental Questions of Marxism," 140, 153), which he illustrated with examples taken indifferently from natural or social reality, preferring to start with the former (140). The "leap" is thus inscribed within "evolution," which it accelerates, the "social revolution" being only a variety of the universal category of "leap" (153). The notion of "catastrophe" is certainly absent from this line of reasoning. It is only logical that it should resurge with the approach to the culminating point of the revolutionary process of 1917, particularly in Lenin's text "The Impending Catastrophe and How to Combat It," *Collected Works*, 25:323–69.

27 Lenin, "Theses on Feuerbach," in *Collected Works*, 21:53.

28 It is scarcely an exaggeration to say that the materialism professed by Plekhanov, and

supported by a host of illustrations and examples drawn from all kinds of scientific works, from geology, physics, and chemistry through to the history of the oldest or "savage" civilizations (this display of erudition, pedantic as well as profoundly amateur, perfectly illustrating the kind of culture with scientific pretensions so typical of late nineteenth-century scholars) was based on a single idea, that of *determination* of human action and all natural processes by the natural and sociohistorical *environment*. To specify somewhat the mechanisms of "social evolution," Plekhanov constructed a schema of successive determinations (from the geophysical environment to the stages of development of the productive forces, and on to the enigmatic human psyche) in conformity with the idea he had of "monism." Faced with the classic question of the status of ideas, Plekhanov did not hesitate to annex to his scheme the a priori and hardly "materialist" notion, still less compatible with "monism," of the "psychology of social man" and "human psychism," simply making sure that the order of determinations remained unchanged: this was the celebrated "theory of factors." It is hardly credible to the eyes of a contemporary reader that this strange vision, a dilettantist mixture at once scientistic and idealist, flirting with all kinds of spiritualist and mystical elements (Social Darwinism, that is, the "struggle for life" which was seen as a principle valid for human society; the "animism of matter" and a fascination with electromagnetism; Taine's vision of history, which was seen as very similar to that of Marx; and a naïvely folkloric vision bordering on racism of "savage societies," "ancient civilizations," and so forth), could have served for decades in the workers' movement as an authority for "Marxist philosophy." This kind of "materialism," by its total inability to grasp the real significance of social practice and the work of the sciences, demonstrates the very opposite of what it claims, that it is simply a cobbled-together metaphysics in which "matter" and "environment" take the place of "God" or "spirit."

29   Cf. Alexandre Koyré, "Alexandre Ivanovitch Herzen," in *Études sur l'histoire de la pensée philosophique en Russie* (Paris: Vrin, 1959), 189ff. Cf. also Franco Venturi, *Roots of Revolution: A History of the Populist and Socialist Movements in 19th Century Russia* (London: Phoenix Press, 1972), in particular chapter 1, "Herzen" and chapter 4, "Chernychevsky"; also Claudio S. Ingerflom, *Le citoyen impossible: Les racines russes du léninisme* (Paris: Payot, 1988).

30   The expression appeared in the course of Marx's letters to Vera Zasulich. Ernst Bloch gave it a considerable significance in *Heritage of Our Times* (Oxford: Polity, 1991).

31   Cited in Ingerflom, *Le citoyen impossible*, 21. Cf. N. Machiavelli, "I have decided to take a path as yet untrodden by anyone, [even] if it brings me trouble and difficulty" (*Discourses on Livy* [Chicago University Press, 1996], 5).

32   Cf. Koyré, "Hegel en Russie," in *Études sur l'histoire*; and Planty-Bonjour, *Hegel et le pensée philosophique*. As Franco Venturi sums up, "Russian socialism in the 1840s had had a thorough grounding in the philosophy of Hegel, and this gave it a very special character" (*Roots of Revolution*, 16).

33   Compare, by way of example, in Plekhanov, "The Fundamental Questions of Marxism," 141 ("algebra of revolution") and 153 ("algebra of evolution").

34   As Venturi emphasizes, "During the czarist empire, the spirit of 1848 had survived, while it has disappeared or been transformed in European countries" (*Roots of Revolution*, 1).

35   Herzen shared this position with other '48ers, Moses Hess in particular, and also in a sense Engels.

36   Lenin, "Remarks on G. V. Plekhanov, *N. G. Chernychevsky*, Petersburg: Shipovnik,1910," *Collected Works*, 38:501–37.

37   Lenin, "In Memory of Herzen," *Collected Works*, 18:25–31.

38   Plekhanov wrote in fact: "Like his teacher [Feuerbach], Chernychevsky directs his attention almost exclusively to the 'theoretical' activity of mankind, and as a result, mental development becomes for him the most basic cause of historical movement" (cited and annotated by Lenin in about 1910; *Collected Works*, 38:538). The "germs" of the break with Plekhanov thus preceded the *Notebooks*, even though they were not yet conceived as such.

39   Cf. two texts of Marx published posthumously that have become among the most famous in his corpus, the Theses on Feuerbach and the Paris manuscripts of 1844, as well as Pascal's *Pensées* and Nietzsche's *Will to Power*, or again, closer to our time, the *Passagenwerk* of Walter Benjamin.

40   Cf. Henri Lefebvre and Norbert Guterman, *Lénine: Cahiers sur la dialectique de Hegel* (Paris: Gallimard, 1967, orig. ed. 1935).

41   Apart from a secondary literature devoted to Hegel, this essentially comprised the sections on the Greeks in Hegel's *Lectures on the History of Philosophy*, Aristotle's *Metaphysics*, Lassalle's book on Heraclitus, and Feuerbach on Leibniz, along with some works on the history and philosophy of science.

42   F. Engels, "Ludwig Feuerbach and the End of Classical German Philosophy," in K. Marx and F. Engels, *Selected Works* (Moscow: Progress Publishers, 1976), 3:342.

43   Cf. in particular the first thesis: "The chief defect of all hitherto existing materialism (that of Feuerbach included) is that the thing (*der Gegenstand*), reality (*die Wirklichkeit*), sensuousness (*die Sinnlichkeit*), is conceived only in the form of the *object* (*der Objekt*) *or of contemplation*, but not as *sensuous human activity* (*als sinnlich menschlich Tätigkeit*), *practice* (*Praxis*), not *subjectively* (*nicht subjektiv*). Hence, in contradistinction to materialism, the *active* side (*die tätige Seite*) was developed abstractly by idealism—which, of course, does not know real, sensuous activity as such (*die wirkliche, sinnliche, Tätigkeit als solche*)" (K. Marx and F. Engels, *The German Ideology* [Moscow: Progress Publishers, 1964], 645).

44   Slavoj Žižek, *Revolution at the Gates* (London: Verso, 2002), 179–80.

45   Cf. the essential demonstration of Fredric Jameson in *Late Marxism: Adorno and the Persistence of Dialectics* (London: Verso, 1990).

46   Lenin, Hegel notebooks, in *Collected Works*, 38:104.

47   Ibid., 233. Emphasis in original.

48   It is precisely this transformation of Lenin by his reading of *The Science of Logic* that is denied in Dominique Lecourt's interpretation. Launched on a perilous exercise of defense and illustration of Althusser's theses aiming to disqualify Lenin's references

to Hegel (by setting up *Materialism and Empirio-Criticism* as the definitive model of Marxist intervention in philosophy), Lecourt resorts to an extraordinary rhetorical contortion: if Lenin applied the Hegelian Absolute against Kant (a point that, in his view, forms "almost exclusively" the content of the 1914 "Notebooks"), this was by "preserving the polemical function of the Absolute" while "eliminating the specifically Hegelian content of the notion" (D. Lecourt, *Une Crise et son enjeu: Essai sur la position de Lénine en philosophie* [Paris: Maspero, 1973], 66). This conceptual miracle is performed by interposing "Lenin's final operation vis-à-vis Hegel: he eliminates the absolute subject, refuses to keep the Absolute as a subject" (ibid.). This in no way prevents Hegel, in a good orthodox Althusserian manner, from being credited with elaborating the concept of the "process without a subject." Can anyone make sense of this?

49   Lenin, Hegel notebooks, *Collected Works*, 38:110.

50   "The basic ideas . . . that of the universal, all-sided, vital connection of everything with everything and the reflection of this connection—*materialistisch auf den Kopf gestellter Hegel*—in human concepts, which must likewise be hewn, treated, flexible, mobile, relative, mutually connected, united in opposites, in order to embrace the world" (ibid., 146).

51   Ibid., 147, my emphasis.

52   Cf. Engels, "Ludwig Feuerbach," 362.

53   "Leaps!," "Breaks in gradualness," "Leaps!" (Lenin, Hegel notebooks, *Collected Works*, 38:123). Cf. Daniel Bensaïd's text in the present volume.

54   Lenin, Hegel notebooks, *Collected Works*, 38:92.

55   Ibid., 38:130. Emphasis in original.

56   "'Die Reflexion is the showing of Essence into itself' (27) "(translation? Reflectivity? Reflective determination? *Reflektsia* is not suitable" (134). It is clear here that Lenin does *not* confuse "reflection" and *Reflexion*, contrary to what Roger Garaudy maintained (R. Garaudy, *Lénine* [Paris: PUF, 1968]).

57   Lenin, Hegel notebooks, *Collected Works*, 38:135.

58   Ibid., 141.

59   "The 'treatment' and 'twisting' of words and concepts to which Hegel devotes himself here is a struggle against making the concept of *law* absolute, against simplifying it, against making a fetish of it" (ibid.,151).

60   Ibid.

61   Engels, in "Ludwig Feuerbach," made this conception of reflection by successive approximations the touchstone of the "materialist theory of knowledge"—followed in this by Plekhanov, and by Lenin in *Materialism and Empirio-Criticism*.

62   Lenin, *Materialism and Empirio-Criticism*, in *Collected Works*, 14:188, my emphases.

63   "The most important thing is that the *laws* of these changes have been discovered, that the *objective* logic of these changes and of their historical development has in its chief and basic features been disclosed—objective . . . in the sense that social being is *independent* of the *social consciousness* of people. . . . The highest task of humanity

is to comprehend this objective logic of economic evolution (the evolution of social life) in its general and fundamental features, so that it may be possible to adapt *to it* one's social consciousness and the consciousness of the advanced classes of all capitalist countries in as definite, clear and critical a fashion as possible" (ibid., 325). This is why it is quite impossible, as Lecourt seeks to do (*Une Crise et son enjeu*, 44–47), to draw from the variations of *Materialism and Empirio-Criticism* on the theme of the approximate and gradual character of "reflection" a theory of the "activity of the reflection" or the reflection as "process," categories that are absolutely not to be found in this work. Henri Lefebvre is far more honest. Equally trying to "save" some elements of *Materialism and Empirio-Criticism*, he also speaks of "active reflection," but makes clear that "this is only an interpretation of Lenin's thought" (*Pour connaître le pensée de Lénine* [Paris: Bordas, 1957], 156).

64   Lenin, Hegel notebooks, in *Collected Works*, 38:153 and 155. Emphasis in original.

65   "Thought proceeding from the concrete to the abstract—provided it is *correct* (NB) (and Kant, like all philosophers, speaks of correct thought)—does not get away *from* the truth but comes closer to it. The abstraction of *matter*, of a *law* of nature, the abstraction of *value*, etc., in short *all* scientific . . . abstractions reflect nature more deeply, truly and *completely*" (ibid., 171). Žižek (*Revolution at the Gates*, 315) believes that in this passage Lenin temporarily breaks with his idealist theory of "reflection" before immediately falling back into it and returning to the metaphor of asymptotic approximation. In my view, on the contrary, the very persistence of resistances and regressions attests to the pursuit of the work of a dialecticization, the transformation of the category of "reflection" providing an indicator of this. Even if reintroduced, the metaphor of knowledge by approximation no longer denotes adaptation to an "objective" given. This question was settled, as I see it, soon after Lenin wrote these notes on the *Logic*, in his manuscript "On the Question of Dialectics," where he identifies the trajectory described by human knowledge not as a straight line asymptotic to a "material world," but rather as a "spiral," a curve moving "endlessly" in a "series of circles" (Lenin, *Collected Works*, 38:361).

66   "The formation of (abstract) notions and operations with them *already* includes idea, conviction, *consciousness* of the law-governed connection of the world. . . . Consequently, Hegel is much more profound than Kant, and others, in tracing the reflection of the movement of the objective world in the movement of notions. Just as the simple form of value, the individual act of exchange of one given commodity for another, already includes in an undeveloped form *all* the main contradictions of capitalism,—so the simplest *generalization*, the first and simplest formation of *notions* (judgments, syllogisms, etc.) already denotes man's ever deeper cognition of the *objective* connection of the world" (Lenin, *Collected Works*, 38:178–79).

67   Ibid., 179.

68   Althusser is thus quite right to emphasize the reprise of Hegel's critique of Kant as a decisive point in Lenin's reading of *The Science of Logic*. But he manages to "forget" both the novelty of this position and the reasons that Lenin evoked to support it. He thus reduces this approval of Hegel to the assertion that "Lenin criticize[s] Kant

from the viewpoint of science" (Althusser's emphasis), whereas Hegel had criticized Kant "from the viewpoint of the Absolute Idea, i.e., provisionally, of 'God'" (*Lenin and Philosophy* [London: New Left Books, 1971], 115).

69   *Materialism and Empirio-Criticism* refers constantly to Feuerbach as an authority, his "views" being described as "consistently materialist" (Lenin, *Collected Works*, 14:155) and cited, at page length and first hand, to counter the positions of the "Kantian" and "agnostic" adversaries. Lenin even speaks of "the *entire school* of Feuerbach, Marx and Engels" (204), and systematically cites the triad in this order, establishing the strictest continuity in their materialism. The fundamental thesis hammered home in this work is that it is precisely the "*same* materialism" (336) that Marx and Engels simply "applied to the social sciences" (ibid.) or "to history" (242), the questions of "gnoseology" having already been settled by the materialists who preceded them (the French of the eighteenth century, but Feuerbach above all others). Marx and Engels thus "crowned" the "materialist philosophy" (329), "complet[ed] the edifice of materialist philosophy *up to its summit*" (242), built up by their materialist forerunners, always "growing out" of Feuerbach (329). There is nothing at all original in all of this: it is a literal reprise of themes developed *ad abundantiam* by Plekhanov, particularly in "The Fundamental Questions of Marxism," according to which "Feuerbach . . . worked out the philosophical foundations of what can be called the world-outlook of Marx and Engels" (120). In the same order of ideas, Marx's "gnoseology" is "the same gnoseology as Feuerbach's, but deepened thanks to the corrective of genius that Marx brought to it," while his "Theses on Feuerbach" "in no way eliminate the fundamental propositions in Feuerbach's philosophy, but only correct them, and—what is most important—call for an application more consistent" (135). As for Hegel, and Marx's relationship to him (rapidly dealt with), and the critique of his *Philosophy of Right*, the author of *Capital* was able to undertake this "*only because* Feuerbach had completed his criticism of *Hegel's speculative philosophy*" (128). And the Hegelian dialectic "could be 'turned right side up' *only* by one who was convinced of the soundness of the basic principle of Feuerbach's philosophy, viz., that it is not thinking that determines being, but being that determines thinking" (139). But is that not already giving too great an honor to a "philosophical idealism" that "present-day ethnology" teaches us "descends, in the historical sense, from the *animism* of primitive peoples" (132)? As we see, Leon Brunschwig was not alone in believing that the syllogisms of Hegelian logic corresponded to the mental age of an elementary school pupil. Besides, Plekhanov strongly insisted on the continuity that linked the materialism of Marx, Engels, and Feuerbach with that of the French Enlightenment, of La Mettrie, Diderot, D'Holbach, and Helvétius, and even beyond these, with Hobbes or a Spinoza "released from his theological tatters." See also Plekhanov's *Essays on the History of Materialism*, significantly made up of three sections, devoted respectively to D'Holbach, Helvétius, and Marx.

70   Cf. Lenin, "On the Question of Dialectics," in *Collected Works*, 38:359.

71   Lenin, Hegel Notebooks, *Collected Works*, 38:180. Lenin stresses that "it is impossible completely to understand *Capital* . . . without having thoroughly studied and

understood the *whole* of Hegel's *Logic*" (ibid.). This simple point is sufficient to refute Althusser's thesis according to which, for Lenin, recourse to Hegel was only necessary for the first section of *Capital*, in which Marx "pastiched" Hegel (Lenin uses this term in the "Notebooks" in reference to the famous "coquetting" that Marx mentions in his 1873 preface), a section that has to be read "from a materialist standpoint." Thus there is again here nothing new in relation to Lenin's positions of 1909. In Althusser's view, "Lenin did not need to read Hegel in order to understand him, because he had already understood Hegel, having closely read and understood Marx" (*Lenin and Philosophy*, 109). If this reasoning is followed, the months passed in reading and annotating Hegel in the midst of the First World War would have been nothing more than a pastime, both gratuitous and perverse. Besides, in a manner that is far from Althusserian, Lenin seems to have been equipped with the almost mystical virtue of "reading and understanding Marx" at a single stroke, without the least discontinuity (not to say "break") affecting this definitive revelation.

72   This is particularly one of the major theses of Kevin Anderson (*Lenin, Hegel and Western Marxism*), who makes this return to Hegel, or to dialectics, the distinctive sign of what he persists in calling (in the wake of his homonym Perry Anderson) "Western Marxism," by which he means all the heterodox European Marxisms. Now if there is one single conclusion to be drawn from the dialectical resurgence in Marxism that Lenin's "Notebooks" attest, it is that such distinctions between a "Western Marxism," supposedly philosophical and somewhat Hegelianizing, and a "non-Western Marxism" ("Oriental," perhaps?) have little real application. For Lenin, Gramsci, or Lukács, placing the dialectic back at the heart of Marxism was in no way a sign of "heterodoxy" or "Hegelianism," but rather of combating revisionist positions and rehabilitating Marxism as a revolutionary theory.

73   Lenin, "Play of the Dialectic (Logic) of Hegel," *Collected Works*, 38:318.

74   Ibid., 182. Lenin realizes, or begins here to realize, something that is effectively "not reflection in a mirror" (Lefebvre, *Pour connaître*, 174). Dominique Lecourt, in formulations that at one time encountered a certain popularity, spoke of "reflection without a mirror" as a "historical process of acquisition of knowledge" (*Une Crise et son enjeu*, 47). It is strange at least, as we have seen, to see Lecourt stubbornly place this definition in terms of process back in *Materialism and Empirio-Criticism* (ibid.), without giving any indication of his support for this assertion—and rightly so, as he would find it hard to find the slightest reference to the category of process in the work in question!

75   Hegel cited in Lenin, Hegel notebooks, *Collected Works*, 38:182.

76   Lenin, Hegel notebooks, *Collected Works*, 38:189–90. Lenin's emphasis—the whole phrase triply underscored—has been omitted.

77   Ibid., 191. The second of Marx's theses on Feuerbach runs: "The question whether objective truth (*gegenständliche Wahrheit*) can be attributed to human thinking is not a question of theory but is a *practical* (*praktisch*) question. Man must prove the truth, i.e., the reality (*Wirklichkeit*) and power (*Macht*), the this-sidedness of his thinking in practice (*in der Praxis*)" (Marx and Engels, *The German Ideology*, 645).

78 Lenin, Hegel notebooks, *Collected Works*, 38:216.

79 Ibid., 211.

80 Ibid., 211 and 212.

81 Marx and Engels, *The German Ideology*, 645.

82 Lenin, Hegel notebooks, *Collected Works*, 38:213. Emphasis in original. In contrast to Lenin, Hegel spoke of "transcending the determinations of the external world" entirely.

83 Ibid., 217–18.

84 I draw inspiration here from the words of T. C. Clark: "Painting is . . . a means of investigation; it is a way of discovering what the values and excitements of the world amount to, by finding in practice what it takes to make a painting of them. . . . Does the 'realization' extend and intensify . . . the meanings and appearances, or disperse and qualify them? Does it even show them becoming (in practice, in miniature, as they are flattened and detailed and juxtaposed) something else? Is there anything out there (or in here) that can pass the test of representation? If I draw it, will it survive?" (T. J. Clark, *The Painting of Modern Life: Paris in the Art of Manet and His Followers* [London: Thames and Hudson, 1990], xxi).

85 Lenin, Hegel notebooks, *Collected Works*, 38:219. Emphasis in original.

86 Ibid. Emphasis in original.

87 "The difference is not clear to me, is not the absolute equivalent to the more concrete?" (ibid., 229).

88 Engels, "Ludwig Feuerbach," 340.

89 Slavoj Žižek, *Le plus sublime des hystériques* (Paris: Point hors ligne, 1988), 17. Emphasis added.

90 Lenin, Hegel Notebooks, *Collected Works*, 38:233. Emphasis in original.

91 On the question of war and revolution, one should consult Georges Haupt, "Guerre et révolution chez Lénine," reprinted in G. Haupt, *L'Historien et le mouvement social* (Paris: Maspero, 1980), 237–66, and the chapter by Etienne Balibar in the present volume. On the question of the transformation of the democratic revolution into a proletarian revolution, see the studies by Michael Löwy and Daniel Bensaïd already cited, as well as Slavoj Žižek, afterword to *Revolution at the Gates*. For an overall view, cf. the second part of Kevin Anderson's "Lenin on the Dialectics of Revolution 1914–1923," in K. Anderson, *Lenin, Hegel and Western Marxism*, 123–70.

92 See S. Žižek, *Revolution at the Gates*, 7–10.

93 Cf. Fredric Jameson, "Max Weber as Storyteller," in *The Syntax of History*, vol. 2 of *The Ideologies of Theory: Essays 1971–1986* (Minneapolis: University of Minnesota Press, 1988), 3–34.

PART III | **war and**
         | **imperialism**

10

The Philosophical Moment in Politics Determined by War:

Lenin 1914-16

Etienne Balibar

I have chosen this complicated—and restrictive—title to mark what is singular about the place of Lenin in this comparison of philosophers in the face of war. Evidently not being himself a professional in philosophy, he was not in a position to discover or assign himself a mission in this field (not even that of "preparing revolution"). And yet he should not be considered as belonging to the category of amateurs. For his relation to war and philosophy shows the very essence of the politics to which he devoted himself. It is this that on reflection struck me as particularly significant: in the strong sense of the term, *there is only one philosophical moment in Lenin, and it is precisely war that determines it*, by its issues at stake and its immediate consequences. This could be important for philosophy, if it is true that its object cannot be isolated from that of politics. It certainly is important in any case for understanding Lenin's position in history, including the history of the social movement that came to call itself "Leninism." We can in fact assume right away that this label covers more of a contradiction than an unproblematic continuity.

The difference between Lenin in the years before 1914 and those after 1917–18 is in a certain sense common knowledge. Many people have noted this and described its effects in different ways.[1] And yet it remains difficult to interpret, for the reference points have not stayed fixed on either side of the great divide marked by war and revolution. For contemporaries, however, these two events, between which Lenin himself proclaimed the existence of a necessary link, immediately went together. The "new Lenin"—the man who appeared as the inspirer of the Third International, hailed by Sorel in the republication of his *Reflections on Violence*, or even the man who inspired the "decisionist" philosophy of Carl Schmitt or Keynes (in the opposite camp)—was the Lenin of October, perceived against the background of the disasters of the war in which a whole world had collapsed, and from which he emerged as a challenge and a prophet. This was the figure around whom "Leninism" would be organized.

But can we not proceed to a closer analysis? For our present concern, the period that is particularly relevant is that from August 1914 to the first months of 1917, from the text "The Collapse of the Second International" to the "April Theses."[2] It was during this period that philosophy came into play, yet only to disappear immediately after. We might rather say that everything happened as if, in the context of war and emergency, Lenin had himself run through the stages of an "end of philosophy," which was realized outside its own field but still had to emerge initially for itself, in a specific work that sought to grasp its essence and practice writing it.

Let us note that before 1914-15, Lenin had already written philosophical books and articles (not counting the use he made of Marxist philosophical concepts throughout his writings). The two most important of these were his study of 1894, *What the "Friends of the People" Are*,[3] which developed an epistemology of historical materialism based on the dual critique of "objectivism" and "subjectivism," and *Materialism and Empirio-Criticism* of 1908,[4] directed against the philosophy of Bogdanov, which is completely honorable in its handling of conceptual techniques and rests on a wide investigation of various philosophers (Berkeley, Diderot, Kant, Mach, and so forth). I shall maintain, however, that in these studies Lenin was not a philosopher in the strong sense of the term. What he produced, in his own way, were ideological arguments in a pre-existing philosophical debate, where he occupied one of the possible positions in the field of variants of "Marxist philosophy" that formed the cement of social democracy. Whereas, in the *Philosophical Notebooks* of 1914-15—simple reading notes, sketches at a definition of the dialectic, drafted for private purposes, at the same time as other notes in preparation for his studies on imperialism—we see paradoxically (but unequivocally) the question of the "foundations" of Western metaphysics, or the meaning of its constitutive categories, confronted for its own sake. But this exercise in critical reading (Aristotle, Hegel) does not lead to *a philosophical discourse* and was not intended to do so. On the contrary, after 1915 *Lenin never wrote any further philosophical work.*[5]

In reality, by way of this very short experience, it was Lenin's whole relationship to philosophical discourse that was completely transformed. In this sense, the philosophical moment determined by the conjuncture of the war had no successor, even if it was far from having no effects. This is clearly something that "Leninist" ideology in its different variants has totally misunderstood. To constitute the figure of a "philosophy of Lenin," this ideology had to have wholesale recourse to his prewar works (in particular *Materialism and Empirio-Criticism*). When it referred to the *Philosophical Notebooks*, raising these from the status of private notes to that of fragments of a finished work, or aphoristic writings, it had to offer a selected and biased reading, denying in practice their essentially unstable character.[6] The same holds, perhaps even more so, for the "dialectical" and "Hegelian" tendency (Deborin, Lukács, Lefebvre) that sought in these *Notebooks*, at the risk of fetishizing them, the instruments for an alternative to official dogma, against the "mechanicism" of *Materialism and Empirio-Criticism*.[7]

It is the very existence of this unique "moment" that should first of all attract our attention. A precise chronology will emphasize its strange character.

1. August 1914. The European war breaks out, and in the different belligerent countries, within a few weeks or even days, a *union sacrée* is established that breaks the unity of European socialism and defeats all its plans to resist "imperialist" war, let alone "use . . . the economic and political crisis created by war . . . to precipitate the fall of capitalist domination," in conformity with the resolutions of the Stuttgart (1907) and Basle (1912) congresses. With a handful of other dissidents from what struck him as a disastrous renegation, Lenin was at that point totally isolated in Switzerland. The war excluded him: from both itself and from politics.
2. What did Lenin do in these conditions? At the end of 1914 he took

part in some meetings of refugees who were opposed to "social-patriotism," finished writing an encyclopedia article on Marx, and before anything else, *set himself to reading the metaphysicians.* This was also the moment at which, for the first time, he proposed to abandon the name of "Socialist" for the revolutionary party and return to that of "Communist."

3. In 1915–16, in contrast, we see him involved in political as well as theoretical activity. The conferences of Zimmerwald (September 1915) and Kienthal (April 1916) were prepared by a series of texts on the "collapse of the Second International" and formulation of the slogan of the "transformation of imperialist war into a revolutionary civil war," implying not only a polemic against the "social-chauvinists" but also against the pacifist current. This was the period in which he wrote the booklet "Imperialism, the Highest Stage of Capitalism,"[8] and the period of the debate on "the right of nations to self-determination."

4. In late 1916 and early 1917, a new series of texts (above all the extraordinary study "A Caricature of Marxism and 'Imperialist Economism,'" published in 1924 after his death), and "The Military Programme of the Proletarian Revolution" inflected his analysis of imperialism.[9] These texts were directed against "left-wing" radicalism, which saw the world war as heralding a definitive effacement of the national problem in favor of class antagonism. Criticizing this idea, and showing the need to distinguish, from the standpoint of both causes and effects, between the democratic nationalism of the oppressed peoples (both outside and inside Europe) and that of the great powers contending with each other for the "division of the world," Lenin put forward the idea that every revolution is "impure," combining both class movements and national political demands. This analysis went together with the denunciation of "bourgeois pacifism" à la Wilson: the "imperialist peace" that was looming on the horizon of secret negotiations and would be imposed by the defeat of the Central Powers was denounced in advance as a "continuation of imperialist war by other means."[10]

This chronology enables us to note a fundamental turning point in Lenin's political thought, but one produced belatedly; economic evolutionism based on an extrapolation of historical "tendencies"—which had dominated socialist thought in the period of the Second International (and would soon make a return in that of the Third), either in a progressive or a catastrophist form (gradual transformation or breakdown of capitalism)—still essentially inspired Lenin's texts of 1915-16 (including the *Imperialism* booklet), even though this was increasingly out of phase with Lenin's new "tactics." With the analyses of late 1916 and early 1917, immediately preceding the revolutionary moment, this evolutionism was profoundly rectified. Not only was all historical development now conceived as "uneven," but the complexity of the political field appeared definitively irreducible to a logic of "tendencies." Following Althusser, we can call this the discovery in the theoretical and strategic field of the *overdetermination* intrinsic to class antagonisms.

Comparison with the thought of Rosa Luxemburg is particularly significant here. In 1914, when both Lenin and Luxemburg were faced with the "collapse" of institutional socialism, they shared the view that the war constituted a "vital test," dissipating the appearance of a peaceful evolution of capitalism and the illusions of parliamentarism, and thus placing socialism against the wall and effecting a practical "self-criticism" of its reformist tendency. Luxemburg's view was that the situation was back to that described by Marx in the *Communist Manifesto*: that of a final crisis with no other issue than revolution, arising from a radical *simplification* of the conditions of class struggle.[11] Lenin, however, increasingly distanced himself from this literally apocalyptic vision, to situate the revolutionary perspective in the element of the duration and complexity of conjunctures. Certainly the a priori of a philosophy of history (expressed particularly in the perspective of a world communist revolution that he constantly maintained) never disappeared. But at the price of an extreme tension, this coexisted and sought linkage with a strategic "empiricism," an "analysis of concrete situations" that assumed incorporating into the concept of the revolutionary process the *plurality of forms* of proletarian political struggle ("peaceful" and "violent"), and the *transition* from one form to another (hence the question of the specific duration and successive contradictions of the revolutionary transition).

It is impossible not to connect this intellectual development immediately with the "philosophical moment" of 1914-15, as the dialectical themes that emerge here are exactly those insisted on in the *Notebooks*. Certainly there can be no question of "deducing" or "reflecting" one of these aspects on the basis of the other. We must start by simply describing the combination of efforts by which Lenin simultaneously sought to enter into the material of philosophy and that of war, to the profit of a new politics.

It is equally impossible not to emphasize the coincidence between this development and the change in style that in fact characterized the postwar Lenin as compared with his prewar self. Without being a dogmatist, the prewar Lenin was nonetheless marked by a stable doctrine and philosophical position, even after the "lessons of 1905" (which appeared above all as the confirmation of the radical position he had taken in the debates within the Social Democratic Party). There was a fundamental continuity, in this respect, between *The Development of Capitalism in Russia* and the "Theses on the National Question" of 1913, or even the analysis of "The Collapse of the Second International," indicating the proletariat as the homogeneous and potentially hegemonic force that had to assure both the tasks of the "bourgeois revolution" in backward Russia and those of the socialist revolution.[12] After 1915, and still more so in the course of the three successive revolutions (those of February and October 1917, and later that of the NEP) in which he was involved, not to say thrown, we see on the contrary how *Lenin did not cease to change*, not simply his "tactics," but his definitions and analyses of the role of the proletariat and the party—even concerning their very composition—and consequently, in the last analysis, of the identity of the "revolutionary subject." This last has remained a constant problem, appearing as the result of a complex political construction instead of constituting an established *socioeconomic presupposition* (including its form of awakening consciousness, the "translation" of the class-in-itself into a class-for-itself). In my view, in fact, we can see this permanent interrogation, which eventually leads (in dramatic fashion) to a "disappearance of the proletariat" in the classical sense,[13] beginning to enter Lenin's thought already during the course of the war, under the effect of the questions that the war raised, but also the effect of the philosophical rethinking that the war immediately aroused. In philosophical terms, we would say that the relationship between theory and practice was no longer seen simply as one of *application*, but instead as one of non-predetermined constitution.

A brief reminder of the contents of the *Philosophical Notebooks* is necessary here, all the more so as it raises an interesting question of historiography (or, as we more correctly say nowadays, of "reception"). Those who have read the official edition (*Collected Works*, vol. 38) will be aware what is to be found here: a summary of Hegel's *Logic*; notes on Hegel's *History of Philosophy*, limited to the Greeks; a summary of the introduction to Hegel's *Philosophy of History* (for the rest of the book, Lenin held that it did not contain anything very important, except "the idea of universal history," which had passed into Marxist science); a summary of Lassalle's book on Heraclitus (the Hegelian assumptions of which Lenin criticized at length); a brief summary of Aristotle's *Metaphysics* ("Clericalism killed what was living in Aristotle and perpetuated what was dead");[14] a summary of Feuerbach's book on Leibniz; and *at the end* a five-page sketch titled "On the Question of Dialectics." The essence of this turns around the question of contradiction, and the historical (or cyclical) relation that connects Hegel's "logical" formulations (on the identity of opposites, essence and appearance, necessity and change, absolute and relative, universal and singular) with the debates within Greek philosophy (above all, the opposition between Aristotle and Heraclitus, the philosophy of Epicurus as presented by Hegel also being an object of particular interest).

This edition, however, betrays an astonishing lacuna: it does not contain Lenin's exactly contemporary notes on Clausewitz's *Vom Kriege* (absent indeed from the *Collected Works* as a whole), even though in his writings of the following period explicit references and allusions to both Hegel and Clausewitz almost always go together. What is the reason for this dissociation, this unequal treatment on the part of the publishers? It may be a case of ideological censorship; there were others as well in the establishment of the Leninist "corpus." It certainly shows a total incomprehension, both of the meaning of Lenin's reflections on the "basis of dialectics," drafted in the wake of his selective reading of the "fundamental" philosophers, and of the use that Lenin subsequently made of this.[15]

What was Lenin looking for in his reading of Hegel? Although his immediately contemporary critique of Kautsky's "ultra-imperialism" and the pacifism that this led to both relate to a refutation of Kantian cosmopolitanism (Kant being the number one target of Lenin's attacks in the *Notebooks*), the Hegel that particularly mattered to him was not the Hegel of "Weltgeschichte ist Weltgericht." The place that Hegel himself was able to assign war in history, in relation to his philosophy of the state, did not play the decisive role. This is why, in particular, there is not here even a verbal encounter with the Hegelianism that German historicism appealed to (and that the French critics of "philosophical pan-Germanism," forerunner of the totalitarianism theory, sought to refute).[16] Nor was it even—as Raymond Aron showed very well in his book on Clausewitz—in the sense of a theory of "total war," of which class struggle would be a particular form, that Lenin attempted the combination of Hegelian and Clausewitzian formulas.[17] This combination is in fact the essence of the matter (Lenin retrospectively projects it into history, maintaining on several occasions the evidently mistaken view that Clausewitz had been a "disciple of Hegel").[18] But he did this in the context of a double rectification: of Hegelian speculation (*Vernunft*, reason) by Clausewitzian pragmatism, and of the latter (as an application of *Verstand*, analytical understanding) by the Hegelian dialectic.

What Lenin corrected in Clausewitz was the idea of military strategy or tactics as an instrument of a state "politics" invariable in substance, or which remained autonomous in its appreciation of the conjuncture. War (or rather wars, their characteristics changing with the times) is a form that contains the essence of politics, and thus becomes the very form of its realization, in conformity with the dialectic of the "immanent genesis of differences" and the "objectivity of the appearance." By continuing politics "by other means," in the famous formula, war does no more than express it, also transforming its course, conditions, and actors.

What Lenin symmetrically corrected in Hegel was the idea of a dialectical contradiction that permits the location of "the absolute in the relative" *independently of the conjuncture*, and of the "contingent" form that the mobilization of the masses themselves assumes: the *practical* translation of the historical dialectic thus does not simply involve reading Hegel through Marx, but also through Clausewitz.[19] This could be summed up as follows: not only is there a primacy of politics over war within war itself (which means that the class struggle *does not cease* to produce its effects, even if "by other means" and "in other forms"), not only does the complexity of class struggle thus always exceed the "simplification" imposed by the military moment, but it always also exceeds a simplified representation of the class struggle itself as a simple "duel." To conceive the conjuncture (in order to intervene in it) is to reject a double simplification of the historical process: that imposed by war (or rather that which war appears to realize) by temporarily "crushing" class politics, and that of the "orthodox" Marxists ideally opposed to it (including those who, like Rosa Luxemburg, did not betray their camp) who proposed simply to *substitute* class struggle once more in place of national war.

We can observe this dialectic at work in the texts of 1914–15. The first "application" that Lenin made of Clausewitz's formula was to link the split in European socialism determined by the war (between "chauvinists" or champions of the *union sacrée* and internationalists) to the previously existing tendencies in socialist politics: that is, seeing this as a continuation of the conflict between the reformist and revolutionary wings of Marxism (independent of particular individuals).[20] This "explanation" was in fact a retrospective rationalization, as if the *union sacrée* had been predictable, and in this sense was still evolutionist. It went together with the idea that this "betrayal" signaled the presence of a "foreign body" in the workers' movement, in thrall to the bourgeoisie, and with the theory of the "crumbs" from imperialist exploitation that served to corrupt the labor aristocracy. It implicitly presupposed therefore the existence of a "pure" proletarian mass, intrinsically hostile to the war, even though the turnaround of the political and trade-union leaderships and the constraints of mobilization had temporarily atomized this and reduced it to impotence.

With the systematic elaboration of Lenin's slogan of the "transformation of the imperialist war into a revolutionary civil war," a noticeably different argument came to light. Far from this being a second best,[21] we can see it rather as the rigorous application of the basic idea that *the war was not a catastrophe but a process*, with specific contradictions that had to be analyzed.[22] The comparison with Marx and Engels is instructive. Lenin was not interested (as his predecessors had been) in the detail of military operations, but rather in the fact that *the masses were involved in the war*. From the idea of "total war" or "people's war" he retained only that war is a fact of society and cannot be reduced to a confrontation of states. This enabled him to maintain that the war had a double character right from the start: a confrontation between the imperialist powers, but also the "use" by each belligerent of the adversary's forces to tame "its own" proletariat. These forces, however, are themselves made up in the last analysis of proletarians or proletarianized masses. The duration of the war was a decisive factor, bringing not only an aggravation of suffering but the transformation of both the objective and subjective conditions of the conflict. If the conflict stirred up national hatreds, like any other war, it was occurring in a period of "mature" capitalism. The war would thus have a double result: *to involve the masses in the war*, not just as a mere manipulable "object" but as a power that in the long run would be impossible to control. The military constraint and the failure of strategies of rapid annihilation would arouse in reaction a formidable democratic aspiration on the part of the masses, which would make impossible a pure and simple restoration of social and bourgeois "discipline." At the same time, however, the tendency of imperialism to transform itself into "state capitalism" by the centralization and militarization of production would cross a decisive threshold. We should note that Lenin introduces here two aspects that would constitute the unity of opposites of the dictatorship of the proletariat as he redefined it in the years 1917–23.[23] We should also note that it is in the last instance, this analysis of the historical "productivity" of war in terms of social forces and social conflicts, that justified Lenin's conviction that it was possible to make war on war in practice, to get a grasp on it (and as far as his personal destiny was concerned, to "enter" it as a factor of disturbance of its purely military logic), whereas pacifist ideology (or the pacifist version of internationalism) had given proof of its impotence.

If we return then to the agonizing question of how war could "produce" socialism, since socialism had been unable to prevent war, we see that the response to it is an open one. Socialization of the economy and latent revolt of the masses at the front and in the rear only determine a *revolutionary situation*, which may or may not develop in the direction of an actual break. What becomes capital here is the fact that war has a history. To know what kind of "class consciousness" war can arouse, starting from its opposite, what is needed is a differential analysis of the internal divisions of the proletariat and the manner in which these are developing. The ambivalent effects of "national feeling" in Europe thus have also to be taken into account. The principled (democratic) position in favor of the "right of nations to self-determination," and thus the call to dismantle, at least provisionally, the multinational empires resting on the caste privileges of a dominant nation, appears as a politically inescapable moment of the transformation of the revolutionary situation into an anti-capitalist civil war.[24]

To determine whether there is anything in Lenin other than a *denial of nationalism* as a mass phenomenon, it is thus not sufficient simply to note his brutally reductive criticism of "patriotism" (presented as the ideological mask of imperialist interests) and his refusal to enter into the casuistry of "aggressors" and "aggressed." We must follow the progressive transformation of the concept of imperialism itself, especially in Lenin's discussions with the supporters of pacifist positions and the projects of disarmament that arose in the course of the war. It seems clear that Lenin's major objection to these projects rested on their Eurocentric "partiality," something that was particularly highlighted by Wilson's slogans. A United States of Europe, Lenin showed, was at the present time "either impossible or reactionary," that is, it represented the idea of a transformation of the imperialist war into an "imperialist peace,"[25] or of a new division of the world: continuation of the process under way, under the appearance ("metaphysical" as Lenin calls it) of an absolute antithesis between peace and war. In actual fact the European war was not purely European, but was determined by a total global structure that irreversibly differentiated nationalisms. Even in Europe itself it was possible from this standpoint to identify situations of a colonial type (witness the Irish uprising of 1916).

It is true all the same that it was only after he had returned to Russia (after the February Revolution) that Lenin actually attempted a "class analysis" of the nationalism of the masses—in particular the peasant nationalism in Russia, that is, the relationship of dependence that existed between the masses and the national state in an emergency situation. And he still did not do so in a "psychological" perspective— doubtless for lack of concepts that would enable him to break the symmetrical standoff between ideologies of "race" or "national character" and those of "class consciousness"—but solely, in a rather doubtful fashion, in terms of the social composition of the peasant or petty bourgeois bloc. This is why the question did not in the end receive any theoretical solution, but only successive tactical ones, starting with that which Lenin applied in 1917 against the supporters of "revolutionary *jusqu'au-boutisme*" and those of a proletarian "coup d'état."[26]

In conclusion, it appears that the war profoundly transformed the very notion of a revolutionary situation. This was no longer a postulate bound up with the idea of a certain "maturity" of capitalism (of which war was the symptom), but rather the result of an analysis of the effects of the war itself on a differentiated global structure, in which the "advanced" and "backward" countries coexisted and interpenetrated (which was especially the case in Russia). This is why, at the same time, Lenin constantly maintained the thesis of a world revolution and conceived the utilization of a "separate peace" unilaterally decreed by the country in which contradictions had reached the breaking point as a means of acting on the balance of forces *as a whole*. Yet he never accepted, for all that, the idea of "socialism in one country." What is more, he ceased to identify the revolution, in these conditions, with the "establishment of socialism." The revolution as this resulted from the fact of the war was in one sense *less* than socialism (expression of the democratic revolt of the masses, a national movement, or even the continuation of state capitalism), and in another sense *more* (immediately bound up with the Communist project, even under the form of "war Communism"). In short, it was an overdetermined historical break, and the point of departure of a new dialectic, in agreement with the lesson drawn from a "practical" reading of Hegel and Clausewitz.

We have to admit, however, that this intellectual shift was only a tendency, which was not without its contrary movements. To convince oneself of this it is only necessary, for example, to reread *The State and Revolution*[27] in this perspective. This work was an attempt to relocate the singularity of the Russian Revolution in a logic of the universal, of which it was, however, symptomatic only in that it remained *incomplete*, not only because of circumstances and their urgency ("more pleasant to go through the experience of the revolution than to write about it"), but perhaps also as a result of the impossibility of the project itself. From 1914 onward, Lenin the "philosopher" advanced beyond Lenin the revolutionary, but Lenin the "theorist" of the revolution still remained behind his own practice.

Notes

This text first appeared as "Le moment philosophique déterminé par la guerre dans la politique: Lénine 1914–16," in *Les philosophes et la guerre de 14*, edited and with an introduction by Phillippe Soulez (Saint-Denis: Presses Universitaires de Vincennes, 1998)—hence the reference to comparing philosophers in the face of war.

1   Cf. in particular Moshe Lewin, "Lénine et bolshevisme à l'épreuve de l'histoire et du pouvoir," in *Les Aventures du marxisme*, ed. René Gallissot (Paris: Syros, 1984). George Haupt's study "Guerre et révolution chez Lénine," from which I borrow some essential elements, notes at the start that "a cleavage can be seen in Lenin's thought between the periods before and after 1914" (reprinted in G. Haupt, *L'Historien et le mouvement social* [Paris: Maspero, 1980], 237–66).

2   Both "The Collapse of the Second International" and the "April Theses" are reprinted in Lenin, *Collected Works* (Moscow: Progress Publishers, 1960), vols. 21 and 24 respectively.

3   Lenin, *What the "Friends of the People" Are*, in *Collected Works*, vol. 1.

4   Lenin, *Materialism and Empirio-Criticism*, in *Collected Works*, vol. 14.

5   I do not consider as such the articles Lenin wrote after the revolution to exhort the study of dialectics and materialism, taking a position in the debates around *Proletkult*, the final somersaults in the Bolshevik-Menshevik conflict, or the first episodes in the discussion on science and technology, all of which went on to play a role in the formation of Soviet philosophy. (Cf. René Zapata, ed., *Luttes philosophiques en U.R.S.S.* [Paris: PUF, 1983].)

6   Cf. the preface by the CPSU Central Committee's Institute of Marxism-Leninism to the volume of the *Collected Works* containing the *Philosophical Notebooks*: "It may be presumed that the preparatory material of *Notebooks on Philosophy* is evidence of Lenin's intention to write a special work on materialist dialectics, a task which he had no opportunity to fulfil. . . . The study of the great ideological content of *Philosophical Notebooks* is of tremendous importance for a thorough grasp of Marxist-Leninist philosophy, the theoretical foundation of scientific communism" (38:18).

7   Cf. H. Lefebvre and N. Guterman, introduction (dated 1935) to *Cahiers sur la dialectique de Hegel* (Paris: Gallimard, 1967), the themes of this being taken up again by Lefebvre in *Pour connaître la pensée de Lénine* (Paris: Bordas, 1957). It seems that Lefebvre was unaware of Lenin's notes on Clausewitz.

8   Lenin, "Imperialism, the Highest Stage of Capitalism," in *Collected Works*, vol. 22.

9   Lenin, "A Caricature of Marxism and 'Imperialist Economism,'" and "The Military Programme of the Proletarian Revolution," both in *Collected Works*, vol. 23.

10 Lenin, "On the Disarmament Slogan," "Bourgeois Pacifism and Socialist Pacifism," and "A Turn in World Politics," all in *Collected Works*, vol. 23.

11 Cf. the "Junius Pamphlet," that is, *The Crisis of Social-Democracy* (1916), abridged translation in P. Hudis and K. Anderson, eds., *The Rosa Luxemburg Reader* (New York: Monthly Review Press, 2004). Compare it to Lenin, "The Situation and the Tasks of the Socialist International," in *Collected Works*, vol. 21. Lenin's critique of

Luxemburg, "On the Junius Pamphlet," can be found in his *Collected Works*, vol. 23.

12   Lenin, *The Development of Capitalism in Russia* (1899), in *Collected Works*, vol. 3; "Theses on the National Question" (1913), in ibid., vol. 19; and "The Collapse of the Second International" (1915), in ibid., vol. 21.

13   Cf. my commentary in É. Balibar, *On the Dictatorship of the Proletariat* (London: NLB, 1977), and especially that of Robert Linhart, *Lénine, les paysans, Taylor* (Paris: Seuil, 1976).

14   Lenin, *Philosophical Notebooks*, in *Collected Works*, 38:365.

15   Lenin's notes on Clausewitz were published in 1930 in *Leninskij sbornik*, vol. 12; the German edition edited by Otto Braun (a former Comintern delegate in China during the Long March) is W. I. Lenin, *Clausewitz' Werk 'Vom Kriege'* (Berlin: Verlag des Ministeriums für nationale Verteidigung, 1957). Raymond Aron (*Penser la guerre, Clausewitz* [Paris: Gallimard, 1976], 2:61) cites a French translation that I have not been able to consult, in Berthold C. Friedl, *Les fondements théoriques de la guerre et de la paix en U.R.S.S.* (Paris: Médicis, 1945).

16   Cf. Charles Andler, *Le Pangermanisme philosophique* (Paris: Conard, 1913).

17   In his commentary (*Penser la guerre, Clausewitz*, 61ff., 213ff., 330ff.), Raymond Aron noted the close link between Lenin's notes on Clausewitz and his reflection on dialectics, but he restricted the significance of this in considering that the "fusion" of Marxist and Clausewitzian themes that Lenin had effected amounted to making war the *instrument* of revolution, requiring a "flexibility" of tactical utilization. The reading I propose here is different. However, Aron was right to raise the question of the limits of Lenin's analysis of nationalism. And he refutes very clearly any assimilation of Lenin's interpretation of Clausewitz to that of precursors of National-Socialism such as Ludendorff, a ridiculous notion still maintained under more or less scholarly aegis. (Cf. C. Roig, *La Grammaire politique de Lénine* [Lausanne: L'Age d'Homme, 1980].)

18   "With reference to wars, the main thesis of dialectics . . . is that 'war is simply the continuation of politics by other (i.e., violent) means'" (Lenin, "The Collapse of the Second International," in *Collected Works*, 21:219). Other explicit references to Clausewitz occur in Lenin, "Socialism and War," *Collected Works*, 21:304, and Lenin, "The War and Revolution" (May 1917), *Collected Works*, 24:399 and 402.

19   Cf. Bertolt Brecht, *Mé Ti, Livre des retournement*, translated into French by Bernard Lortholary (Paris: l'Arche, 1979). "'Basing ourselves on the *great method* that the masters Hü Yeh and Ka Meh taught, we speak too much of the perishable character of all things,' Mé Ti said with a sigh. 'Many people consider this language already too subversive. This perishable character of things is in their eyes a threat addressed to the rulers. But it is wrong to call it the *great method*. What is needed is to speak of the way in which certain things can be led to perish'" (53).

20   Cf. Lenin, "The Collapse of the Second International," in *Collected Works*, vol. 21, and "Opportunism and the Collapse of the Second International," in ibid., 22:438–53.

21 This is the interpretation of Marc Ferro among others: "Lenin, unable to oppose the patriotic current, proposed the transformation of the European war into a civil war" ("Première Guerre Mondiale" in *Encyclopaedia Universalis* [Paris: Encylopaedia Universalis]). Preferable is the painstaking analysis of George Haupt ("Guerre et révolution chez Lénine," 251ff.) on the origin of this slogan based on the double analysis of the conjuncture and the structural transformations of imperialism in the war.

22 I summarize here the sense of the analyses contained in vol. 23 of Lenin's *Collected Works*, in particular 22ff., 77ff., 152ff., 175ff., 229ff., 297ff. What is notable here is how much more Clausewitzian Lenin actually was here, in the "dialectical" use he made of *Vom Kriege*, than the strategists (Foch, Schlieffen) who claimed this ancestry. (Cf. R. Aron, *Penser la guerre, Clausewitz*, 28ff.)

23 Cf. Balibar, *On the Dictatorship of the Proletariat*; and Balibar, "Dictature du prolétariat," in *Dictionnaire critique du marxisme*, ed. G. Labica and G. Bensussan, 2nd ed. (Paris: PUF, 1985).

24 Lenin, "The Discussion on National Self-Determination Summed Up" (1916), in *Collected Works*, 22:320ff.

25 Cf. Lenin, "On the Slogan for a United States of Europe," in *Collected Works*, 21:344ff.), and "Bourgeois Pacifism and Socialist Pacifism," in ibid., 23:175–94.

26 This double critique lay at the heart of his "April Theses," "The Tasks of the Proletariat in Our Revolution," and "Draft Resolution on the War," in *Collected Works*, vol. 24.

27 Lenin, *The State and Revolution*, in *Collected Works*, vol. 25.

11

From Imperialism

Georges Labica | **to Globalization**

Lenin's booklet "Imperialism, the Highest Stage of Capitalism (A Popular Outline)," which appeared in 1917, was written in Zurich, the author tells us, in spring of the previous year.[1] It responded to an emergency situation. It was necessary to comprehend the nature of the world war and explain its characteristics in order to determine the attitude that socialists should take toward it. The war corresponded to a new stage that capitalism had reached; it was now *imperialist* and its objective conditions represented the "prelude to the socialist revolution." Such was the thesis that Lenin put forward. It was both economic, asserting that imperialism was the product of the development of capitalism and not just a "policy" that could be opposed, and political, denouncing the social-chauvinism that rallied to the bourgeois cause not just as a betrayal of socialism, but as having proved incapable of understanding that the war could provide the proletariat with an occasion for victory. Lenin's analysis rejected any kind of neutrality. It diagnosed, on the contrary, a "split in socialism," opposing the reformist currents symbolized by the eminent figure of Karl Kautsky, Engels's heir and leader of the German Social Democrats, to the revolutionary current whose intransigence was represented, despite certain mistaken views, by Rosa Luxemburg. The theory of imperialism formed the point of articulation of a many-sided struggle, both ideological and strategic, which would culminate in the October Revolution. This means that it combined all of Lenin's various interventions concerning the specific character of wars, the national question and the right of nations to self-determination, the conditions for the socialist revolution and "full democracy,"[2] the "two camps" that divide the world,[3] and internationalism. "It goes without saying that there can be no concrete historical assessment of the current war, unless it is based on a thorough analysis of the nature of imperialism, both in its economic and political aspects."[4] Georg Lukács was the first to maintain, in 1924, that "Lenin's superiority—and this is an unparalleled theoretical achievement—consists in his concrete articulation of the economic theory of imperialism with every political problem of the present epoch, thereby making the economics of the new phase a guideline for all concrete action in the resultant decisive conjuncture."[5]

The modest subtitle of Lenin's work—"A Popular Outline"—should not lead us to underestimate the enormous preparatory work that went into it. This is to be found in the "Notebooks on Imperialism," which fill nine hundred pages of his *Collected Works*, volume 39, and only cover the period 1915-16. These notebooks, numbered from "alpha" to "omicron," and supplemented by various other notebooks on particular themes (for example "Marxism and Imperialism," "Material on Persia," and "Various Notes"), contain commented extracts from nearly 150 books, as well as 240 articles that appeared in forty-nine different periodicals, in German, French, English, and Russian, together with full bibliographical lists drawn up chiefly on the basis of the stocks of the Zurich library, the city where Lenin lived at this time.[6] On several occasions Lenin worked there on the plan of the "Imperialism"[7] booklet, as well as the articles "Imperialism and the Right of Nations to Self-Determination"[8] and "Imperialism and the Split in Socialism."[9] He extracted every piece of information concerning trusts (electricity, petrol, coal, iron, cinema), the struggles for hegemony between the great powers, the banks, the various imperialisms, the colonial system. He paid particular attention to two works that formed his main sources. One of these was J. A. Hobson's *Imperialism*, first published in London in 1902, to which Notebook Kappa devotes his longest summary (405-36). He paid particular attention to examples of parasitism, for example, England having Indian troops make war on its behalf (418). He noted that the dominant state set out to corrupt the lower classes in order to keep them quiet, and that the "white races" had been freed from labor and were "living as a sort of world aristocracy by the exploitation of the 'lower races'" (420), also that "China may awaken" (428). He indicated that capital had succeeded in international collaboration much more quickly than the workers (428), that imperialism used its economic superiority to prevent the development of the dominated countries (430), and that inequalities between countries were an asset for imperialism (430). But it was the Marxist Rudolf Hilferding's book *Finance Capital*, published in 1910 with a Russian edition in 1912, to which Lenin was closest and to which he owed most. While particularly approving such important lessons as that "the reply of the proletariat to the economic policy of finance capital, to imperialism, can only be socialism, not free trade" (337), he does not hesitate to stress the "defects" that his own book was to rectify, that is, a theoretical error on money; the almost total failure to recognize the division of the world between the great powers; misunderstanding of the correlation between finance capital and parasitism, and between imperialism and opportunism.[10] In connection with his central preoccupation with imperialism, Lenin also reread certain writings of Marx and Engels concerning Europe, Russia, the national question, internationalism, the Paris Commune, and Ireland.[11] Among the Marxists whose texts he perused, Lenin reserved a particular place for Kautsky, preparing the plan of the pamphlet he would devote to him later on.[12] Hobson's work, he writes, "is especially useful because it helps to reveal the basic falsity of Kautskyism on this subject" (116). Kautsky had committed a double error. On the one hand, he imagined it possible to oppose, to the pillage of the banking monopolies and colonial oppression, a "'healthy,' 'peaceful' capitalism," in other words a "petty-bourgeois reformism in favour of a cleanish, sleek, moderate and genteel capitalism" (ibid.), and thus ceased to see imperialism as an economic stage; on the other hand, with his thesis on *ultra-imperialism*, Kautsky maintained the illusion of a future pacified thanks to the union of capitalist powers.

We shall confine ourselves here to noting the exemplary character of Lenin's method of working. It is in no way different from that which he had employed somewhat earlier in preparing his pamphlet on *The State and Revolution*. In my introduction to the Blue Notebook, I wrote:

> Practical activity: struggle against the war at the conferences of Zimmer-
> wald and Kienthal. Theoretical activity: theses on the right of nations
> to self-determination, on socialism and war, the collapse of the Second
> International, imperialism as the highest stage of capitalism. Public and

private activity: this propagandist and activist was a library bookworm, filling notebook after notebook with his reading notes. . . . Concrete analysis of the concrete situation: whilst Lenin's political practice forged the scientific instruments for a transformation of the world, in the strictest sense, in which we are still engaged, elsewhere the noise of other weapons, which unmasked the violence inherent in capitalist relations of production, took hold of the workers' movement itself and struck its best minds with blindness.[13]

This was already the lesson of *Capital*.

A final precision is necessary to avoid a misunderstanding that has become classic. The term "highest" in the title of Lenin's work should not be understood as "last" or "final," in any ontological sense, that is, the stage after which there could be no further development. It simply means "contemporary" or "present." The author himself made this clear on a number of occasions. In considering a title, he initially opted for "Imperialism, the highest (modern) stage of capitalism."[14] Elsewhere he wrote "modern (recent, the recent stage of)" (230). He took over, in fact, the subtitle of Hilferding's *Finance Capital*: "the recent phase in the development of capitalism" (333).[15] We shall see that in this sense, the present globalization can be equally considered as belonging to the imperialist stage or as representing a new expression of it. Lenin, in a similar spirit, evoked the "new imperialism" when he copied out Hobson's sentence: "The new imperialism differs from the older, first, in substituting for the ambition of a single growing empire the theory and practice of competing empires, each motived by similar lusts of political aggrandisement and commercial gain; secondly, in the dominance of financial interests or investing over mercantile interests."[16] He gave a chronology of it, this time following the book by E. Ulbricht, *Puissance mondiale et État national (Histoire politique 1500–1815)*: the old imperialism had died with Napoleon on St. Helena; the new imperialism corresponded to the foundation of a new world empire by Great Britain, which led other nations to follow suit and thus to economic competition with other peoples.[17]

What were the most striking features of this imperialism, according to Lenin? The most explicit presentation of these is given in "Imperialism and the Split in Socialism," which can serve as a grid for the reading of the other texts. Here are the essential points.

1) Imperialism is a particular historical stage of capitalism, the stage of monopoly capitalism, which is expressed in five main phases:
    a) cartels, employers' associations, trusts, these being products of the concentration of production;
    b) the big banks;
    c) the seizure of sources of raw materials by the trusts and the financial oligarchy. N.B.: finance capital = monopolized industrial capital + banking capital;
    d) the economic division of the world by the international cartels. N.B.: export of goods, characteristic of non-monopoly capital, has been followed by export of capital;
    e) the territorial division of the world (colonies) has been completed.

    We should add that, historically, imperialism was fully established between 1898 and 1914 (reference points being the Spanish-American War of 1898, the Anglo-Boer War of 1899–1902, the Russo-Japanese War of 1904–05, and the European economic crisis of 1900).

2) Imperialism is a parasitical or rotting capitalism. N.B.: These terms differ from those under the first heading in that they appear to express a value judgment, but they are also economic, while the political implications of the analysis are beginning to be drawn. Thus:
    a) the imperialist bourgeoisie, despite the often rapid development of certain branches of industry, is rotting because it has turned from being republican and democratic (under free competition) to being reactionary;
    b) formation of a broad stratum of *rentiers* living from "coupon clipping";
    c) export of capital, which is "parasitism squared";
    d) political reaction is specific to the nature of imperialism; it is a principle of venality and corruption, and produces "Panamas of all kinds";
    e) exploitation of oppressed nations: the "civilized" world lives parasitically on the body of the noncivilized. N.B.: this is true also for a privileged stratum of the proletariat in Europe.

3) Imperialism is *capitalism in its agony, marking the transition toward socialism*, owing to the socialization of labor, which is far more advanced than in the previous stage.

To summarize again some of these features, imperialism is a necessary product of the development of capitalism:

capitalism = free competition = democracy
imperialism = monopoly = reaction.

We can immediately note here the intimate connection of the two levels, economic (status of the productive forces) and political (nature of the social relations), which in the event makes clear the fact that there is a contradiction between imperialism and democracy. Lenin himself draws a conclusion from this: to separate foreign policy from domestic, he writes, is anti-scientific, since in each case imperialism seals the triumph of reaction.

"Imperialism is a superstructure of capitalism"; this formulation was used by Lenin in his "Report on the Party Programme" (19 March 1919).[18] The essence of his proof of this was as follows. Taking up Marx's verdict when he declared that manufacture was a superstructure of mass-scale petty production (*Capital*, vol. 1), he put forward three propositions:

1) there is no imperialism without previous capitalism;
2) with the collapse of imperialism "the foundations are laid bare";
3) it is necessary therefore to take account of an "immense lower layer of previous capitalism."

Lenin had set out to demonstrate this, for the Russian case, in his book *The Development of Capitalism in Russia*, when he analyzed the mutual entanglement of different modes of production as characteristic of the country's economic structure. The term "superstructure" came to specify the nature of imperialism, which is indeed, as Henri Lefebvre wrote, "at the same time as being a form of capitalism (economic element), a form of class activity of the bourgeoisie (social element) and a form of state (political element), the whole being inseparably combined."[19]

We shall not deal here with the various debates that took place at that time around the features of imperialism and its definition. Even among "left-wing" Marxists the differences were significant: with Bukharin, whom Lenin took issue with despite having written a preface to his pamphlet;[20] with Rosa Luxemburg over her *Accumulation of Capital* even if in an indirect manner;[21] or with Anton Pannekoek, who "posits the problem of reformism badly."[22]

We shall rather investigate the question of the topicality of Lenin's theses today, without falling into the coquetry of postponing the answer that the reader will already have expected: contemporary globalization is nothing other than Lenin's "new imperialism," now reaching a still higher stage of development. With due apologies to postmodern mockers, always in a hurry to dismiss as prehistoric any language that does not reflect their own submission to the dominant order, there are certain terms whose ability to grasp reality has lost nothing of its effectiveness. *Imperialism* is one of these and continues to govern a constellation of concepts, in which *capitalism, exploitation, property, classes and class struggle, social democracy*, and *revolutionary transition* still keep their full meaning. There is no lack of analogies and similarities that translate the same essence. Besides those already noted, we can offer some new ones. Today's lively discussions bearing on the definition and periodization of globalization recall the arguments that accompanied the recognition of imperialism in the early twentieth century: relationship to capitalism, determining features, reciprocal roles of economics and politics, forms of competition, appearance in the 1960s (or earlier or later), even so early that some people reject any originality for a phenomenon that they see as coextensive with capitalism. It is certainly true that the world market coincided with the advent of capitalist relations of production; Marx and Engels stressed this fact in their *Manifesto*.[23] And Marx returned to this point in *Capital*: "Capitalist production creates the world market," and the formation of this is one of the specific features of capitalism.[24] As for the predominance of finance capital, we know that Marx had already shown how "with interest-bearing capital, the capitalist relation reaches its ultimate point," that is, M—M, what Marx calls the "automatic fetish," "self-valorizing value, money breeding money." "Thus it becomes as completely the property of money to create value, to yield interest, as it is the property of a pear tree to bear pears."[25] Whereas in all cases—need we recall?— "it is profit based on productive capital that is the root of the profits of finance capital."[26]

None the less, the specificity of the new imperialism that is globalization should not be underestimated, whatever the nuances that are applied in its definition or periodization. Undoubtedly the features already noted by its first theorists—Hobson, Hilferding, Lenin—have been continued, but they are accelerated by the conjunction of three recent phenomena: the predominance of speculative finance capital, the technological revolutions, especially in the field of information and communications, and the collapse of the so-called socialist countries. Flows of capital certainly played a role already at the start of the twentieth century, but they have now come to the point of triggering a systemic integration that enables the monopolies to consider the world as a global field in the service of their interests, relayed by the international institutions under their control that fulfill the function of a planetary government (the IMF, the World Bank, the WTO, and so forth). The end of any competition between antagonistic "blocs," whatever their regimes and forms, also leaves the field open to a single superpower, the United States of America, whose hegemony is exercised in every domain—economic, military, strategic, political, legal, scientific, technological, linguistic, and cultural. Endowed with an omnipotence never before attained by any nation, the United States now holds the place once occupied by Great Britain. While noting the role of this last, Lenin foresaw the transition of power already in 1915 when he wrote that the United States was the "leading country of modern capitalism . . . [and] is in many respects the model for our bourgeois civilization and is its ideal."[27] There is no division of the world that is not the object of a redivision,[28] with the difference that the competing imperialisms of today's "triad" (the United States, Europe, and Japan) are not in a relation of equality; the last two are very much in a subaltern position vis à vis the former dominant power, being now completely vassalized and playing only a subcontracting role.[29] Globalization is thus one and the same as Americanization—or *U.S.-Americanization* as it should rightly be called.[30]

In this list of complementary analogies, we should not forget the orders of politics and ideology. A few brief remarks will suffice, as things have become so clear since the aftermath of the fall of the Berlin Wall, when liberalism sung a victory whose days were numbered.

For the political order, three elements should be considered:

1) The "reaction," which, far from signaling a retreat of state prerogatives, surreptitiously places the state in the service of the needs of the multinationals, whether the object is to privatize, increase flexibility, downsize, or finance by an ongoing reduction of taxes, and proceeds

to the abandonment of sovereignty needed by economic concentra-
tions (competitivity) and political ones (European Union). The destruction of public services, the dismantling of the right to work, the
suppression of cultural autonomy (the "French exception" in films),
and junk food are all part of the price paid.

2) The rallying of Social Democratic and, more recently, Communist
parties to the management of capitalism, so that far from preserving
"social gains" they devote themselves to the quest for civic "consensus," but in a covert fashion. Kautsky would not believe his eyes.

3) The defeat, followed by the decomposition, of the revolutionary
(workers,' socialist) movement under the double impact of globalization and the collapse of the "socialist camp," which no longer seems
to authorize a "split" in the direction of a socialist offensive, as in
1915–16, but rather to signal the death of a hope.

As for the second order, the ideological, this emphasizes "democracy" pure and simple, offered as a "model" especially to the countries
of Eastern Europe (and we know what use they make of it), and assimilated to the market, along with the discourse on rights—human rights,
the *Rechtsstaat*, international law, recently supplemented by the "right
of intervention," the sole objective of which is to inculcate the reign of
TINA (There Is No Alternative), the Thatcherite deity of submission to
the fatality of neoliberalism. The other side of the coin, which in fact
is simply a replica of the same, is political abstentionism, religious and
nationalist regression, community and ethnic assertion, to say nothing of the daily growth in inequality that does not spare any domain,
from income to education to health. Clearly the gift box in which the
package is wrapped has a different image, that of a "happy globalization" (as we are assured by a licensed sycophant), guaranteeing at
least in *virtual* fashion (which *is* the fashion) growth for all, respect
for differences, promotion of sociality, free access to information, and
unobstructed movement in the "global village." This image has succeeded to the point that some people, with good faith or bad, manage
to think and even maintain that a choice remains possible between bad
and good globalization. All that is needed is to "weigh in on the right
side" and "anchor to the left" governments that are still undecided.[31]

What then is the present situation? We have learned well enough what Empire means (this already applied to Rome), and the whole twentieth century has taught us the sense of the "new imperialism." Certainly Zbigniew Brzezinski would not pretend otherwise. To take some snippets from his book: "The defeat and collapse of the Soviet Union was the final step in the rapid ascension . . . of the United States, as the sole and, indeed, the first truly global power"; "the American political experience tends to serve as a standard for emulation"; "to put it in a terminology that hearkens back to the more brutal age of ancient empires, the three grand imperatives of imperial geostrategy are to prevent collusion and maintain security dependence among the vassals, to keep tributaries pliant and protected, and to keep the barbarians from coming together"; "[we need] to manage the rise of other regional powers in ways that do not threaten America's global primacy"; "a wider Europe and an enlarged NATO will serve well both the short-term and the longer-term goals of U.S. policy."[32]

But "globalization . . . is no more than a mystifying term for imperialism,"[33] "the unequal spread of capitalism on the planetary scale."[34] Not only do specialists concerned with analyzing the reality of our time not hesitate to use the term *imperialism*,[35] several expressly refer to Lenin's theses. S. de Brunhoff and W. Andreff emphasize the actuality of the law of unequal development.[36] D. Collin writes: "Neo-liberalism is not the expression of a revitalization of the free-market capitalism of the previous century, it is above all the theorization and legitimization of what can more properly be called imperialism in the sense of Hilferding and Lenin."[37] A. Catone, for his part, notes: "All the characteristic aspects of imperialism noted by Lenin have undergone a tremendous development: monopolies, cartels, trusts have become mega-monopolies."[38] And what about parasitism? "As for the tentacular development of a widely parasitical financial oligarchy, it is not necessary to read Lenin's *Imperialism* to be convinced of this; George Soros, the celebrated speculator, explains it himself in his books."[39] Perhaps "putrefaction" is a little strong? This is quite evident, however, in the "countries rich in capital," declares G. de Bernis, its symptoms including a brake on technical progress, a large number of *rentiers* still living on "coupon clipping," not to mention "*rentier* states" oppressing "creditor states." "It is in no way surprising that . . . the present manifestations of the 'rottenness' of capitalism are more numerous and deeper than Lenin observed at the end of a period of (relative) stability."[40] We should not miss the allusion to our own fine country when Lenin copies out the following passage from M. Sembat: "The modern financial history of France, if it were ever sincerely written, would be the history of a multitude of acts of plunder, like the sack of a conquered city!"[41]

It is unfortunately necessary to go a step further in this characterization, and maintain that the situation engendered by our "new imperialism" is worse than that which prevailed in the 1910s. As we have just seen, the situation at that time was marked by a relative stability, which is no longer the case in the present crisis, and prevented Lenin from speaking of unemployment or mass poverty. Besides, not only did the phenomenon of multinationals not then present "this ubiquity that it has acquired today,"[42] but many other features have grown considerably more acute, including the steady diminution of the state's functions of social regulation, the decline of the nation-state, which is no longer what it still was in the aftermath of the First World War, the concentration and fusion of firms, the circulation of capital, and the role of stock exchanges.[43] A possible way of updating Lenin's text would be to substitute for the data he presented what we have available today. The result would be illuminating on the "monopolists throttling those which do not submit to their yoke" (206), on the "domination and violence that is associated with [monopoly capital]" (207), on "combination," on the banks, on the interpenetration of banking capital and industrial capital (223), on the financial oligarchies, joint-stock companies, and the illusion of their "democratization" (228), on the contamination of politics and other fields by monopoly capital (237), on the export of capital, on the debt (242–43), on the hunt for raw materials (260), on the dependence of countries that are in principle independent (263–64), on inter-imperialist rivalries, on the project of a United States of Europe,[44] on the "increase in immigration into these countries from the more backward countries where lower wages are paid" (282), or on the defense of imperialism by "bourgeois scholars and publicists" (286).

We may add that the insertion of data from the most official statistical sources would demonstrate really stupefying gaps. To give just one example concerning speculative capital, which as we know is at the center stage of "globalization": after the abandonment of the Bretton

Woods agreement and the end of the monetary system based on the gold standard, the 50 billion Eurodollars of 1969, already considered disturbing, have risen to 8,000 billion, though this is only "a small share of world finance."[45] If we finally take into account elements unknown to the old "new imperialism," since they simply did not exist, or at least in some cases not on such a scale, such as the weight of debt controlled by the international monetary institutions, which has led to the ruin of an entire continent (Africa), we have such things as the threat of nuclear weapons, the dangers to the environment, the foreseeable shortage of drinking water, and the general commodification that extends to the sale of organs and the massive prostitution of children, so that we should not be afraid to speak of a regular "criminalization of the world economy."[46] The drug trade, another element previously unknown, stands at the head of world commerce, narcotics being the commodity with the highest rate of profit. This is the basis not just for economic networks such as "tax havens" and banking establishments specializing in money laundering, but for the whole system being gnawed away from within. Despite their moral denials and repressive simulacra (destruction of drug plantations), the developed countries, rich and powerful, protect the circuits from which they derive such great profit, this manna being legally integrated into the most official activities. So-called dirty money can now no longer be distinguished from clean. From its marginal origins, corruption penetrates all the driving wheels of the social body, especially politics, which is one of the reasons it is so discredited.[47]

A final question: How do things stand with the relationship that Lenin established between imperialism and the transition to socialism? Is not this the point that refutes his entire theory, when historical science assures us that the revolutionary process begun in 1917 has not kept its promise, and has even collapsed with the Soviet system in 1989, while capitalism, giving proof of an unsuspected vitality, has succeeded in overcoming its crises and re-establishing with globalization an equilibrium that enables it to fulfill its essence, conferring on it a geostrategic mastery without precedent? This argument, however, does not hold water, for a series of reasons that are closely interconnected. We can mention the familiar historical fact that globalization is a process under way, that its career is in no way completed and is difficult to predict; that this process, by general opinion, is contradictory, determined by the well-known "surprises" of the market that confound economists, the "invisible hand" acting in the last instance as it wills (from the Mexican crisis via the Asian crisis to the Nasdaq crash); and that this process is affected less by rivalries within the triad than by what might happen with the so-called emerging countries, from Brazil to China.[48] Brzezinski himself scarcely expects the reign of the "indispensable nation" to last more than a generation, and he does not rule out "that a genuinely pre-revolutionary situation is in the process of taking shape."[49] If it is true, in contrast, that Lenin expected a great deal of socialization as imperialism accelerated, in relation to the old capitalism of competition between small and medium-sized firms, if he expected—not without hard struggles—the opening of a revolutionary period as a function of the world conflict,[50] if he even betrayed a weakness, soon rectified, for the *political* slogan of a United States of Europe,[51] this cannot be attributed to any predisposition to optimism in his temperament, but rather to the conjuncture in which he lived, to the "concrete situation" that was his. This is where the difference lies. Lenin was still a man of the Enlightenment, nearer in this to his *maîtres à penser* than we are, witnesses and heirs to a century of blood, massacre, and ruins, of which he saw only the beginnings—what we dare to call "modernity" has forced us to renounce any form of inevitability, even of a revolutionary kind. It is none the less the case that this pessimism, if it should be called that, is also anchored in a particular context. It is the reflection of this imperialism of despair that is globalization, for although the positive possibilities of this may well be discerned, lucid attention is necessarily focused on the extraordinary power of the negative inherent in the system. But this is why, in a seeming paradox, Lenin's diagnosis maintains its pertinence, even in its *different* conclusion. For it is a system that is in question, and this system of *capitalism* has remained the same in nature from Marx's *Capital* to its imperialist avatars, which, by way of the considerable revolutions these have brought and which have changed our ways of seeing the world, and by way of the rhythm of these revolutions, have only confirmed its deleterious nature, to the point of giving the necessity of changing it a genuinely emergency character. The novelty is not to be sought elsewhere, and it is radical. Poorly equipped and disorganized as the forces against it might be, for apparent conjunctural reasons, they face the very same task. The most recent symptoms multiply to the point of suggesting that convergences will occur, are indeed in the process of happening, and which have an unquestionable finality even if their program is certainly not already cut and dried.

Globalization in the true sense, such as every *internationalist* has dreamed of, is still something to be won. The judgment of Rosa Luxemburg, for whom imperialism had no more secrets, reaches us like a clenched fist: capitalism is incapable of achieving globalization, as its internal contradictions will devour it before this point; only socialism can do so.[52]

Notes

This chapter was originally published as the introduction to *L'impérialisme, stade suprême du capitalisme*, by Vladimir Ilich Oulianov Lénine (Pantin: Le Temps des Cerises, 2001).

1 The text is cited here from Lenin's *Collected Works* (Moscow: Progress Publishers, 1960), 22:185–304. All subsequent citations in this chapter to Lenin's *Collected Works* are cited by volume number, and page number(s), with title and year of original publication included when not mentioned specifically in the text.

2 "It would be a radical mistake to think that the struggle for democracy was capable of diverting the proletariat from the socialist revolution or of hiding it, overshadowing it, etc. On the contrary, in the same way as there can be no victorious socialism that does not practise full democracy, so the proletariat cannot prepare for its victory over the bourgeoisie without an all-round, consistent and revolutionary struggle for democracy" ("The Socialist Revolution and the Right of Nations to Self-Determination" [1916], 22:144).

3 "There are now actually two parties all over the world. There are in fact already two Internationals" ("Split or Decay?" [1916], 22:181).

4 "Preface to N. Bukharin's Pamphlet, *Imperialism and the World Economy*," 22:103. See below.

5 G. Lukács, *Lenin: A Study in the Unity of His Thought* (London: NLB, 1970), 41.

6 Cf. also "Imperialism and Socialism in Italy," in which Lenin examined the works of R. Michels and T. Barboni (21:357–66).

7 Cf., among other passages, 39:100, 218, 757–58.

8 See 39:735–42.

9 See 39:754–55 and "Imperialism and the Split in Socialism," 23:105–20. It should be noted that the "Notebooks on Imperialism" (39:27–786) give full references to the works in other volumes that contain the main interventions on imperialism.

10 These "defects" are mentioned in Notebook Beta, where the themes "On the Ques-

tion of Imperialism" are listed (39:201–2). The analysis of Hilferding's work as such is found at the start of Notebook Theta (333ff.). Cf. also "Hilferding (Kautskyite Views)" (613–15).

11   On the last two of these questions, the interest of which is self-evident, Lenin himself made a connection with his own reflection on "Marxism and the State" (the Blue Notebook); cf. 39:583.

12   "The Proletarian Revolution and the Renegade Kautsky" (1918), vol. 28; but Kautsky is regularly targeted in all the writings of the previous period.

13   Cf. V. I. Lenin, Le Cahier bleu (Le marxisme quant à l'État), ed. G. Labica, trans. (from Russian) B. Lafite (Brussels: Complexe, 1977), 5.

14   Notebook Beta, 39:206.

15   Cf. also "modern," 39:420, the preface to Bukharin's pamphlet, 22:107 and below.

16   "Notebooks on Imperialism," 39:428 (Lenin's emphases omitted); also Imperialism, 22:269 and below.

17   Cf. "Notebooks," 39:607.

18   Cf. "The VIIIth Congress of the C(B)PR," 29:168.

19   Cf. H. Lefebvre, Pour connaître la pensée de Lénine (Paris: Bordas, 1957), 236.

20   Scarcely a year later, Lenin was led to criticize Bukharin in "The Nascent Trend of Imperialist Economism" (August–September 1916), 23:13–21. See also, for more details, "Eighth Congress of the R.C.P.(B)," 29:165ff.; "Notebook 'Gamma,'" 39:247; "Notebook Imperialism," 39:756; and the correspondence of this period with Zinoviev, 43:544–74.

21   Cf. G. Labica, "Dialogue marxiste: Lénine et Luxemburg," La revue Commune 18 (May 2000).

22   Cf. "Notebooks on Imperialism," 39:270. This refers to Pannekoek's article "State Expenditure and Imperialism," which had appeared in Neue Zeit in 1913–14. At the same time, Lenin seems to have drawn usefully on Paul Louis, Essai sur l'impérialisme, which was published in Paris in 1904 ("Notebooks," 250). On conceptions of imperialism, I recall two publications that are certainly unavailable today, but which suffice to show the continuity of imperialism to our own time: L'impérialisme: Colloque d'Alger 21–24 Mars 1969 (Algiers: SNED, 1970); and the Journée d'étude sur l'impérialisme (Paris: Cahiers du C.E.R.M. 1 and 2, 1970).

23   Cf. Marx and Engels, "Manifesto of the Communist Party," in Karl Marx, The Revolutions of 1848 (Harmondsworth: Penguin, 1973), 71. Cf. G. Labica, "Les leçons du Manifeste," in Le Manifeste communiste aujourd'hui (an extract) (Paris: Éditions de l'Atelier, 1998), and in Realitat (Barcelona) 53–54 (1999) (in Spanish).

24   Marx, Capital (Harmondsworth: Penguin 1981), 3:359, 449. The world market is the basis of capitalism and is always present in the capitalist's mind (451); production for the world market is the precondition for capitalist production (205).

25   Cf. ibid., 516.

26   S. de Brunhoff, Mondialisation (Paris: Espaces Marx, 1999), 141.

27   "New Data on the Laws Governing the Development of Capitalism in Agriculture: Part One, Capitalism and Agriculture in the USA," 22:17.

28 Lenin cites a sentence from the book by G. F. Steffen, *World War and Imperialism*, which was published in 1915: "The world is now almost completely 'divided up.' But world history teaches us that empires tend to divide up *each other* after they have more or less divided among themselves the 'no-master' areas in all parts of the globe." In the margin Lenin comments: "well said!" (39:259).

29 G. de Bernis, for example, remarks: "It is no exaggeration to say that British capital has left Britain and is totally in sway to American" (J.-P. Michiels and D. Uzunidis, *Mondialisation et citoyenneté* [Paris: L'Harmattan, 1999], 72).

30 One effect of denoting the United States of America by the name America, and its nationals as Americans, is that these terms condemn all other nations on two continents to nonexistence. This is a completely internalized effect of U.S. hegemony.

31 This is of course the position of the PCF at its latest congress. Cf. Pierre Lévy, *Bastille, République, Nation, La mutation du PCF: Cette étrange défaite* (Paris: Michalon, 2000).

32 Z. Brzezinski, *The Grand Chessboard* (New York: HarperCollins, 1997). The quotations, which are selected almost at random, come from pp. xiii, 24, 40, 198, and 199. The NATO aggression against Yugoslavia had just given a new proof of this hegemony. (Cf. Samir Amin, *Maîtres du monde? Ou les dessous de la guerre des Balkans* [Paris: Le Temps des cerises, 1999].)

33 Cf. Bernard Gerbier, in *Mondialisation et citoyenneté*, 47.

34 Cf. J.-P. Michiels and D. Uzunidis, *Mondialisation et citoyenneté*, 11. Erna Betten notes that the present increased inequalities "were already described by Lenin in his 1917 book on imperialism" ("Where Do We Go from Kosovo?," *Australian Marxist Review* 41 [November 1999]).

35 Cf., for example, J. Magniadas, in *Mondialisation et citoyenneté*, 117, and P. Bourdieu and L. Wacquant, "La nouvelle vulgate planétaire," *Le Monde Diplomatique* (May 2000).

36 Cf. de Brunhoff, *Mondialisation*, 142 and 216.

37 Cf. D. Collin, "Néoliberalisme ou keynésianisme rénové: La fausse alternative," *L'Homme et la Société* (Paris) 135 (2000–2001): 51.

38 Cf. A. Catone. "Ridiscutere di imperialismo," *L'Ernesto* (Novara) 1 (2000): 3.

39 Cf. D. Collin, "Néoliberalisme ou keynésianisme rénové."

40 Cf. G. de Bernis, "Aspects économiques de la mondialisation," *Nord-Sud XXI* (Geneva) 13:1 (1999): 60ff.

41 The reference here is Marcel Sembat, *Faites un roi, sinon faites la paix*, which was published in 1913. ("Notebooks on Imperialism," 438, Lenin's emphases omitted; in the margin, Lenin wrote "NB.")

42 Cf. W. Andreff in *Mondialisation et citoyenneté*, 206.

43 We should note that Lenin held that the replacement of the "old capitalism" by monopolies would actually "reduce the importance of the stock exchange" (218).

44 This question can only be mentioned here. Lenin was hostile to such a perspective, which would have led to the establishment, foreseen by Hobson, of an aristocracy exploiting the rest of the world (cf. "Notebooks," 39:429); he also wrote against

Kautsky (380) and Bauer (626). He did in an almost prophetic fashion, however, retain as one of the tasks attributed to such a United States of Europe by G. Hildebrand that of struggling against "the great Islamic movement" ("Notebooks on Imperialism," 112; repeated in *Imperialism*, 281ff.). Cf. also "On the Slogan for a United States of Europe," 21:339–43.

45   Cf. G. de Bernis in *Mondialisation et citoyenneté*, 31.

46   The expression is found, among other places, in Jacques Chonchol, *Hacia dondé nos lleva la globalizacion? Reflexiones para Chile* (Santiago: Universidad Arcis, 1999), 22. In Latin America, this author tells us, the policy of "structural adjustment" increased the number of people living in poverty during the 1980s from 136 to 196 million. Jean-Louis Levet, for his part, writes: "This criminalization of the economy has become part of the backbone of the economic system and the international monetary system . . . a tool of regulation of the world economic system" (*Mondialisation et citoyenneté*, 356).

47   For further details and the most recent information, see the dossier of *Le Monde Diplomatique* of May 2000 on "The Planetary Archipelago of Financial Crime," especially the investigation by Christian de Brie, the very title of which, "States, Mafias and Transnationals as Thick as Thieves," gives a perfect summary of the process involved.

48   On the contradictions that undermine neoliberalism from within, to the point of preventing it from holding to its own objectives, we can refer to the unchallengeable demonstrations that Susan George gives in her recent book *The Lugano Report: On Preserving Capitalism in the 21st Century* (London: Pluto Press 1999).

49   Z. Brzezinski, *The Grand Chessboard* (New York: Basic Books, 1998), 196–97.

50   This sentiment is present in *Imperialism*. It possibly represents an echo of the enthusiasm of the *Communist Manifesto* for the permanent revolution of relations of production under capitalism, and thus a still teleological vision of progress.

51   Cf. "On the Slogan for a United States of Europe," 21:339–43.

52   "Although [capitalism] strives to become universal, and, indeed, on account of this its tendency, it must break down—because it is immanently incapable of becoming a universal form of production. In its living history it is a contradiction in itself, and its movement of accumulation provides a solution to the conflict and aggravates it at the same time. At a certain stage of development there will be no other way out than the application of socialist principles. The aim of socialism is not accumulation but the satisfaction of toiling humanity's wants by developing the productive forces of the entire globe. And so we find that socialism is by its very nature an harmonious and universal system of economy" (Rosa Luxemburg, *The Accumulation of Capital* [London: Routledge, 1963], 467).

Domenico Losurdo

1.

In Lenin the critique of colonialism and imperialism plays a central role, far beyond the immediacy of politics. What is democracy? Let us see how the classics of the liberal tradition define it.

Tocqueville describes the inhuman treatment reserved for the Indians and blacks in the United States lucidly and without indulgence. With successive deportations, and suffering the "terrible evils" that these involved, the former were by now clearly destined to be wiped off the face of the earth. As for the latter, they were subjected in the South to a more inflexible slavery than in the ancient classical world or Latin America. In the North they were in theory free, but in reality they continued to be victims of a "racial prejudice" that raged in a particularly cruel manner, so that the blacks were deprived not only of political rights but also civil rights, given that society had, in fact, delivered them helpless to racial violence: "Oppressed, you can complain but you will find only whites among your judges."[1] This did not prevent, however, the French liberal from celebrating America as the only country in the world where democracy was in force, "lively, active and triumphant."[2] The tones even become lyrical: "There you will see a people whose conditions are more equal than you will see even among us; in which the social order, the customs and the laws are all democratic; in which everything emanates from the people and returns to them, and where, however, each individual enjoys a more entire independence and a greater freedom than at any other time or in any other country on earth."[3]

And the Indians? And the blacks? Tocqueville responds in advance to these objections in his programmatic declaration at the beginning of the chapter dedicated to the problem of the "three races that inhabit the territory of the United States": "The main task that I imposed on myself has now been completed; I have shown, at least as far as it has been possible for me, what the laws of American democracy are and I have made its customs known. I could stop here." He writes about the relations between the three races only to avoid possible disillusion in the reader: "These arguments, that touch my subject, are not an integral part of it: they refer to America not to democracy, and I wanted above all to paint a portrait of democracy!"[4] However cruel the fate of two of the three races inhabiting the territory of the United States might be, it has nothing to do with the problem of democracy!

Let us take a leap back three decades and turn to an author who Bobbio has elected as the founding father of "liberal socialism."[5] In John Stuart Mill we can read that "*despotism is a legitimate mode of government in dealing with barbarians*, provided the end be their improvement, and the means justified by actually effecting that end. Liberty, as a principle, has no application to any state of things anterior to the time when mankind has become capable of being improved by free and equal discussion. Until then, there is nothing for them but *implicit obedience* to an Akbar or a Charlemagne, if they are so fortunate as to find one."[6]

This declaration is even more significant because it lies in a work thematically dedicated to the celebration of liberty (*On Liberty*). But it is clear that for the English liberal, liberty "is meant to apply only to human beings in the maturity of their faculties," and certainly not to a "race" that can or must be considered as "nonage,"[7] that is sometimes scarcely above the superior animal species.[8] And once again democracy and liberty are defined independently of the fate of the excluded, who are, however, the majority of human beings.

With respect to this world, Lenin represents a break not only at the political level but also at the level of epistemology. Democracy cannot be defined by abstracting the fate of the excluded. It is not just a question of colonial populations. In the imperial metropolis itself, in England, "small" (or allegedly small) details of the electoral legislation "deny political rights to women"[9] and to the "really proletariat inferior strata."[10] But the great Russian revolutionary concentrated particularly on the clause of exclusion of the colonial, or of colonial origin, populations.

2.

The history of the West confronts us with a paradox that can be best understood starting from the history of today's guide-nation: democracy among the white community developed simultaneously in relation to the enslaving of the blacks and the deportation of the Indians. For thirty-two of the first thirty-six years of the United States' life, slave-owners held the presidency, and they were also those who wrote the Declaration of Independence and the Constitution. Without slavery (and successive racial segregation), it is not possible to understand anything about "American liberty": they grew together, one sustaining the other. If the "peculiar institution" already assured an iron grip over the "dangerous" classes at the workplace, the moving frontier and the progressive expansion westward defused social conflict, transforming a potential proletariat into a class of landowners, at the expense, however, of populations condemned to being removed or swept away.

After the baptism of the War for Independence, American democracy experienced a further development in the 1830s under President Jackson: the cancellation, for the most part, of the census discriminations within the white community that went step by step with the vigorous impulse given to the deportation of the Indians and with mounting resentment and violence against the blacks. An analogous consideration can also be made for the so-called Progressive Age that, starting from the end of the nineteenth century, covered the first fifteen years of the twentieth century: it was certainly characterized by numerous democratic reforms (assuring direct election to the Senate, the secrecy of the vote, the introduction of primaries, the institution of referendums, and so forth), but it was at the same time a particularly tragic time for blacks, who were the target of Ku Klux Klan terrorist squads, and for Indians, who were deprived of their residual lands and subjected to a pitiless process of assimilation that aimed at depriving them even of their cultural heritage.

With regard to this paradox that characterizes the history of their country, authoritative U.S. scholars have spoken of *Herrenvolk democracy*, that is, democracy valid only for the "master-race" (to use the language dear to Hitler). The line of demarcation between whites, on the one hand, and blacks and Indians, on the other, favors the development of equality within the white community. The members of an aristocracy of class or color tend toward self-celebration as "peers"; the net inequality imposed upon the excluded is the other face of the relationship of parity installed among those who enjoy the power to exclude the "inferiors."

The category of *Herrenvolk democracy* can be useful also in explaining the history of the West as a whole. During the end of the nineteenth century and the beginning of the twentieth, the extension of the suffrage in Europe went step by step with the process of colonialism and with the imposition of servile or semi-servile work relations upon the subject populations; government by law in the metropolises was closely linked to the violence and arbitrariness of the bureaucracy and the police and with the state of siege in the colonies. It was, after all, the same phenomenon as in the history of the United States, only that in Europe's case it was less evident because the colonial populations, instead of living in the metropolis, were separated from it by the ocean.

3.

It is very difficult to find a critique of this "master-race democracy" in liberal thinking, which is rather often the theoretical expression of this regime. *Herrenvolk democracy* is instead the privileged target of Lenin's struggle. The revolutionary Russian leader stubbornly placed in evidence the macroscopic clauses of exclusion in liberal liberty at the expense of "red and black skins," as well as immigrants from "backward countries."[11] As in a play of mirrors, the West that gloried in government by law was placed before the reality of the colonies: "The most liberal and radical of politicians in free Great Britain . . . transformed themselves, when they became governors of India, into real and proper Genghis Khans."[12]

Giolitti's Italy can well be proud of the extension of citizenship to almost all the adult male population. But once again Lenin's counter-chorus echoes against liberal self-celebration, noting that the extension of the suffrage was aimed at enlarging the base of agreement for the Libyan expedition, that "typical colonial war of a twentieth-century 'civil' state: here is 'a civil and constitutional nation' proceeding in its work of 'civilization' by means of bayonets, bullets, rope, fire and rape," and even with the "slaughter"; it is "a civil, perfect butchery of men, a massacre of Arabs with 'extremely modern' arms . . . almost 3,000 Arabs were massacred, entire families were massacred, women and children massacred." [13]

Yes, Mill could celebrate the British Empire as "a step, as far as it goes, towards universal peace, and general friendly co-operation among nations." [14]

But, even ignoring the conflict between the great powers that finally led to the First World War, this celebration implies a monstrous repression: the expeditions of the great powers in the colonies are not considered wars. They were conflicts in which, even if "few Europeans died," nevertheless "hundreds of men, belonging to the peoples the Europeans were suffocating, lost their lives." And then—continued Lenin sharply—"can you call it war? In the strictest sense no, you cannot call it war and so you can forget it all." Not even the honors of war were allowed the victims. Colonial wars were not considered as such because it was barbarians who were subjected to them and they "did not deserve even being called people (were Asians and Africans people?)" and, they, after all, are excluded from the human community itself. [15]

It was on this basis that the split with Social Democracy took place. It was not determined by the reform/revolution dichotomy. This is a standard image that does not become more credible by being often shared, with contrary value judgments by both the antagonists. In the decades prior to the outbreak of the First World War, Bernstein saluted imperial German expansionism as a contribution to the cause of progress, civilization, and world trade: "If socialists proposed to help savages and barbarians in their struggle against encroaching capitalist civilization prematurely, it would be a throwback to romanticism." [16] Together with the West as a whole, Bernstein, like Theodore Roosevelt for his part, attributed to tsarist Russia too the role of "protecting and dominant power" in Asia. [17]

The German Social Democratic leader went up to the threshold of Social Darwinism. The "strong races" represented the cause of "progress," and so inevitably they "tend to enlarge and expand their civilization," while uncivilized and even peoples "incapable of civilizing themselves" conduct a useless and retrograde resistance; by "uprising against civilization" they must be fought even by the labor movement. If, on the one hand, he struggled for democratic reforms in Germany, on the other hand, Bernstein demanded an iron fist against barbarians: the logic is the same as that already analyzed of "master-race democracy."

The subjection of colonial peoples cannot be impeded by sentimental obstacles nor by abstract juridical considerations. Strong and civilized races cannot be made the "slaves of legal formalities." It was precisely the Social Democratic leader who theorized a superior substantial legality, starting from the philosophy of history dear to colonial tradition, and who then expressed his complete horror at the lack of respect for the rules of the game during the October Revolution.

That this represented a radical change with respect to an ideological and political tradition, in the setting of colonial arrogance and racial prejudice, is an obvious and self-evident fact. In these conditions, the appeal for a struggle for emancipation directed at the slaves of the colonies, and at the "barbarians" present in the capitalist metropolises themselves, could not but appear as a mortal menace to the white race, the West, and civilization as such.

Starting from that, the gigantic conflict that took place in the twentieth century can be understood. The fate reserved for centuries in the United States for Indians and blacks is a declared Fascist and Nazi model. In 1930, a prime ideologue of Nazism such as Rosenberg expressed his admiration for *white supremacy* America, that "splendid country of the future" that had had the merit of formulating the happy "new idea of a racial State," an idea that it is time to put into practice, "with youthful force," by expulsions and deportations of "Negroes and yellow-skins."[18] If, on one hand, the Third Reich presented itself, with its "Aryan" rhetoric, as the attempt, carried out in the conditions of total warfare, to create a *white supremacy* regime on a world-wide scale under German hegemony, on the other hand the Communist movement gave a decisive contribution to overcoming racial discrimination and colonialism, whose inheritance Nazism intended to assume and radicalize.

4.

In his struggle against *Herrenvolk democracy*, Lenin radicalized the lesson of Marx and Engels: "The profound hypocrisy, the intrinsic barbarity of bourgeois civilization stand unveiled before us the moment that from the great metropolises, where they take on respectable form, we turn our eyes toward the colonies where they go around naked."[19] The great capitalist and colonialist powers can well abandon themselves to self-celebration, but a people that oppresses another cannot be considered really free.[20] Meanwhile, enormous changes have taken place at the world level: Is Lenin's lesson remanded to a closed chapter of history by now?

To reply to this question, let us look at some of the conflicts that characterize today's world. The international press is full of articles or attitudes committed to celebrating, or at least justifying, Israel: after all—they say—it is the only country in the Middle East in which the freedom of expression and association exist, in which there is a democratic regime operating. In this way a macroscopic detail is suppressed: government by law and democratic guarantees are valid only for the master race, while the Palestinians can have their lands expropriated, be arrested and imprisoned without process, tortured, killed, and, in any case under a regime of military occupation, have their human dignity humiliated and downtrodden daily. We are here placed before an alternative, epistemological rather than political. Do we rely upon "democracy" in Israel in recognizing this country's right to domination, plunder, and colonial or semi-colonial oppression; or do we consider from this reality of domination, plunder, and oppression precisely the character quite other than democratic of Israel?

Analogous considerations can be made of Israel's great ally and protector. Inaugurating his first presidential mandate, Clinton declared: America is "the world's oldest democracy," and it "must continue to lead the world"; "our mission is timeless."[21] The patent of democracy attributed to the United States at the very moment of its foundation authorizes ignoring in silence the genocide of the indigenous populations and black slavery (in any event the descendants of these two groups make up 20 percent of the total population). The same logic is used when looking at the present and the future. Not too long ago, the "commission for truth" instituted in Guatemala accused the CIA of having decisively helped the military dictatorship to commit "genocide" against the Maya Indians, who were guilty of having sympathized with the opponents of the regime dear to Washington.[22] But, being the most ancient and greatest democracy in the world, the United States has no problem in repressing all of this. Conserving its good conscience, it can continue to claim the right to bombard or dismember any state, having been superbly defined by Washington as a "pariah" or "rogue" state, thus condemning its population to hunger or starvation. But, it is precisely the treatment inflicted yesterday upon the Indians and the blacks and today upon the Mayas or "pariahs" and "rogues" in every corner of the world that demonstrates the ferocious anti-democratic nature of the United States.

At the same time, the terminology used is significant. As far as the expression "pariah state" is concerned, it clearly goes back to the history of societies divided by caste, where no equality, indeed no contact was permitted or possible between the members of a superior caste on the one hand, and the untouchables on the other. But the expression "rogue state" is perhaps even more eloquent. For a long time, during the seventeenth and eighteenth centuries in Virginia, indentured servants, white-skinned temporary semi-slaves, when caught after escaping, which they often did, were branded with the letter R (for "rogue"): made immediately recognizable, they no longer had a means of escape. Later, the problem of identification was definitely solved by replacing the white semi-slaves by black slaves: the color of their skins made branding superfluous, the black was in himself synonymous with "rogue."

In order to bend or force "pariah or rogue states" into capitulation, there is no hesitation in using the practices that, before invading the heart of the West itself during the twentieth century, have tragically characterized the history of the colonial tradition. The embargo is a kind of postmodern version of the concentration camp. In the epoch of globalization, there is no longer any need to deport a people: it is enough to block the influx of food and medicine, and with some "intelligent" bombing, you succeed in destroying aqueducts, sewage systems, and sanitary infrastructures, as indeed happened in Iraq.

5.

We have seen Clinton claim an eternal mission for the United States and we are led back to the history of colonialism and imperialism. At the beginning of the twentieth century, in arguing against the American and European prophets of imperialism, J. A. Hobson, a left-wing English liberal, ironically characterized them as the "manifest destiny" and "mission of civilization" party.[23] Using this information, too, Lenin formulated a political program of a "complete break with the barbarous policies of bourgeois civilization" that legitimized and celebrated the dominion of "a few elect nations" over the rest of humanity.[24] Has this vision and this imperial pretension dispersed? In the course of his election campaign, George W. Bush did not hesitate to proclaim a new dogma: "Our nation is chosen by God and commissioned by history to be a model for the world."[25] In his time, his father had declared: "I see America as leader, as the only nation with a special role in the world." Let us listen to other voices. Said Henry Kissinger, "World leadership is inherent in America's power and values."[26] *Dixit* Madeleine Albright, the United States is the only "indispensable nation."

This eternal "mission" or leadership is claimed in the name of "the rights of man." We are led to think of the history of British imperialism, which, as it expanded, felt committed to "making wars impossible and promoting the best interests of humanity." This was how Cecil Rhodes expressed himself, synthesizing the philosophy of the British Empire as "philanthropy + 5 percent,"[27] where "philanthropy" is synonymous with "human rights" and the 5 percent indicates the profits that the English capitalist bourgeoisie made or intended to make by colonial conquest and waving the banner of "human rights." Let us now see how an American journalist describes and celebrates globalization: it serves to export, first of all, the products, technology, ideas, values, and style of American capitalism; "to swift China," the United States has to know how to combine "gunboats, trade and Internet investments," other, naturally, than the password of "democratizing" the economy and politics.[28] The formula dear to Rhodes, the voice of British imperialism, can therefore be reformulated with extra precision and frankness: "philanthropy (or human rights) + 5 percent + gunboat policies."

6.

But should we not be talking by now of overcoming the nation-state? It was with this slogan that the war against Yugoslavia was launched. The process of recolonizing the Third World and its periphery with respect to the West goes ahead with universalistic slogans that proclaim the absolute transcendence of ethical norms over state and national borders. But this, far from being a novelty, is a constant of the colonial tradition. At the same time, it is clear that, in claiming the right to declare the sovereignty of other states surmounted, the great powers attribute themselves an enlarged sovereignty, to exercise well beyond their own national territories. The dichotomy that had scanned colonial expansion, in the course of which its protagonists have constantly refused to recognize as sovereign states the countries subjected or transformed step by step into protectorates, is reproduced in a scarcely modified form. The outlines of a "new international order" clearly emerge: on the one hand, there are those who have the right and obligation to launch "international police actions," and on the other, "rogue states," outlaw states, or more exactly nonstates, whose illegal behavior must be struck down with every means. In the kind of world state that is being evoked here, the West completes the monopoly of legitimate violence, and this renders de-emancipation explicit, consumed at the expense of the excluded.

7.

Claiming the modernity of Lenin does not mean, however, ignoring or undervaluing the elements of innovation that have taken place in the international situation. Certainly, in some cases the national question continues to be put in the classic fashion, such as the struggle for liberation from colonial domination and to construct an independent nation-state (the Palestinian case). At other times, the national question is linked to the struggle to defend the results achieved following the process of decolonization.

Compelled to recognize the independence of countries that have escaped from their control, the great capitalist powers now try to disintegrate them by appealing to ethnic and tribal rivalry. It is an easy maneuver. Newly independent countries, often with uncertain, badly drawn, or arbitrary borders, do not have a unitary history behind them. In itself the colonial inheritance is fertile soil for the emergence of separatist and secessionist movements, where imperialism easily has a hegemonic role. "Hence the constant, and eventually often vain calls of the leaders of such new States to surmount 'tribalism,' 'communalism' or whatever forces were made responsible for failure of the new inhabitants of the Republic X to feel themselves to be primarily patriotic citizens of X rather than members of some other collectivity."[29]

The events that took place in the Congo between the end of the 1950s and the beginning of the 1960s are exemplary. Compelled to concede independence, Belgium immediately committed itself to promoting the secession of Katanga. Was it not in the name of self-determination that the Congo (like all Africa) had claimed and continued to claim independence? Well, this same principle ought to apply also to the rich mining region controlled by the Union minière. A "revolutionary" ready to wave this banner was immediately found for the occasion: Moise Chiombe, "son of the first Negro millionaire" of Katanga. Secessionists and colonial forces captured Lumumba, the leader of the National Congolese Movement, who supported "a unitary, progressive inter-tribal program." He was therefore guilty of opposing the secession and "self-determination" of the rich region that the colonists did not intend to relinquish; he was therefore massacred.[30]

Moreover, colonial domination has left its mark: on the economic level, the inequality of development among different regions has been accentuated; while the hegemonic presence at every level of the great powers and the policy of ethnic engineering, often promoted by them, has accentuated cultural, linguistic, and religious fragmentation. Secessionist tendencies of every kind are once again lying in wait, regularly fed by the ex-colonial powers. When it wrested Hong Kong from China, Great Britain certainly did not conceive of self-determination, and it did not remember it even during the long years in which it exercised its dominion. But, suddenly, on the eve of Hong Kong's return to China, to the motherland, the governor sent by London, Chris Patten, a conservative, had a species of illumination and improvised conversion: he appealed to the inhabitants of Hong Kong to claim their right to "self-determination" against the motherland, thus remaining within the orbit of the British Empire.

Analogous considerations are true for Taiwan. When, at the beginning of 1947, the Kuomintang, which had fled from continental China and the victorious People's Army, let loose a terrible repression that provoked about ten thousand deaths,[31] the United States was careful not to invoke the right to self-determination for the inhabitants of the island; on the contrary, it sought to impose the thesis according to which Chiang Kai-shek's government was the legitimate government not only of Taiwan but also of the whole of China. The great Asian country had to remain united but under the control of Chiang Kai-shek, reduced to a simple pro-consul of Washington's sovereign imperialism. As the dream of reconquering the mainland slowly faded away, and the stronger became the aspiration of the whole Chinese people to achieve full territorial integration and independence, ending the tragic chapter of colonial history, so the presidents of the United States experienced an illumination and a conversion similar to that of Chris Patten. They too began to caress the idea of "self-determination." Incoherence? Not at all: "self-determination" is the continuation of imperial policy by other means. If it was not really possible to get their hands on China as a whole, it was, meanwhile, convenient to secure control of Hong Kong or Taiwan.

Finally, it needs to be kept in mind that, in determinate circumstances, the national question can be made acute even in the heart of the West. On the basis of recently declassified U.S. documents, the CIA was ready, on the eve of the April 1948 elections, in case of a left-wing victory, to support secessionist movements in Sardinia and Sicily and dismember Italy.[32] Unduly claiming the right to declare the sovereignty of other states surmounted, the great powers attribute themselves a monstrously dilated sovereignty. This radical inequality among nations is an essential characteristic of imperialism, that is, that political-social system characterized, according to Lenin, by the "enormous importance of the national question."[33] In proclaiming their "mission," the United States and the great imperial powers can well wave the flag of "democracy"; it still remains a *Herrenvolk democracy*, constituting the constant target of Lenin's action.

Notes

1 A. de Tocqueville, *De la démocratie en Amérique*, in *Oeuvres complètes*, ed. J. P. Mayer (Paris: Gallimard, 1951ff.), vol. 1, 358–59.

2 Speech to the Constituent Assembly, September 1848, in A. de Tocqueville, *Oeuvres complètes*, ed. by the widow Tocqueville and G. de Beaumont (Paris: Michel Lévy Frères, 1864–67), 9:544–55.

3 Ibid., 288.

4 Tocqueville, *De la démocratie en Amérique*, vol. 1, 331.

5 See in particular N. Bobbio, *Stuart Mill, liberale e socialista*, in "La lettera del venerdì," supplement to *L'Unità* (31 May 1991), 26–27.

6 J. S. Mill, "On Liberty" (1858), in *Utilitarianism, Liberty, Representative Government*, ed. H. B. Acton (London: Dent, 1972), 73.

7 Ibid.

8 J. S. Mill, *Considerations on Representative Government* (1861), in ibid., 197.

9 Lenin, "Stato e Revoluzione" (1917), in *Opere Complete* (Rome: Editori Riuniti, 1955ff.), 25:433. Subsequent references to *Opere Complete* cite the specific title included in the work, the year of its initial publication, the volume number, and the page number.

10 Lenin, "Imperialismo fase suprema del capitalismo" (1917), 22:282.

11 Ibid., 181–82.

12 Lenin, "Sostanze infiammabili nella politica mondiale" (1908), 15:178–79.

13 Lenin, "La fine della guerra dell'Italia contro la Turchia" (1912), 18:322–23.

14 Mill, *Considerations on Representative Government*, 380.

15 Lenin, "La guerra e la rivoluzione" (1917), 24:417.

16 E. Bernstein, "Die deutsche Sozialdemokratie und die türkischen Wirren," in *Die Neue Zeit* (1897), 1:110.

17 E. Bernstein, "Sozialdemokratie und Imperialismus," in *Socialistische Monatshefte* (1900) (reprint Bad Feilnbach: Schmidt Periodicals, 1986), 1:238–51.

18 A. Rosenberg, *Der Mythus des 20: Jahrhunderts* (1930) (Munich: Hoheneichen, 1937), 673.

19 K. Marx, "Die künftigen Ergebnisse der britischen Herrschaft in Indien" (1853), in K. Marx and F. Engels, *Werke* (Berlin: Dietz Verlag, 1955ff.), 9:225.

20 F. Engels, "Reden über Polen," in *Werke*, 4:417; and F. Engels, "Auswärtige deutsche Politik," in ibid., 5:155.

21 Davis N. Lott, ed. *The Presidents Speak: The Inaugural Addresses of the American Presidents, from Washington to Clinton* (New York: Henry Holt and Company, 1994), 366–69.

22 M. Navarro, "U.S. Aid and 'Genocide': Guatemala Inquiry: CIA's Help to Military," *International Herald Tribune*, 27–28 February 1999, 3.

23 J. A. Hobson, *Imperialism: A Study* (Ann Arbor: University of Michigan Press, 1965), 77.

24 Lenin, "Dichiarazione dei diritti del popolo lavoratore e sfruttato" (17 [4] January 1918), 26:403.

25 R. Cohen, "No Mr. Lieberman, America Isn't Really God's Country," *International Herald Tribune*, 8 September 2000, 7.

26 H. Kissinger, *Diplomacy* (New York: Simon and Schuster, 1994), 834.

27 B. Williams, *Cecil Rhodes* (London: Constable and Company Ltd., 1921), 51–52.

28 T. L. Friedman, "On Key Foreign Policy Issues, the Differences Are Narrowing," *International Herald Tribune*, 11–12 March 2000, 8.

29 E. J. Hobsbawm, *Nation and Nationalism since 1780* (Cambridge: Cambridge University Press, 1990), 179.

30 E. Santarelli, *Storia sociale del mondo contemporaneo: Dalla Comune di Parigi ai nostro giorni* (Milan: Feltrinelli, 1982), 511–12.

31 M. A. Lutzker, "The Precarious Peace: China, the United States, and the Quemoy-Matsu Crisis, 1954–1955, 1958," in *Arms at Rest: Peacemaking and Peacekeeping in American History*, ed. J. R. Challinor and R. L. Beisner (New York: Greenwood Press, 1987), 178.

32 M. Molinari, "1948, guerra civile a Roma," *La Stampa*, 14 September 1999, 23.

33 Lenin, "Della fierezza nazionale dei grandi russi" (1914), 21:90.

PART IV   **politics and its subject**

13

Lenin and the Party,

Sylvain Lazarus   **1902–November 1917**

The Twentieth Century and Politics

The twentieth century saw the development of a new figure of politics, in which the notion of the party is central. Whether this is parliamentarism and its parties, the Leninist vision of the Social Democratic Party as presented in 1902 in *What Is to Be Done?*, the Stalinist form of the party, the Italian Fascist Party, the Nazi Party—the notion of the party is decisive in the century's political space.

This developed into the form of state parties, not only the various forms of single-party state, but also parliamentary multi-partyism. In my view this is the case in France at the present time, with parliamentary parties being internal to the state, and consequently state organizations in the sense that it is entirely within the state and its categories that these parties act, with a view to acceding by way of elections to the management or direction of the state.

One characteristic of twentieth-century politics is its organized character. There is no politics that is not organizational, and the word *party* denotes this.

This is a completely new situation in relation to that of the nineteenth century through to the Paris Commune of 1871, when the basis of politics was insurrection. We may say therefore that in the nineteenth century the idea of politics was insurrectionary, while in the twentieth century it was party-like. And it is within the forms of party that relations to the question of classes and the seizure of power have been redeployed. The parties of the Third Republic were explicitly formed against the Paris Commune at the same time as they presented themselves as parties of the whole people, seeking in other words to recruit and rally all strata and classes of the population. The *class reference* of parties thus becomes *ideological* and *programmatic*: the question of class is no longer judged according to the social origin of the members of a party, since it recruits in all classes of society, but rather by its ideological and programmatic positions.

Lenin was to make the establishment of a new conception of the party the condition of a revolutionary strategy in the age of imperialism. Stalin subsequently organized and theorized the form of the Soviet state party. Both Mussolini with the Fascist Party and Hitler with the Nazi Party had the party as the support of their strategy for seizing power, and to some extent also in their exercise of power, at least for a certain time. To analyze the different sequences and situations of politics in the twentieth century requires an analysis of the central role that the party form has played.

To proceed to this investigation, it is indispensable to identify properly, to separate properly, and to distinguish properly between the space of politics in the nineteenth century and that in the twentieth; this is all the more so the case in that political problematics are at work that aim not to distinguish these two sequences that must be considered as heterogeneous in order to understand them, but on the contrary to connect and combine them. The most patent example was Stalin's creation of the category Marxism-Leninism, which claimed to combine a conception of politics in which the guiding idea was that of the revolutionary capacity of the proletarians with that of the party as the constitutive kernel of the revolutionary process. In French parliamentarism, the notion of the republic likewise combined the nineteenth and twentieth centuries. It collapsed with Pétain. De Gaulle abandoned it in favor of the theme of France, and we are familiar with the avatars of its present resurgence.

This disjunction between the nineteenth and the twentieth centuries has considerable effects. The end of the nineteenth century saw the lapsing of the category of class as the sole bearer of politics, and the end of the twentieth century saw the lapsing of the party form, which can take no other form than the state party.

Hence we have these theses on a *politics without party*, and a mechanism not aiming at power and the state but *on the side of the people*, though still capable of prescribing for the state, that is, taking a position in its vicinity while remaining external and radically heterogeneous to it.

Lenin between Singularity and Subjectivity

My first point is that there is Lenin's work, accessible in the form of his *Collected Works*, which in no way means that one can decide a priori that the theses in these thousands of texts are internally homogeneous and coherent. The existence of such a work does not mean continuity, homogeneity, unity. This issue is important for two reasons. The first is that we can raise vis-à-vis Lenin's writings the same question that Althusser raised in relation to Marx, that is, what are the first texts in which we can say that Marx was a Marxist—the sequence that Althusser called the "works of maturity," in relation to which the works of the "young Marx" were still marked by Hegelian idealism.[1] We know that Althusser worked with the notion of epistemological break, which he took from the Bachelard tradition. But it is not this epistemological break that I propose to deploy in relation to Lenin. My own mode of analysis consists rather in presenting problematic sequences in order to examine what might be their specific singularities. This is the first issue at stake. The second, which is not unconnected to the first, focuses on the difficulty of the notion of Leninism, which I maintain is a Stalinist theme. Stalin's text *Problems of Leninism* is the most well-known illustration of this: Lenin's work allegedly had a common core that was both identifiable as such and pervaded the entire corpus. I argue that the thesis of the existence of Leninism leads on to the relevance of Marxism-Leninism. To opt at the start for a sequencing procedure in Lenin's texts, in contrast, will necessarily lead to displaying the radical break that Lenin effected in relation to Marx and to showing that Stalinism arose not in this hypothesis of a break with Marx but rather in that of a continuity and combination of Marx and Lenin. The rejection of a break between Marx and Lenin is the condition here for the thesis of combination and continuity between Lenin and Stalin. An approach to Lenin's texts in terms of singular sequences also has the extremely positive effect of separating right away the names of Lenin and Stalin, which makes it possible to return later on to the question of their connection.

My second point is that Lenin's major work, which founded and established the sequence that I consider that of Lenin's politics—what I call the Bolshevik mode of politics—is *What Is to Be Done?* (1902). This sequence, which I call the historical mode of politics, here in its Leninist variant, runs from 1902 to October 1917. It was closed by the victory of the insurrection, the creation of the Soviet state, and the renaming of the Bolsheviks as the Communist Party in 1918. The sequence in question thus includes, at the most general chronological level, the final phase of tsarism, the Russian Social Democratic Labor Party, the 1905 Revolution, the First World War, and the revolutionary sequence from February to the seizure of power and victory of October.

Certainly no one interested in history and politics will challenge the fact that *What Is to Be Done?* is a major text. But this is only the beginning.

On the one hand, we have to take a position on what theses put forward in *What Is to Be Done?* make it an important work, a founding text in terms of political practice and political thought. On the other hand, if we seriously apply this theory of sequentiality and accept that the seizure of power was a major break that, in itself, signaled both the end of one sequence and the beginning of another, then this means that the theses of *What Is to Be Done?*—in their historicity, that is, their political modernity and even their political effectiveness—ceased to apply after the seizure of power. The question of what exactly was closed in this closure is evidently of the greatest importance.

To privilege *What Is to Be Done?* because it bears on politics, its conditions and its thought—rather than the works on imperialism ("Imperialism, the Highest Stage of Capitalism," published in the spring of 1917) or on the state (*The State and Revolution*, written in August-September 1917 and published in 1918)—is thus highly significant in my perspective. At all events, I think it absolutely essential to separate radically the texts before the seizure of power from those of the period of the exercise of power.

My personal thesis is thus as follows.[2] In *What Is to Be Done?* Lenin broke with the thesis of Marx and Engels in the *Communist Manifesto* (1848) with regard to the spontaneous character of the appearance of

Communists within the modern proletariat. In contrast to the Marxist thesis that can be stated as "Where there are proletarians, there are Communists," Lenin opposed spontaneous consciousness and Social Democratic (that is, revolutionary) consciousness and stretched this opposition to the limit.

The tension is not between what is a Communist for Marx and a conscious revolutionary for Lenin. We may recall that three character- istics are proposed in the *Manifesto*: to have a scientific vision of the course of history, to privilege in all struggles national over local inter- ests, and to privilege the interest of the world proletariat in relation to that of the national proletariat. The tension lies rather in the fact that, for Marx, the appearance of Communists is something internal to the existence of the workers as a class. Lenin distances himself from this thesis by his critique of what he calls spontaneous consciousness. Revo- lutionary consciousness, the appearance of revolutionary militants, is not a spontaneous phenomenon. It is a very particular phenomenon, and it requires a break with spontaneous forms of consciousness. The political core of nonspontaneous consciousness is antagonism to the entire existing social and political order. As for the mechanism of real- ization of the conditions that will permit the emergence of a political consciousness, it is the party.

With Marx, in fact, there is no theory of organization, nor can we speak of a real theory of political consciousness. There is a theory, major and fundamental, of historical consciousness and of conscious- ness as historical consciousness—the history of humanity is the history of class struggles. I hold that Lenin brings the foundation of modern politics in the fact that revolutionary politics is required to announce and practice the conditions of its existence.

The sequence of the Leninist mode of politics was closed in 1917. That is, the political sequence that has the category of revolutionary party as its core was closed, and hence, in a certain fashion, "revo- lutionary party" is the name of this politics. From now on, "party" would be assigned to power, to the state. Already with Lenin, therefore, there is the start of something that refers to the state party. We have to understand, therefore, that "party" does not mean at all the same thing before and after 1917, any more than do other important words such as revolution, class, and consciousness.

As a result, we need new terms to properly distinguish the period up to 1917 from that which follows. This could be an argument for two separate colloquia today, one up to November 1917 and the other from 1917 to the death of Lenin.

My third point is that for this period, in particular in the texts between February and October 1917, there is the separation that Lenin clearly makes between politics and history. I have described this opposition as follows. History is clear (analysis of the war), politics is obscure. (In March 1917 Lenin maintained that the future character of the revolution that had begun was undecidable. He wrote that "no one knows and no one can know.") History and politics are thus out of phase, and we are extremely far from the mechanism of historical materialism and dialectical materialism that Stalin was to theorize and that Althusser paradoxically took over as well.[3] Politics, in this sequence, is in a never-ending discussion with history, just as with philosophy, while maintaining disjunctive relations with both. Politics is charged with assuming its own thought, internal to itself. This is the condition for its existence, and it is also this point that requires the disjunctions. As we know, the Stalinist mechanism was quite different: circulation of notions between politics, philosophy, and history, the party no longer being the system of conditions for politics but the real subject of all knowledge and decision.

To sum up, with the victory of the October Revolution, the sequence in which the category of party disposed the conditions of revolutionary politics was closed. After 1917 it would become an attribute of the state, or even its center. We enter the global era of state parties: Stalinism, Nazism, parliamentarism—multi-partyism being an *intrastate multipartyism*. At all events, parties exist only as state parties, which means that in the strict sense, these parties are not political organizations but state organizations.

It is possible to understand, therefore, that from China at the time of the Long March and the anti-Japanese war through to the Vietnamese war of liberation, the subsequent organizational mechanism would be the revolutionary army, and within it the question of people's war, rather than the pattern "clandestine organization plus mechanism for urban insurrection." Already in certain texts of Lenin from the period of the Civil War, and above all in some texts of Stalin from this period, we find this question in terms of the theme of partisan warfare. When Trotsky sought to militarize the trade unions, this similarly meant that his organizational model was the Red Army, of which he was of course the great leader.

The lapsing of the party form, in its political efficacy, was thus complete after November 1917. From this moment on, we enter a historicist problematic of politics in which the key word becomes *revolution*. The question of Leninism today finally raises two questions: the political lapsing of the party form and the obsolescence of the category of revolution.

Revolution, a Singular Term

For me the term revolution is not a generic term denoting an insurrection against the established order, or a change in the structures of a state—and a state of things. It is on the contrary a singular term. And it is a term whose occurrence, in the sense in which I understand it, can only refer to one thing as a category of political doctrine. The extension of the term to other situations that can be described otherwise, and of the name of the new political category that is both thought and applied in what I call a political sequence, is thus unwarranted. "Revolution" is not a generic term to describe any kind of overthrow or measure its importance. It is a singular noun that I accept only when the word appears and constitutes the central category of acting consciousnesses, the sole occurrence being what I have called the revolutionary mode, the political sequence of the French Revolution.

This way of conceiving the validity of the term, only on the basis of the moment at which it enters subjectivity and is effective as a central category of thought and practice, follows from my conception of politics as unusual and sequential, and not having the state as its object— that is, when it is not thought on the state that fuels political thought, but specific and singular categories "invented" by the political sequence in question—even when the state is at issue. The question about the word "revolution" is to know what space it is inserted into: in a statist doctrine that I here call historicist, or in a political doctrine?

There are two points to note. First, the distinction I make between state and politics removes the conception of revolution as a change in the structures of a state and assigns it, in a theory of sequences or *modes* of politics, to the sole occasion when "revolution" was a term of consciousness and subjectivity—the revolutionary mode.

Second, the general and constant use of the term is its historicist and statist use. "Revolution" for me, however, is paradoxically not identical to the notion of politics. This is so much so that the debate here bears on the relations between politics and revolution, as well as on knowing which of the two to choose.

This choice bears on the maintenance or abandonment of the historicist vision of politics. The historicist vision of politics is one that assigns it to great events. The matter of politics is then the event and not subjective phenomena and capacities. Politics then belongs to the order of the event and not to that of thought.

To take the event as paradigm rather than subjectivity has the consequence of centering politics on the question of the state and its power—in other words, considering that the field of politics is state power. People have believed that this doctrine was specific to Leninist Marxism, but it is just as much that of parliamentary democracy, in which only the state—and not programs or reforms, for example—is the issue at stake in politics, and parties are in reality statist parties with no other goal than state power, rather than being representative parties.

"Revolution" then is at the end of the day the major, paroxysmic event of what can happen to state power or the interior of state power: its subversion, its transitory cessation. In actual fact, revolution is the unheard-of experience that the end of a state is possible. It is unheard-of because the state itself asserts its inalienable perpetuity, whether this derives from divine right, or in today's terms from its place as the natural foundation of freedom, this last being given as a combined space of capitalism and parliamentary democracy.

To close this historicism, in my view, the two sides of which have been the Marxist class-based vision on the one hand and the parliamentary and capitalist vision on the other, means breaking with the category of revolution. This presents itself as the horizon in the class-based vision but continues to function in the form of its empty place and site, in the form of its impossibility or its certain defeat—proof that historicism keeps a place for the word "revolution"—in postsocialist parliamentarism following the fall of the Berlin Wall.

This empty place partly explains the destitution and criminalization of the "revolutions" of the twentieth century. Contemporary parliamentary historicism, which is made up of competitive capitalism, commodities, and money presented as voluntary choices of our freedom, has as its condition of possibility the lapse of the idea of revolution and its structurally criminal character, offering in exchange the collapse of thought, reduced to microeconomics and the philosophy of John Rawls, or rendered coextensive with the political philosophy of the rights of man in a senile appropriation of Kant. The fall of the Soviet Union and socialism has fully confirmed the good historicist conscience of parliamentarism in its rightful place and considerably reinforced its arrogance, its violence, and its legitimacy, allowing it to treat any reservation and criticism, worse still any other project, as crazy and criminal.

Revolution, whether to be made or proscribed, is thus not a notion specific to socialism and the emancipation attempts of the twentieth century; it belongs as a category to the historicism that is fuelled by both defunct socialism and parliamentarism. By way of the category of the state, and still more so by the state as major event, whether this is something to come or already represents in its parliamentary form "the end of history," historicism equally thrives. For socialism, the major state event lay in the future and was called revolution, while for the other option the state event was already there, with its place in the form of parliamentarism. As Churchill supposedly said, democracy is the worst political system apart from all the others. Whether the major event is a change in the state or the state itself, it is the state that prevails in thought.

My thesis is that "revolution" is intrinsically bound up with the historicist vocabulary, and that its use, any reference that can be made with it, is necessarily inscribed in historicism and consequently in the present hegemonic form of historicism that is parliamentarism. To add to a reflection on historicism the desire for revolution is an attempt to extract revolution from this capturing mechanism. I do not, however, believe that this is possible, for the following reason: seen from today, the capture of revolution by historicism is only one of the elements and symptoms of a far more fundamental capture, which is that of politics by the state. Is this then a thesis of a fundamental historicism of the state? No, but it is a thesis in which it is historicism that marks out the state as the sole and essential issue at stake in politics.

The only contemporary question, at the same time theoretical, political, and personal, since each is required, is to undo this unnecessary capture of politics by the state and historicism, and thus to dismiss the category of revolution. This dismissal is a complex business, for the closure by itself does not break historicism. What is involved is in no way closing a previous stage and moving on to the following one (which is the case with historicism), but rather maintaining that any closure requires the re-examination of the era whose closure is to be pronounced. This is what I call saturation, a method that traces the subjective spaces of the categories of the sequence to be closed. It is not just a question of closing the October Revolution and the idea of proletarian revolution, but of re-examining the political space of revolution in the French Revolution, in what I call the revolutionary mode, in order both to identify the singularity of the politics at work in this mode and to remove from October the description of revolution, to give it back its originality and its unprecedented political power—that of being the invention of modern politics. I will readily grant the political power of a sequence the name of a work: it has a specific readability and it is its propositions that dispose the new field and the break. This is not in the order of before and after, but in a new present that leaves the preceding one behind. The lapse imposes identification of the sequence, the presentation of its specific propositions, treating it as a singularity that alone gives the event its readability.

In historicism, on the contrary, the caesura does not support a readability of the event, what I call an identification in interiority. Most often the event character is left obscure, is not considered in itself, and serves only as a marker between anterior and posterior. In other words, every great event fundamentally divides (and this is the wellspring of historicism) a "before" and an "after," while in other respects the investigation of the event itself remains open and is not resolved, to use the textbook terms, either in its causes or its consequences. Historicism introduces a typological periodization and comparativism: there is the French Revolution as event, there is the *ancien régime* society as a strictly chronological "before" and of a particular type, and there is an "after" in these two dimensions. The event becomes a break of order in the social mechanism. From the moment at which there is this caesura on each side of an event, there is a "before" and an "after," and it is the great defect of the would-be social disciplines that the boundary between description and analysis is accordingly very difficult to trace: the descriptive and the analytical are confused. In the historicist mechanism, therefore, there can never be an idea of singularity, but only of differentials or comparisons that are standardized by before and after. In this sense, the historicist procedure is necessarily dialectical; it requires a mechanism of coherence, liaison, and "bridging" between the subjective and the objective (between the precarious and the invariant, the sequential and the structural), and it is by this transition that the descriptive becomes analytical. Furthermore, this is why the notion of state is needed for this procedure.

I shall therefore speak of an *event character in exteriority*. As opposed to this, one can also speak when it is examined for itself of an *event character in interiority*, when it is the specific material that gives rise to identification, the study of deployment and cessation. The operative terms are then sequence and political sequence. The material of the event character then becomes that of a politics, and a singular politics at that, which is no longer just an overthrow in the order of the state but consists only of effects. An event character in interiority is political and not statist. The term revolution has the unfortunate property of always remaining in exteriority (limits, caesura). In the nineteenth and twentieth centuries, the attempt to internalize "revolution," that is, to subjectivize it and make it a principle of mobilization of subjectivities, was the mechanism of "class" and "class party," to the extent that the present, chimerical use of the term is that of imagining it possible to divide it from the party form that was the very condition of its subjectivization and its condition of political possibility. To substitute "desire for revolution" for "party of revolution" does not deploy an alternative subjectivity to these existing ones.

In my view, the root of the problem is not the lack of a party or a revolution, the mourning for this, but on the contrary the need for an intellectuality of politics without party or revolution, something that does not prevent radicalism or prescribe resignation to the order of things but imposes the hypothesis of other possibilities. Revolution for its part is a nonpolitical, historicist notion, reducing the thought of politics, its condition of possibility, to that of an event character in exteriority, and placing this latter in a chain in which "party" and "state" also figure. Party, revolution, and state form a triptych.

"Revolution," moreover, is a category that was rendered obsolete in 1968, as far as France is concerned, when despite being the key word there was no question of insurrection, of state power. If the question of the state is no longer raised, it is because it is no longer the common legacy, even when it is cited in the propositions of antagonistic classes. What is apparent here is a workerist classism in which the working class and the political vision of the state are separated. The end of the nation-state, which must be dated from 1968, is basically the end of the state as object of an "inherited" conflictuality. From this point on, the end of the nation-state goes by the name of consensus and cohabitation.

Classism died in 1968. We can call classism the space of the state in (antagonistic) inheritance, and it is this that could be called the nation-state. The lapsing of classism, that is, an approach to politics in terms of class, took place when it appeared very precisely that "class" and "class party" carried no particular proposition on the state and did not aim at any event, either in exteriority or in interiority: this was the figure of the PCF and CGT in 1968. At this point something essential came to an end, an end that was signaled here by the obsolescence of the party-state-revolution triptych.

At the same time, the freedom and decision that then opens is that of making the hypothesis of a new intellectuality and a new practice of politics in which we break with "party" and "revolution," and the state is an important question without being the heart of politics.

How does the past history of "revolutions" appear in the approach that I am proposing? First, "revolutions" are identified by politics, and each one by a remarkable inventiveness. Revolutions do not exist in the plural, except in the illegitimate idea that "revolution" simply denotes great changes touching the government and the state as a general case, but each time with singularities of an extremely specific character. For the Russian Revolution, *What Is to Be Done?*, the "April Theses," the decision on insurrection, the professional revolutionaries, and the separate peace were inventions and discoveries. We certainly find a break here, but in the sense of the work.

Second, in the strict sense in which "revolution" bears the political capacity, there was only a single occurrence: the French Revolution. In other words, this was the sole occasion when "revolution" was a category of thought for the political subjectivity at work. In October 1917, on the contrary, it was not revolution that was the category of thought, but the dictatorship of the proletariat.

In China during the Long March, the category of thought was the people's war of national liberation with its three components of party, army, and united front. We can see how, from the point of active categories of subjectivity and thought, these are disparate processes that have been enveloped under the same name.

I have spoken of the freedom and decision of a new intellectuality of politics. To leave behind the way of thinking of historicism, which is tied to the state party in both its parliamentary and socialist forms, means believing that politics can be conceived as a subjective category—as a thought—on its own basis. The issue today is not some hypothetical capsizing of the balance of forces, or the emergence of a great financial crisis, something that may well happen but without therefore mechanically giving rise to great politics. Before proving itself in a conjectural adjustment to situations, politics must first exist in thought. This is the central point: to accept that there is a new intellectuality of politics, and to refrain from the previous one—hegemonic and disastrous—in which parties, historicism, and parliamentarism are dominant. We are in an event-type situation in exteriority, the only rhythm of which is an occasional one, the eruption of movements such as that of 1995, certain interpretations of which fuel parliamentarist leftism. A new intellectuality, that says it all: I propose the category of *mode of politics*, maintaining that non-statist politics, that is, non-historicist politics, is uncommon, sequential, and identified by what I call its mode: a mode of politics is the relation of a politics to its thought, the bringing to light of its specific categories that permit an identification of the subjective on its own basis. Politics does not have to be conceived by way of a hypothetical object, the content of which is the state and power. A political sequence in interiority creates its categories, its theorists, its sites. To give two examples: the political sequence that I call the revolutionary mode was the sequence 1792–94, its theorists were Saint-Just (the major figure in this sequence) and Robespierre, its sites were the

Convention, the clubs, the *sans-culotte* societies, and the revolutionary army. For what is abusively called the Russian Revolution, the sequence was from 1902 to October 1917, its major theorist being Lenin (also Trotsky and Bukharin), and its sites being the RSDLP and the soviets. In the theory of modes, when a site disappears, the mode and the sequences come to an end.

Third, politics precedes and fashions, carries and supports historical factuality. We are faced with the need to finish with historicism, but to do so we have to reopen its sequence, re-examine its terms (which are revolution, party, and state), and pronounce in our name, and no longer that of historicism, its identification and closure.

Notes

1   In Louis Althusser, *Pour Marx* (Paris: Maspero, 1965), and Althusser, *Lire "le Capital"* (Paris: Maspero, 1965).
2   Cf. Sylvain Lazarus, "Lénine et le temps," *Conférence du Perroquet* 18 (March 1989), and *L'Anthropologie du nom* (Paris: Seuil, 1998).
3   Cf. Sylvain Lazarus, *Althusser, la politique et l'histoire* (Paris: PUF, 1993), and "Althusser et Lénine," paper presented at the Vienna colloquium in 1996.

14

Lenin the Just, or Marxism Unrecycled

Jean-Jacques Lecercle

What interest can a philosopher of language find in reading Lenin today? Is there a point in reviving an *oeuvre* that was once an absolute worldwide bestseller (Lenin was for a long time the most translated of all authors) and is now almost impossible to find except on the dusty shelves of public libraries? I intend to give a strongly positive answer to both questions, for a reason indicated by my title: Lenin is the very embodiment of Marxism unrecycled, or rather of a form of Marxism that is radically *irrecuperable*.

There is, of course, a personal aspect to this statement. When a middle-aged academic proclaims his attachment to Lenin, he is nostalgically looking back to the giddy days of his youth. Having decided at the age of sixteen that I was a Communist, and not having seen fit, in spite of the vicissitudes of history, to change my mind on that point, I look up to Lenin as one of the major gods in the pantheon of my youth. And since I am an atheist, and know that gods are mere hypostatizations of human virtues or qualities, I shall contend that my continued admiration for Lenin is due to the fact that he is the incarnation of the virtues of firmness, of hardness, and of subtlety, virtues that incite me to call him "Lenin the Just," in that they are the virtues that keep Marxism unrecycled in an age when everything, from old bottles to militant Marxists, is endlessly recycled.

That militant Marxists should recycle themselves is as trivial as it is frequent. I had the dubious privilege of being for several years a member of the same branch of the French Communist Party as someone who became vice-chairman of MEDEF, the French CBI, a man actively engaged in dismantling the system of unemployment benefits, not to mention pensions, in France. And so on and so forth: the list could be endless—it was already the case at the time of Lenin. What is perhaps even more disquieting is the recycling of Marxist theorists. Thus Voloshinov is (at least in France) republished under the name of Bakhtin, and Bakhtin himself is torn between his phenomenological youth and his mystical old age (Todorov is the main agent of this transformation); Gramsci is admired and made use of by Roger Scruton in Britain and Alain de Benoist and his likes in France. Marx himself has become meat for academic syllabi, he is endlessly humanized and eschatologized, if you pardon me the coinage. I should not exaggerate the novelty of this: on the first page of *The State and Revolution*, Lenin already deplores the canonization of Marx.

But there is one Marxist theorist who has totally escaped such recycling (except of course in TV ads and on adolescent t-shirts)—Lenin himself. With him, the dominant ideology hesitates between execration (he is the prime mover of the Gulag)—this is good news to me: the enemy of my enemy is my friend—and a form of grudging respect (he, after all, gave world capitalism the worst fright it ever had). Among academics and intellectuals today Lenin is unrecycled because he is deeply unrespectable: he is hardly a philosopher (we still remember the frisson caused by Althusser's conference); he is a dogmatist (remember the narrowness of his reading before he wrote *The State and Revolution*: neither Aristotle nor Hobbes or Locke, not even Spinoza, only the classics of Marxism), which makes him merely a vulgarizer; he is a totalitarian (there is no elegant cult of failure for ethical reason in him: he not only seized power but kept it, and actually smashed the bourgeois state apparatus in the process); and lastly, he is a clever opportunist, who never hesitated to contradict himself whenever opportunity called.

I mean to take these insults as indirect celebrations of the three virtues that Lenin embodies. I do not mean to damn Lenin with faint praise, I mean to praise him with strong damnation.

The Many-Virtued Lenin, or Marxism Unrecycled

I am not the best person to tell you what in Marxism is still alive, what should not be recycled. I work in a field, the philosophy of language, where Marxism is at best marginal, at worst absent: a few cryptic remarks by the founding fathers, a disastrous intervention by the pseudo-Stalin (it is now known that the pamphlet on Marxism and linguistics that Stalin signed was actually written by a Soviet academician called Alexandrov), and a few fragments shoring up those ruins (chief among which are the Voloshinov book and the semantics of Michel Pêcheux—and I am very fond of the essay on the origins of language by the Vietnamese Marxist Tran Duc Thao). Lenin himself is no better than the rest: his contribution to the philosophy of language is more or less limited to the famous marginal annotation to Hegel's *Logic*, in the *Philosophical Notebooks*: "history of thought = history of language??," surrounded by a square surrounded by a circle.

Yet it can be said that, in this field also, Lenin is important. First, as I shall contend in a moment, he gives us a glimpse of what a Marxist philosophy of language might be. Second, his very virtues give us a sense of what we miss in a cultural conjuncture in which Marxism is, if not entirely missing, at least marginalized. The time has come to celebrate Lenin's virtues in more detail.

The first is the virtue of *hardness*. Lenin was an unceasing and unflinching polemicist. There is a certain *méchanceté* in him, which keeps his occasional texts alive today. He never hesitates to give offense where offense is due. He does this not out of innate crabbiness, but because he is, in his own terms, waging a war. He never rejects a compromise, but he never makes concessions; he never hesitates to defend the right slogan, even if that makes him unpopular. In short, he always strikes where it hurts, because he is lucid about who and where the main enemy is. This is what we miss in the present conjuncture of recycled, that is, watered-down or faint-hearted, Marxism (in which Marxists are apt to turn their weaknesses into illusory strengths): Marxism on the offensive (as you know, this is a Leninist principle: always keep on the offensive!), Marxism able and willing to expose the dominant ideology and its innumerable hypocrisies (need I mention the concept of democracy in its bourgeois version, or the ideology of human rights, of which recycled Marxists are the most enthusiastic supporters?). This is where Lenin is hard: he unremittingly advocates the dictatorship of the proletariat, and he is not tender toward petty-bourgeois morality either.

The second of Lenin's virtues is his *firmness*. He is entirely clear about the strategic force of Marxism. He knows that Marxism offers, is the only theory to offer, a global critique of capitalism, with a hierarchy of objectives. In other words, Lenin, being a dogmatist, never forgets that his positions rest on a firm grounding of theory—this is another well-known Leninist principle: without a revolutionary theory, there is no revolutionary practice.

The qualities of hardness and firmness account for Lenin's *solidity*. In matters of Marxist theory, Lenin is a totalitarian dogmatist, in other words a tower of strength. But he is not only that. For he has a third quality, the quality of *subtlety*. What we miss in the present disarray of Marxism is the instrument for decision that Marxist theory provides, the capacity to perceive the crucial elements in the historical conjuncture, the capacity to identify potential allies as well as the main enemy. There, as we all know, lies Lenin's specific genius, his main contribution to Marxist theory, inscribed in the theory of the weakest link and the famous slogan about the necessity of a concrete analysis of the concrete situation.

There is a structure, or a hierarchy, in Lenin's virtues: he is hard, that is critically operative and successful, because he is both firm and subtle. His contribution to Marxism is the dialectics of strategy and tactics, of the general theory or the strategic program and the detailed analysis of the concrete conjuncture.

All of this, I am aware, is trivially true. I am only rehearsing the convictions of my youth, points that, thirty years ago, were so entirely obvious they hardly needed spelling out. But they need spelling out now, in a cultural conjuncture where Marxism is in retreat. And this is where what I have to say is less obvious and probably contentious: the ideological offensive of capitalism, and the consequent retreat of Marxism is, at least in part, due to the fact that Marxism has never thematized the question of language, never produced a theory of language, and therefore has been left disarmed in a period when the struggle on the ideological front became of prime importance. And I believe that

Lenin, even if he obviously does not have a full-fledged theory of language to offer, because of his three virtues, gives us an inkling of the Marxist philosophy of language we need. At least we can hope that, being hard or *méchant*, he will give us the instruments of a thorough critique of what passes today for a philosophy of language.

In the field of philosophy of language, Lenin's embodiment of un-recycled Marxism has an incarnation in the theory of slogans. The source for this is well-known: in July 1917, at a time when he was outlawed by the provisional government and was in hiding in the pastoral surroundings of Lake Razliv, Lenin, at that moment of extreme political crisis, devoted some of his energy to a short pamphlet on the nature and choice of slogans.[1] The pamphlet is not of course a general theory of slogans, but it is a concrete analysis of the political conjuncture, from the point of view of the determination of the right slogans, the slogans that are just.[2] I shall just stress the most important point of the pamphlet, with a view to the construction of a Marxist philosophy of language.

The main thesis is, naturally, that slogans exert performative power, or force. There is nothing new or exciting in this. This is, after all, what slogans are for: a slogan is etymologically a war cry. Lenin's specific contribution lies in the characterization of such force, which has nothing to do with the rather vague notion of "force" evoked in such expressions as "illocutionary force" (an important concept in speech-act theory). The pamphlet makes it clear that force is exerted by the right slogan in three ways. First, the right slogan *identifies* the *moment* in the conjuncture (in this case: on 4 July 1917, the first, potentially peaceful, phase of the revolution has ended, and the slogan that named it, "All power to the soviets," is, therefore, no longer correct). Second, as a result of this, the right slogan *names the task* associated with the moment in the conjuncture: the task is now to prepare for the "decisive struggle" of violently overthrowing a government that has turned counter-revolutionary. The right slogan enables one to name the *decisive* element. Third, as such, the right slogan exerts force in that it *condenses* and *embodies* the concrete analysis of the concrete situation. The implicit Leninist principle at work here is "without the correct slogans, no revolutionary success."

This centrality of a concrete force has consequences for what could be a Marxist philosophy of language. This, the pamphlet only evokes, of course, *au détour d'une phrase*. Here are the main points. First is a concept of *meaning* as linked to the conjuncture in which the utterance is produced: meaning is the result of a *rapport de forces*, not of a cooperative language-game but of political struggle (with no fixed rules, or rather rules in a state of constant variation, which must be reappraised with every change in the conjuncture). Second, a consequence of this is that the utterance is not a description of a state of affairs in the conjuncture, but is an *intervention* in it: it reflects, but also modifies, the *rapport de forces* that gives it its meaning. We understand the importance of slogans: they, and not descriptions or constatives, are the building bricks utterances are made of. Third, the right slogan is the slogan that is *just*, that fits in with the conjuncture in that it works in it. There is a reflexive circularity between the slogan that names the relevant moment in the conjuncture and the conjuncture that allows it to make sense. This conjuncturality of meaning is captured in the concept of justness—the right slogan is not true, but just. Fourth, the word truth, however, is used by Lenin in the pamphlet, as the people "must be told the truth," that is they must know who (the representatives of which class or subpart of a class) are the real holders of state power in the conjuncture. But such truth is strictly dependent on the justness of the slogan, it is an effect, perhaps also an affect, of justness: illocutionary justness, to borrow the language of speech-act theory, causes perlocutionary truth. It is the combination of truth and justness that guarantees the efficacy of the sense that is made of the situation. Lastly, what is suggested here is a *political concept* of discourse—of discourse as intervention. The pamphlet insists on the illusions of petty-bourgeois morality, on the obfuscation of "the substance of the situation," which is political, by moral questions. The question is not to be kind to the Mensheviks and Social Revolutionaries, to allow them to understand the error of their ways and improve their behavior; the question is to tell the masses that they have betrayed the revolution. And the opposition between politics and morality is the opposition between the concrete and the abstract. Hence another of those Leninist principles: in the revolutionary period the most grievous and most dangerous sin against the revolution is the substitution of the abstract for the concrete.

My cursory reading of this text, from which I shall try to derive another philosophy of language (by which I mean other than the philosophy of language that underpins most, if not all research programs in mainstream linguistics), does not occur in a void. It has been preceded by two strong readings, one notorious, the other less well-known.

The passage in *Mille Plateaux* where Deleuze and Guattari read Lenin on slogans is well-known.[3] They make much of the date of 4 July, the date at which the revolution reaches a turning point (before, a peaceful accession to power was possible, and the slogan "All power to the soviets" was just; after, only the violent overthrow of the provisional government could save the revolution, and the main slogan had to be modified accordingly). They hail the "incorporeal transformation," an effect of language, but of language endowed with singular performative power, that achieves this. And their analysis goes further: the power of the slogan is not only performative, it is constitutive of the class it interpellates into existence. The genius of the First International had been to extract from the masses a class, with the slogan "Workers of the world, unite!" Likewise, Lenin's slogan institutes a vanguard, a party, out of the proletarian mass. The slogan is in advance of the political body it organizes. And they insist that such considerations do not concern only the language of politics, but the very way language in general works, in that language is always worked through by politics. The linguistic nexus, or regime of signs, or semiotic machine they describe is an unholy mixture of utterances (in this case slogans), implicit presuppositions (the acts that follow the effect of the slogans), and incorporeal transformations (affected by the performative, or naming power of the slogan): such are the internal variables of the assemblage of enunciation of which the slogan is a crucial part.

The context of this disquisition on Lenin is the critique of mainstream linguistics and its postulates in the fourth plateau of *Mille Plateaux*, and more specifically the refutation of the first postulate according to which language is about information and communication. The critique produces a cluster of concepts (force, machine, assemblage, minority, style, and stuttering), which I think do provide a first attempt at a Marxist philosophy of language—although of course Deleuze and Guattari would never claim that theirs is either a philosophy of language or a Marxist attempt. But we may take the reference to Lenin as a symptom, especially if we replace it in the context of another, little known text by Deleuze, his preface to Guattari's first collection of essays, *Psychanalyse et transversalité*, where Deleuze addresses the question of what he calls the "Leninist break,"[4] The definition he gives of the break is the following: Lenin (with his correct slogans) turned the military, political, and economic dissolution of Russian society into a victory for the masses. The only problem was that this possibility of victory, this turning that amounted to a revolution, was achieved at the cost of turning the agent of the revolution, the party, into a state apparatus in rivalry with, and therefore modeled on, the bourgeois state. And the outcome of that was not only Stalinism but the eventual defeat of "real" socialism (which Deleuze could not foresee at the time, but which he makes intelligible). He attempts to provide a solution to this problem, which has always plagued the Communist movement (it still does), in terms of the distinction, put forward by Guattari, between *groupe assujetti* (the subjected group, which will do anything to ensure its own survival) and *groupe sujet* (the subject group, which is always calling for its own demise).

I have strong doubts about the political relevance of Deleuze's solution—it is too close for comfort to the left-communist deviation in the early days of Soviet power that was lambasted by Lenin in pamphlet after pamphlet, article after article. But I deeply agree with the link between politics and language, and the role ascribed to language in revolutionary social change.

There is another strong reading of the Lenin pamphlet. It is to be found in issue 9/10 of a short-lived publication, *Cahiers marxistes-léninistes*. It is boldly entitled "Vive le léninisme."[5] The texts are unsigned, but they are widely attributed to Althusser. (They are obviously lecture notes: whether noted down by the master himself, or given as a series of public lectures and piously noted down by a member of the audience is of little import—"Althusser" here is the name of a collective assemblage of enunciation.) The journal was published by the Ecole Normale Supérieure branch of the Union of Communist Students, which soon after gave birth to the UJC m-l Maoist sect. The text, therefore, belongs to the period before the break between Althusser (who was unwilling to leave the French Communist Party) and his Maoist disciples. It reflects the *Zeitgeist*, in that the object of the analysis is what the text calls a number of Leninist "sciences."

Althusser identifies the core of Leninist science with the concept of conjuncture: the sole object of Lenin's thought is the correct description of the conjuncture, of its class determinants, of its *rapports de force*, and of the exact moment at which the analyst finds himself. The concept is another name for the dialectics of general scientific principles and concrete analysis that is Lenin's specific contribution to Marxism. Hence the structure of the "three sciences" of Leninism. There is one dominant science, the science of concrete analysis, which proceeds in five stages: 1) the description of the elements of the conjuncture, given by class analysis; 2) the determination of the limits of the conjuncture, that which necessitates its violent transformation; 3) the recognition of the impossibility of certain combinations between the elements — certain alliances are *contre nature*, which *a contrario* establishes the possible combinations, or possible alliances; 4) the determination of the variations of the conjuncture, which provide guidelines for political action; 5) the taking into account of the constraints of the strategic perspective of the proletariat. Conjuncture, then, is a double constraint (it has limits, it is the object of a strategic perspective). This dominant science is complemented by two dominated or secondary sciences that govern its adaptation to political practice: the science of slogans (not individual slogans, but rather, an articulated set that justly names the moment of the conjuncture), and the science of leadership, or how to make the masses realize the justness of the slogans. So Leninist science is an articulated hierarchy of disciplines or fields, which enable the successful revolutionary to negotiate the three levels of the party's activity and program: the general level of theory (and the principles on which the Communist program is based: the theory of modes of production, the tendential laws of capitalism, the current stage of social development); the level of the concrete analysis of a social formation; and the level of strategic and tactical analysis that determines the tasks to be fulfilled in day-to-day political action. And Lenin's contribution is to have shifted the center of the structure from the general level of theory (that is Marx's, or the Mensheviks' theory of the strongest link), to the dialectic relationship between the second and the third levels, the level of the analysis of the concrete social formations and of the determination of the political tasks the moment in the conjuncture requires. In other words, he substitutes, for Marx's theory of the strongest link, the theory of the weakest link, and of the complexity of the real structure of the social formation, which means that the path to revolution is not like the Nevski perspective; it is never a straight line.

The scientistic language of Althusser's reading of Lenin has gone out of fashion, and calling Lenin a scientist, even a political scientist, is of little help. Besides, if we compare this reading with Deleuze's and Guattari's, we cannot but confess that the role of language in political action and revolutionary change is downgraded to the secondary science of slogans: first comes the science of concrete analysis, then the secondary science of adaptation of the analysis to political practice; first comes the theory of the conjuncture and the *rapports de force* between classes within it, then comes its translation into an array of slogans that are just. The production of a class or group by the slogan that anticipates it has disappeared, and language belongs to the realm of representation rather than performativity and intervention. Nevertheless, I believe the theory of the three levels of articulated theory and practice still offers a framework for another philosophy of language.

Lenin and the Philosophy of Language

Let us metaphorically take the three levels of the Communist program as levels for a research program (which I hesitate to call scientific) into the workings of language. The program starts with the general level of theory, of principles. Lenin's solidity (the combination, if you recall, of critical hardness and firmness in the attachment to theoretical principles) being what it is, we need to define at this level what a *materialist philosophy of language* might be. It is, after all, the Marxist philosopher's task, a task briskly fulfilled by Lenin himself, to intervene on the materialist side in the philosophical struggle. And here we immediately have a problem. The dominant program in linguistics, the one that makes the strongest claim to scientificity, the Chomskyan research program, does belong to a form of materialism, except that it is the kind of materialism that the Marxist tradition calls "vulgar," the materialism that reduces language to physical changes in the brain's neurons. This *reductionism* is encapsulated in Chomsky's notion of the "mind-brain." And it is, of course, not an established scientific theory with consequent scientific practice, but a philosophical gesture, a gesture of confident expectation that one day the rules of grammar will be stated in terms of neuron connections. At present, and for the foreseeable future, the mind-brain is still, as far as language is concerned, a black box, and the claim to scientificity a form of philosophical terrorism.

But Lenin's theory of slogans enables us to conceive of another form of *materiality of language*, so that linguistic materialism need not be vulgar reductionism. This materiality is the materiality of forces and *rapports de force*. It is not the vague concept of force that lies behind the Anglo-Saxon pragmatic concept of performativity (where the "force" of the utterance is left undescribed, being merely a pretext for classification — what type of speech-act is this? — and the calculus of implicit meaning — she can't mean this, so what does she really mean?), but it is a concept of force as collectively exerted, in the course of political action, in the creation of *rapports de force*. What Lenin's solidity, his firm reliance on historical materialism, teaches us, is that language is material not only in that it can exert physical or bodily force (we might call this the Castafiore principle), but also in that it is material with the same materiality as institutions. There is a causal chain, we might call this the Althusserian chain of interpellation, that goes from institution to ritual, from ritual to practice, and from practice to speech-act: each element of the chain is endowed with its own materiality, and with the materiality of the whole chain.

We understand why, against Chomsky and mainstream linguistics, Deleuze and Guattari maintain that the elementary type of utterance is not the declarative sentence, embodying a proposition, but the slogan. It is not even the imperative, another type of sentence, but the *mot d'ordre*,[6] an utterance and not a sentence, issued in an always already political context. The utterance, then, is not a representation of a state of affairs but an intervention in it: this intuition was central in Austin's invention of the performative, but was hopelessly caught up in typically Anglo-Saxon methodological individualism (collective action is nothing but the composition of individual decisions) and intentionalism (the meaning of the utterance is what the utterer means it to mean, provided it is recognized as such by the hearer). Slogans, in contrast, are always collective, and their meaning derives not from their author's political genius (for they have no author, not even Lenin) but from their capacity to intervene in the conjuncture they analyze, but also, in naming it, to call it into being. If this analysis of language is right, we understand why Deleuze and Guattari claim that Chomsky's grammatical markers are markers of power. And we understand another reason why the pragmatic analysis of language must be ultimately rejected (although not to the same extent as the Chomskyan research program): it is based on an irenic concept of language, of language as means of exchange of information and as means of communication, conforming to the cooperative principle that governs scientific discussion. But it does not: Lenin's theory of slogans enables us to understand that linguistic "exchange" is not an exchange at all, that it is not about Habermassian communicative action or Gricean cooperation, but about struggle, the claim for discursive positions and the ascription of places. And we understand why Harold Pinter is a materialist playwright. In other words, where Anglo-Saxon theories of pragmatics are always based on ethics (it is noteworthy that Grice's lexicon of principles and maxims is borrowed from Kant's second critique), materialist theories of language are based on politics: Lenin the just is the natural antidote to both Chomskyan reductionism and the pragmatic idealism of speech-act theory.

The second level in the Communist program is the level of the concrete analysis of social formations. In the field of language, this means the analysis of natural languages as national languages. And here we meet Chomsky again—his philosophy of language is wrong but consistent. Because he believes that linguistics is about the laws of nature that describe the workings of the mind-brain, he believes in universal grammar (the universal wiring of the human brain, which is immune to cultural and historical differences). This, of course, offers certain advantages for a progressive political position in the field of language: it undermines the traditional linguistic racism or xenophobia about the superiority of certain languages over others. But it has disastrous consequences: it gets rid of the very concept of a national language. There is no solution of continuity between German, Dutch, and English, only a few switches more or a few switches less activated in the mind-brain. This utter ahistoricism is difficult for a Marxist to swallow—it takes to its logical extreme the Saussurean principle of synchronicity, which at least provided a place, albeit a marginal one, for historical phenomena under the name of diachrony. Here, Lenin's subtlety (I have no time to rehearse the intricacies of his positions on the question of nationality) and his solidity help us realize the importance of the concept of natural-national language as the proper object of study for linguistics. If language is structured like a *rapport de force*, the natural site for such *rapport de force* is this or that natural language, or their clash: concepts of glottophagy (as advanced by Louis-Jean Calvet), of minorization (as proposed by Deleuze and Guattari), and the whole idea, defended by Bourdieu, of an external linguistics, are of the essence. Perhaps the Marxist philosophy of language that is to come has already found two of its founding concepts: the Deleuzean concept of *assemblage* ("agence-ment" in French, as in "agencement collectif d'énonciation") and the Althusserian concept of interpellation. Such concepts enable us to understand the linguistic concept of subject (utterer versus grammatical subject, *sujet de l'énonciation* and *sujet de l'énoncé*) not as unanalyzed central notions but as end-of-chain effects.

The third level of the Communist program is the level of strategic and tactical analysis, the level that directly informs political action. This is where Lenin's subtlety comes to the forefront. If, as Althusser claims, Lenin operates a reversal of Marx by privileging the second and third levels of the Communist program (the analysis of the concrete social formation and the political analysis in terms of strategy and tactic) over the first (the general principles), it follows that there is no analysis of the moment of the conjuncture that is sufficiently stable, predictable, and derived from general principles to be called *true*. What we have is a series of political propositions, incarnated as slogans, that are *just*, in other words an interpretation. Lenin the just, this is the second mean-ing of my title, is a master of interpretation, of a just interpretation, adapted to the concrete moment in the situation, a moment that is de-cidedly deciduous—the essence of the concrete analysis of the concrete situation is that the slogan that was just yesterday is wrong today. This does not mean, since it appears that the main political task of the mo-ment is the production of an interpretation, that there are as many in-terpretations as there are interpreters, or that there is a choice between several, equally just, interpretations. We are not in the field of aesthetics, and each moment calls for its just appraisal: it must be apprehended, struggled for, embodied in a slogan, so that it will be the object of an effective intervention producing effects of truth in the masses. In the matter of interpretation, the just logically and chronologically precedes the true.

There are two important consequences of this for the construction of a Marxist philosophy of language. The first is that, contra Deleuze and Guattari, who are hostile to interpretation as part of their general hostility to psychoanalysis, the meaning of an utterance is given in its interpretation (in the struggle to achieve it, in the *rapport de force* it establishes). The second is that we need a concept of *linguistic conjuncture*, a combination of the state of the encyclopedia, the state of the language, and the possibilities for interpellation and counterinterpellation (Deleuze would say countereffectuation) that exist in it. An interpretation is an intervention in the linguistic conjuncture: it is constrained by it and it transforms it, so that the final meaning of the utterance is a function of the interpretation it embodies like a slogan, and of its intervention in the conjuncture it transforms.

Conclusion

This is what I think Lenin enables us to do in the field of philosophy of language: to criticize the pseudo-scientific apparatus of mainstream linguistics in its two aspects of the vulgar materialism of the reductionist Chomskyan program and the idealism of Anglo-Saxon pragmatics. There is no need to repeat Lenin to achieve this: I am only too aware that historical repetition usually turns into a farce. But there is every need to make Lenin's concepts, his strategies and tactics, reverberate in a field so far unreceptive to them.

Notes

1 V. I. Lenin, "On Slogans," in *Collected Works* (London: Lawrence and Wishart, 1964), 25:183–90.

2 I am aware that in the English text, this word appears as "correct" ("juste" in the French version).

3 G. Deleuze and F. Guattari, *Mille plateaux* (Paris: Minuit, 1980), 105–6.

4 G. Deleuze, "Trois problèmes de groupe," in F. Guattari, *Psychanalyse et transversalité* (Paris: Maspero, 1972), i–xi.

5 "Vive le léninisme," in *Cahiers marxistes-léninistes* 9/10 (Paris: SER, 1966).

6 The translation of the French "mot d'ordre" by the translator of *Mille Plateaux* as "order-word," a coinage, not only loses the Leninist connection but also the political and collective implications of the word.

15

Lenin and the

Lars T. Lih   **Great Awakening**

Explanation of Title

Let me start off by explaining my title: "Lenin and the Great Awakening." I chose this title, first, because "awakening" is a key metaphor in *What Is to Be Done?* Central to the outlook expressed in this book is the idea that the masses are *spontaneously awakening* to the socialist message. Unfortunately, this central image is not only overlooked but denied, thanks to misinterpretation of some of Lenin's polemical phrases. Later on I shall present some of the eloquent passages in which Lenin evokes the great awakening of the workers.

I also chose this title because of its evangelistic overtones: The Great Awakening is the name commonly given to an important episode of evangelistic revival in eighteenth-century America. I think that if we compare Lenin to an evangelistic revival preacher, we will get a good grasp of what he was up to. I like to set out the contrast between my view of Lenin and the standard view of Lenin by describing two missionaries, both intent on spreading the word of God to the heathen. Both are convinced that there is no salvation outside the word. Both are convinced that the heathen will not receive the word unless it is preached to them. Both are convinced that the correct interpretation of holy writ is necessary for this work: they are quick to denounce heretics. In these respects, I agree with the standard view of Lenin.

But the standard view goes on to describe Lenin as a missionary who emphasizes the irredeemable sinfulness of man. Many are called, he thinks, but few even respond. And he expects that even among those who respond with enthusiasm there will be much backsliding: such are the powerful lures of the World, the Flesh, and the Devil. Perhaps, unconsciously, he is repelled by the natives' "uncultured" ways. He therefore insists on tight control of the natives by professional agents of the church. Despite his cheerless version of the good news, he is an indefatigable preacher and organizer—one suspects, in order to still his inner doubts.

This is the standard Lenin: elitist and pessimist to some, realist and insightful to others. I believe Lenin is much more of an enthusiast than either critics or admirers realize. I picture Lenin as a missionary of a very different type: a Bible-thumping, table-pounding revivalist. This type of missionary has such strong belief in the power of the word that he expects mass conversions. He is fully aware of the power of worldly temptations and the lures laid by evil men who scorn God's chosen as dogmatic enthusiasts—yet he is sure they have no real chance of success when face to face with the word well and truly preached. He is seeking to inspire not only the crowd but a corps of fellow revivalists who tour the high roads and the byroads, seeking to inspire others as they have been inspired. This revivalist missionary does not hide his belief that God has started to move in this world and that he and his fellow revivalists are his chosen instrument. His indefatigable energy is fueled by a confident belief in the coming Great Awakening.

This contrast between two missionaries leads to my central contention: Vladimir Lenin was a socialist missionary intent on spreading the good news that the proletariat had been chosen for a heroic historical mission, namely, taking political power in order to introduce socialism. Lenin's career cannot be understood apart from his conviction that he and his fellow Social Democrats were *needed* and would be *heeded*—that inspiring leadership was not only *necessary* but *sufficient* for the relatively quick growth of socialist consciousness among the workers and even beyond. His triumph and his failures, his achievements and his crimes, all stem from this awe-inspiring, even bizarre confidence.

Preaching the Socialist Word: The Underlying Narrative

Lenin's outlook was structured by an underlying narrative to which I attach several labels. One of these labels is "the inspired and inspiring leader." This label points to the central character in the narrative: a person who hears the message that emanates from the sacred source and then turns around and spreads that message further. For example, Lenin himself is inspired by Marx's message of the world-historical mission of the proletariat. He in turn dedicates himself to inspiring "the conscious worker," another key character in the narratives of the Russian revolutionaries. Lenin expects the conscious worker to spread the word further, to the regular mass of workers. And the current of inspiration does not stop at the boundaries of the class of industrial workers, for this class is called upon to exercise leadership for *all* the exploited and oppressed.

Another label for the same narrative is "the expanding circle of consciousness." This phrase points exactly to the same process that we have just seen, except that the role of individual leaders, agitators, propagandists, and activists is not so visible. What needs to be brought out is the way that for Lenin the spread of "consciousness," of socialist awareness, is akin to enthusiastic religious revival: it is an acceptance of a high calling, a new way of life. Perhaps I can bring this out by listing some of the key words and metaphors that litter the writings of Lenin and his cohort of Russian Social Democrats. First of all, of course, is "awakening" (*probuzhdenie*); also "light versus darkness"; "education" (the Russian word *vospitane* has more uplift to it than the English term); "leadership" and "hegemony," both of which centrally include the idea of being able to inspire people; "disseminator" (*rasprostranitel'*); "inspirer" (*vdokhnovitel'*); "mission"; "the path and the task," "calling"; "profession of faith" (*ispoved'*); and the "banner" (*znamia*), upon which is emblazoned one's profession of faith (this last is an incredibly important symbol for Lenin). All of these symbols cling together, forming a system. The meaning, say, of "leader," cannot be grasped apart from the others.

I can also bring out the semi-religious intensity of the leadership process by citing the words of Grigorii Zinoviev, Lenin's faithful lieutenant, in a party history published in the early 1920s about the party controversies that swirled around *What Is to Be Done?*: "[Lenin's economist critics] would say: 'So what, in your opinion, is the working class, a Messiah?' To this we answered and answer now: Messiah and messianism are not our language and we do not like such words; but we accept the concept that is contained in them: yes, the working class is in a certain sense a Messiah and its role is a messianic one, for this is the class which will liberate the whole world. . . . We avoid semi-mystical terms like Messiah and messianism and prefer the scientific one: the *hegemonic proletariat*." [1] As this citation brings out, "scientific" terminology such as "hegemony" and so on was a very thin covering to an intense process of conversion to a higher calling, of inspiring the chosen class with a sense of its mission.

In *What Is to Be Done?*, Lenin is addressing the Social Democratic activists of Russia and telling them: you too have a heroic task: you too are *needed* and you will be *heeded*. The masses are spontaneously awakening, and so, despite all the obstacles put in your way by tsarist Russia, you *will* be able to inspire them, you *will* be able to accomplish great things.

It's now time to let Lenin speak for himself. There are four or five standard quotations from *What Is to Be Done?* — "consciousness from without," "diverting spontaneity," and the like, I'm sure you're very familiar with them — but the following quotations *should* be the famous ones.

Lenin says to his critics: "[I object to this] belittling of the initiative and energy of conscious activists, since on the contrary, Marxism gives a gigantic incitement to the initiative and energy of the Social Democrat [that is, the party activist and/or leader], turning over to his disposal (if I may express myself this way) the mighty forces of the millions and millions of the working class 'spontaneously' [*stikhiino*] rising up for struggle!" [2]

He uses the example of earlier Russian revolutionary leaders to tell the story — the same story he tells over and over again — of the inspired and inspiring leader: "A circle of real leaders such as Alekseev and Myshkin, Khalturin and Zheliabov [of the People's Will] are capable of political tasks in the most genuine and practical sense of the word — capable precisely because their impassioned profession of faith [*ispoved'*] meets with an answering call from the spontaneously [*stikhiino*] awakening masses—and the leaders' boiling energy is taken up and supported by the energy of the revolutionary class." [3]

In another place, Lenin tells us what he learned from his great teacher Georgii Plekhanov: "Plekhanov was a thousand times right when he not only identified the revolutionary class—not only proved the inevitability and unavoidability of its spontaneous [*stikhiinyi*] awakening—but also presented to the 'worker circles' a great and noble political task." [4] In this statement we see the inextricable combination of the high calling of the socialist *leaders*, their "great and noble task," and the expectation of mass *awakening*.

Because of this awakening, inspired leaders can perform miracles, or, as Lenin tells his critics who thought he was a doctrinaire divorced from reality: "You brag about your practicality and you don't see (a fact known to any Russian *praktik*) what miracles for the revolutionary cause can be brought about not only by a circle but by a lone individual." [5] Just remember this quote the next time you hear about Lenin's "pragmatism" and "realism."

Lenin's Sacred History

We now must ask ourselves: where did Lenin himself get his inspiration? He got it from Marx, to be sure, but more concretely and effectively from *Marx as incarnated by European Social Democracy and the German SPD in particular*. There is a certain amount of resistance from both the Right and the Left to this fact, since both the Right and the Left prefer to set up a strong contrast between Social Democracy and Lenin. For the Right, this is because Social Democracy is pictured as a democratic mass labor party that was the very opposite of a vanguard party; for the Left, this is because the Marxism of the Second International was revisionist, weighed down by the baleful influence of Friedrich Engels, not sufficiently dialectical, and a host of other reasons.

For Lenin, the history of the SPD in particular was a sacred history. Let me make more precise what I mean by "sacred history" by considering the relation between New Testament and Old Testament as seen by the Christian tradition. The New Testament tells us about a series of events as *secundum prophetas*, according to the prophets—as a confirmation and incarnation of what the Old Testament was really saying. In a similar way, the history of the SPD became a sacred history for Lenin by the combination of an Old Testament—the *Communist Manifesto*—and a New Testament—Karl Kautsky's *The Erfurt Program*. The birth of the SPD from the energy of leaders such as Lassalle and Bebel, its miraculous growth under extremely unpropitious conditions, its triumph over Bismarck's Anti-Socialist Laws, and its solid base in the German working class: this history is set out in Kautsky's *Erfurt Program* as a stunning confirmation of the basic rightness of Marx's *Manifesto*.

And this sacred history is what inspired Lenin as a young Russian revolutionary in the early 1890s. For him, the basic prophecy laid out in the *Manifesto* and confirmed by the history of the SPD is *the merger of socialism and labor*. According to this formula, socialism and the labor movement started off separately but then joined together. Separately, both are weak; together, they are invincible. This formula—the merger of socialism and labor—is central to everything Lenin writes in the 1890s, up to and including *What Is to Be Done?*

There is a lot to be said about the consequences of this formula, but I will restrict myself here to showing the way it becomes part of Lenin's sacred history. In 1899, he writes: "Social Democracy cannot be reduced to simply providing services for the worker movement: it is 'the unification of socialism with the worker movement' (to use K. Kautsky's expression that reproduces the basic ideas of the *Communist Manifesto*): its task is to bring [внести] definite socialist ideals to the *stikhiinoe* worker movement . . . to merge this *stikhiinoe* movement in one unbreakable whole with the activity of the *revolutionary party*."[6] Around the same time he writes: "The central contribution"—the *central* contribution, mind you—"of K. Marx and F. Engels was to direct socialism toward a merger with the worker movement: they created a revolutionary theory that explained the necessity of this merger and gave socialists the task of organizing a class struggle of the proletariat."[7]

In Germany, socialism followed the behest of Marx and Engels, because—and only because—(as Lenin put it in 1894 in his first published writing) "a series of talented and energetic disseminators of that doctrine in the worker milieu were found."[8] Particularly inspiring was the example of Lassalle. Lassalle is Lenin's paradigm example in *What Is to Be Done?* of what he means by "struggling with spontaneity":

What historical service for the German worker movement was performed by Lassalle? This: he drew away [*sovlek*—the Russian word mis-
translated as "divert" in the standard translation] the movement from
the path of the Progressive Party's tred-iunionism and cooperativism—
the path along which it was moving in *stikhiinyi* fashion (with the benign
participation of [liberal democrats such as] Schulze-Delitzsch and his
like). . . . This task required a desperate struggle with *stikhiinost*, and
only as a result of this struggle carried out over many long years were
results obtained like this one: the worker population of Berlin changed
from a basic support of the Progressive Party to one of the best fortresses
of Social Democracy.[9]

The phrase "desperate struggle with *stikhiinost*" should not mislead
us: Lassalle accomplished miraculous results just by preaching the socialist word—only that, and nothing more—and he couldn't have succeeded in his mission without the *stikhiinyi* awakening of the German
workers.

Lenin's point is that Russian Social Democrats should be inspired
by Lassalle's example to spit on their hands, get down to work, and
accomplish similar miracles in Russia. Lenin explicitly draws the appropriate moral from his sacred history in this statement from his first
published writing, in 1894, a statement that in some sense sums up his
whole outlook: "Social Democracy—as Kautsky says with complete
justice—is the unification of the worker movement with socialism. And
for the progressive work of capitalism to appear among us as well as
elsewhere"—that is to say, to create a worker class capable of introducing socialism—"our socialists must get down to their own work with
all energy"—that is, they must duplicate the miracle of the SPD.[10]

Lenin's Crusade Against the Social Democratic
"Mr. Worldly Wise"

As with any enthusiastic evangelical, Lenin's worst enemy is John Bun-
yan's character, "Mr. Worldly Wise," especially when he makes his appearance among the faithful. The common label for Lenin's polemical
target in *What Is to Be Done?* is "economism," but this label puts a
misleading focus on a relatively subsidiary issue. What really enraged

Lenin and his friends about these people was their worldly-wise denial that Social Democratic preaching could have much effect. This quotation is from a German revisionist, Edouard David, but it was used by a Russian Social Democrat, Sergei Prokopovich, to make his own point: "We didn't obtain the sympathy of the masses in the way described by Kautsky: revolutionizing minds. . . . The revolutionizing of minds will get us only a few students. We can't get the sympathy of the masses by awakening hopes for the future in them or by ideas that are not so easy to understand. The revolutionizing of the masses doesn't start from the mind but from the stomach." [11]

Mr. Worldly Wise says: don't bother preaching to the masses, they can't be converted by mere words, they can't be inspired by a sense of mission. Lenin says: Give me that old time Social Democracy—it was good enough for Marx, it was good enough for Plekhanov and Kautsky, and it is good enough for me. We Russian Social Democrats *can* and *will* revolutionize minds.

Recall Lenin's admiration for Lassalle, and then read Prokopovich's attack on Lassalle as a self-deceiving demagogue—and this from a Social Democrat! Prokopovich strikes at the heart of Lenin's sacred history when he writes, apropos of Lassalle: "The masses are not conscious of any 'grand historical ideas' that they are supposed to carry out—and indeed, are the masses even capable of striving in a conscious fashion to carry out such ideas?" [12]

I could give a number of these attacks on the very possibility of a merger of socialism and the worker movement, but I will close with one that Lenin ran across in the fall of 1901 at the very time that he was writing *What Is to Be Done?* This particular statement determined the whole polemical framework of Lenin's book. It states: "*Iskra* [Lenin's political newspaper at the time] takes little account of that material environment and those material elements of the movement whose interaction creates a specific type of worker movement and determines its path. All the efforts of ideologues—even though inspired by the best possible theories and programs—cannot divert [*sovlech*] the movement from this path." [13]

In other words, inspirational-type leaders are useless, futile: they can rhapsodize about the great cause all they want, they can try to inspire workers all they want, but the effect will be essentially nil. In response,

Lenin structured his entire book around the counterassertion that you *can* divert spontaneity, that is, that preaching the socialist word *will* have an effect. Leaders are needed, and they will be heeded.

Today we tend to think of Social Democracy, both then and now, as essentially unheroic, prosaic. But if you read Lenin for any length of time, you will see that the very words "Social Democracy" had a kind of aura for him: they were inscribed on the banner under which he marched into battle. In order to bring this out, I will give a description of Social Democracy by a contemporary of Lenin who probably didn't know who Lenin was. In 1908, an American socialist named Robert Hunter wrote a book called *Socialism at Work* about European Social Democracy. His opening words may seem melodramatic and overwrought to us, but they serve all the better as a clue to Lenin's mindset:

> Almost unknown to the world outside of Labor a movement wide as the universe grows and prospers. Its vitality is incredible, and its humanitarian ideals come to those who labor as drink to parched throats. Its creed and program call forth a passionate adherence, its converts serve it with a daily devotion that knows no limit of sacrifice, and in the face of persecution, misrepresentation, and even martyrdom, they remain loyal and true. . . . From Russia, across Europe and America to Japan, from Canada to Argentina, it crosses frontiers, breaking through the carriers of language, nationality, and religion as it spreads from factory to factory, from mill to mill, and from mine to mine, touching as it goes with the religion of life the millions of the underworld.
>
> Its converts work in every city, town and hamlet in the industrial nations, spreading the new gospel among the poor and lowly, who listen to their words with religious intensity. Tired workmen pore over the literature which these missionaries leave behind them, and fall to sleep over open pages; and the youth, inspired by its lofty ideals and elevated thought, leave the factory with joyous anticipation to read through the night.[14]

Robert Hunter and Vladimir Lenin thought that the mass of workers could be inspired by "lofty ideals and elevated thought," while Edouard David and Sergei Prokopovich thought they could not. That is the nub of the issue, as Lenin saw it.

What Is to Be Done? Is Not a Breakthrough Document

It follows from all that I've said that *What Is to Be Done?* is not a break-through document, not the founding document of Bolshevism, not an example of Lenin's secret revisionism, not the invention of the vanguard party. I'm not sure exactly where and why this idea came about, but I can report that it was not shared by Lenin or the people who knew him best. Lenin himself said later that *What Is to Be Done?* was a compendium of the *Iskra* outlook, nothing more, nothing less—that is, it was the expression of the outlook of a whole cohort of Russian Social Democratic activists who were inspired by the stunning example of a powerful German workers' party.

Nadezhda Krupskaya, Grigorii Zinoviev, and Lev Kamenev were the people who worked closest with Lenin in the years before the war and they were also the first party historians. In their accounts of the first decade of Lenin's career, they place great emphasis on Lenin's first publication in 1894 as the expression of his basic outlook, one that remained with him to the end of his days. They treat *What Is to Be Done?* as historically important, as a book that shows Lenin's fiery revolutionary temperament, but certainly not as a breakthrough document or one that is key to Lenin's outlook.

Nikolai Bukharin, the foremost theorist, wrote a couple of fascinating articles about Lenin as a theorist. He realized that for his readers in 1920 there was something paradoxical about the very idea of Lenin as a theorist. In these articles, Bukharin does not mention *What Is to Be Done?* In fact, he does not mention the whole subject of party organization as one in which Lenin made any particular theoretical contributions.

Finally, I might add in the party debates of the early years of the Bolshevik regime, when Lenin was of course quoted on all sides as the ultimate authority, we find that *What Is to Be Done?* is conspicuous by its absence. In fact, it was this absence—the theoretical dog that didn't bark, as it were—that first led me to suspect that something was wrong with the image of *What Is to Be Done?* with which I had grown up.

Where did this idea about the primordial importance of *What Is to Be Done?* originate? I am not completely sure, but one important landmark was the publication in the late 1940s of Bertram Wolfe's *Three Who*

Made a Revolution. In this book, the writing of *What Is to Be Done?* becomes the event where Lenin finds himself, where he really becomes Lenin. In contrast, in serious English-language studies of Lenin written before the war—and they are very few—we find an account that is much more like the one proposed by Krupskaya and Zinoviev.

The Fundamental Outlook Expressed in *What Is to Be Done?*

I have argued that *What Is to Be Done?* is not the great innovation it is commonly held to be. It is one expression among many of the outlook Lenin had been propounding throughout the 1890s—one that he took over in basic respects from international Social Democracy and one that he shared as well with a whole cohort of Russian Social Democratic activists. Lenin stands out, if at all, for the intensity of his devotion to this outlook. But one reason that it is important to see this relative lack of originality is precisely to bring out the fundamental importance for Lenin of the *outlook* that he set forth in *What Is to Be Done?*

Let us call it the *Iskra* outlook, after the newspaper that Lenin and his friends founded just prior to the writing of *What Is to Be Done?* I have argued that the essence of the *Iskra* outlook is belief in the Great Awakening of the workers—the belief that *if* Social Democratic activists preach the socialist word with energy and enthusiasm, the spontaneously awakening masses will respond. Activists are *needed* and will be *heeded.* I will now make the claim that this same belief lies behind all the major positions of Lenin's political career, all the decisions that make up the profile of Lenin as a political leader. Among these are his scenario for the 1905 Revolution; his insistence on maintaining an illegal party in the years before the revolution; his insistence, after the war started, that a socialist revolution was now in the making; his slogan, "turn the imperialist war into a civil war"; his idea in 1917 that Soviet democracy was the proper form for the dictatorship of the proletariat; his rationale for signing the Brest-Litovsk Treaty; his hopes for world revolution afterward.

I of course cannot go in to any detail to back up this claim, but I will add one revealing statement made by Lenin during World War I in one of his writings on the national question. Inspired by Kevin Anderson, I recently turned to Lenin's writings on this issue, which became important for him only during the war. I first of all noticed that Lenin himself hammered home the continuity of his stand on the national issue—that is, his insistence that socialist revolutionaries had to guarantee the right of national self-determination up to and including the right of secession—with the *Iskra* outlook. In one article, he argued that while premature national uprisings would probably fail, the long, drawn out revolutionary process was also a good thing because it was a learning process. And what was the basic lesson learned? "The masses will acquire experience, will learn, will gather strength—and they will see their true leaders [*nastoiashchie vozhdi*], the socialist proletariat."[15]

The masses will recognize their true leaders—this is the basic narrative, the basic axiom behind Lenin's political career. First, it is the workers themselves who recognize *their* true leaders, namely, the inspired and inspiring party activists. In turn, the workers will themselves become a leader-class: an inspired and inspiring leader for *all* the oppressed. The course of events, the process of revolution itself, teaches the masses a lot and in a hurry—and the fundamental lesson it teaches is the identity of their true leaders.

Is Lenin Still Relevant?

Does this interpretation of Lenin render him relevant or irrelevant for those of us interested in political struggle today? That is for you to decide: my job as a historian is merely to identify the main themes of Lenin's basic outlook. I will only say that as far as I am concerned, there are two positions that someone would have to hold today in order for it to make sense to call his position "Leninist" in even a figurative sense. First, he or she must believe that some identifiable group is (to use Zinoviev's words) something like a Messiah class: a group of people to whom history has entrusted the high calling, the world historical mission, of fundamentally reordering society. Second, he or she must have an evangelistic confidence that preaching the word will awaken this group to its calling. These two positions are Lenin's baby. If we can't accept them, we'll have to make do with his bath water.

Epilogue

I will close with one more citation, this time from Krupskaya's funeral eulogy of Lenin in 1924. I was struck by this passage when I first read it, since most academic commentators on Lenin would not only disagree with it—they wouldn't even comprehend what Krupskaya was talking about: "Work among the workers of Piter [that is, St. Petersburg], conversations with these workers, attentive listening to their speeches gave Vladimir Ilich an understanding of the grand idea of Marx: the idea that the working class is the advance unit of all the laborers and that all the laboring masses, all the oppressed will follow it: this is its strength and the gage of its victory. The working class can only be victorious as the inspiring leader [*vozhd*] of all the laborers."[16] This is what Vladimir Ilich understood as he worked among the workers of Piter. And this idea, this thought illuminated all his further activity and each step he made.

Appendix: "From Without" and "Diverting Spontaneity"

The standard view of *What Is to Be Done?* is that in it Lenin expresses his relative pessimism and *lack* of confidence in the ability of the workers to acquire socialist consciousness. This view rests essentially on two famous phrases from the book, in which Lenin asserts that the workers must acquire "consciousness from without," and also that it is necessary to "divert spontaneity." A detailed historical and textual analysis is required to show that these phrases do not mean what they seem to mean. "From without" [*izvne*] is straightforward: Lenin used this word to evoke the merger narrative ("Social Democracy is the merger of socialism and the worker movement") that was a constitutive formula of European Social Democracy. To see why Lenin went on so much about "diverting spontaneity" we have to go into the details of the immediate polemical context of the book. Briefly, Lenin concocted this phrase from statements made by his foes: the main statement was the one about the inability of "ideologues" to "divert" the worker movement from the path determined by the material environment. When Lenin says "we must divert spontaneity," he is essentially affirming that leaders *can* make a difference. And why?—because the workers are spontaneously awakening. This train of thought is made explicit in the following passage from *What Is to Be Done?*:

> True, in the stagnant waters of "an economic struggle against the bosses and the government," a certain moldy film has unfortunately formed—people appear among us who get down on their knees and pray to spontaneity [*stikhiinost*], gazing with beatitude (as Plekhanov puts it) on the "behind" of the Russian proletariat. But we will be able to free ourselves from this moldy film. And it is precisely at the present time that the Russian revolutionary—guided by a genuinely revolutionary theory and relying on the class that is genuinely revolutionary and is undergoing a spontaneous [*stikhiinyi*] awakening—can at last—at last!—draw himself up to his full stature and reveal all his heroic strength.[17]

Notes

1   Grigorii Zinoviev, *Istorica Rossiskoi Kommunisticheskoi Partii (Bol'shevikov)*, fourth edition (Leningrad: Gosizdat, 1924), 74.

2   V. I. Lenin, *What Is to Be Done?*, in *Polneo sobranie sochineniia* [Collected works], fifth edition (Moscow: Gospolizdat, 1958–65; henceforth *PSS*) 6:48.

3   Lenin, *What Is to Be Done?*, in *PSS* 6:106–8.

4   Ibid.

5   Ibid.

6   Lenin, *PSS* 4:189.

7   Lenin, *PSS* 4:244–47.

8   Lenin, *PSS* 1:332–33.

9   Lenin, *What Is to Be Done?*, in *PSS* 6:40–41.

10 *PSS* 1:332–33.

11 Quoted in S. Prokopovich, *Rabochee dvizhenie na Zapade: Opyt kriticheskogo issledovaniia. Tom 1. Germaniia. Bel'giia* (St. Petersburg: Izdanie L. F. Panteleeva), 166.

12 *PSS* 1:16.

13 *PSS* 1:360–62.

14 Robert Hunter, *Socialists at Work* (New York: Macmillan, 1908), v–vi.

15 "The masses will acquire experience, will learn, will gather strength—and they will see their true leaders [*nastoiashchie vozhdi*], the socialist proletariat" (*PSS* 30:56).

16 Lenin, article in *Pravda*, 27 January 1924.

17 For readers who wish to read more about the "scandalous passages" in *What Is to Be Done?*, see Lars T. Lih, *Lenin Rediscovered: "What Is to Be Done?" in Context* (Leiden: Brill Academic Press, 2006), 613–67.

What to Do Today with

What Is to Be Done?, or

Rather: The Body of the

Antonio Negri | **General Intellect**

The weak link in the imperialist chain is where the working class is at its strongest.
—Mario Tronti, *Lenin in England*, 1964

The Biopolitical Aspect of Leninism

"To speak of Lenin is to speak of the conquest of power. Whether one exalts or criticizes them, it is pointless to collocate his work or actions on any other horizon: the conquest of power is the only Leninist theme." Thus Western political science pays homage to Lenin, paradoxically exalting his *sombre grandeur*. Might it not be said that even Mussolini and Hitler dreamed of being Lenin? What is certain, however, is that at the end of the civil wars that marked the twentieth century, bourgeois political science has finally granted its acknowledgment to Lenin, the victor of October 17, the man of untimely decision and unshakeable determination.

A Disgusting Acknowledgment

In what indeed consists this notion of seizing power in revolutionary Marxism? Both in the workers' movements of the nineteenth and twentieth centuries and in the Communist movement itself there is in fact no seizing of power that is not connected with the abolition of the state. Lenin is no exception, since his own extraordinary adventure is linked to just such a project, which alone is enough to place his achievement a million miles from bourgeois political science's ambiguous exaltation of it. Undoubtedly Lenin's project was only ever half-realized: though succeeding in its conquest of power, it failed to abolish the state. Undoubtedly too the very state that should have withered away has instead become so strong and vicious as to dispel for entire generations of Communist militants the hope that the conquest of power can be conjoined with the abolition of the state. And yet the problem remains. To return to the question of Lenin means asking ourselves once again whether it is possible to take up that path which at once subverts the existing order of things and invents a new world of freedom and equality, destroying the West's metaphysical *arché*—both as principle of authority and as tool of social exploitation—along with its political hierarchy and control of the forces of production.

Phrasing the question thus, we must immediately add a further note, given that capitalist power is composed of two indistinguishable poles—state control and a social structure based on exploitation—and that it is the aim of revolution—when it is Communist—to attack and destroy both. It is that for Lenin (as for revolutionary Marxism in general) the Communist struggle is necessarily biopolitical. It is so because it involves every aspect of life, but above all because the Communists' revolutionary political will attaches itself to the *bios*, which it critiques, constructs, and transforms. In this sense Lenin removes political science from any idealistic simplification or notion of "reason of state" as he does from the illusion that the political can be defined in terms of bureaucracy or quick decision making. Yet even more radically he refuses any separation of the political from the social and human spheres. In terms of his own political thought, Lenin begins by freeing the analysis of the state from the (ancient, oft-repeated, and invariably mystificatory) theory of forms of government. He then proposes an analysis of the political sphere that goes beyond the naïve hypothesis of its mirroring economic forms, and he does this by freeing himself from millenarian pulsions, as well as from secular utopian visions that, in terms of a theory of revolution, might confound our sight. Contrariwise, he mixes, hybridizes, shakes up, and revolutionizes both forms of theory: what must always emerge triumphant is the political will of the proletariat in which body and reason, life and passion, rebellion and design may constitute themselves in the form of a biopolitical subject. And that subject is the working class and its vanguard, the soul of the proletariat *in its body.*

Rosa Luxemburg, though in many ways very different from Lenin, is on this point of the Communist project's biopolitical character extremely close to him. By their different routes, the curve of Luxemburg and the straight line of Lenin intersect in regarding the life of the masses and the entire articulation of their needs as a physical, corporeal potential that alone can ground and give content to the abstract violence of revolutionary intellectuality. Such a progress in Communism's political ontology is undoubtedly mysterious though nonetheless real for that—showing, through its biopolitical aspect, the extraordinary modernity of Communist thought, particularly in terms of the corporeal fullness of the freedom it expresses and desires to produce. And this is where we find the real Lenin, in this materialism of bodies that strive to free themselves and in the materiality of life, which revolution (indeed only revolution) permits to renew itself. Lenin thus represents not an apology for the autonomy of the political sphere but the revolutionary invention of a body.

Lenin beyond Lenin

But exploitation and the struggle against exploitation: What do these things mean for us today (and not yesterday or a century ago)? What is the present status of that body which transformed itself during the adventures and civil wars of the twentieth century? What is the new body of Communist struggle?

It was during the early 1960s (and afterward with ever increasing intensity) that these questions came to the fore, questions there seemed no great possibility of resolving. And yet there remained the conviction that regarding such questions, not only must Lenin's thought be reexamined with exegetic fidelity, but it must also be reframed—as it were—"beyond Lenin."

The first problem was therefore that of preserving the sense of Leninism within the ongoing transformation of conditions of production and the power relations that informed them, along with the accompanying mutation of subjects. A second problem, which arose from the first, was how to render Leninism (that is, the demand for the organization of a revolution against capitalism and for the destruction of the state) adequate to the current consistency of productive reality and to the new insistence of subjects. Today this means asking how the conquest of power and abolition of the state are possible in a historical period that sees (to anticipate a key point) capital establishing its hegemony over the general intellect.

Everything has changed. With respect to Lenin's own experience and theories the technical and political composition of the work force involved in today's systems of production and control is entirely new, with the result that the experience of exploitation has itself been completely transformed. These days, in fact, the nature of productive labor is fundamentally immaterial, while productive cooperation is entirely social: this means that work is now coextensive with life just as cooperation is with the multitude. It is therefore within society as a whole (and no longer simply in the factories) that labor extends productive networks capable of renovating the world of consumer goods, putting to work the complex of man's rational and affective desires. The same extension determines exploitation. So much for technical composition. But the problem returns when we consider also the political composition of this new workforce since (qualified by the incorporation of the utensil, which in terms of immaterial labor is the brain) it presents itself on the market as extremely mobile (a mobility that is also a sign of its flight from disciplinary forms of capitalist production) and highly flexible—a sign of political autonomy, the search for self-evaluation, and a refusal of representation. How can we posit Leninism within these new conditions of the workforce? How can the flight and self-evaluation of the immaterial worker be transformed into a new class struggle, in terms of an organized desire to appropriate social wealth and liberate subjectivity? How can we connect this wholly different reality to the strategic project of Communism? How can the old be remodeled in terms of a radical opening toward the new, which is nonetheless—as Machiavelli demanded of every real revolution—a "return to origins," in this case to Leninism?

Marx's own thinking was tied to the manufacturing phenomenology of industrial labor. As a result, his conception both of the party and of the proletariat's social dictatorship was fundamentally one of self-management. Lenin was, right from the outset, bound to a vanguardist notion of the party, which in Russia—even before the revolution—was to anticipate the passage from manufacturing to "large-scale industry," which it would then give itself the strategic objective of governing. For Lenin as for Marx the relationship between the technical composition of the proletariat and political strategy went by the name of "Commune" or "Communist Party"—and it was this "Commune" or "party" that effected recognition of the real and that proposed a full circulation between (subversive) political strategy and (biopolitical) organization of the masses. The party was the engine that powered the production of subjectivity—or rather, it was the utensil employed to produce subversive subjectivity.

Our question is thus: What production of subjectivity for seizing hold of power is possible for today's immaterial proletariat? Or put another way: If the context of present-day production is constituted by the social cooperation of immaterial labor—which we shall term the general intellect—how can we construct the subversive body of this "general intellect," for which Communist organization would be the lever, the point of generation of new revolutionary corporealities, the powerful base of the production of subjectivity? At this point we move into the realm of "Lenin beyond Lenin."

The Subversive Body of the General Intellect

It is inevitable that we introduce this point here, almost in the form of a parenthesis. But as sometimes happens in Socratic argument, such a parenthesis may provide evidence of the concept itself. There is a famous chapter in Marx's *Grundrisse* in which Marx appears to construct a "natural history" (that is to say one that is linear, continuous, and necessary) of capital, which evolves toward the general intellect wherein the general intellect is the product of capitalist development, a conclusion that is not without its ambiguities for us as it was already for Lenin himself (who evidently was not familiar with the *Grundrisse*, though he possessed the logic of rupture that Marxist thought exalted and that rendered impossible any natural continuity of capitalist development).[1] In effect, aside from the objectivist illusion that often finds its way into the critique of political economy, for Marx too this is the way things are: the development that generates the general intellect is in his view a process that is anything but natural. It is, on the one hand, bursting with life (all the vital forces of production and reproduction that go to make up the biopolitical context of capitalist society); it is, on the other hand, intensely contradictory (the general intellect is in fact not merely the product of the struggle against wage labor but also represents that anthropological trend embodied in the refusal of work). Lastly it is also the revolutionized result of the tendential decline of capitalism's rate of profit.

Here we find ourselves in an entirely biopolitical situation. What unites the Marx of the general intellect with Lenin and ourselves is this: the fact that we are all actors, men and women, in that world of production that constitutes life—that we are in essence the *flesh* of development, the very reality of capitalist development, this new flesh in which the powers of knowledge are inseparably mixed with those of production, as scientific activities are—in the most singular and voluptuous manner—with passions. Now, this *bios* (or rather this bio-political reality that characterized the post-1968 industrial revolution) certain authors and *maîtres à penser* (who when the night got darker declared themselves to be Communists) chose to call the cso—*Corps sans Organes*. But I continue to call it *flesh*. Perhaps it has the strength to become a body and to constitute for itself all the organs it requires—but only perhaps. In order to make the event real, what is required is a demiurge, or rather an external vanguard that can transform this flesh into a body, the body of the general intellect. Or perhaps, as other authors have suggested, might the becoming body of the general intellect not be determined by the word that the general intellect itself articulates, in such a way that the general intellect becomes the demiurge of its own body?

I myself do not believe that we have the power to identify which road to take; only a genuine movement of struggle will be able to decide that. What is certain, however, is that in terms of the maturation of the general intellect, we must anticipate its experimentation. Only in this way, by opposing to the natural history of capital those indissoluble contradictions that Marx invented, will the genealogy of the general intellect be constituted as a subversive force. Defining the body of the general intellect is in fact tantamount to affirming the power of the subjects who populate it, the violence of the crises that shake its ambiguity, the clash of teleologies that traverse it—and to deciding where we stand in this chaos. If we decide that in the general intellect the subject is powerful because it is nomadic and autonomous; that therefore the forces of cooperation win out over those of the market; and that the teleology of the commune predominates over that of the private individual—then we will have taken a stand over the question of the body of the general intellect. It is a constitution born from the militancy of individuals constructed through immaterial and cooperative labor who have decided to live as a subversive association.

We thus find the "biopolitics of Leninism" embedded within the new contradictions of the "beyond Lenin." It is with Lenin that we decide to make the body of the general intellect the subject of the organization of a new way of life.

Spaces and Temporalities

However, "beyond Lenin" does not simply mean the recognition of a new reality and thus a renewed discovery of the urgent need for organization: there must also be the spatial and temporal determination of a liberatory project. The body is always localized just as it always exists in this or that particular time. The production of subjectivity—in order to be effective—requires spatial and temporal determination. In the case of Russia—a particular place in a particular time—for Lenin this determination will be absolute—here and now, or never! But what space and time are open to the subversive organization and possible revolution of an immaterial proletariat that is "exodic" and autonomous?

Identifying the spatial dimension of a new Leninist project is a task that is fraught with difficulties. Living in the Empire, we know that any revolutionary initiative that limits itself to a confined space (even if this be a large nation-state) is doomed. It is clear that the only recognizable Winter Palace we have nowadays is the White House, which, it must be admitted, is somewhat difficult to attack. Moreover, the more imperial power reinforces itself, the more complex and globally well-integrated its political representation becomes. Though its summit may be in the United States, the Empire itself is not American—it is rather the Empire of collective capital. Contrariwise, recognizing that there is no space for the party if not the International is tantamount to uttering a banality, if not something wholly inessential. No longer decisive for the renewal of Leninism, in fact, is the theoretical reaffirmation of a particular point of leverage by which the forces of subversion can be multiplied. What is of interest to us in considering "Lenin beyond Lenin" is to concretely identify the point in the imperial chain where it may be possible to force reality. Now, this is no longer a weak point, nor will it ever be again: rather it will be where resistance, insurrection, and the hegemony of the general intellect—that is to say the constituent power of the new proletariat—is at its strongest. Thus while the formal base of the revolutionary device of production of subjectivity is still the International, in concrete, political, and material terms there is no longer a space but a place, no longer a horizon but a point, the point at which the event becomes possible.

For the party, therefore, the subject of space is subordinated to a specific *kairos*, the untimely power of an event. This is the arrow shot by the general intellect so as to recognize itself as a body.

Regarding the temporality of the neo-Leninist party in the epoch of post-Fordist globalization, the discourse is in certain ways analogous to what we have said so far. The same goes for time as for space; determinations have fallen away. Economic and political history become increasingly harder to define according to rhythmic sequences, while the regular cyclic alternation between epochs of exploitation and creative periods of class struggle has altered beyond all recognition, despite the fact that it is what characterized an entire century from 1870 to 1970. What temporality therefore is given to today's Leninist party that it may take control of, use, and transform? Here too the confines are extremely blurred: just as in reasoning over the question of spatiality and place we saw how the nation-state had become a feud of the Empire and how the developed Northern Hemisphere and the underdeveloped Southern Hemisphere were by now inside one another, interwoven in the same destiny, so too temporalities have become indistinguishable. Only a specific *kairos* will enable the body of the general intellect to emerge.

But what does all of this actually mean? Regarding these considerations we can come to no theoretical conclusion. Never as in this case has there been so great a need for militant action and experimentation.

It is by now clear to all of us that the Leninist device of intervention on a weak point at a critical, objectively determined moment is completely ineffective. It is just as clear that it is only where the immaterial workforce's energy is higher than that of the forces of capitalist exploitation that a project of liberation will become possible. Anti-capitalist decision becomes effective only where subjectivity is at its strongest, where it is able to build a "civil war" against the Empire.

Dictatorship without Sovereignty, or "Absolute Democracy"

At this point we have to admit that our reasoning has not been as convincing as our initial Socratic appeal would have the right to expect. While it is true that—to reaffirm the figure of the Leninist party (which involves itself in power and constitutes freedom through an untimely and absolute decision)—we have established several important premises (the emergence of the general intellect and the possibility of giving it body; the tendential centrality of immaterial labor; the phenomena of flight and nomadism, autonomy and self-evaluation that this context gives rise to; and lastly the contradictions that mark the relationship between globalization and the complex interweaving of its internal devices with forces of resistance and subversion)—we must at the same time acknowledge that in the wake of all this we have failed to reach any real conclusions. If we cannot provide a content, a determination and a singular power with which to fill in the picture, in entrusting ourselves to the *kairos* we risk losing the essential. For while this appeal to the *kairos* may give form to the production of subjectivity, without subversive utterances and contents it is at the same time terribly exposed to pure tautology. It is our task then to give content to the *kairos* of the general intellect, to give food to its revolutionary body. What, therefore, we might ask, would constitute a revolutionary decision today? By what contents is such a decision characterized?

To respond to this question we must first make a short detour. We must bear in mind the limitations (which nonetheless constituted an enormous leap forward from the manufacturing culture of Russian Social Democracy) of the Leninist point of view, whose revolutionary decision, establishing itself as constituent power, was in reality informed by a particular model of industry: the Western—more specifically American—model. Modern industrial development was the skeleton in Bolshevik revolutionary theory's closet. The model of revolutionary management—or rather the work of the Russian people who constituted it—was determined, and in the long run perverted, by this premise.

Today the situation has radically altered. There is no longer a working class to cry over the lack of a management program for industry and society, whether this be direct or mediated by the state. And even were such a project to be reactualized, it could no longer gain hegemony over the proletariat or the intellectuality of the masses; nor could it have any effect on capitalist power, which has by now shifted to other levels (financial, bureaucratic, communicational) of command. Today then, revolutionary decision must be grounded on a completely different constituent scheme: no longer positing a preliminary axis of industrial and/or economic development, it will propose instead the program of a liberated city where industry bends to the needs of life, society to science, and work to the multitude. Here, the constituent decision becomes the democracy of the multitude.

And so we come to the conclusion of this essay. What is required of the party is a great and sweeping radicalism in order to transform the movement into the practice of constituent power. In so far as it anticipates law, constituent power is always a form of dictatorship (but then there is dictatorship and dictatorship: the Fascist form is not the same as the Communist, though we do not consider the latter preferable to the former). The fact remains that political decision is always a question of production of subjectivity, which in turn involves the production of concrete bodies, of masses and/or multitudes of bodies—thus every subjectivity is necessarily different from others.

Today what is of interest to us is the subjectivity of the general intellect, which in order to transform the world around it must use force—a force that shall be organized by the constituent power. Of course, this exercise of constituent power may also have both positive and negative effects. There is no measure we can use to decide in advance the criteria for what the multitudes will create. However, so as not to be misunderstood, nor to be accused of working for an indiscriminate dictatorship that is veiled by a language of hypocrisy and that is today more dangerous than ever—since it lies hidden in the vulgarity of a social sphere ruled by homogenous consumption—we shall say that the dictatorship we desire and that we believe to be the treasure of a rediscovered Lenin may also be termed "absolute democracy." This is the term Spinoza used to describe the form of government that the multitude exercised over itself. Spinoza showed great courage in adding the adjective "absolute" to one of the equivalent forms of government that had been passed down through the theory of the ancients: monarchy against tyranny, aristocracy against oligarchy, democracy against anarchy. This is because Spinoza's "absolute democracy" has nothing to do with the theory of the forms of government, for which it deserved to be, and indeed has been, covered with negative epithets. However, "absolute democracy" is a term particularly suited to describing the invention of a new form of liberty, or better, the production of a people "to come."

But if there is one fundamental reason that supports our proposal of "absolute democracy" it is the realization that this term is wholly uncontaminated (on account of the very nature of the spaces and times of the postmodern) by the modern concept of sovereignty. We must therefore—and we can, provided that we acknowledge its biopolitical nature—bear Lenin's thought out of the modern universe (the sovereign industrial model) in which it has so far dwelt and translate its revolutionary decision into a new production of Communist and autonomous subjectivity within the postmodern multitudes.

Note

1 K. Marx, "Fixed Capital and Continuity of the Living Process: Machinery and Living Labor," in *Grundrisse* (Harmondsworth: Penguin, 1973), 702–44; see especially 704–12.

17

Lenin and Hegemony:

The Soviets, the Working

Class, and the Party in the

Alan Shandro | **Revolution of 1905**

Most thoughtful treatments of leadership understand it as a complex relationship between leader and led. If the literature on Lenin is to be relied upon, the preeminent practical leader of the Marxist working-class movement would have little of theoretical importance to contribute to an understanding of leadership. For the predominant tendency in this literature suggests that the distinctive conception of the vanguard party developed by Lenin merely reassigns revolutionary agency from the working class to a vanguard organization led by intellectuals of bourgeois provenance. Lenin's project, on this sort of reading, was to identify an agent capable of substituting its revolutionary consciousness for the alleged incapacity of the working class for revolutionary activity. But by framing Lenin's position in terms of the categories of his opponents, this reading misidentifies it. Lenin's core thesis, that Social Democratic consciousness must be introduced into the spontaneous working-class movement from without, might now be reformulated as the idea that the working-class movement cannot, absent the organized intervention of Marxist theory in its struggle, generate revolutionary socialist consciousness.[1] I claim that the effect of his thesis was to reorganize the categories with which Marxists could approach the phenomena of leadership and to do so in a way that yields some conceptual purchase upon the complex dynamics of the relation between leaders and masses.

The Vanguard and Socialist Consciousness

If the spontaneous working-class movement is equated with the economic base and Social Democratic consciousness with the superstructure, then Lenin's thesis amounts to a voluntarist reversal of the Marxist primacy of the base; revolution is no longer grounded in a materialist analysis of class relations and becomes instead the expression of the will of the conscious revolutionary intellectuals. These categories provide little conceptual space in which to grasp the phenomena of leadership: revolution is accomplished *either* by the working class *or* by the vanguard party; *either* the working class spontaneously generates a consciousness of its revolutionary vocation *or* the self-professed vanguard of revolutionary intellectuals substitutes itself for this spontaneous process. Situated in this context, leadership could only consist in imparting consciousness of a revolutionary vocation. Politics is thus effectively equated with education and the essential political division rests upon whether or not the educator respects the autonomy of the learner.

Lenin's thesis, however, resists any simple identification of the distinction between spontaneity and consciousness with that between base and superstructure. In the course of his argument, the conscious vanguard is called upon both to foster the spontaneous working-class movement and to combat it. The apparent ambivalence of this stance is grounded in an assessment of spontaneity itself as at once embryo of socialist consciousness and repository of bourgeois ideology, a contradiction Lenin states pointedly as follows: "The working class spontaneously gravitates towards socialism; but the most widespread (and continuously and diversely revived) bourgeois ideology none the less spontaneously imposes itself upon the worker to a still greater degree."[2] Marxist sense can be made of this claim only by examining the dialectical process whereby the ideological dominance of the bourgeoisie is established in struggle with the spontaneous socialist tendencies of the working class.

The terms of the problem (spontaneity versus consciousness, bourgeois spontaneity versus socialist spontaneity) must be set within a dynamic of struggle. This requires two levels of analysis. At an initial level, abstraction is made from the influence of ideology—that is, of "consciousness"—upon the spontaneous struggle of social forces, a struggle characterized in terms of the social relations of production.

Since, at this level, the interests of the working class can be shown to be in irreconcilable conflict with the fundamental social relations of the capitalist mode of production, the workers may be expected, in virtue of these social relations, to gravitate spontaneously toward Marxist theory for an explanation of their situation and orientation in their struggle. But Lenin argues that the spontaneous movement is not only determined by the socioeconomic base of the class struggle. The claim "that ideologists (i.e., politically conscious leaders) cannot divert the movement from the path determined by the interaction of environment and elements . . . ignore[s] the simple truth that the conscious element *participates* in this interaction and in the determination of the path. Catholic and monarchist labour unions in Europe are also an inevitable result of the interaction of environment and elements, but it was the consciousness of priests and Zubatovs and not that of socialists that participated in this direction."[3]

Reckoning with this "simple truth," Lenin analyzes the spontaneous movement as the movement of the working class, not simply as it is determined by the relations of production, but also as it is subjected to the influence of the ideological apparatuses of the bourgeoisie (institutional vehicles of ideas and information, such as political parties, government offices, newspapers, and churches, whose operation simply assumes or otherwise accepts the dominance of capitalist interests). Understood in these terms, the spontaneous movement is that which confronts the socialist consciousness of the would-be vanguard of the proletariat, within its field of action but beyond its control. Only at this second, more concrete, level of analysis does Lenin locate the dominance of bourgeois ideology; what is thus subject to this domination is not the working class as such but the spontaneous unfolding of its movement, that is, the working-class movement considered in abstraction from its revolutionary socialist vanguard, from those intellectuals and workers whose political activity is informed by Marxist theory and is, in this sense, conscious.

There is no need, on these assumptions, to suppose that the dominance of bourgeois ideology is perfect or that the workers are incapable of spontaneous resistance, political struggle, or, indeed, innovation. The logic of spontaneous struggle generates a dynamic through which bourgeois ideology and proletarian experience come to be partially constitutive of each other. The limitation of the spontaneous struggle consists, not in an absolute incapacity of the working-class movement to generate any particular form of political activity, but in its inability, in the absence of Marxist theory, to establish a position of strategic independence vis-à-vis its adversaries. Lenin's thesis of consciousness from without can thus be restated as the following three claims: first, the working-class movement cannot assert its strategic independence without attaining a recognition of the irreconcilability of its interests with the whole of the politico-social system organized around the dominance of bourgeois interests; second, such recognition implies that attempts to reconcile proletarian with bourgeois interests be assessed in the context of the Marxist critique of capitalist political economy; hence, third, this recognition cannot be brought to bear effectively upon the class struggle in the absence of an organized leadership informed by Marxist theory. An implication, not immediately drawn by Lenin, is that revolutionary consciousness must be open to the ability, not only of the bourgeoisie, but also of the workers, to innovate spontaneously in the course of the struggle.

This set of assumptions, which sustains the thesis of consciousness from without, is needed in order to conceive the political project of a Marxist vanguard as a determinate intervention within a complex, uneven, contradictory logic of struggle for hegemony. But this is just what the circumstances of class struggle in tsarist Russia called upon the Russian Marxists to do. While the extension of capitalist social relations eroded the feudal and patriarchal foundations of absolutism, the unfettered growth of capitalism and the prospects for proletarian socialism made a thoroughgoing democratic transformation of the institutions of tsarism and landlordism imperative. But the dependence of the Russian bourgeoisie upon the state and upon international finance rendered it an unlikely leader of a consistent democratic revolution; the precocious strength of the working-class movement made tempting a "moderate" political settlement between bourgeois liberals and the more progressive landlords. A thoroughgoing bourgeois-democratic revolution seemed to depend upon the political initiative of the proletariat. But this would require not a simple and straightforward polarization along class lines but the orchestration of a revolutionary-democratic alliance of diverse social and political forces. The struggle for leadership, for hegemony in the democratic revolution was thus a struggle over the constitution and the political orientation of alternative systems of political alliances.

Consciousness, as conceived by Lenin, had reflexively to grasp the complex and uneven process of the struggle for hegemony. In focusing upon the contradiction between the conscious vanguard and the spontaneous working-class movement, the thesis of consciousness from without enabled Lenin, paradoxically, to situate himself, as Marxist theorist and political actor, within the class struggle. It assumes a conceptualization of class struggle in which both conscious vanguard and the spontaneous movements of the masses are capable of effective and sometimes of innovative action, although different, even contradictory modes of action are characteristic of each and a certain conjunction, even "fusion" of the two is needed to sustain a hegemonic position in the process of revolutionary transformation. The claim that socialist consciousness must be imported into the spontaneous working-class movement from without does not signify the substitution of one collective actor for another but serves to open a conceptual space in which the relations between different actors, and hence the complex and contradictory relation between leaders and led, can be subjected to critical examination.

Through an examination of Lenin's response to the emergence of the soviets in the revolution of 1905, I will trace some of the contours of this space. In so doing, I will argue that sense can be made of Lenin's stance vis-à-vis the spontaneous working-class movement and the soviets only in the context of the politico-strategic logic of the struggle for hegemony that sustains his thesis of consciousness from without. The shifts in Lenin's stance do not indicate an abandonment of this thesis but actually depend upon it. Situating the demands of leadership in relation to the logic of a political struggle for hegemony that implicated adversaries and allies as well as leaders and masses, his strategic analyses produced a richer appreciation and a more effective grasp upon the dynamics of the relation between leaders and led than did the principal alternative available to the Russian working-class movement, the one represented by Lenin's adversaries in the moderate wing of the Russian Social Democratic Labor Party (RSDLP), the Mensheviks. I will suggest, further, that Lenin's stance in the struggle for proletarian hegemony represents a more effective coming to grips with the diversity of revolutionary mass movements and the complexities of the leadership relation than does the influential "post-Marxist" notion of "counter-hegemony."

The Theory and the Practice of Revolution

The Russo-Japanese War of 1904–5 brought to the surface the tensions that pervaded the social and political structures of tsarist Russia. Taking a cue from liberal intellectuals campaigning to extend the bounds of free political speech, the priest Father Gapon led a procession of St. Petersburg's workers to present Tsar Nicholas himself with a petition to remedy their grievances. When the tsar's troops responded by gunning down hundreds of the petitioners, the tsarist faith of even the most backward workers was shattered. A process of revolutionary struggle was unleashed, punctuated by waves of mass political strikes, mutiny in the armed forces, land seizures and persistent disorders in the countryside, and concessions by the authorities, followed by brutal repression. Revolution would shift the ground upon which politics moved in Russia and Lenin's political thought would move with it. But just how it moved is a matter of controversy. Lenin would formulate the relation between the spontaneous working-class movement and the conscious vanguard party in somewhat different terms than he had used before the revolution. Struck by a shift in emphasis, tone, and formulation, a number of writers have tried to counterpose, more or less systematically, a Lenin of the mass democratic revolution of 1905 to the pre-revolutionary party politician of *What Is to Be Done?* Foremost among them, Marcel Liebman has characterized this shift as "Lenin's first revolt . . . against Leninism."[4] Captivated by the spontaneity of the proletariat, Lenin, it is claimed, would now discard his previous distrust for the spontaneous working-class movement. His calls for a thoroughgoing democratization of the Russian Social Democratic Labor Party (RSDLP) are supposed to belie his earlier "elitist conception of the party."[5] Reliance upon professional revolutionaries from the intelligentsia is said to give way to enthusiasm for the influx of revolutionary workers into the party as a tonic to relieve the bureaucratic lethargy of the committee-men. Whereas intervention on behalf of centralized control from above had seemed so essential in the underground, in the light of revolutionary reality Lenin would make himself the spokesman for creative initiative from below. The previous supposition that revolution "must necessarily be the work of a vanguard group rather than a mass party" would now be replaced by a recognition of the soviets, broad organizations of the power of the working masses, as vital centers of revolutionary activity.[6] Thus was 1905 "a revolution that shook a doctrine."[7]

Do Lenin's reformulations of 1905 amount to a theoretical reversal or do they merely represent an adaptation of the available analytical tools to altered circumstances? Liebman's approach, which abstracts spontaneity and consciousness, workers and intellectuals, democracy and centralism, party and class, and so on from the context of Lenin's thinking on the strategic problems of the revolution, is not well designed to judge the issue. Thus abstracted, these concepts no longer occupy a determinate place in Lenin's Marxist project of grasping theoretically, so as to transform politically, the complex and shifting constellation of class forces; they figure, instead, as a set of essentially moral distinctions, each of whose terms represents a contrasting value, repeated shifting of emphasis between which merely serves to enact the drama of a soul torn between the demands of conflicting political moralities. But these terms may also be approached in light of Lenin's strategic orientation to political struggle, an orientation shaped by an appreciation that the identity of political forces, movements, institutions, policies, issues, ideas, and so forth is not a simple reflex of the socioeconomic class position of the actors, but responds as well to the conduct of the actors in the struggle and is therefore always subject to re-evaluation in relation to the logic and the development of the political (and ideological) struggle itself. I use the expression "politico-strategic logic of the struggle for hegemony" to designate this Leninist insight, and I argue that without such an organizing concept it is possible to account neither for the play, the dramatic shifts in emphasis, nor for the learning, the real theoretical movement, in Lenin's political thought.

"Undoubtedly," Lenin would write, "the revolution will teach us and will teach the masses of the people. But the question that now confronts a militant political party is: shall we be able to teach the revolution anything?"[8] Something new could be learned from the revolution and from the masses in the course of revolution only by grasping them in a conceptual framework capable of responding to conjunctural variations in the revolutionary process and consequently of formulating the appropriate questions. To express the same point somewhat paradoxically, it was only because he was ready to teach the revolution something that he was able to learn from it what he did. By incorporating the experience of the spontaneous revolutionary movements of the workers and peasants into his analyses of the politico-strategic logic of the struggle for hegemony Lenin would work out a Marxist conception of proletarian hegemony in the bourgeois-democratic revolution. In so doing he would come to grasp his own Marxism reflexively as itself situated in the midst of the struggle for hegemony and thus to rectify his account of the relation of spontaneity and consciousness. He would do so, not by abandoning the thesis of consciousness from without, but precisely by pursuing its logic, the politico-strategic logic of the struggle for hegemony.

Lenin's response to the peasant movement of 1905 cannot be extensively considered here but perhaps the following incident can serve to indicate that his response to the spontaneous working-class movement can be fully understood only in conjunction with it. The Inaugural Congress of the All-Russian Peasant Union held in August 1905 proposed to send greetings to "our brothers the workers, who have for so long been spilling their blood in the struggle for the people's freedom." But when a Social Democratic delegate intervened in the discussion with the claim that "'without the factory workers the peasants will achieve nothing,' he was met with shouts from the floor that 'on the contrary, without the peasants the workers can achieve nothing.'"[9] Apparently, proletarian hegemony was not exercised just in being asserted, even where there was a measure of good will and a recognition of common interests. The sophistication of Marxist socioeconomic analysis and political calculation would seem a thin thread, in historical materialist terms, upon which to hang a claim to proletarian leadership in the bourgeois-democratic revolution; and even if the organization of the RSDLP had responded reliably to these calculations, it would still have been in no position to bring their insight to bear in the villages. The hegemony of the proletariat would have to be spread through a more extensive and more deeply rooted network than the party. It would require, therefore, a reappraisal of the spontaneous working-class movement, a reappraisal occasioned by the emergence of the soviets.

The Spontaneous Movement and the Soviet

The most prominent exemplar of the institution of the soviet, the St. Petersburg Soviet of Workers' Deputies, emerged at the height of the general strike of October. The workers of the capital were acquainted with the idea of representatives elected in the factory. Under a law of 1903 factory elders (*starosti*) could be chosen by management from candidates nominated by the workers to negotiate their grievances; committees of deputies had been organized in a number of factories since the January strike; and in the aftermath of Bloody Sunday, the workers took part in two-stage elections for representatives to the abortive Shidlovsky Commission, established by the government to investigate the causes of unrest among the factory workers.[10] In addition to this practical experience, the workers had been exposed during the summer to Menshevik efforts to popularize slogans in favor of a "workers' congress" and "revolutionary self-government."[11]

As the strike wave reached St. Petersburg deputies were spontaneously elected in a number of factories. When the Mensheviks initiated a workers' committee to lead the general strike and, seeking to broaden its representation, agitated for the election of one deputy for each five hundred workers, it was under the rubric of "revolutionary self-government." The Soviet of Workers' Deputies thus came into being as a strike committee but one that was already animated by a broader political vision.[12] In response to the practical imperatives of the general strike, the soviets began to act like a "second government," ruling on matters of everyday life and issuing instructions to the post office, railroads, even policemen.[13] The momentum of the strike movement was such that the tsar felt obliged, in order to bring the moderate opposition into the camp of order and pacify the situation, to concede civil liberties, a representative assembly with legislative powers, ministerial responsibility, and universal suffrage. The revolutionary impetus of the working class was not broken. The soviets continued to spread through urban Russia. In taking up the everyday concerns of the masses, they won the allegiance of broad strata of workers and attracted sympathy and support among the non-proletarian population of the cities. They renewed strike activity against state repression and martial law, and for the eight-hour day and "a people's government," and encroached more and more upon the prerogatives of the state. In accordance with the logic of an illegal confrontation with the tsarist state, they began to assume a new dimension as an agency of insurrection and an organ of revolutionary state power. Before the autocracy could restore its order and deploy its forces against the peasant risings in the countryside, it would have to put down workers' insurrections in Moscow and other cities.[14]

By the time Lenin returned from exile in early November, the terms had already been defined in which the Russian Social Democrats, both Mensheviks and the more intransigent Bolsheviks, debated the significance of the soviet. Partially constitutive of the new institution were the Menshevik watchwords calling for "revolutionary self-government" and a "workers' congress." They entered, through the early influence of the Mensheviks in organizing the soviet, into its self-conception. A plan for revolutionary self-government called upon workers' organizations to take the initiative in organizing, parallel to the official Duma elections, an electoral process open to the masses. This would bring the pressure of public opinion to bear upon the official electors and the people's representatives could, at an auspicious moment, declare themselves a constituent assembly. Whether or not it reached this "ideal objective," such a campaign would "organize revolutionary self-government, which will smash the shackles of tsarist legality, and lay the foundation for the future triumph of the revolution."[15] The idea of a workers' congress, as presented by the Menshevik theorist, P. B. Axelrod, was to embody proletarian self-activity. The congress would be composed of delegates elected by assemblies of workers to "adopt specific decisions concerning the immediate demands and plan of action of the working class." It would debate the stance to be adopted toward "the government's caricature of a representative assembly," the appropriate terms for agreements with liberal-democratic bodies, the summoning of a Constituent Assembly and the kinds of economic and political reforms to be advocated in elections to that body, and other such current public issues. Agitation around this idea, Axelrod wrote, could "captivate tens of thousands of workers," a mass large enough in a period of revolution to "endow the congress, its decisions and the organization set up by it with tremendous authority, both among the less conscious masses of the proletariat and in the eyes of the liberal democrats." Even if the

congress did not come to fruition, by contributing to "the political enlightenment of the working masses, strengthening their combative spirit
and developing their ability and readiness to meet force with force in
defense of their rightful demands," such agitation might occasion an
uprising.[16]

The Mensheviks hoped that such proposals, by providing a forum for
working-class self-activity, might culminate in the formation of a mass
party of labor. What was most fundamentally at stake in the institution
of the soviet was thus the relation between the working class and its
political party rather than the more inclusive political agenda of the
democratic revolution. Unable to grasp the new institutional form in
terms different from those proposed by the Mensheviks, the Petersburg
Bolsheviks reacted defensively. Fearful that the influence of an amorphous, non-socialist political organization could undermine the political evolution of the workers toward Social Democracy, they greeted
the formation of the soviet with suspicion. Their leader, Bogdanov,
favored setting the soviet an ultimatum: accept the program and leadership of the RSDLP or the Bolsheviks would withdraw. In the end they
stayed in the soviet with a view to correcting spontaneous anti–Social
Democratic tendencies and expounding the ideas of the party. Perhaps
mindful of Lenin's earlier warnings about the danger of nonpartisan
political organizations serving as conduits for bourgeois influence over
the proletariat, they sought to distinguish the need for the soviet as
"the executive organ for a specific proletarian action" from presumptuous "attempts on its part to become the political leader of the working
class."[17] But by the time Lenin arrived, the soviet had concluded the
"specific proletarian action" for which it had been formed and showed
no sign of withdrawing from the field of political action.

Lenin's Intervention

Read in terms of the debate between Mensheviks and Petersburg's Bolsheviks over the soviet, Lenin's intervention must seem unstable, ambivalent, and ultimately incoherent. It is this appearance, I believe, that
has occasioned the invention of Lenin's alleged "revolt against Leninism." I will argue on the contrary that, by setting the soviet in the context of the strategic logic of the struggle for hegemony, Lenin was able

to conceive it as an apparatus for the exercise of proletarian hegemony and thereby to shift the terms of the debate. Once this shift is recognized, the case for his "revolt against Leninism" simply collapses. Once the relation between the spontaneous working-class movement and the Marxist party is re-examined in light of it, the real movement in his thought can be established.

Lenin cautiously advanced his reading of the situation in a long letter, "Our Tasks and the Soviet of Workers' Deputies," submitted to the editorial board of the Bolshevik *Novaya Zhizn* but not published. Beginning as a strike committee, the soviet had spontaneously assumed the features of a hub of revolutionary politics, capable of unifying "all the genuinely revolutionary forces" and serving as the medium for an uprising against the state. It should be regarded, consequently, as "the embryo of a *provisional revolutionary government*." But considered in this light, the broad, nonpartisan composition of the soviet was no disadvantage. On the contrary, "We have been speaking all the time of the need of a militant alliance of Social Democrats and revolutionary bourgeois democrats. We have been speaking of it and the workers [in bringing forth the soviet] have done it." The question as to whether the soviet or the party should lead the political struggle was ill conceived: both the party and a reorganized soviet were equally necessary. Indeed, the soviet, considered "as a revolutionary center providing political leadership, is not too broad an organization but, on the contrary, a much too narrow one." It must constitute a provisional revolutionary government and must "enlist to this end the participation of new deputies not only from the workers, but . . . from the sailors and soldiers, . . . from the revolutionary peasantry, . . . and from the revolutionary bourgeois intelligentsia." [18]

This estimate of the soviet was accompanied by a call for the reorganization of the party in line with the new, albeit precarious, conditions of political liberty. While its secret apparatus would have to be preserved, the party must be opened up to Social Democratic workers. Their initiative and inventiveness would have to be engaged in the task of devising new, legal, and semi-legal forms of organization, broader and less rigid than the old circles and more accessible to "typical representatives of the masses." Accordingly, the party must adopt democratic practices, including the election of rank and file delegates to the forthcoming congress. The workers who join the party would be dependable socialists or amenable to socialist influence. "The working class is instinctively, spontaneously Social-Democratic, and more than ten years of work put in by Social-Democracy has done a great deal to transform this spontaneity into consciousness." The workers, better than intellectuals at putting principles into practice, must take the issue of party unity in hand.[19]

The soviet figured in Lenin's analysis not only as an organizer of the general strike but also as a nonpartisan political organization. Within days of this assessment, however, he would support the Bolshevik critique of "'non-partisan' class organizations" by declaring "Down with non-partisanship! Non-partisanship has always and everywhere been a weapon and slogan of the bourgeoisie";[20] and shortly thereafter he would pronounce the soviet "not a labour parliament and not an organ of proletarian self-government, nor an organ of self-government at all, but a fighting organization for the achievement of definite aims."[21] He had pronounced the soviet just as necessary, in order to provide the movement with political leadership, as the party and had indicated that the party was itself in need of revitalization through the influx of "typical representatives of the masses." Yet he could, at the same time, issue a warning that the "need for organization which the workers are feeling so acutely will," without the intervention of the Social Democrats, "find its expression in distorted, dangerous forms." He could acknowledge that, were the party inclined to demagogy or lacking a solid program, tactical precepts, and organizational experience, a sudden influx of untried and untested new members could threaten the dissolution of the conscious vanguard of the class into the politically amorphous masses.[22] Though the workers were "instinctively, spontaneously Social-Democratic," it was still necessary to reckon with "hostility to Social-Democracy within the ranks of the proletariat," hostility that often assumed the form of nonpartisanship. The transformation of the proletariat into a class was dependent upon "the growth not only of its unity, but also of its political *consciousness*" and the transformation of "this spontaneity into consciousness" was still envisaged in connection with the intervention of the Marxist vanguard in the spontaneous class struggle.[23]

Considered in abstraction from the logic of the struggle for hegemony, Lenin's response to the soviet and to the spontaneous working-class movement that had called it into being would seem to collapse into a welter of conflicting formulations. His discourse can then be partitioned into elements reflective of the reality of the spontaneous class struggle and those marked by the resistance of the Bolshevik apparatus. This procedure, which reduces Lenin's discourse to a battleground for contending political forces, is most systematically deployed by the Menshevik historian Solomon Schwarz, but it is implicit in Liebman's interpretive apparatus of Leninist "doctrinal rebellion." It becomes superfluous, however, once Lenin's stance toward the soviet is re-examined in the context of the struggle for hegemony.

The Soviet and the Struggle for Hegemony

The "instinctively, spontaneously Social-Democratic" disposition Lenin ascribed to the working class in the immediate triumphant aftermath of the general strike did not consist in its pursuit of specifically socialist objectives. In an essay written to explain the prevalence of nonpartisan ideology and institutions in the revolutionary movement, he characterized "the striving of the workers towards socialism and their alliance with the Socialist Party . . . [even] at the very earliest stages of the movement" as a consequence of "the special position which the proletariat occupies in capitalist society." He claims at the same time, however, that an examination of the petitions, demands, and instructions emanating from factories, offices, regiments, parishes, and so on throughout Russia would show a preponderance of "demands for elementary rights" rather than "specifically class demands": "purely socialist demands are still a matter of the future. . . . Even the proletariat is making the revolution, as it were, within the limits of the minimum programme and not of the maximum programme."[24] If the working-class movement was spontaneously Social Democratic, it was so not in virtue of its consciousness but of its practice, not in virtue of what it thought but of what it did and how it acted. In order to grasp how this could be so, the practice of the spontaneous working-class movement must be situated in relation to the politico-strategic logic of the struggle for hegemony, specifically in relation to the struggle between the two possible paths of the bourgeois-democratic revolution, the landlord-bourgeois path and the proletarian-peasant path.

First, the general strike rendered unworkable the proposed Duma, thereby disrupting the compromise it represented between tsar and bourgeoisie. The revolutionary struggle of the workers thus escaped the strategic hegemony of the liberal bourgeoisie spontaneously—by its fighting spirit, its tenacity, and its "plebeian" methods—although not yet consciously and not, therefore, durably. In the aftermath of "the first great victory of the urban revolution," it was incumbent upon the proletariat to "broaden and deepen the foundations of the revolution by extending it to the countryside. . . . Revolutionary war differs from other wars in that it draws its main reserves from the camp of its enemy's erstwhile allies, erstwhile supporters of tsarism, or people who blindly obeyed tsarism. The success of the all-Russian political strike will have a greater influence over the minds and hearts of the peasants than the confusing words of any possible manifestoes or laws."[25]

Not only did the spontaneous movement of the general strike open up the possibility of a decisive revolutionary transformation, in so doing it exemplified the exercise of hegemony materially through the production and/or imposition of *faits accomplis* and not only ideologically through the generation and transmission of consciousness, of belief and conviction. It foreshadowed the hegemony of the proletariat as a reorganization of the system of alliances of social and political forces, both destabilizing the adversary's forces and mobilizing an incipient revolutionary coalition. The working class was "spontaneously Social-Democratic" to the extent that its spontaneous struggle was congruent with the strategic orientation of Russian Social Democracy toward the hegemony of the proletariat in the bourgeois-democratic revolution.

Second, the soviet thrown up in the course of the general strike provided an institutional form through which the alliance of revolutionary democrats could be concluded on a mass scale. Since the political independence of the proletariat from the influence of the liberal bourgeoisie required it to ally with other revolutionary democrats, especially with the peasantry, to effect the thoroughgoing destruction of the foundations of tsarism, the soviet constituted the form in which the "imprint of proletarian independence" could be placed upon the path of the revolution. Though it emerged from the working-class movement, Lenin did not treat the soviet as a specifically proletarian class institution, a form of organization exclusive to the workers. Indeed, what was decisive in his analysis was that, as a mode of organization, the soviet constituted an opening to the masses of workers and peasants, intellectuals and petty bourgeois, sailors and soldiers, a political terrain upon which a coalition of revolutionary democrats could take shape. As such and only as such did it represent an embryo of revolutionary-democratic state power.

This estimate of the soviets was pointedly formulated in a Bolshevik resolution prepared for the April 1906 Unity Congress of the RSDLP and elaborated more fully in a lengthy pamphlet, "The Victory of the Cadets and the Tasks of the Workers' Party," which was distributed to congressional delegates. According to the resolution, soviets, arising "spontaneously in the course of mass political strikes as non-party organizations of the broad masses of workers," are necessarily transformed, "by absorbing the more revolutionary elements of the petty bourgeoisie, . . . into organs of the general revolutionary struggle"; the significance of such rudimentary forms of revolutionary authority was completely dependent upon the efficacy of the movement toward insurrection.[26] In the context of this movement, however, the "Soviets of Workers,' Soldiers,' Railwaymen's and Peasants' Deputies" really were new forms of revolutionary authority:

> These bodies were set up exclusively by the *revolutionary* sections of the people; they were formed irrespective of all laws and regulations, entirely in a revolutionary way, as a product of the native genius of the people, as a manifestation of the independent activity of the people which . . . was ridding itself of its old police fetters. Lastly, they were indeed organs of *authority*, for all their rudimentary, spontaneous, amorphous and diffuse character, in composition and in activity. . . . In their social and political character, they were the rudiments of the dictatorship of the revolutionary elements of the people.[27]

Established in struggle against the *ancien régime*, the authority of the soviets and kindred institutions derived neither from the force of arms nor from the power of money nor from habits of obedience to entrenched institutions, but from "the confidence of the vast masses" and the enlistment of "all the masses" in the practice of government. The new authority did not shroud its operations in ritual, secrecy, or professions of expertise: "It concealed nothing, it had no secrets, no regulations, no formalities. . . . It was an authority open to all, . . .

sprang directly from the masses, and was a direct and immediate instrument of the popular masses, of their will." Since the masses also included those who had been cowed by repression, had been degraded by ideology, habit, or prejudice, or were simply inclined to philistine indifference, the revolutionary authority of the soviets was not exercised by the whole people but by "the revolutionary people." The latter, however, patiently explain the reasons for their actions and "willingly enlist the *whole* people not only in 'administering' the state, but in governing it too, and indeed in organizing the state."[28] The new authority thus constituted not only and not so much an embryonic state as an embryonic anti-state. This implication was not yet drawn, but a certain dissolution of the opposition between society and the apparatus of politics, between the people and the organization of state power, does emerge. The soviet provided an institutional form in which the social, economic, and cultural struggles of the masses, workers, and peasants could be combined with the revolutionary struggle for political power, amplifying and reinforcing each other.

Self-Government or Revolutionary Hegemony?

Properly understood, not only does Lenin's criticism of "revolutionary self-government," the "workers' congress," and the principle of nonpartisanship not contradict his analysis of the soviet in 1905–6, it follows logically from it. To invoke the theme of "revolutionary self-government" in order to characterize the soviets was to invoke the political orientation of those, the Mensheviks, who gave it currency. As Lenin saw it, they simply juxtaposed the exercise of "revolutionary self-government" with cooperation in the rites of the tsarist government without strategic forethought as to the inevitability of counter-revolutionary repression. Thus conceived in abstraction from the logic of the struggle for hegemony, "self-government" represented a denial of the need to organize the revolutionary insurrection or, at best, a refusal to take the initiative in organizing it. In this context, it does not signal a call for the dictatorship of the revolutionary people but subordinates it to an experiment in political pedagogy. This was the target of Lenin's criticism.

The same holds *a fortiori* for such formulations as "labor parliament" and "workers' congress," which bear the additional disadvantage of identifying the soviets as nonpartisan organizations of the working class. Framed in this way, the soviets would exclude the non-proletarian masses and depreciate the leadership of the Social Democratic Party. The nonpartisan structure of the soviet was essential, in Lenin's analysis, precisely because it provided a political arena in which a coalition of the proletarian, petty-bourgeois, and peasant masses could take shape. Nonpartisanship was indeed a bourgeois principle but inasmuch as the revolutionary process called for an alliance of the workers with bourgeois democrats, this was not a drawback but an asset. In order to preserve the political independence of the working class the leadership of the Social Democratic Party remained essential and, paradoxical as it may seem, this leadership was exercised precisely in orchestrating a class alliance around the organization of a revolutionary insurrection and, consequently, in unraveling the strategic confusion represented by the notion of a "workers' congress" and so on.

As demonstrated in the emergence of the soviets, the spontaneously Social Democratic bent of the working-class struggle was more than receptivity to the political lessons of Marxist class analysis. The workers had not simply put into practice advice supplied by Marxist theory; they had shown themselves capable of political innovation and, in so doing, generated a solution in practice to a key problem on the agenda of Marxist theory. But what they had done in Social Democratic fashion was done spontaneously, not consciously. It was Lenin who, by situating their innovation in the context of the politico-strategic logic of the struggle for hegemony, would provide the theory of their practice. Just what had the working class done? Not only had it momentarily disrupted the hegemony of the liberal bourgeoisie and gained for itself some political experience, it had erected a new institutional form through which the diverse revolutionary-democratic forces could mesh together in a coalition of the masses, the worker-peasant alliance, and assume state power. It had thereby demonstrated its own aptitude for hegemony in the bourgeois-democratic revolution.

This hegemonic potential of the soviet form of organization could be durably realized only through action in conformity with the politico-strategic logic of the struggle for hegemony. It would require, therefore, the deployment of armed force to meet and defeat the violence of the counter-revolution and the deployment of Marxist analysis to seize the shifting conjunctures of the political struggle and hold the springs of

ideological confusion in check. The soviet could not render the intervention of the Marxist vanguard party superfluous, but the soviet and
similar forms of organization had come to embody an aspect of the
struggle for proletarian hegemony that was hardly less requisite. Dis-
placing the conventions that gave politics its shape and texture, soviets
reorganized the space of political life: opening the process of political
decision making to the scrutiny of the popular masses, they encouraged
the masses to enter politics; merging the social, economic, and cultural
demands and grievances of the people in the assault upon the autocratic
regime, they palpably expanded the range of the political struggle; dis-
pensing with formalities that barred the path to participation in the
struggle, they facilitated the confluence of popular forces in all their
contradictory diversity. In all these ways, they restructured the terrain
of political struggle along lines that enabled the Marxist vanguard party
to pursue the political project of proletarian hegemony more effectively.
In thus transforming the terrain of struggle, the institution of the soviet
represented a connection between the idea of proletarian hegemony as
the project of a party and the material inscription of proletarian hegemony in the path of the bourgeois-democratic revolution. Theorizing
the soviet in this context enabled Lenin to pull together a coherent historical materialist conception of the hegemony of the proletariat.

Some years later, he would have recourse, albeit without specific reference to the soviets, to a spatial metaphor in order to define the idea of
proletarian hegemony:

> He who confines the class to an arena, the bounds, forms and shape of
> which are determined or permitted by the liberals, does not understand
> the tasks of the class. Only he understands the tasks of the class who
> directs its attention (and consciousness, and practical activity, etc.) to
> the need for so reconstructing this very arena, its entire form, its entire
> shape, as to extend it beyond the limits allowed by the liberals. . . . The
> difference between the two formulations . . . [is] that the first *excludes*
> the idea of "hegemony" of the working class, whereas the second delib-
> erately defines this very idea.[29]

The politico-strategic logic of the struggle for hegemony was grounded
in the struggle of social classes. It dictated preparedness for armed conflict, readiness to deploy the arts of insurrection. It engaged a battle of
ideas, waged with the science of Marxist analysis and the arts of per-

suasion. But it could not be disengaged from a struggle over the very shape, the contours and dimensions, of the battlefield. This struggle might be waged consciously according to the arts of organization, but it would most often unfold spontaneously, the product of impromptu variations upon or challenges to established convention whose bearing is reinforced or transformed in unforeseen ways by the sheer weight of popular involvement. The conventions governing political actors' expectations of each other, deployed in the material environment of politics, shape an arena for political action that, although subject to change at the hands of those implicated in it, both offers various possibilities for action and exerts a kind of structural constraint upon the plans of actors; this arena is encountered by individual actors, like baseball players having to adjust to an idiosyncratic stadium, not exactly as persuasion and not exactly as coercion, but as something like the force of circumstance. Thus, the exercise of hegemony could make itself felt not only in consent to persuasion or fear of coercion but also in adaptation to circumstance. The spontaneous working-class movement, in throwing up the soviets, had transformed the circumstances of political action in ways that made some constraints more pressing and others less so, some possibilities more real and others less so, some threats more plausible and others less so, some arguments more persuasive and others less so; reconstructing the political arena, it enabled and/or required actors, not only workers themselves but also peasants, soldiers, sailors, employees, intellectuals (and, of course, landlords and bourgeoisie), to reorient themselves in relation to the political struggle of the working class for hegemony in the bourgeois-democratic revolution.

Practice and the Theory of Hegemony

Applying the politico-strategic logic of the struggle for hegemony to the analysis of the spontaneous revolutionary movements of the peasants and the workers, Lenin was able to endow the project of proletarian hegemony with a more concrete orientation. Prior to the revolution, he had characterized the exercise of hegemony by analogy with a tribune of the people, whose function it was to articulate any and all popular grievances against the regime; this universal role is preserved, but the emergence of a revolutionary peasant movement required that hegemony take the specific form of an alliance between the working class and the peasantry. Hegemony figured earlier as a kind of generalized proletarian influence, liable to be confused in practice with the mere dissemination of party propaganda; but with the emergence of an institutional form, the soviet, capable of enacting the proletarian-peasant alliance and exercising revolutionary state power, hegemony could be conceived concretely as embracing the mass action of the working class.

The politico-strategic logic at work in Lenin's political analyses called for receptiveness to conjunctural variations in the class struggle. This endowed his theoretical stance with a certain reflexivity, permitting him to bring the practical experience of the spontaneous mass movements to bear upon the lacunae of Marxist theory. The idea of proletarian self-activity that formed the substance of the Menshevik notion of hegemony was adaptable in quite another sense. Conformable to the limits of any situation, it manifested itself differently in accordance with variations in the circumstances of the class struggle. Whatever form it assumed, however, since the self-activity of the working class was never situated in relation to the strategic logic of the struggle for hegemony, what typified it was that it prefigured the socialist aim, contained it in intention. In this sense there was no distance between theory and reality, no theoretical lacunae but also no possibility of theoretical growth. The form of self-activity appropriate to the given situation would have to develop spontaneously, in an ad hoc fashion. The call for proletarian self-activity would be adjusted to an arena of struggle imposed by the defeat of the revolution, and, instead of contesting the boundaries of that arena, the Mensheviks would allow the illegal apparatus of the party to fall into disuse and disrepair. Menshevism had long figured, on Lenin's strategic map, as a conduit for the hegemony of the liberal bourgeoisie but this, he claimed, amounted to an abandonment of the very project of proletarian hegemony in the bourgeois-democratic revolution. The Mensheviks would increasingly abandon the language of hegemony. But they had never held, and so could not have abandoned, the concept of hegemony as Lenin had come to employ it.

The Menshevik discourse of hegemony might be characterized more accurately from Lenin's standpoint as simply another form of subaltern insertion in the deployment of bourgeois hegemony. And in this optic the Menshevik analysis of the soviets as organs of workers' self-government presents an unlikely homology with contemporary "post-

Marxist" discussion of hegemony and counter-hegemony.[30] Where
Menshevik self-government signifies, not a struggle to overthrow the
autocratic power of the state, but a forum where the workers could
educate themselves politically, sheltered hot-house fashion from state
power, post-Marxist counter-hegemony signifies, not a project for the
reconstruction of the bourgeois social order along new lines and under
new leadership, but a critique of any hegemonic project as an over-
weening claim to foreclose the innovative diversity of the process of
individual self-definition and thereby "suture" the social order. Indeed,
the very substitution of "counter-hegemony" for the Leninist (and
Gramscian) term "proletarian hegemony" suggests that the alternative
to bourgeois rule is no social order at all but a universe of autonomously
self-defining individuals. Marx's sardonic pronouncement in the "Critique of the Gotha Programme" that the bourgeois have good reason to
attribute "supernatural creative power" to labor[31] suggests, however,
that just as one cannot simply produce oneself, neither can one simply
define oneself. One always finds oneself already in context and so one
is always already defined, even if the terms by which one is understood
and/or understands oneself are contested. In class society, the material
available for the arduous work of transforming contexts and redefining
political projects, aspirations, and identities is supplied by the historical
movement of the class struggle and in this context the social, political,
and ideological relations of capital do not represent a mere static back-
drop against which workers and revolutionary intellectuals strive to
fashion a socialist project: just as the workers spontaneously innovate
in the course of their struggles, the ruling class innovates, through its
political and ideological representatives, in response to working-class
struggles. The process of working out a socialist project, of elaborating
the political self-definition of the working-class movement, is one in
which the adversary is inevitably and actively present. To reckon without this presence is to take the contours of the political arena as given
and thereby to assume, in the very terms of one's counter-hegemonic
struggle, the position of the subaltern. It is to make political leadership,
strictly speaking, unthinkable.

Lenin's persistent refusal to equate politics with pedagogy establishes, by contrast, a conceptual field that opens to analysis the nuances
of the relation of leadership. Part of leadership is the political education
of the led—but only part: vanguard and masses play different, poten-

tially complementary but sometimes essentially contradictory parts in the class struggle. The very weight of organized numbers in motion, of the masses, can lead to the emergence of unforeseen political forces, possibilities, and positions. But a position staked out today can always be invested and transformed tomorrow in accordance with the strategic calculation of an adversary. So the struggle for hegemony presumes the ability to adapt to the changing conjunctures of political struggle, to combine awareness of the underlying forces that shape the logic of struggle with openness to the ways in which different actors, vanguard and masses, adversaries and allies, can innovate in the struggle. Leadership in the class struggle thus demands a conscious vanguard that is sensitive to the struggles of the masses yet willing where necessary to counterpose its political analyses to their spontaneous movement. It might be objected that this opposition between leader and led simply provides a sophisticated rationale for minority dictatorship. But this objection would be persuasive only if the concepts and distinctions that inform Lenin's approach to leadership did not afford a superior analysis of the logic of class struggle. The question of the truth of the analysis is, in this sense, unavoidable. And if Lenin's analysis does illuminate the logic and dynamics of mass movements, then the real question is the one posed by Gramsci: "In the formations of leaders, one premise is fundamental: is it the intention that there should always be rulers and ruled, or is the objective to create the conditions in which this division is no longer necessary?"[32]

Notes

1   See Alan Shandro, "'Consciousness from Without': Marxism, Lenin and the Proletariat," *Science and Society* 59:3 (fall 1995): 268–97.

2   V. I. Lenin, *What Is to Be Done?* (1902), in *Collected Works* (Moscow: Progress Publishers, 1961), 5:386n.

3   V. I. Lenin, "A Talk with Defenders of Economism" (1901), in *Collected Works*, 5:316.

4   Marcel Liebman, "Lenin in 1905: A Revolution That Shook a Doctrine," *Monthly Review* (April 1970): 73.

5   Marcel Liebman, *Leninism Under Lenin* (London: Jonathan Cape, 1975), 29.

6   Ibid., 29–31.

7   Liebman, "Lenin in 1905," 57–75.

8   V. I. Lenin, "Two Tactics of Social-Democracy in the Democratic Revolution" (1905), in *Collected Works*, 9:18.

9   See Maureen Perrie, *The Agrarian Policy of the Russian Socialist-Revolutionary Party* (Cambridge: Cambridge University Press, 1976), 110–11.

10 See Sidney Harcave, *First Blood: The Russian Revolution of 1905* (London: Bodley Head, 1965), 181–86; and Oskar Anweiler, *The Soviets: The Russian Workers, Peasants, and Soldiers Councils, 1905–1921* (New York: Pantheon Books, 1974), 24–27, 32–37.

11 Anweiler, *The Soviets*, 45–46.

12 See Solomon Schwarz, *The Russian Revolution of 1905* (Chicago: University of Chicago Press, 1967), 168–78.

13 See Anweiler, *The Soviets*, 55–58.

14 See Harcave, *First Blood*, 233–42; and Leon Trotsky, *1905* (Harmondsworth: Penguin Publishers, 1973), 249–64.

15 Cited in V. I. Lenin, "A Most Lucid Exposition of a Most Confused Plan" (1905), in *Collected Works*, 9:224; see Schwarz, *The Russian Revolution of 1905*, 168–71.

16 P. B. Axelrod, "The People's Duma and the Workers' Congress" (1905), in *The Mensheviks in the Russian Revolution*, ed. Abraham Ascher (Ithaca, N.Y.: Cornell University Press, 1976), 65–67.

17 Cited in Schwarz, *The Russian Revolution of 1905*, 186, 187; see V. I. Lenin, "A New Revolutionary Workers' Association" (1905), in *Collected Works*, 8:507–8.

18 V. I. Lenin, "Our Tasks and the Soviet of Workers' Deputies: A Letter to the Editor" (1905), in *Collected Works*, 10:21–23. Emphasis in original.

19 V. I. Lenin, "The Reorganisation of the Party" (1905), *Collected Works*, 10:34, 32.

20 V. I. Lenin, "Learn from the Enemy" (1905), *Collected Works*, 10:61.

21 V. I. Lenin, "Socialism and Anarchism" (1905), *Collected Works*, 10:72.

22 Lenin, "The Reorganisation of the Party," 10:29, 32.

23 Lenin, "Learn from the Enemy," 10:60. Emphasis in original.

24 V. I. Lenin, "The Socialist Party and Non-Party Revolutionism" (1905), in *Collected Works*, 10:76, 77.

25 V. I. Lenin, "The First Victory of the Revolution" (1905), in *Collected Works*, 9:433.

26 V. I. Lenin, "A Tactical Platform for the Unity Congress of the RSDLP: Draft Resolutions" (1906), in *Collected Works*, 10:156.

27 V. I. Lenin, "The Victory of the Cadets and the Tasks of the Workers' Party" (1906), in *Collected Works*, 10:243. Emphasis in original.

28 Ibid., 244–45, 247. Emphasis in original.

29 V. I. Lenin, "Fundamental Problems of the Election Campaign" (1911–12), in *Collected Works*, 17:422, 423. Emphasis in original.

30 Ernesto Laclau and Chantal Mouffe, *Hegemony and Socialist Strategy: Towards a Radical Democratic Politics* (London: Verso, 1985).

31 Karl Marx, "Critique of the Gotha Programme" (1875), in *The First International and After* (Harmondsworth: Penguin Publishers, 1974), 341.

32 Antonio Gramsci, *Selections from the Prison Notebooks*, ed. Quintin Hoare and Geoffrey Nowell Smith (New York: International Publishers, 1971), 144.

Contributors

Kevin B. Anderson teaches political science at Purdue University, Indiana. He is the author of *Lenin, Hegel and Western Marxism* (1995) and the co-editor, with Janet Afary, of *Foucault and the Iranian Revolution* (2005).

Alain Badiou teaches philosophy at the Ecole Normale Supérieure in Paris. His latest publications include *Logiques des mondes* (2006) and, in English, *Being and Event* (2006) and *Infinite Thought: Truth and the Return to Philosophy* (2005).

Etienne Balibar teaches philosophy at the University of California, Irvine. His latest publications include *We, the People of Europe? Reflections on Transnational Citizenship* (2003) and *L'Europe, l'Amérique, la guerre: Réflections sur la médiation européenne* (2005).

Daniel Bensaïd teaches philosophy at the University of Paris 8. He is the author of *Marx for Our Times* (2002). His latest publications include *Fragments mécréants* (2005) and *Karl Marx: Sur la question juive* (2006).

Sebastian Budgen is a member of the editorial board of the journal *Historical Materialism*.

Alex Callinicos is chair of European studies at King's College, London. His latest publications include *Resources of Critique* (2006) and *The New Mandarins of American Power* (2004).

Terry Eagleton teaches cultural theory at the University of Manchester. His latest publications include *Holy Terror* (2005) and *Myths of Power: A Marxist Study of the Brontës* (2005).

Fredric Jameson teaches comparative literature at Duke University. His latest publications include *Archaeologies of the Future* (2005) and *A Singular Modernity* (2002).

Stathis Kouvelakis teaches political theory at King's College, London. He is the author of *Philosophy and Revolution: From Kant to Marx* (2003) and the co-editor, with Vincent Charbonnier, of *Sartre, Lukacs, Althusser: Des marxistes en philosophie* (2005).

Georges Labica is professor emeritus of philosophy at the University of Paris 10. He is the editor of the *Dictionnaire Critique du Marxisme* (2001) and the author of *Démocratie et revolution* (2004).

Sylvain Lazarus teaches anthropology at the University of Paris 8. He is the author of *L'anthropologie du nom* (1998) and the editor of *Politique et philosophie dans l'oeuvre de Louis Althusser* (1993).

Jean-Jacques Lecercle teaches linguistics at the University of Paris 10. His latest publications include *Marxism and the Philosophy of Language* (2006) and *The Force of Language* (2005).

Lars T. Lih has taught at Duke University and Wellesley College and is now an independent scholar living in Montreal. He is the author of *Lenin Rediscovered: "What Is to Be Done?" in Context* (2006).

Domenico Losurdo teaches philosophy at the University of Urbino. His latest publications include *Nietzsche, il ribelle aristocratico* (2002), *Hegel and the Freedom of the Moderns* (2004), and *Heidegger and the Ideology of War* (2001).

Savas Michael-Matsas is an independent writer and scholar living in Athens. He is the author of *Forms of the Messianic* (2006) and *Forms of the Wandering* (2004), both in Greek.

Antonio Negri has taught philosophy and political science at the universities of Padua and Paris 8. His latest publications include *Multitude* (2006), *The Politics of Subversion: A Manifesto for the Twenty-First Century* (2005), and *Books for Burning: Between Civil War and Democracy in 1970s Italy* (2005).

Alan Shandro teaches political science at the Laurentian University, Canada.

Slavoj Žižek is a senior researcher at the Institute for Social Studies in Ljubljana, Slovenia. His latest publications include *The Parallax View* (2006), *Interrogating the Real* (2006), and *Iraq: The Borrowed Kettle* (2005).

Index

Sebastian Budgen is a member of the editorial board of the journal *Historical Materialism*.

Stathis Kouvelakis teaches political theory at King's College, London. He is the author of *Philosophy and Revolution: From Kant to Marx* (2003) and the co-editor, with Vincent Charbonnier, of *Sartre, Lukacs, Althusser: Des marxistes en philosophie* (2005).

Slavoj Žižek is a senior researcher at the Institute for Social Studies in Ljubljana, Slovenia. His latest publications include *The Parallax View* (2006), *Interrogating the Real* (2006), and *Iraq: The Borrowed Kettle* (2005).

Library of Congress Cataloging-in-Publication Data
Lenin reloaded : toward a politics of truth / edited by Sebastian Budgen,
Stathis Kouvelakis, and Slavoj Žižek.
p. cm.
Includes bibliographical references and index.
ISBN-13: 978-0-8223-3929-8 (cloth : alk. paper)
ISBN-13: 978-0-8223-3941-0 (pbk. : alk. paper)
1. Socialism. 2. Communism. 3. Marxian economics. 4. Capitalism.
5. Lenin, Vladimir Il'ich, 1870–1924. I. Budgen, Sebastian. II. Kouvélakis,
Eustache, 1965– III. Žižek, Slavoj.
HX73.L423 2007
320.53′22—dc22   2006034547